Son of Classics and Comics

CLASSICAL PRESENCES

General Editors

Lorna Hardwick   James I. Porter

The texts, ideas, images, and material culture of ancient Greece and Rome have always been crucial to attempts to appropriate the past in order to authenticate the present. They underlie the mapping of change and the assertion and challenging of values and identities, old and new. Classical Presences brings the latest scholarship to bear on the contexts, theory, and practice of such use, and abuse, of the classical past.

Son of Classics and Comics

EDITED BY

George Kovacs and C. W. Marshall

OXFORD

UNIVERSITY PRESS

OXFORD
UNIVERSITY PRESS

Oxford University Press is a department of the University of
Oxford. It furthers the University's objective of excellence in research,
scholarship, and education by publishing worldwide.

Oxford   New York

Auckland   Cape Town   Dar es Salaam   Hong Kong   Karachi
Kuala Lumpur   Madrid   Melbourne   Mexico City   Nairobi
New Delhi   Shanghai   Taipei   Toronto

With offices in

Argentina   Austria   Brazil   Chile   Czech Republic   France   Greece
Guatemala   Hungary   Italy   Japan   Poland   Portugal   Singapore
South Korea   Switzerland   Thailand   Turkey   Ukraine   Vietnam

Oxford is a registered trademark of Oxford University Press
in the UK and certain other countries.

Published in the United States of America by
Oxford University Press
198 Madison Avenue, New York, NY 10016

Library of Congress Cataloging-in-Publication Data
Son of classics and comics / edited by George Kovacs and C.W. Marshall.
pages cm — (Classical presences)
Includes bibliographical references.
ISBN 978-0-19-026889-3 (pbk.) — ISBN 978-0-19-026888-6 (hardback)
1. Comic books, strips, etc.—United States—History and criticism.   2. Classical literature—Influence.
I. Kovacs, George, 1976-   II. Marshall, C. W., 1968-   III. Series: Classical presences.
PN6725.S66 2015
741.5'973—dc23
2015008772

1 3 5 7 9 8 6 4 2
Printed in the United States of America
on acid-free paper

Contents

List of Illustrations

Introduction

C. W. Marshall and George Kovacs

Among the many delights of American comic books from the 1960s to the 1980s were the advertisements, promising inexpensive gimmicks and toys to their excited readers, all in return for a self-addressed stamped envelope and their allowances. None held the same promise, however, as the complete plastic armies that were offered by anonymous companies with ads illustrated by Russ Heath, whose confident line work in war comics of the 1960s inspired Roy Lichtenstein (among others). Heath's illustration of Roman soldiers was the first image of the ancient world for many North American children, and, with *Asterix* comics, they have helped shape expectations for Roman history courses in subsequent generations (figure 0.1).[1] The plastic toys that one received were inevitably disappointing; they were not quite as three-dimensional as the adolescent brain imagined, and the stark blue and yellow plastic figures required considerable creative effort by the Greek-less, Latin-less ten-year-old to reconstruct a Roman battlefield, especially when the figures could barely remain upright on the narrow stands included. The power of illustration in Heath's drawings seems not even to have been realized at first; the earliest ads used the illustration only as part of the background, against which one was shown replicas of the actual figures. This no doubt limited sales, and truth in advertising gave way to a more fanciful, imagined glory-that-was-Rome.

In those days, before the Internet and before trade paperbacks collecting entire story arcs under a single cover, when "research" into comics consisted of reading what one could borrow from friends or learn by reading the relevant letters column, the appearance of a collection of reprinted superhero origin stories—*Origins of Marvel Comics*, by Stan Lee (Fireside, 1974)—was a heady delight. Here was the otherwise unavailable source material; here was where one could learn how one's favorite characters came to be. Not just one collection, either; sequels followed, including *Son of Origins of Marvel Comics* in 1975, which reprinted the first issues featuring the X-Men, Daredevil, and the Silver Surfer (figure 0.2). Reading and rereading these volumes were a delight and an education, and it is in tribute to that era of the late 1970s

---

1. Some details of the history of these advertisements can be found in this unexpected essay on a model train website: <http://www.thortrains.net/milihistriot/comictoys/comicbooktoysoldiersintro.html>

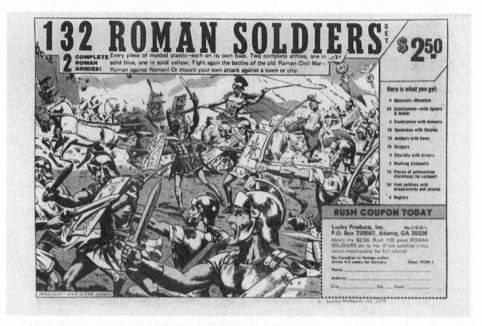

FIGURE 0.1 Advertisement for plastic Roman soldiers, 1968. Art by Ross Heath.

when one of us first became aware of comics as a medium that we have named this book *Son of Classics and Comics*.[2]

As this book demonstrates, the intersection of classics and comics remains a fertile ground for the meaningful exploration of antiquity.[3] The essays in this volume expand the purview of its predecessor, with more emphasis on European, Japanese, and independent comics. No study can be exhaustive, and so in this introduction we look at a number of classical comics that are not considered in the main chapters, some of which certainly warrant future critical study.

History Comics

The imaginative realm of comics is nearly without limits, and the medium allows the creation of "classical" stories that can defy logic, probability, or historical facts. Consider "The Last Shrill Laugh of the Phantom," a seven-page story in a 1970s horror comic, *Ghosts* 22 (DC, January 1974). No writer is credited, but the art by Filipino Jess Jodloman is dark and shadowed, which makes the ancient Roman ghost that appears to Benito Mussolini in 1922 even more spectral, as pale blue shading and particularly fine black lines leave a white, uninked background in many of the panels; the ghost's substance is signaled on the page with visible absence. The specter

2. The other, younger editor began reading these same issues, found at the back of his cousin's closet, a few years later.

3. Interest in the topic has lead to fruitful study elsewhere. See Lochman (1999); Espino Martín (2002); Herreros Tabernero (2002); Geus and Eickhoff (2006); Hernándes Reyes (2008); Pitcher (2009); Moula (2012); Marshall (forthcoming). The role of Latin comics in the (German) classroom is considered by Fuhrmann (1976); Frings (1978); Graf von Rothenburg (1989).

FIGURE 0.2 One of the earliest means of "researching" the Marvel Universe. *Son of Origins of Marvel Comics* (Fireside, 1974). Cover art by John Romita, Sr.

spurs Il Duce to ambition, and his rise to power and allegiance with the Nazis will help "build the second Roman Empire . . . and I will be the greatest Roman who ever lived" (14.2).[4] Only as Mussolini dies by hanging in 1945 does the ghost reveal his identity as Julius Caesar, laughing maniacally at the successor who eventually succumbed to the same grievous fault that had destroyed him.

Another Roman ruler appears, equally unexpectedly, in *Incredible Hulk* 5 (January 1963) by Stan Lee (w.) and Jack Kirby (a.), when the Hulk battles a subterranean sorcerer named Tyrannus. Tyrannus, it emerges, is an immortal sorcerer from ancient Rome named Romulus Augustus. Historians will therefore shudder to discover that the last emperor of the western Roman Empire, reigning from 475 to 476, was a usurper magician before he was deposed by Odoacer. Ancient sources are silent on Romulus Augustus' ultimate fate, but few have suspected his superhuman longevity, his psionic powers, or his mastery of advanced technology which he uses to battle the Hulk in the 1960s. Although it is off the wall, *Incredible Hulk* 5 shows how gaps in the historical record can leave space for speculative fiction.

The interaction of history with a present era is more meticulously explored in *Pax Romana* (Image Comics, 2010) by Jonathan Hickman (w./a.), in which the Catholic Church uses time travel to aid Constantine in securing an empire and Christianity's future.[5] The selection of Constantine is preceded in the comic by intense historical debate on the part of church elders. Within the imagined world, the timeline may only be altered once, at which point the present-day decision-makers effectively cease to exist. It is therefore imperative that they choose the most significant moment in their timeline to disrupt. *Pax Romana* is a demanding, text-heavy comic, but it prompts an informed reader to consider some big questions about a key moment in Western history.

Comics adaptations of historical lives and events can, like the sources on which they are based, adopt fictionalizing approaches. In the 1950s, *Valor* 1–5 (EC, March–December 1955, collected 1988), a short-lived anthology series that focused on historical drama, consistently included a story set in Rome.[6] Events during the Second Punic War are presented in three Italian albums by Giovanni Brizzi (w.) and Sergio Tiselli (a.): *Occhi di lupo. Un'avventura ai tempi di Annibale* (Savena Setto Sambro, 2004), *Foreste di Morte* (2006), and *Ad portas – La battaglia del Trasimeno* (2013); the earlier conflict between Regulus, the Carthaginians, and a giant snake is presented in *Bagradas*, by Valerio Massimo Manfredi (w.) and Diana Manfredi

---

4. As in *Classics and Comics*, references will be made where appropriate to page and panel number thus: "14.2" here refers to panel 2 on page 14 of *Ghosts* issue 22. Comics are a collaborative medium, and it is frequently important to distinguish writer (w.) from artist or penciller (a.), though at times both tasks are completed by the same person (w./a.).

5. Hickman's work is discussed in Marshall (2015).

6. "The Arena," *Valor* 1: 1–7, Carl Wessler (w.), A. Williamson and A. Torres (a.), with the prose essay "The Guardians of Empire" on p. 8, describing the Roman army; "The Champion," *Valor* 2: 1–7, A. Williamson (a.), with the prose essay "No Survivors" on p. 8, on the Spartans; "The Cloak of Command," *Valor* 3: 1–7, Otto Binder (w.) and A. Williamson (a.); "The Pyramid," *Valor* 3: 17–21, B. Krigstein (a.); "Gratitude," *Valor* 4: 1–7, J. Orlando (a.); and "Dangerous Animal," *Valor* 5: 1–7, W. Wood (a.). All published by EC, 1955. Both Williamson and Wood had long, prolific careers that transcended studios and genres and survived the censorship pressures that forced EC to cancel most of its series and focus instead on *MAD Magazine*.

(a.) (Ailiberti, 2011). *Caligula* 1–6 (Avatar, January–October 2011, collected 2012) and *Caligula: Heart of Rome* 1–6 (Avatar, October 2012–July 2013), by David Lapham (w.) and German Noble (a.), combine an ultraviolent presentation of Rome during the reign of Caligula with supernatural horror. Other, less violent examples exist. Designed for schoolchildren and billed as "graphic nonfiction" (a phrase meant to provide an implicit contrast with "graphic novel"), a series of forty-eight-page biographies appeared in 2005, with volumes on Cleopatra, Julius Caesar, Spartacus, and Alexander the Great.[7] These are accompanied by illustrated overviews of geography and the aftermath of the events presented, along with a glossary and a short bibliography. In spite of the somewhat rough art, the storytelling attempts to create some literary touches (as when young Alexander shows a beautifully drawn damselfly to Aristotle, over a page and a half, 8.1–9.2).

More ambitious is *Marathon* (First Second, 2012), by Boaz Yakin (w.) and Joe Infurnari (a.). The careful pen work and dynamic use of panel layout help create a sense of tension and constant, urgent movement, and the sepia coloring conveys (if through an anachronistic association) a sense of depth and authenticity to the world presented. Yakin opts for Eucles as the name of the runner rather than Pheidippides, following Plutarch and his sources (*Moralia* 347C), and makes him the same man who conveyed news of the imminent Persian attack between Athens and Sparta (the role Herodotus 6.105 ascribes to Pheidippides). Although it stands successfully as an independent work, there can be no doubt that *Marathon* would not exist if Frank Miller's *300* had not come first for Persian War stories in the comics medium; and *300* itself continues to attract scholarly attention.[8]

As will be clear from this handful of examples, the presence of a historical figure does nothing to ensure actual historical content within a modern adaptation in any medium. A young Cleopatra can have time-travel adventures in the future, as in *Cleopatra in Space* by Mike Maihack (w./a.), without interfering with the attested historical facts.[9] Similarly, there can be entirely fictional narratives located within a convincing historical setting. In *Pompeii* (Picturebox, 2013), creator Frank Santoro (w./a.) presents the separate romantic entanglements of a painter and his apprentice in the lead-up to the eruption of Vesuvius in 79 CE. The rough sketchbook-like illustration is presented uncompleted, unlinked, and uncolored, suggesting initial raw sketches rather than a finished work of art, as if the events of the narrative have prevented the comic's completion. The warmth of the brown ink on cream paper invites the reader's complicity to fill out the ancient world. At the same time, the organization of panels and composition within panels display an awareness of formal balance that would seem to expect a more finished product. Like the works of art created within the story, *Pompeii* presents the process of creation as it is happening.

---

7. *Cleopatra: The Life of an Egyptian Queen*, Gary Jeffrey and Anita Ganeri (w.) and Ross Watton (a.); *Julius Caesar: The Life of a Roman General*, Gary Jeffrey and Katie Petty (w.) and Sam Hadley (a.); *Spartacus: The Life of a Roman Gladiator*, Rob Shone and Anita Ganeri (w.) and Nick Spender (a.). *Alexander the Great: The Life of a King and Conqueror*, Rob Shone and Anita Ganeri (w.) and Chris Odgers (a.). All published by Rosen, 2005.

8. Fotheringham (2012); Kovacs (2013); Marshall (2014). See also the parody by Leo Ortolani, *299+1* (Panini Comics, 2011; originally in *Rat-Man* 62–63, September–November 2007).

9. Based on a web comic, Book 1, *Target Practice* (Graphix, 2014), finds Cleo destined to fulfill an ancient prophecy and overthrow a galactic overlord, Xaias Octavian. She also attends a space high school.

Mythic Figures

The *Olympians* series by George O'Connor (w./a.) continues to appear, now numbering seven volumes.[10] O'Connor, who generously provided the cover art for *Classics and Comics* and for this book, structures each volume around a particular god but often uses this frame as a means to retell narratives of heroes. *Poseidon* presents stories of both Theseus and Odysseus, and this juxtaposition also allows a parallelism to emerge between the Minotaur and the Cyclops that is not explicit in antiquity; similarly, *Hera* features Heracles and Jason, inviting further comparison of those two heroes. Although these volumes also contain some pedagogical apparatus, the storytelling is strong and offers a nuanced and sometimes touching vision of classical myth.

Figures from myth regularly appear in other comics, too, although not all of these appearances are substantial.[11] The four stories in *The Savage Axe of Ares* (Marvel, June 2010), a single-issue black-and-white anthology, allude through the title to the long-running *The Savage Sword of Conan* (Marvel, 235 issues, 1974–1995), but the focus on the war god independent of a larger superheroic context was unsuccessful. It followed another series, *Dark Avengers: Ares* (Marvel, three issues, 2009–2010) by Kieron Gillen (w.) and Manuel Garcia (a.). Neither seems to have had the larger impact of the earlier series, *Ares: God of War* (five issues, collected 2006) by Michael Avon Oeming (w.) and Travel Foreman (a.).[12] Its presentation of Ares as a struggling father has been absorbed into the larger Marvel continuity, as discussed below.

In *Olympus*, a one-off trade paperback (2005) by Geoff Johns (w.), Kris Grimminger (w.), and Butch Guice (a.), a teacher scuba diving with three undergraduate students discovers Pandora's box with the lid open. The lesson for university professors is clear: never take students to the Mediterranean on your own. Shortly after, they are hijacked by diamond smugglers, and the entire group is washed up on a mysterious island on which dwell all the mythical creatures of Greek myth. There is little sophistication to the narrative, and the Cyclopes and the Minotaur, meaningfully juxtaposed in O'Connor's *Poseidon*, appear as narratively disposable obstacles and a cheap motivation for violent action sequences. Although it is implied that the cultural knowledge of the teacher and her students is of value in negotiating the perils of Olympus, said knowledge is highly superficial in this Hollywood version of Greek myth. As with the films *Clash of the Titans* (2010), *Immortals* (2011), and *Wrath of the Titans* (2012), *Olympus* clearly demonstrates the lengths to which Greek myth must be distorted to accommodate the modern action-film template.

Bearing the same title was *Olympus* (Image, 1–4, collected 2009), by Nathan Edmondson (w.) and Christian Ward (a.). Castor and Pollux are modern-day bounty hunters for Zeus; they enforce the laws of Olympus and chase down renegades, including those who escape from the Underworld. The characters are better developed here, but the series again failed to find a following.

---

10. *Zeus: King of the Gods* (First Second, 2010); *Athena: Grey-Eyed Goddess* (2010); *Hera: The Goddess and Her Glory* (2011); *Hades: Lord of the Dead* (2012); *Poseidon: Earth Shaker* (2013); *Aphrodite: Goddess of Love* (2013); *Ares: Bringer of War* (2015).

11. Marshall (2011a) discusses a surprise appearance of Athena in an intergalactic boxing ring.

12. See Simms (2011). *Ares: God of War* was republished in a trade paperback along with *Dark Avengers: Ares* in 2010.

In a similar vein is *Greek Street*, by Peter Milligan (w.) and Davide Gianfelice (a.). It, too, was canceled after a short run of only sixteen issues (2009–2010). Named after Greek Street in London's Soho, the series is a gritty crime comic following the interconnected lives of the criminal underworld as the legends of Greek tragedy supernaturally impose themselves on the lives of the characters (Uncenta Gómez 2012). Gianfelice's artwork, with strong, thick lines and printed in panels separated by black gutters, renders a dark and often claustrophobic world appropriate to Greek tragedy. As modern analogs of Oedipus, Agamemnon, Cassandra, Medea, and other major figures of Greek myth are propelled inexorably toward their gory fates, the police inspector Dedalus (*sic*) attempts to make sense of it all, assisted by a lieutenant who possesses a classical education from Oxford (*Greek Street* 7, 18.1: "Well remembered, sir. We'll make a Classicist of you yet.").[13] *Greek Street* often loses its narrative thread in its attempt to outgore its tragic exemplars, and the amount of sex and violence is a byproduct of the creators' reliance on voyeurism to attract readers.

The standout story of *Greek Street* is "Ajax," a three-issue arc (*Greek Street* 12–14) largely separated from the events of the primary storyline, although some characters, including Dedalus, make cameo appearances. Soldier Alex Jackson has returned from Afghanistan, suffering posttraumatic stress disorder (PTSD) from an event revealed over the course of the story.[14] He blames the minister of defense for blocking proper recognition of his military honors. As a private, Alex's wartime experience is not exceptional, but his assumptions of his own importance and demands for acknowledgment from a figure of importance resonate well with readings of Sophocles' *Ajax* that explore the link between thinking big (ambiguously linked to the concept of hubris) and its consequences.[15]

As a popular and creative medium, comics also hold the potential to develop Greek myth, rather than simply transplant it, as is the case in many of the examples above. More innovative still is *Hybrid Bastards!* by Tom Pinchuk (w.) and Kate Glasheen (a.), a three-issue miniseries (Archaia, 2007–2008). In revenge for Zeus' innumerable infidelities and as an extension of the creative forms of his mythical seductions and rapes (swans, bulls, golden showers), Hera and Hypnos enchant Zeus for a single evening, during which he has sex with a wide range of inanimate objects. Since Zeus' fecundity is infallible, these objects give birth to hybrid creatures, crosses between Zeus' human form and whatever object served as the unwilling parent. The series chronicles the attempts of a small group of these offspring as they seek revenge and achieve recognition as Zeus' heirs. Similarly, the short stories in *Rage of Poseidon* (Drawn and Quarterly, 2013), by Anders Nilsen (w./a.), give postmodern takes on classical and Judeo-Christian figures and events (including Isaac, Prometheus, Athena, and the Flood) accompanied by simple but striking black-and-white

13. The direct narrative resonance between the ancient world and the modern exemplified in *Greek Street* is anticipated in *Testament* (22 issues, Vertigo, February 2006–March 2008) by Douglas Rushkoff (w.) (art by Liam Sharp, Gary Erskine, and Dean Ormston). *Testament* juxtaposes stories set in antiquity (Pentateuch-era narratives combined with alternative traditions and mythologies) with a primary near-future narrative in which Jake Stern and his friends fight a totalitarian American government.

14. The use of Greek myth as a vehicle for understanding PTSD, both for modern-day veterans and for their psychiatrists, has seen meaningful exploration; see Shay (1994); Shay (2002); Meineck (2009).

15. Winnington-Ingram (1980, 11–56); Cairns (1994); Cairns (2005).

images, in an accordion-fold book, in which the structure proclaims an ultimate unity of myth.[16]

As with the examples of history comics already discussed, works in this category can exhibit a range of relationships with the depiction of antiquity. This book begins with a series of examinations of Homeric adaptations. C. W. Marshall (chapter 1) uses *The Infinite Horizon* (Image, 2012), by Gerry Duggan (w.) and Phil Noto (a.), to consider the history of adaptations of the *Iliad* and the *Odyssey*. Building on other recent work,[17] George Kovacs (chapter 2) describes the ambitious approach to re-presenting myth in *Age of Bronze* by Eric Shanower (w./a.). *Asterios Polyp* (Pantheon, 2009), by Dave Mazzucchelli (w./a.), traces the existential crisis of its title character, a paper architect. The experiences of Asterios are both implicitly and explicitly associated with the trials of Odysseus, Orpheus, and other figures of Greek myth. *Asterios Polyp* is the magnum opus of an established mainstream comics practitioner.[18] In this book, Abram Fox and HyoSil Suzy Hwang-Eschelbacher (chapter 3) explore the impressively complex network of cultural and literary allusions at play in this work.

Superheroes

Over the course of time, the many characters that make up the larger continuities of the Marvel and DC universes proliferate, and they often are relegated to the background for years at a time, only to reemerge and be redeployed by a new writer. The bulk of the readership itself might not be familiar with the character, but there is a sense that some measure of attention to previous continuities rewards the intrepid reader. Such cross-references are much easier to accomplish (and detect) in the age of the Internet than they were when they depended on the memory of the reader, when at times the editor would include an actual footnote to inform readers where this character might previously have appeared.[19] Such reminders were a key element in the success of Marvel Comics, when writer-editor Stan Lee (and his successors) would point out links to other issues or series, generating a spirit of collusion through which the series editors invite the readership into an insider's world. The practice was immensely popular with readers, and creators have been using the tactic ever since.

16. One other example not discussed in this book is the first issue of Matt Fraction (w.) and Christian Ward (a.), *Ody-C* (Image, November 2014). This psychedelic reimagining places the *Odyssey* narrative in deep space. Its science-fiction themes and sexual content are reminiscent of the *Heavy Metal* adaptations (see chapter 1 in this book), but its most defining feature must be its adherence to "Rule 63," a modern adage suggesting that for every male character in popular culture, there exists, or could exist, a female counterpart. Almost all the figures of *Ody-C* are female.

17. Shanower (2011); Sulprizio (2011).

18. We discuss some of Mazzucchelli's other work in Marshall and Kovacs (2011). Another important Orpheus adaptation is that of Dino Buzzati's *Poema a fumetti* (1969); see González Delgado (2010).

19. This signals one of the primary differences between myth building in ancient myth and myth building in modern comics. Greek myth grows organically, with individual creators drawing on a shared mythographic history and amending or emphasizing certain details in each iteration of a myth's telling. In comics, the myth is consciously built, with a controlling creative (and financial) interest guiding and reshaping the narrative as necessary. Thus, even classical heroes will appear differently in modern comics. See Uncenta Gómez (2007).

For example, Walt Simonson (w./a.) displayed his myth-making abilities in such narratives with *The Judas Coin* (DC, 2012), which follows through time one of the thirty pieces of silver given to Judas Iscariot as it motivates or intersects with six DC characters in tales of treachery. The first of these, a thirteen-page story called "Blood Peace," concerns the death of Marcus the Golden Gladiator during the reign of Vespasian. The Golden Gladiator had first appeared in *Brave and the Bold* 1 (DC, August–September 1955), an anthology series that would eventually introduce the Justice League in issue 28 (February–March 1960). Although the storytelling in that first appearance was overshadowed by Joe Kubert's art in "Viking Prince" (a character also reimagined in Simonson's *Judas Coin*), the character of Marcus (living in an imprecise era of the Roman Empire) was not widely used within the early DC comics continuity[20] and has appeared only occasionally in the past three decades.[21] Most readers will not have had direct familiarity with the character previously, but the inclusion of the Golden Gladiator in *The Judas Coin* helps reinforce the grand sweep of the DC Comics universe, tying one of its most popular characters, Batman, with some of the least known.

One of the givens within the world of hero comics is that a character's death can always be revisited, either through retconning (retroactively changing the narrative continuity) or simply by recognizing that for superpowered beings, including the divinities of classical mythology, death is not the final barrier that it is in life. When Triton kills his father, Poseidon, in *Aquaman* 42 (DC, March 1998), by Peter David (w.) and J. Calafiore (a.), no reader genuinely expects this to be the end of Poseidon within the DC continuity, and indeed the status quo is restored following a *katabasis* by Aquaman a mere four months later in *Aquaman* 46 (DC, July 1998).[22]

Both Marvel and DC, the two biggest producers of hero comics in North America, have developed the Greek pantheon and integrated these gods into their larger meta-narratives. The reach of any of these works would require much more extensive study, but a quick survey focusing on a few individuals is both possible and informative. Mars, Venus, and Hercules (the Roman names are more typically used in comics, though both are found) are familiar enough as mythological figures that both companies have felt they could appropriate them into their larger mythic tapestries (they are, after all, out of copyright and fall within the public domain).[23] As we have seen, there is a strong internal incentive within these large publishing houses to maintain continuity over time, with the events in one comic having an impact on the

---

20. *Brave and the Bold* 1–3, France Herron (w.), Russ Heath (a.); *Brave and the Bold* 4, Robert Kanigher (w.), Russ Heath (a.); *Brave and the Bold* 6, Bill Finger (w.), Russ Heath (a.). Finger had been instrumental in the creation of Batman in the 1930s and Green Lantern in the 1940s. These early issues also included little two-page comics essays on historical subjects, including the legions of Rome (1), siege weapons (2), Caesar in Gaul (3), Roman galleys (5), and the siege of Troy (6).

21. *All-Star Squadron* 54–55 (February–March 1986), *The War That Time Forgot* 2–9 (August 2008–March 2009), and now *The Judas Coin*.

22. Aquaman, like many oceanic denizens in comics, is associated explicitly with Atlantis, a fictional location that is almost totally removed from its classical context in North America, though not in Europe; see Kaelin (1999).

23. For example, *Venus*, a romance comic, ran for 19 issues (August 1948–April 1952). The goddess comes to earth and becomes editor of Beauty magazine, though later episodes transform the narrative into "strange stories of the supernatural" (beginning with issue 11). This transition occurs just before the evolution of the publishing company transforms from Timely Comics to Atlas Comics (it will later become Marvel), see Kovacs (2011, 16–18). *Venus* 1–9 were collected in 2011.

events in others. Even if the serial nature of comics narrative is such that stories and characters are expected to persist (even after the cancellation of an individual series), this uncoordinated narrative practice reinforces itself so that certain individuals also persist. Depending on the whims of a current writer, previously minor figures can be granted new life and new promi-nence (for a time) within the fictional universe.

At Marvel, one example of this comes from Greg Pak, who began writing *The Incredible Hulk* in 2006, a series featuring one of the (physically) strongest figures in the Marvel Universe. Hulk, perhaps surprisingly, is a challenge to write if one is to avoid page after page of punching, and Pak's six years writing the character saw a fascinating development, even if the nature of comics "events" (cross-title stories that help drive sales) meant that the narrative crossed mul-tiple titles and resulted in confusing numeration.[24] Following the excellent sword-and-sorcery tale "Planet Hulk" (issues 92–105), Pak reduces the role of the Hulk within the primary series, and this facilitates a transition that leads to renaming the series *The Incredible Hercules*, begin-ning with issue 112.

The Incredible Hercules, coauthored with Fred Van Lente and using a variety of artists, maintained a lighter tone than the previous series but foregrounded the son of Zeus in a con-tinuing series for the first time (*Incredible Hercules* 112–141, January 2008–April 2010).[25] Marvel's Hercules had appeared regularly as an antagonist to the Norse god Thor, beginning with *Journey into Mystery* annual 1 (October 1965), by Stan Lee (w.) and Jack Kirby (a.), and regularly since then.[26] He headed a Los Angeles-based superteam in the 1970s called the Champions, for which Pluto, the god of the Underworld, was a principal villain (*Champions* 1–17, October 1975–January 1978). He also appeared in a number of limited series by Bob Layton (w./a.) set in the future, in which he wanders the Andromeda Galaxy in a space chariot as he learns the meaning of humility.[27]

While some of the story arcs in *The Incredible Hercules* were weaker because they, too, were tying into "events," narratives could be both entertaining and classically aware. Issues 112

24. Pak wrote *Incredible Hulk* 92–111 (April 2006–December 2007) with Carlo Pagulayan, Aaron Lopresti, Gary Frank, Leonard Kirk, et al.; *World War Hulk* 1–5 (August 2007–January 2008) with John Romita Jr,; *World War Hulk: After Smash* 1 (January 2008) with Rafa Sandoval; *World War Hulk Aftersmash: Warbound* 1–5 (February 2008–June 2008) with Leonard Kirk and Rafa Sandoval; *Skaar: Son of Hulk* 1–12 (August 2008–August 2009) with Ron Garney, Ron Lim, et al.; *Incredible Hulk* 601–611 (October 2009–October 2010) with Ariel Olivetti and Paul Pelletier; *Incredible Hulks* 612–635 (November 2010–August 2011) with Tom Raney, Barry Kitson, Paul Pelletier, Dale Eaglesham, Tom Grummett, et al. Other related short series were also created at this time with other writers.

25. These were followed by *Hercules: Fall of an Avenger* 1–2 (May–June 2010), by Greg Pak and Fred Van Lente (w.) and Ariel Olivetti (a.), and *Heroic Age: Prince of Power* 1–4 (July–October 2010), with Reilly Brown (a.).

26. Several of these encounters were collected in *Thor versus Hercules* (Marvel, 2010), collecting material from *Journey into Mystery* annual 1; *Thor* 126, 221, 356, 400, 437, annual 5; *Thor: Blood Oath* 3–4; and *Incredible Hercules* 136.

27. *Hercules, Prince of Power* 1–4, by Bob Layton (w./a.) (September–December 1982); series 2, 1–4 (March 1984–June 1984); *Hercules, Prince of Power: Full Circle* (1988); *Hercules: Twilight of a God* 1–4 (August–November 2010), by Bob Layton (w.) and Ron Lim (a.). These narratives seem inspired in part by the cinematic space fantasy of the *Star Wars* films, with Hercules being accompanied by the Recorder, an android evocative of C-3PO. See also *Hercules and the Heart of Chaos* 1–3, by Tom DeFalco (w.) and Ron Frenz (w./a.) (August–October 1997), and *Hercules: The New Labors of Hercules* 1–5, by Frank Tierl (w.) and Mark Texeira (a.) (June–September 2005), which are even less promising.

to 115, as Herc and boy genius Amadeus Cho fight Ares and ally themselves with Athena, are regularly punctuated by flashbacks to thirteenth-century BCE Greece, and this is a technique that returns sporadically through the remainder of the series. The presentation of Ares and the other Olympians in the series draws heavily on the ground cleared in *Ares: God of War* 1–5. *Incredible Hercules* 121–125 feature Gorgons, Amazons, and the Titan Atlas using the Washington Monument as a club (issue 124, p. 9). The presence of humor in the series at this point reinforces the ambivalent place that Heracles held in fifth-century Athenian thought: he could be hero, god, drunkard, or glutton, as needed (Silk 1985), and certainly all of those qualities are evident here. Readers are given a prepubescent reincarnated Zeus (131–142) and Hercules pretending to be Thor on a visit to Svartalfheim, the land of the Dark Elves in Norse mythology (131–36). Pak and Van Lente even show their work, as it were, by having Cho read up on Joseph Campbell's theories about the hero's journey (issue 133, pp. 2–6). This narrative self-awareness allows the authors to deviate from the pattern meaningfully when, in issues 138 to 141, Hercules and Cho take on Hera and the "Olympus Group" (the Greek gods' corporate holdings on Earth), who are supported by the Titan Typhon (Typhoeus). Following *Incredible Hercules* was another short-lived continuing series, *Herc* 1–10, by Pak and Van Lente (w.) with various artists.[28]

By having Herc and the Greek and Norse mythological pantheons active in the world of superheroes, Marvel makes an implicit statement about the nature of the stories it tells in its superhero comics; the transition from Hulk to Hercules in Pak's tenure as writer, without interruption of issue numbers, suggests that the two characters are both somehow operating at the same level of engagement with the readership's consciousness. (One can even argue that the eventual decline in sales suggests that Hercules was an unworthy successor to Bruce Banner and the Hulk.) More interesting, though, is the exploration of the stories one tells about a paradigmatic hero of strength. Both Hulk and Hercules are presented as being exceptionally strong physically, even though (as it emerges) the narrative interest for Pak resides in Athena's mentorship of Amadeus Cho, a hero of intellect. Cho serves as a counterpoint to the intellectual superheroes who had exiled the Hulk to space at the beginning of Pak's run on *The Incredible Hulk*, offering a rehabilitation of the academic, even if it comes at the cost of the more iconic figures of strength within the Marvel Universe.

A similar development can be observed with the treatment of Greek mythological figures within the DC Universe. Hercules first appears in a flashback within the first Wonder Woman story, published in December 1941 (*All Star Comics* 8, December 1941), by William Moulton Marston (w.) and H. G. Peter (a.). Hercules, along with Aphrodite, Athena, and Ares, who all first appear in *Wonder Woman* 1 (Summer 1942), regularly informs the celestial politics that must be faced by the Amazons of Paradise Island throughout the coming decades. In the 1970s, DC's Hercules was given a short-lived series called *Hercules Unbound* 1–12 (November 1975–September 1977),[29] but this seemed to develop a separate continuity. Set after the nuclear strikes of World War III in 1986, Hercules frees himself from a Promethean punishment to

28. Frustratingly, there were eleven issues published, numbered 1–6 (June–October 2011), 6.1 (October 2011), and 7–10 (November 2011–January 2012).

29. Issues 1–6 by Gerry Conway (w.) and Jose Luis Garcia-Lopez (a.); 7–9 by David Michelenie (w.) and Walt Simonsen (a.); 10–12 by Cary Bates (w.) and Walt Simonsen (a.).

help survivors of the devastation (figure 0.3).[30] By issue 9, the inking of this comic (producing the finished art from the pencils supplied by the initial artist) had been handed over from veteran Wally Wood to his apprentice (Wood had worked at *Mad* in the 1950s, and at Marvel, he introduced Daredevil's striking red costume). The apprentice was Bob Layton, who would then proceed to ink Marvel's *Champions* and then write and draw Marvel's own versions of Hercules in the future.[31]

There are many possible points of entry to contemporary Wonder Woman stories. Greg Rucka's run on *Wonder Woman* 195–226 (October 2003–April 2006, collected in five volumes 2004–2006) offers a well-paced extended story that has much to offer the classically minded reader.[32] Set against a background in which Athena usurps the throne of Olympus from Zeus, the plot renders bare the political machinations of the gods through a consistent anchoring of the story with *Iliad* 1. Zeus' throne is even protected by Briareos, one of the Hecatonchires (the Hundred-Handed Ones), who is presented as a surprisingly plausible antagonist. A retelling of the Perseus myth as a bedtime story (issue 200, March 2004, with Drew Johnson [a.]) is followed by a duel with a reincarnated Medousa (the spelling is Rucka's) in Yankee Stadium (issue 210, January 2005), while a subplot follows the latter-day adventures of the Minotaur (a chef named Ferdinand[33]), whom Wonder Woman takes on a *katabasis* (issues 215–217, June–July 2005, with Rags Morales [a.]). At the same time, the story is firmly grounded in the roots of Wonder Woman and features encounters with traditional villains Silver Swan, Doctor Psycho, Cheetah, Giganta (in passing), Circe (the witch from *Odyssey* 10 who is a recurring Wonder Woman villain), and, of course, Ares.

Ares had been an antagonist to Wonder Woman and the Amazons on Paradise Island since *Wonder Woman* 1. From the following issue until 1987, writers used the Roman form Mars; the Greek name returned during the seminal 1980s run of George Perez (w./a.), in which many of the elements in Rucka's run find their origin. Perez's relaunch (tied closely with the momentous events in comics generally in the mid-1980s) reinvigorated the series (issues 1–24, February 1987–Winter 1988).[34] Paradise Island was renamed Themyscira, and the divine framework was made considerably more complex, with Diana (Wonder Woman's given name) receiving patronage from several female Greek divinities. Following the first two years (collected in four volumes published during Rucka's run, 2004–2006), many of the stories are not strong, as artists change and Perez gives way as writer to William Messner Loebs (63–100) and then John Byrne (101–136). Other individuals take up the title of Wonder Woman (the official representative of Themyscira to the Patriarch's World),

---

30. Although the cover of *Hercules Unbound* 1 belies its postapocalyptic setting, it does pay clear homage to the Hercules films of Steve Reeves, the poster for which depicted the hero in chains.

31. Other companies have also created comics versions of Hercules. *Hercules: The Thracian Wars* 1–5 (Radical Comics, May–September 2008, collected 2008), by Steve Moore (w.) and Admira Wijaya (a.), is set in antiquity after the completion of the labors. It became a film in 2014.

32. Rucka's stand-alone Wonder Woman story *Hiketeia* is discussed by Marshall (2011b).

33. Ferdinand's name alludes to the bovine protagonist in the 1936 children's tale *The Story of Ferdinand*, by Munro Leaf (w.) and Robert Lawson (a.).

34. Perez continued to write the series until issue 62 (February 1992; he coauthored it with Mindy Newell for issues 36–46 and 49).

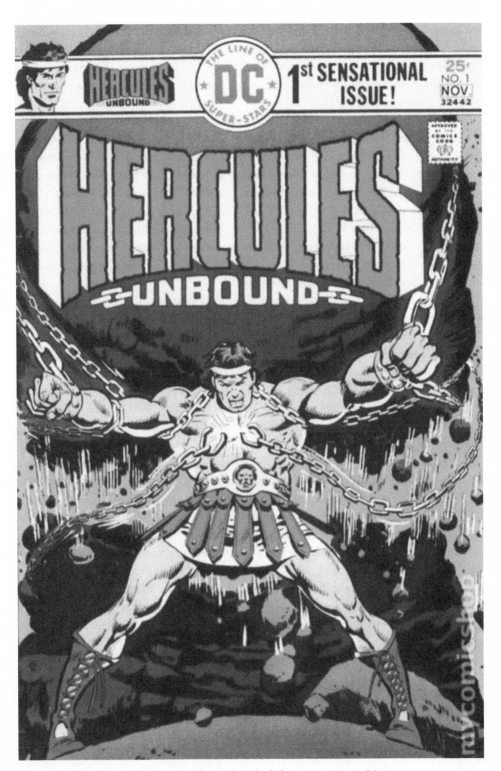

FIGURE 0.3 *Hercules Unbound* 1 (July 1976). Pencils and inks by José Luis García-López.

and in the years that followed, Diana briefly became a goddess ruling from Olympus. Some invigorating breath was given to the series when Phil Jimenez became cowriter (with J. M. DeMatteis) and artist, and his first storyline featured Eris, Phobos, and Deimos—all children of Ares—taking over the bodies of Batman villains, until Ares himself appeared (issues 164–167, January–April 2001).[35]

The integration of Greek mythology into superhero comics is not always seamless. While classically themed heroes frequently face classically themed villains, the same classical heroes team up with Norse heroes and indeed are often deployed interchangeably (as with Hercules and Thor, who are both established powerhouses on superteams; both have tenure, for example, as members of the Avengers). There is typically a single mythological figure on the DC and Marvel superteams (Thor in Marvel's Avengers, Wonder Woman in DC's Justice League, and Wonder Girl in DC's Teen Titans).[36] There is often a sense that the characters somehow belong to another world and are simply being borrowed by the DC and Marvel Universes. It is arguable that not enough writers and artists are invested in the classical material, and consequently, its use as window dressing can at times disappoint.

Further, not everything from the big publishers fits securely into this category. Consider another short-run comic set in Rome, *Sweet XVI*, by Barbara Slate (w./a.) (Marvel, May 1991–November 1992). The story, told over six issues and a "back to school" special, features a handful of teenage characters in ancient Rome facing problems that may as well be shared by the teens of Riverdale in *Archie* comics: misplaced birthday invitations, romantic jealousy, and who will win the debate for student senate. References to the Roman setting are contextually superficial (a teacher lectures to bored students in Latin class, "As Tacitus says, blah, blah, blah, blah, blah . . ."; special 1, 59.3), and that is part of the fun for these comics targeting young female readers: "Dad said if I ace my Latin test, I can borrow the chariot Saturday night." "Awesomeus!" (issue 4, 22.1). Issues also offer short didactic comics on Roman numerals or how to read a sundial and encourage readers to write letters to Aria and Princess [*sic*] Cornelia, the Betty and Veronica substitutes who are rivals for Antony's affections.

Or consider the untold and unexpected function that classical narratives played in underground comix of the 1970s. *Gay Hearthrobs* 1 (Funhorne Productions, 1976) was a revolutionary comic from San Francisco, and it included an extended adaptation of Sophocles. "Oedipus Ritz" (pp. 10–21), by R. W. Borg (w./a.), utilizes a classical frame to set up what becomes an increasingly improbable but still violent variation on the familiar narrative, culminating in a night of sex between Oedipus and his daddy, followed by the appearance of Elektra and the Virgin Mary. The next issue, *Gay Heart Throbs* 2 (Larry Fuller Presents, March 1979), has a

---

35. More recent prominent writers of *Wonder Woman* include Gail Simone (issues 14–43, January 2008–July 2010) and by Brian Azzarello (issues 1–35, November 2011–December 2014). For a survey of Wonder Woman's history, see Gindhart and Gietzen (2015).

36. The Teen Titans are a group of superhero sidekicks, often exploring coming-of-age themes and the challenges of living in the shadow of adults; it consequently has an obvious appeal for teenage readers. Wonder Girl (Cassandra Sandsmark in the current storyline) is a protégée of Wonder Woman. A serious attempt to distinguish her narrative from that of Wonder Woman was made by giving her Ares as an ambiguous patron, beginning with *Teen Titans* 4 (December 2003), by Geoff Johns (w.) and Mike McKone (a.).

cover that promises, "In this issue . . . Spartans: the lusty saga of men in love and war" (M. Kuchar [a.]). "Spartans" (pp. 36–41, finishing on the inside back cover), by Ericuus Ashfil (w.) and Mike Kuchar (a.), tells a story of Manzer and Cayer fighting against Granolu, "debaucher of a thousand virgins," and his army of a thousand barbarians (none of these, needless to say, is an actual classical name). Fighting naked leads to sex following military victory. Cayer, however, has fled the battle, and Manzer chases him down to kill the deserter. The two friends have sex, during which Manzer stabs Cayer with a sword. Two classical narratives are found in *Gay Heart Throbs* 3 (Inkwell, Summer 1981), which contains both a gladiatorial narrative ("and still they come," pp. 1–9 and the back cover) and a short adaptation of myth ("Narcissus," pp. 17–21). Actual knowledge of classical sources is, of course, unimportant here. This countercultural use of classical narratives provided an expression of social rebellion for the gay community of the late 1970s and claimed a legitimizing heritage and legacy for what was then an underground lifestyle. At the same time, the violence and death that conclude all four of the classically inspired narratives can be read as a bleak prophecy for fuller social integration in America.[37]

Manga

The appeal of the Greek gods as blocking characters in comics narratives appears to transcend cultures. The Western academic study of Japanese comics has been limited, and the uncertain relationship between Japanese culture and an understanding of classical antiquity makes it especially problematic (Theisen 2011). Why should the Japanese be concerned with ancient Greece and Rome in the first place? Further challenges are posed by methodology. Many successful manga are adapted and translated for international markets (or become anime), so that disentangling the question of which text is being analyzed can be a substantial task.

Consider *Saint Seiya: Knights of the Zodiac*, by Masami Kurumada (w./a.). Twenty-eight volumes were published by Shueisha after individual chapters appeared in *Weekly Shônen Jump*, 1986–1991 (these were translated and published by Viz, 2004–2010). Armored warriors fight and serve Athena wearing armor inspired by the constellations. The hero, thirteen-year-old Seiya, wears the "Pegasus Cloth," which provides him with his supernatural abilities. Later volumes in the series involve extended stories centered around the gods Poseidon (14–18) and Hades (19–28). The success of the manga was exceptional, and versions and adaptations appeared in other media, including anime (including direct-to-video adaptations, known as OVAs, for "original video adaptations"), novels, video games, musicals, soundtracks on CD, and other merchandising. Even if the classical content were to be seen as more than simply cosmetic, this huge and diverse body of work would be a challenge to assemble into a straightforward narrative. Two sequel series, one by Kurumada and the other by Shiori Teshirogi, remain untranslated.

---

37. Also of interest from this period is the single issue of *Cyclops Comics* (Print Mint: December 1969), by John Thompson (w./a.). In 19 pages (plus a 2-page epilogue in Tibetan), what starts with a Hesiodic narrative of cosmogony becomes surreal imagery from Hebrew, Hellenistic Greek, and Tibetan mysticism and astrology. The comic is reprinted without its last page, but with an introduction in Nadel (2010, 198–216).

More straightforward is *Bride of Deimos* (*Akuma [Deimos] no Hanayome*), by Etsuko Ikeda (w.) and Yuhu Ashibe (a.) (published by Akita Shoten in *Princess*, 1975–83; seven of the series' seventeen volumes have been translated into English by ComicsOne, 2002–2004). *Bride of Deimos* is a *shôjo* (girls') horror manga, about a schoolgirl, Minako Ifu, who is pursued by Deimos, the Greek personification of fear, whose presentation is layered with Christian overtones that also equate him with the devil (*akuma* in Japanese). His twin sister, Venus, trapped in the Underworld, occasionally escapes in the form of a white butterfly. She looks just like Minako, and Deimos's pursuit is understood as a surrogate for his incestuous desire.[38]

Many manga are not (yet) translated from Japanese, and this has led to the emergence of online communities who crowdsource fan translations of works that may not otherwise receive a wider audience. These "scanlations" typically do not clear issues of copyright and can vary in tone significantly, even from page to page. For example, *Aries*, by Rurika Fuyuki (w./a.) (also published in *Princess*, beginning in 1987 and collected in twenty volumes), has been only partly scanlated. A *shôjo* romance, the series presents the Greek gods in a modern-day Japanese school, all in the bodies of (well-dressed, long-haired) students. Hades, disguised as a schoolboy named Amano, is trying to recapture the love of Persephone, in the form of school-girl Arisa. Alone of the gods, she is unaware of her mythological ancestry. A similar fate faces a character in a Korean comic (manhwa) with a similar name, *Ares* (also known as *Vagrant Soldier Ares*), by Ryu Kum-chel (w./a.) (twenty-six volumes, published by TeamMania and BB Comics, 2001–2007). Here, a young swordsman named Ares serves as a temple mercenary in the fictional country of Chronos. Many character names have classical pedigrees (Helena, Ariadne, Icarus), and the fantasy world depicted shares many features with (a modern, popular understanding of) ancient Rome. This series has been scanlated, but authorized translations in print form are unlikely ever to find a market, in part because of the existence of the scanlations online, in a self-perpetuating cycle wherein market demand is met by an unofficial product that in turn reduces demand for something official.

The most recent contribution in this category is the truly spectacular *Thermae Romae* (six volumes, 2008–2013), by Mari Yamazaki (w./a.), a *seinen* (young men's) manga translated into English in three hardcover collections (Yen Press, 2012–2014). During the reign of Hadrian, a young architect named Lucius is drawn to modern-day Japan, where his observations about bathing give him revolutionary ideas when he mysteriously returns to Rome. Yamazaki's jux-taposition of second-century Rome with modern Japan is carefully observed, and the humor emerges from the shared values of water and bathing, which are contrasted with, for example, the two cultures' differing senses of modesty and decency. Part of the fun is Yamazaki's treat-ment of cultural obstacles, as when Lucius adopts a legionary pose with a wooden bathmat as his shield and challenges some inebriated foreigners during one of his visits to Japan (figure 0.4). *Thermae Romae* has been adapted for television as an anime and for cinema as a live-action film

---

38. The story shares ideas with a ninety-six-page comic called *Headache*, by Lisa Joy (w.) and Jim Fern (a.) (Kickstart, 2011), in which Sarah Pallas, a nineteen-year-old girl in a modern American asylum, remembers that she is, in fact, the goddess Athena. The title alludes to the unique circumstances of the classical Athena's birth.

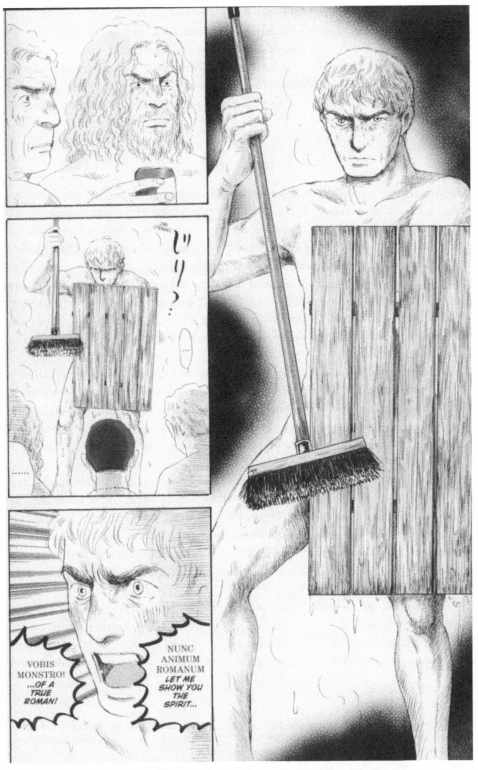

FIGURE 0.4 Lucius the gladiator in *Thermae Romae*, chapter 7 (w./a. M. Yamazaki).

(both in 2012).[39] These works are understated and ambitious and should be considered necessary reading for any interested in the intersection between classics and comics.

Three of the most familiar manga outside of Japan are studied in this book. Gideon Nisbet explores the classical content in *Appleseed* (chapter 4); Nicholas Theisen considers the nature of Homeric allusion in *Nausicaä of the Valley of the Wind* (chapter 5); and Sara Raup Johnson explores the image of the Persian king Xerxes in *Fullmetal Alchemist* (chapter 6).

Euro Comics

Continental Europe represents the third major region of the development of comics (Britain, though it has its own comics tradition, is typically more in line with North American comics) and has been the subject of an important scholarly collection based on an exhibit in Basel.[40] As in Japan, comics enjoy greater market penetration and are regarded more widely as literature in their own right, without the pejorative associations or defensive gestures that seek to claim legitimacy (such as the use of the term *graphic novel*), often still attached to American comics. Unlike in Japan, however, Greco-Roman antiquity is not the product of a foreign culture and occupies a much more foundational space. As such, European comics practitioners are able to rely on greater cultural literacy and demand deeper engagement in a more traditional way.

Attempts have been made to bring European comics to a broader North American market (the magazine *Métal Hurlant*, or *Heavy Metal*, is the best known of these). *Scourge of the Gods*, by Valérie Mangin (w.) and Aleksa Gajic (a.), recasts the fifth-century downfall of the western Roman Empire as space opera. In this series, space-faring Huns begin to systematically conquer colonized planets within the galactic "Roman Orbis." Originally published in France from 2000 to 2005, *Scourge of the Gods* was brought to an American audience by Marvel Soleil in 2009–2010. Roman history is a common subject in European comics, and *Scourge of the Gods* offers a cerebral tale, focused not only on the action of battle but also on the machinations of the political elite, as the series traces the rise and fall of significant historical figures such as Flavius Aetius, Valentinian III, and Atilla. A detailed knowledge of late antiquity is not a prerequisite for enjoyment of this comic, but the informed reader will be able to fill in many gaps in the narrative of the story by transposing historical details into the space-age story.

In this book, the discussion of the influence of European comics is clustered around one of its most influential representations. Three chapters on the *Asterix* series reveal the many ethnographic concerns that fueled the formation of the most widely distributed comic book in the world. Eran Almagor explores how cultural perceptions both ancient and

---

39. *Thermae Romae* also provides an example of how narratives span media, as the literary texture draws on different genres. The manga is inspired in part by the HBO series *Rome*, and the live-action film was able to use the *Rome* set. Increasingly, comics influence cinema in all the major markets.

40. Lochman (1999); see Carlà (2014).

modern allow *Asterix* to maintain a continuity between our world and the past (chapter 7). Stuart Barnett deconstructs the often contradictory claims of national independence made by the Gauls who fight Rome (chapter 8). Issues of nationalism and the intricacies of word play intersect in the discussion of translations of *Asterix* by Siobhán McElduff (chapter 9).[41] Together, these chapters represent a variety of approaches that can be integrated into a larger context of the use of comics to create a sense of national identity.[42]

Always More Comics

The dynamic possibilities of the comics medium are not limited when they encounter classical material. Opportunities exist for comics creators, whatever their background knowledge in classics. The growth of comics in the twentieth century allowed the medium to stand as a metonym for modernity. In that respect, comics are like cinema and television, genres that we have seen influence each other.[43] The engagement that results when the medium chooses to represent the past can be direct or indirect and can challenge the reader aggressively. In different ways, four chapters in this book interrogate the limits of that representation. Ian Runacres and Michael K. Mackenzie explore the rich use of classical reference in British political cartoons (chapter 10). Frederick Williams and Edward Brunner explore the introduction of classical material into a comics adaptation of that central text for modernism, T. S. Eliot's *The Waste Land* (chapter 11). The importance of Alexander the Great as a role model for the fictional character Ozymandias in *Watchmen* (DC, 1987), by Alan Moore (w.) and Dave Gibbons (a.), is discussed by Matthew Taylor (chapter 12). Finally, Kate Polak extends the discussion to biblical narrative as she expands on her earlier work on the DC comic *Lucifer* and considers alternatives to the Garden of Eden (Polak MacDonald 2012) (chapter 13).

As the presentation of classical material within the medium of comics continues to develop, there will continue to be a need for thoughtful scholarly engagement with it. The chapters in this book contribute to that study, expanding both the methodologies employed and the range of texts being examined. By introducing new scholarly voices, *Son of Classics and Comics* can model a number of different ways forward within this branch of classical reception studies. Our hope is that in doing so, it will encourage new contributions from other scholars, illuminating further the magnificent juxtaposition of printed words and static image that defines comics.[44]

41. For very different examinations of *Asterix* comics, see Kamp et al. (2011b), with Lloyd (2011) and Kamp et al. (2011a); see also Fuhrmann (1976); Lüthje (1979); Brenne (1999); Gentry (2004).

42. Moula (2012); see also Schnitzler (1999).

43. See also Fotheringham and Brooker (2013) for a discussion of comics, cinematic storyboarding, and the nature of epic.

44. Thanks are due to Melissa Funke, Sarah Chan, Corey Creekmur, and Jack Swan for identifying comics discussed in this introduction.

About the Cover

The cover for this book comes from George O'Connor, author and illustrator of the *Olympians* series. It is inspired by a late-sixth-century black-figure prize amphora from the Panathenaic games by Euphiletos, and the inclusion of superheroes in the race points to their embodiment of the pinnacle of human accomplishment.[45] Successful ancient athletes were compared to mythological heroes in epinician poetry (such as the songs of Pindar and Bacchylides) but were always warned against being too confident in their own abilities, lest they incur divine wrath (*phthonos*). At the same time, the notion of superheroes racing one another has been a staple of comics since August 1967, when the United Nations asked the Flash to race Superman for charity.[46] In this image, it is the speedster hero who naturally is the victor.

45. Metropolitan Museum of Art, New York, 14.130.12, c. 530 BCE. The cover image also bears similarity to another Panathenaic prize vase (in that each only has four runners), Staatliche Antikensammlungen, Munich, 1451, c. 530 BCE.

46. This and subsequent races between 1967 and 2002 were collected in *Superman vs. the Flash* (DC Comics, 2005). The stories come from *Superman* 199 (August 1967), *Flash* 175 (December 1967), *World's Finest Comics* 198–199 (July–October 1978), *Adventures of Superman* 462 (February 1990), *DC First Flash/Superman* (July 2002). More recent stories in this vein include *Flash* 209 (June 2004), *Flash: Rebirth* 3 (August 2009), and *Superman* 709 (May 2011). See also *Action Comics* 314 (July 1964), "The Day Superman Became the Flash." Of course the Flash is faster.

PART ONE

Postmodern Odysseys

1

Odysseus and *The Infinite Horizon*

C. W. Marshall

"Getting back home to her was my greatest achievement," the opening panel of Gerry Duggan and Phil Noto's comic *The Infinite Horizon* declares, and in so doing, it reveals its explicit debts to Homer's *Odyssey*. "Getting back home" embraces both *nostos* in *Odyssey* 1.5 and *nostimos* in *Odyssey* 1.9; the emphasis on the speaker's reunion with his wife ("to her") additionally offers a charged interpretation of the poem's first word, *andra*, as "husband." At the same time, the three inset panels on the page present the shutting of a door, closing off the possibility of homecoming for the Odysseus figure anytime soon (figure 1.1). *The Infinite Horizon* (w. Gerry Duggan, a. Phil Noto)[1] reconceptualizes Homer's *Odyssey* in the light of post-9/11 American foreign policy. Over six issues, the series, while not critical of the military, nevertheless encourages identification with the isolation of soldiers and the implications of foreign wars for their families. By providing a deep resonance and reinterpretation to the Homeric narrative, *The Infinite Horizon* invites a new understanding of the Iraq War and the traumatic costs of military violence for the individual. As an example of the reception of Homer for modern audiences, *The Infinite Horizon* may serve as an ideal site for an examination of the intersection between high and low culture, embodied respectively in Homer and comic books.

This discussion begins with a survey of adaptations of Homer in comics (section I) and is followed by an introduction to the Homeric aspects of *The Infinite Horizon* (section II). From

I wish to thank George Kovacs and Tony Keen for their incisive comments. This research was supported in part by the Social Sciences and Humanities Research Council of Canada.

1. The series appeared at a glacial pace from Image Comics; the first two issues were published with cover dates of December 2007 and January 2008, the third April 2008, the fourth April 2009, and the last two October and November 2011. A collected trade paperback appeared with a March 2012 date, but no new reader of the series will experience the long-delayed unresolved anticipation that accompanied the original publication—feelings that coordinate strongly with Homeric *nostos*. The serial format is crucial to the experience of reading comics and could be felt here particularly, as the ever-absent conclusion stretched into an unresolved future. A new selection of comics appears weekly, and for two and a half years, there was weekly anticipation of the arrival of the fifth issue. Because the pages in the collected edition are unnumbered, I refer to them here by "chapter" (issue) and page number (with individual panels noted where relevant). The six chapters are as follows: "Journey into Misery" (twenty-two pages), "Red Sky at Morning" (twenty-four pages), "Nobody's Invincible" (twenty-eight pages), "That Which Does Not Kill Us" (twenty-three pages), "Red Sky at Night" (twenty-six pages), and "Homecoming" (twenty-six pages). The collected edition adds a twelve-page "Prelude"—spoiling the effect of the powerful opening page of chapter 1 (figure 1.1)—and a one-page introduction by Duggan.

FIGURE 1.1 The prominence of *nostos* is stressed on the very first page of *The Infinite Horizon* 1.1 (Image, December 2007). Art by Phil Noto.

this, I develop a taxonomy of classical reception that emphasizes the degree of classical knowledge expected of the reader (section III). This taxonomy is then modeled in a consideration of the final chapters of *The Infinite Horizon* (section IV).

I

The Infinite Horizon is not the first adaptation of Homer into the comics medium. In November 1950, the series *Classics Illustrated* produced a forty-four-page adaptation of the *Iliad* (issue 77, art by Alex A. Blum), which emulated the narrative shape of the *Iliad* to a remarkable degree. The events of *Iliad* 1 are presented early (3–5), and for the most part, the story proceeds from there; even the Doloneia (*Iliad* 10, often believed to be a post-Homeric intrusion) receives full treatment (28–30). Consider the presentation of *Iliad* 22 on a single page (43; see figure 1.2, as Hector and Achilles fight). In panel 2, the circular panel shape provides a visual echo that replicates the shape of the shields the panel depicts, and this framing reinforces the clash of combat. The heroes appear to fight on clouds, removing any specific sense of topography from their timeless conflict. In panel 4, after Hector's dying curse, "Beware the anger of the gods" (*Il.* 22.356–360), Achilles answers, "Die, dog that you are . . . My doom I'll meet when it shall please the gods" (see *Il.* 22.356–366, with the vocative taken from 345); similarly, panel 3 summarizes *Iliad* 22.337–354, and panel 5 evokes many ancient artistic representations of Achilles dragging Hector (though with the inclusion of a charioteer and a modestly clothed corpse). It is not the case that most readers will notice what appears to be a conscious evocation of a specific, identifiable moment in Homer; such side-by-side comparisons are not expected. The entire issue, though, would seem to demonstrate a sincere trust that the Homeric narrative has the capability to communicate powerfully in the comics medium and implicitly that the comic in some way continues to represent Homer's story and not the Trojan War more generally. Or so one might think until the reader turns the page.

The ending of the *Classics Illustrated* version of the *Iliad* is abrupt: after a book-by-book treatment, the final page represents Books 23 and 24 in a single panel that deviates wildly from the Homeric narrative (44.1; see figure 1.3). The caption reads: "Thetis visited the tent of Achilles. She told him that Zeus was angered by Achilles' treatment of the body of Hector." She says, "'Tis the will of Zeus that you give up the body to King Priam." Achilles responds, "Let it be so if the gods will have it." This rewrite misses the funeral games of Patroclus, Priam's heartbreaking supplication of Achilles after having been guided from the city walls to Achilles' tent by the god Hermes, their intense conversation featuring the Parable of the Jars (*Il.* 24.525–551), Priam's return with the corpse of Hector, the mourning of the Trojan women, and finally the burial of Hector. The remaining two panels mention post-Iliadic events such as the death of Achilles and the Trojan horse (as Athena looks on from a battlement), with a scroll in the corner tidily proclaiming, "The end."

Even though the tragedy of Hector is lost completely, someone coming away from the comic will have learned something about the events of the *Iliad*.[2] This didactic purpose is explicit: the bottom of the last page informs the reader, "Now that you have read the Classics Illustrated edition, don't miss the added enjoyment of reading the original, obtainable at your

---

2. For the *Iliad* as tragedy, see Macleod (1982, 1–16).

FIGURE 1.2 The duel of Hector and Achilles from *Iliad* 22 in *Classics Illustrated* 77 (Gilberton, November 1950). Art by Alex A. Blum.

FIGURE 1.3 *Iliad* 23 and 24 (?) in *Classics Illustrated* 77 (Gilberton, November 1950). Art by Alex A. Blum.

school or public library." Four pages of text follow this, providing additional information on Homer and other volumes of the series.

There are other comics versions of Homer. In the 1970s, two versions of the *Odyssey* appeared in *Heavy Metal*, a science-fiction/fantasy/erotica magazine.[3] In 1974, Lob (w.) and G. Pichard (a.), two French creators, offered a science-fiction *Ulysses* in which the gods are technologically superior: Aeolus' gift to Ulysses is a jet engine, and Hermes appears with a helmet and a jetpack. Circe's magic is presented as a drug-induced hallucination ("Trapped by sex and drugs, Ulysses has spent a whole year in Circé's room," one panel declares), but the production values are low, and the comic cannot sustain its conceit.

Better is *The Odyssey* (w. Franco Navarro, a. Jose Saurí), produced from 1979 to 1982 and published in 1983. Its engagement with Homer proves more resonant, and it is clear that the creators chose to include less familiar mythic traditions as they sought character motivations. While Euro-porn comics still exert their influence on the art when Odysseus sleeps with Calypso, for instance, Navarro and Saurí go beyond Homer in incorporating the narrative of Telegonus, reinforcing the themes of homesickness in terms of the loss of family and particularly the absence of his son. When the voice-over proclaims, "I cannot say that the seven years that I remained in Ogygia were totally unhappy," the Homeric scholar is reminded of *Odyssey* 5.151–155, where

οὐδέ ποτ' ὄσσε
δακρυόφιν τέρσοντο, κατείβετο δὲ γλυκὺς αἰὼν
νόστον ὀδυρομένῳ, ἐπεὶ οὐκέτι ἥνδανε νύμφη.
ἀλλ' ἦ τοι νύκτας μὲν ἰαύεσκεν καὶ ἀνάγκῃ
ἐν σπέσσι γλαφυροῖσι παρ' οὐκ ἐθέλων ἐθελούσῃ·

His eyes were not yet

dry from tears, and his sweet life was shed away
lamenting his homecoming, since the nymph was no longer pleasing.
Yes, he would pass the nights with her, and under compulsion,
in her hollow grotto, he the unwilling lay beside her the willing.

This *Odyssey* resonates with the larger mythic context to explore a particularly vexed moment in *Odyssey* 5. The ending, too, leaves unresolved the sexual tension between husband and wife resulting from their long separation. Rather than offering a reunion between them (*Odyssey* 23.295–296, 300–301), Navarro and Saurí instead present "a disconcertingly pensive scene, one in which Odysseus and Penelope stare at each other silently, banished to the background, as the camera zooms away from the garden."[4]

Similar problems of adaptation achieve different realizations in three series published by Marvel and written by Roy Thomas, a veteran in the comics world with a long interest in mythic narratives.[5] Two eight-issue series on the *Iliad* and the *Odyssey* appeared at the same

---

3. See Jenkins (2011).

4. Jenkins (2011, 226, with fig. 16.2 on 227).

5. See Marshall (2011b, 90 n. 7).

time as the initial publication of *The Infinite Horizon* and were followed (beginning in May 2009) with a five-issue series called *The Trojan War*, which recounts stories from the Epic Cycle, the post-Homeric epic poems that survive now only in fragments.[6] As a project, these series demonstrate a fascinating commitment to the presentation of the classics within the comics medium by a large publishing house. It is distinctly Homer's *Iliad* which is being presented, which is not the case for most adaptations of Homer to modern media, where the gods are removed or minimized, and the entire story of the Trojan conflict is presented, rather than the short period in the tenth year, as in the *Iliad*. While there are occasional interpretations of the traditional narrative that bear attention (I am fond of the presentation of the fight with the river in *Iliad* 21, which envisions the river as terrain, a water giant, rolling surf, and a horizontal geyser from one panel to the next, as the fluid mythic form of the supernatural becomes partially rationalized; see *The Iliad* 7 [August 2008], 13–19), the concern to draw buxom women shows a greater dependence on the traditions of hero comics and plays havoc with the Homeric chronologies. This may be acceptable for the appearance of Helen (as in *Odyssey* 4 when she meets Telemachus; see 4.121–122, when she first appears and is compared to Artemis, and *The Odyssey* 1 [November 2008], 14.3), but it undermines the scale and sacrifice of the length of Odysseus' absence when a superheroine's torso is imposed on Penelope (e.g., *The Odyssey* 1 [November 2008], 22.6, 23.1). Thomas's work adapts the Homeric narrative to the tastes and expectations of the hero-comics audience. That said, the stories were collected, and *The Trojan War* must be ranked among the most approachable versions of the material from the Epic Cycle. Marvel granted Thomas a significant amount of space (with the concomitant financial risk) for his Homer adaptations. The collections were also published in a smaller-than-usual digest-sized softcover that may be seen to be targeted at younger audiences and school libraries (even if they remain out of print as of this writing).

An earlier Marvel adaptation, no doubt aiming to compete directly with reprints of the *Classics Illustrated* Homer (which had also produced an *Odyssey* in 1951, drawn by Harley Griffiths), had appeared in 1977: *Marvel Classics Comics* 18 adapted the *Odyssey* (w. Bill Mantlo, a. Jess Jodloman); *Marvel Classics Comics* 26 adapted the *Iliad* (w. Elliot Maggin, a. Yong Montaño). These forty-eight-page adaptations were considerably more substantial than regular single-issue comics.[7] With their sincere messages to the reader on the inside covers, there again seems to be an effort to present something more literary, or at least more elevated, than a traditional hero comic. In that respect, the choice of individuals to create these single-issue stories is significant. *Marvel Classics Comics* was an anthology series, with a different creative team on each, drawing on available talent from the "Bullpen." For the *Iliad*, Elliot Maggin, a wide-ranging author known in comics mainly for his long tenure at DC writing for *Superman* and *Action Comics*, and for comics building on *Dungeons and Dragons* and other role-playing games, was paired with Yong Montaño, an artist known mainly for horror comics in the Philippines and then America (particularly with Marvel's short-run black-and-white

---

6. Roy Thomas (w.) and Miguel Sepulveda (a.), *The Iliad* (Marvel Comics, 2008). Roy Thomas (w.) and Greg Tocchini (a.), *The Odyssey* (Marvel Comics, 2009). Roy Thomas (w.) and Miguel Sepulveda (a.), *The Trojan War* (Marvel Comics, 2009).

7. Both also proclaim "52 pages," a generous total including the front and back cover, inside and out, and boasting on the cover, "no ads."

magazine-length comics, such as *Vampire Tales* and *Monsters Unleashed*). In the 1960s and '70s, many Filipino artists came to the United States to work on comics in the two big houses. While they brought with them a sense of rich line work and distinctive style that were found to be particularly suitable for more adult-targeted comics, financial realities were likely the primary criterion in the selection of these men for the extra work offered by a one-off contribution to an anthology series, since Filipino artists could be hired for less money per page.

For the *Odyssey*, Bill Mantlo was still very early in his career, though he would go on to do masterful work, writing surprisingly credible stories for unlikely properties.[8] He was paired with Jess Jodloman, another Filipino, most of whose American work was in horror and war comics published by DC, especially selected issues of *House of Mystery* (1974–1982) and *Weird War Tales* (1974–1983).[9] Seas and skies are drawn with an exceptional amount of detail, although the printing process of 1970s comics does not always serve the line work well, leaving details smudged. The intersection of these men's sensibilities emerges most clearly in the characterization of the Cyclops (6.3; see figure 1.4). The nonhuman appearance is unusual for visual representations of the creature, and it is possible that it is based on Jodloman's imagined form of the Tagalog one-eyed giant in Philippine mythology, the Bungisngis.[10] This might be too optimistic, however, for the appearance of the creature (also drawn on the cover by fellow Filipino artist Ernie Chan) as a one-horned, one-eyed, purple people eater seems surprisingly close to the creature described in Sheb Wooley's 1958 American novelty song "The Purple People Eater." Even if that was not the intention, American readers were perhaps more likely to make the latter association than the connection with Philippine folklore.

There are, of course, many other comics adaptations of Homer that could be considered here. Eric Shanower's euhemerizing of the Trojan War in *Age of Bronze* works to integrate a variety of ancient sources into a meaningful and consistent sequential narrative.[11] At the same time, he introduces his own concerns (particularly concerning sexuality and the role of the gods) which make it an innovative and creative literary vision of the war at Troy. More typically, adaptations draw on a less diverse array of sources. The opposite impulse is seen in George O'Connor's *Poseidon* and *Ares* volumes, where the gods are foregrounded instead of rationalized. This is seen particularly in *Ares* (2015), which is a retelling of the *Iliad* in which book 5 (in which Ares and Aphrodite are wounded by Diomedes) is especially prominent.[12]

---

8. The true diversity of Mantlo's writing cannot be adequately summarized. Known particularly for the stories he wrote for toy properties about which Marvel had licensed to produce comics, especially *ROM: Spaceknight* (1979–1986) and *Micronauts* (1979–1984), Mantlo also had significant runs on *The Spectacular Spider-Man* (1977–1986), *The Incredible Hulk* (1980–1985), and the Canadian superhero team *Alpha Flight* (1985–1989). By the late 1980s, he had trained as a lawyer and was working as a public defender in the Bronx, but his career was cut tragically short when he suffered permanent brain damage after being hit by a car while rollerblading; see Coffin (2011) and Yurkovich (2007). When I began reading comics, a disproportionate number of my earliest purchases were written by Mantlo.

9. See also Jodloman's art for the story in *Ghosts* 22 (DC, January 1974), discussed in the introduction to this book.

10. Etymologically, *Bungisngis* is connected to the verb *giggle* because of the creature's laugh.

11. Shanower (2001; 2004; 2007; 2008–2012). See Shanower (2011); Sulprizio (2011), and Kovacs in chapter 2 in this volume.

12. O'Connor 2015: 23–41 represents *Iliad* 5; while the events of *Iliad* 11–16 are on a single page (2015: 42). O'Connor 2013: 13–25 presents the Cyclops story from *Odyssey* 9 (with part of book 5 as well).

FIGURE 1.4 A Philippine Cyclops? *Marvel Classics Comics* 18, "The Odyssey" (Marvel, June 1977). Art by Jess Jodloman.

If *Classics Illustrated* was seeking to supplement a child's education with a more or less "straight" retelling (where there is a stated claim that it is reproducing the narrative of the ancient source, even if the accuracy of the claim may be questioned), there are more recent examples that are tapping specifically into the North American market for children's books, which are facilitated by school boards and library purchases. Gareth Hinds's *The Odyssey*, for example, occupies an interesting place in the market. Although for the most part its gentle watercolors depict a safe and less challenging approach to Homer, through its aggressive marketing, it achieved wide sales to children and school libraries. Since many school buyers remain suspicious of comics as a medium, or at least are unfamiliar with it, the unthreatening style serves a marketing purpose. As a result, Odysseus goes through the motions (e.g., a dark-skinned Calypso with dreadlocks wears a revealing sea-blue bikini wrap, as she silently leads the much older Odysseus by his hand into her cave and they begin to kiss; 2010, 53.3–5), but it is hard to assign much purpose behind many of the choices made. More effective in this retelling is the visual juxtaposition between the aged and weary eyes of Odysseus, shown in extreme close-up, and those of the mange-ridden Argus (2010, 176.4–5), which properly highlights the pathetic weakness and frailty of both.[13]

Three other recent *Odyssey* adaptations demonstrate the variety of work that finds its direct inspiration in Homer. *Odysseus the Rebel* (2009, w. Steven Grant, a. Scott Beiser) promises "this is not your daddy's *Odyssey*." While the events are familiar, the dialogue aims not at representing the Homeric narrative but at asserting an even more defiant and willful character, one who would deny the gods their power even though Odysseus knows objectively that they exist. Despite its science-fiction sensibilities and reductively naive art, *Homer: The Odyssey*, "adapted by" Seymour Chwast (2012), follows Homer book by book. Chwast's simplified story dresses many characters in costumes evoking science-fiction serials of the 1930s and '40s (or perhaps the setting of Lob and Pichard), as (for example) two little spaceships are seen passing by in the background as Calypso and Odysseus tan themselves on Ogygia.[14] A more rewarding read is the much more obviously literary *Asterios Polyp*, by David Mazzucchelli (2009), which uses *Odyssey* 9, among many other classical sources, as a touchstone.[15] All of these have their precursors as well, such as the wildly inventive mash-up of the *Iliad* with the *Homeric Hymn to Dionysus* in "Helen's Boys", or the single-panel synopsis of the *Odyssey* in *The Cartoon History of The Universe*.[16]

The Infinite Horizon is not the only comics version of Homer to use the tropes of science fiction as a substitute for myth, and it needs to be understood within the context of these many adaptations of Homer to the comics medium (and this could easily be extended to include

13. See also Dev (2012). Other comics versions of Homer that seem designed to target the school market include two small books published by Pocket Classics (1984), with no author or artist credits at all, Fontes and Purcell's short account of the Trojan War (2007), Macdonald and Sidong's *Odyssey* (2009), and the cartoony but enjoyable *Odyssey* by Caldwell, Mucci, and Lacy (2012).

14. Chwast (2012, 16.1); see also the bubble-domed three-wheeled rocket car used by Telemachus and Pisistratus to travel from Pylos to Sparta (24.1).

15. See chapter 3 in this volume.

16. Messner-Loebs and Keith (2003) and Gonick (1990, 224.1; subsequent panels show Helen and Clytemnestra with duck-bill mouths, presumably to represent their birth from Leda's egg).

other modern media presenting science fiction). It does not follow Homer closely, but its narrative and art do reveal several important and evocative associations that present a new understanding through its representation of the Homeric tale.

II

The Infinite Horizon is set in a near future, with American soldiers having been reassigned from Iraq to Syria. While the exact date is indeterminate, we see green-glowing clipboards (1.4), a Chinese attack in space that has destroyed the global telecommunications networks (1.3),[17] and New York City now partially submerged, suggesting a massive melting of the ice caps (4.4–7). When an airport bomb prevents evacuation, the Captain (who remains otherwise unnamed) begins a ten-year *nostos* leading his troops home on a commandeered ship. The adaptation is relatively free, though it is concerned to represent specific Homeric events. The emphasis on Penelope and her son in the Catskill Mountains and the presence of up to a dozen "suitors," attempting to secure water rights for their neighboring properties, preserve a tension often lacking in modern Homeric adaptations. Penelope, while attractive, is desirable primarily for economic reasons.[18] Penelope as an economic agent is also powerful, and later we see her armed, with allies, and willing to kill (3.14–15, 6.10–11, 6.20–21).

I had originally suspected that the choice of the Catskills was for an implied pun, based on geographic proximity to Ithaca, New York. In his introduction to the collected edition, however, writer Gerry Duggan identifies the choice of location as personal, since his father grew up in the area, near Woodstock, New York. Indeed, there are many details of *The Infinite Horizon* that resonate with Duggan personally. In 1991, when the first Gulf War began, his family had considered sending him to Canada if a draft were introduced. And in the course of writing the comic, both writer and artist became fathers, and both had sons. The *Odyssey* and its themes (including war-weariness and fatherhood) literally grew on them, into them, as they were writing. Duggan's knowledge of the *Odyssey* comes from rereading his future wife's copy (in English translation) around the time of the American invasion of Iraq. *The Infinite Horizon* has its genesis following 9/11, and the interweaving of themes mark it as a personal story for both creators.[19]

A number of elements of *The Infinite Horizon* bear consideration, and even in my description so far, one can see how specific details recreate aspects of the Homeric world. The Catskills are remote, and arrival for Odysseus will likely be by sea. The place of the supernatural is ambiguous. In chapter 2, the Captain stands on deck with one of his crew and sees a shooting star. "Look! That's a good omen, right?" the crewman asks, pointing. The Captain only grunts, "Hnh," while his voice-over ties the sight to the ruined satellites: "Months had passed since the Chinese strike in space . . . and the pieces were still falling" (2.3). The narrative device of the

---

17. See especially panels 3 and 5: "China finally went into Taiwan last night—first thing they did was knock out our satellites. They blinded most everything up there with EMP's and they nailed the hardened military satellites in low earth orbit the old-fashioned way: shot them down."

18. This insight may be aligned with Finkelberg's arguments (1991, 306–307; 2005, 69–71). for matrilineal succession of kingship in heroic Greece.

19. This, admittedly, goes some way in explaining the delays in publication described in note 1 above.

electromagnetic pulse creates the appearance, then, of a supernatural apparatus. Stars fall from the sky, and that is seen as having at least a potential real-world impact; the regression to superstition is quick and easy in troubled times. This in turn invites consideration of how the gods themselves are represented. Those powers that transcend humanity but have a constant impact on many aspects of day-to-day existence are here equated with nations, as an unrelated conflict in Taiwan has impact on the lives of those across the globe in Syria.

In tying the Homeric gods to nationhood, Duggan and Noto point to the helplessness of most ordinary citizens in face of these larger entities, but they nevertheless do allow for other expressions of the supernatural. The falling satellite becomes an omen for the Captain as the ship encounters dozens of corpses floating in the water (2.4), left there by pirates (the scene is given prominence within the narrative by dedicating a whole page to a single panel—a splash page—at 2.5). Later in the same issue, Penelope experiences an omen that operates within a more familiar Homeric frame. When her son is kidnapped, Penelope happens to see a bird of prey snatch a crow in mid-flight (2.21). The page's central panel shows only the crow's corpse, its blood spattered on the winter show, with Penelope's voice-over affirming, "He's coming back" (figure 1.5).

The five-panel layout of the scene means the central, prophetic image is framed by the other four panels, which share a color palette. This precise layout of panels has in fact only been used once previously in the series so far, and that was when the Captain sees the debris fall from the sky as a shooting star (2.3). The panel layout invites the reader to juxtapose the two moments, if only subconsciously.[20] Penelope sees the bird's actions as a sign, and the reader is simultaneously fully aware that this presents an alternative to the nation-state divinities experienced by the Captain and his crew, while still remaining true to one of the ways Homeric gods do clearly communicate. We can think of *Odyssey* 15.525–528, for instance:

> ὡς ἄρα οἱ εἰπόντι ἐπέπτατο δεξιὸς ὄρνις,
> κίρκος, Ἀπόλλωνος ταχὺς ἄγγελος· ἐν δὲ πόδεσσι
> τίλλε πέλειαν ἔχων, κατὰ δὲ πτερὰ χεῦεν ἔραζε
> μεσσηγὺς νηός τε καὶ αὐτοῦ Τηλεμάχοιο.

> Just as he spoke, a bird flew by on the right,
> a hawk, Apollo's quick messenger; and in its talons
> it plucked a clutched dove and rained feathers to the ground
> between the ship and Telemachus himself.

In Homer, Theoclymenus interprets this as a favorable omen, which Telemachus accepts hopefully (*Od.* 15.529–538).[21] Through different and conflicting devices, Homer's theological apparatus continues to operate in *The Infinite Horizon*. The reader is never told the governing frame of reference unambiguously, and the multiple representations of the divine are incommensurate, presenting an ongoing challenge to the engaged reader. Even the title of issue 1, *Journey into Misery*, puns on the comics series *Journey into Mystery* (Marvel, 1952–1966, 1972–1975,

---

20. Subsequent uses of this five-panel layout do not share this supernatural tone.

21. I do not know if we are to make much of the transference from a dove to a crow, beyond the desire to have the plumage stand out against the snowy background.

FIGURE 1.5 Penelope's omen. *The Infinite Horizon* 2.21 (Image, January 2008). Art by Phil Noto.

1996–1998, 2011–2013), the comic best known for introducing the hero Thor and therefore a comic that already possesses an explicit mythological divine apparatus.

There is no doubt that the Captain is a military figure. While still in Syria, he is shown to be a crack shot with his assault rifle (1.7). Two shots become two head wounds on the turbaned enemy and establish the Captain as a sniper, anticipating the association with Odysseus the archer. This in fact becomes a false lead, as becomes clear in issue 6, another narrative element that proves to be overdetermined for the attentive reader (see section IV below). We are also presented with a sort of reverse Trojan horse escape, as the soldiers hide themselves on a departing airplane to provide a target, while they covertly leave before it is destroyed by enemy fire (1.17). "I gave our enemy a flashy exit they can't miss" (1.15), the Captain describes, as we see our first example of his tactical cleverness. The escape from war can only begin after this deception. As in Homer, however, the hero's cleverness has its limits: "The moment I put us on this boat I trapped us" (2.6). This second chapter is titled "Red Sky at Morning," a phrase that serves dual functions, evoking both Homer's rosy-fingered Dawn and the folklore weather rhyme urging that sailors take warning.[22] In the *Odyssey*, of course, Odysseus is cursed by the Cyclops and fated to return home alone. So here, before the issue is complete, there are only four soldiers left accompanying the Captain, all floating on an inflatable raft and landing on a volcanic island.

The art on the page shapes the story Duggan and Noto create. Noto uses a minimum of strokes, and the spare lines and limited color palette present a simplicity in the overall story. The world presented is rough-hewn, carved from the substance of myth, but still not fully realized. This is reinforced with the use of large-grain mechanical stippling to represent shadows. In addition, though, there are smudges, scratches, streaks, and graininess, some of which extend to the gutters between panels; the effect exists outside of the world of the Captain, as if the page itself has been damaged. This suggests the appearance of an older comic or perhaps a document that had survived in a bottle at sea. These extra lines create a texture of weathered survival for the reader of the comic and perhaps suggest something of a traditional tale, something that has been passed down from one generation to the next, like an oral epic or an old comic book.[23]

The tenor of *The Infinite Horizon* is mostly rationalizing, removing supernatural elements, as has already been seen with the presentation of omens. In chapter 3 ("Nobody's Invincible"), the Cyclops becomes a Russian special-forces soldier with single-lens night-vision equipment. As is the case with most *Odyssey* adaptations, the readership's previous familiarity with the Cyclops narrative grants it a disproportionate prominence in the overall story. The Russian's scope allows him to read heat signatures, identify targets, call up aerial views of opponents—all things that offer a technology-based tactical advantage. It is even possible that we might see some debt to the appalling Lob and Pichard adaptation from the 1970s (compare figure 1.6 [Duggan and Noto 3.1] and figure 1.7 [Lob and Pichard 11.4]).

22. The weather rhyme in fact dates to Roman times; it is found in the New Testament (Matthew 16:2–3). The verses are not found in the Syriac or Coptic translations, however, or in the Codex Sinaiticus, which suggests that the passage was likely added as an expansion in the third or fourth century CE.

23. This effect is used regularly but can be seen particularly at 1.8; 2.10–11, 2.18; 3.2, 3.9–10, 3.19, 3.24, 3.27; 4.5–8; 5.2, 5.3, 5.14–23, 5.25–26. Significantly, the effect is not employed in chapter 6, when the Captain returns home. Seeing this can be disconcerting for a reader, and students have told me they thought their copies were soiled or "used" when they first noticed the effect.

FIGURE 1.6 The Cyclops of *The Infinite Horizon* 3.1 (Image, April 2008). Art by Phil Noto.

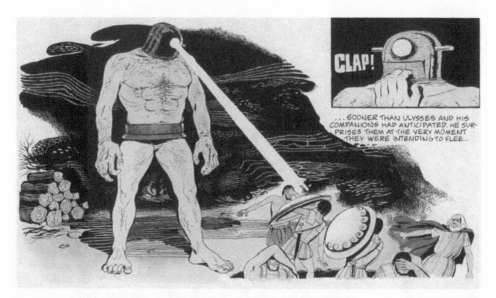

FIGURE 1.7 The Cyclops of Pichard and Lob, *Ulysses*, Vol. 1 (Heavy Metal Press, 1977, reprint 2006). Art by Jaques Lob.

Yet within his cave, many of the captives have lost a single eye: "It was . . . unnerving not knowing if he had taken their eyes or if they had blinded themselves" (3.9). These disfigured inhabitants of the cave are the analogs for the Cyclops' sheep, and their harrowing situation, whether it is seen as a product of madness or maltreatment, is a particular challenge for readers who know the *Odyssey* well. The emotional resonance becomes stronger when we realize that Polyphemus' pastoral existence has been replaced with this uncanny torture. In this light, the blinding of the Cyclops is given a particular prominence, with two consecutive splash pages, both of which bleed right to the edge of the page, eliminating any panel border, following a five-page duel (3.16–20). The first shows the red screen of the scope, with static and indicators of malfunction (3.21); flip the page, and the reader sees the same scene rotated 180 degrees (3.22), with the Captain's knife plunged into the middle of the Russian's eye.

"Who are you?" he is asked twice (3.23, 3.24). "Nobody," the Captain replies (in an answer he will repeat in 4.13 and 5.8 and which provides the chapter with its name), as the survivors get into a plane for an aerial escape. There is not room for everyone, however, and some of the sheeple are left behind. One of these is an old woman who had stayed to watch, perhaps to help, her former captor die. Duggan and Noto ascribe to her Polyphemus' final function. She is one of those freed but left behind by the Captain, and the reader is told, "One of them spits something at me that I can't understand. I'm sure now that it was a curse" (3.25). As the survivors escape, four successive panels on a page depict the Captain sleeping (3.27), unaware of the shattering glass around him as the plane goes down ("It had been such a beautiful dream . . ." says the narrator's voice). The sequence of panels replicates the effect of a slow cinematic close-up, with each image of the Captain's face slightly larger than the one preceding. The reader of the *Odyssey* might perceive analogs with Odysseus' sleep on the Phaeacian ship in Book 13, but this is a false clue, since this is not the end of his journey. More apt, perhaps, as the

Captain finally takes to the air, is the trouble Odysseus faced when he fell asleep after meeting Aeolus, the master of winds, in *Odyssey* 10. He falls, like Icarus, in an issue-ending cliffhanger made more tangible for the comic's first readers by the year-long delay before the publication of issue 4.

The fourth chapter ("That Which Does Not Kill Us") has the crash survivors in North Africa, with the Captain nursing a poorly set broken leg and dulling the pain with a narcotic flower. The presence of the plant evokes the Lotus Eaters encountered by Odysseus (*Od.* 9.82–104), but the reference is casual and jostles for attention amid other potential allusions. "I fought for my life every day of that first year in North Africa" (4.8, panel 1), the Captain's voice-over describes (looking back from the future and so offering to the reader some assurance of the outcome). The Captain hallucinates freely ("I won the struggle to live, but I let my sanity slip away," panel 2), drawing together memories of the past and nightmares of possible futures. Beneath the floorboards of the room where he is recovering, faces appear; their words appear in normal speech balloons (e.g., "Help us!" "Please!" in panel 3), and so are indistinguishable from the speech of characters who are actually in the world being presented. These hallucinations are echoes of drowning captives whom the Captain had earlier abandoned on a sinking ship (2.18–19, especially "Help us!" "Please!" at 18, panel 3). The Circe figure is a red-headed foreign doctor who is dealing with the injuries caused by the armed child soldiers, whom the Captain, though crippled, can overcome through sheer resolve. This is a sympathetic Circe, whose efforts to detain the Captain are motivated by medical concern. This doctor is also an embodiment of Athena, and the owl tattoo below her neckline (seen when she is wearing tank tops; see 4.10, panels 2 and 3; 4.14, panels 2–5; 4.22, panels 1 and 2) provides another manifestation of the supernatural in the story, different again from those already encountered. "Athena" stays with the captain for much of issue 5, and one is reminded of the many guises adopted by Homer's Athena (e.g., *Od.* 1.105, 2.267–268, 2.382–383, 7.20, 8.194, etc.) and also Odysseus' disavowal of her, when he proclaims he was unaware of her presence supporting him on his journey home (*Od.* 13.312–323).

As time passes, the Captain's depression increases, and his hard-hearted military practicality exerts itself. For the reader, these references to time seem to blur together, as they do for the Captain; references to a year (4.8, 4.10) might overlap with one another, but they might not. Duggan and Noto also apparently elide the syncretic Circe-Athena figure with Calypso as one year becomes many: "My injuries kept me down for months . . . but it was the drug that kept me out for years" (4.3). To break this cycle requires an act of will by the Captain, who rebreaks the leg that was poorly set in the plane crash, forcing the doctor to act, to set the bone properly. The closing words in the story at this point come from the Captain and suggest that Book 11's *katabasis* is also to be elided into the North African adventure: "There are worse things than death, and I had survived them. I had finally righted myself, and was on course for home" (4.23).

III

The scrutiny I am applying to *The Infinite Horizon* here is (and perhaps should be) atypical. I am more familiar with the *Odyssey* than most readers of *The Infinite Horizon* and have spent more time thinking about Homer. If I am to argue that this analysis is not completely inappropriate, then, it is worth taking a step back to consider some of the different ways a modern cultural object (a text, such as *The Infinite Horizon*) might relate to a classical model. Perhaps necessarily, this will construct a taxonomy, and with it an implied hierarchy, and so I should be clear about what I hope to accomplish in this section. I am interested in identifying the nature and degree of the knowledge of classical material that is required or expected of a reader at the point of reception. We may ask, required or expected by whom? Rather than defer to the "author" (a concept that has been heavily problematized even when there is only a single creative mind at work and which is made significantly more complex when the work is the product of multiple creative intelligences, as in most comics), it will be sufficient for now to speak only of the expectations of the text itself, and this is determined by the knowledge the reader brings to the text. The classification I propose is basic but useful:

1. Cosmetic reference.
2. Indirect reference.
3. Envisioning.
4. Revisioning.
5. Engagement.

Each of these categories represents a wide range of concepts and possibilities of creative expression, all of which could manifest in many diverse ways.[24]

The first category, *cosmetic reference*, recognizes that not everything that seems classical need be so. A spacecraft may be called *Prometheus* (as it is in Ridley Scott's 2012 film of that name) without reference to Hesiod or the play attributed to Aeschylus and without any expected association with the Titan of myth. The occasional use of classical nomenclature for spaceships in science fiction can be seen to parallel the haphazard labeling of objects in our solar system, but such associations are (for modern astronomers and most readers) essentially mere window dressing. For the most part, the spacecraft would not connote much differently for most readers if they were named after Shakespeare characters (e.g., *Miranda, Caliban*) or Conrad novels (*Nostromo*, as in Scott's 1979 film *Alien*). This is not to say that such significance cannot exist; the ship that falls from the sky in the 1968 film *Planet of the Apes* is called *Icarus*, and that seems as pointed as the protagonist's name in Pierre Boulle's 1963 novel *La planète des singes*, which is Ulysse Mérou, or the name of the chimpanzee revolutionary in the last two *Planet of the Apes* films (1972's *Conquest of the Planet of the Apes* and 1973's *Battle for the Planet of the Apes*), which is Caesar.[25] All of this, however, is nothing more than signposting, providing

24. By focusing on (presumed) audience knowledge, my typology differs from Keen's (2006) similar typology which blurs authorial intent and the narrative being presented. His categorization is nonhierarchical: retellings, allusions, appropriation (i.e., maintaining cultural continuity), interaction (as when individuals use a time machine), (authorial) borrowing (a category that includes elements of allusion), stealing, and ghosting (in which there are no hints of influence). See also Kovacs (2011, 15), which distinguishes "passing references and cosmetic borrowings," "appropriations and reconfigurations," and "direct representations of the classical world" (= my cosmetic reference, revisioning, and envisioning, respectively).

25. For the series generally, see Greene (1998). Caesar was played by Roddy McDowall, who had also played Caesar's father, Cornelius, in the original 1968 film and 1971's *Escape from the Planet of the Apes*, and Galen (a third Roman name) in the 1974 television series.

a hint of the direction that interpretation might follow rather than a hermeneutic key that enriches or unlocks certain readings of the work. Even the Romulan Empire in the *Star Trek* universe, which over time accretes details derived from the Roman Republic (it has praetors and proconsuls, for example), never really uses these terms except as labels. The audience is expected to recognize names, words, or places, but their use is not systematic and may be ill informed.[26] Deviations from classical material therefore may be expected and are to be seen as insignificant.

The second category, *indirect reference*, acknowledges that while there may be a classical source, its use is derivative, and an intermediate source is to be seen as primary. I would place George Lucas's 1977 film *Star Wars* (renamed *Episode IV: A New Hope* in 1981) in this category. Although the narrative describes a galactic empire with an emperor and a senate and memories of an earlier republic, and while the narrative of the hero can be shown to correspond closely with the quest narrative of heroes such as Perseus and Theseus, the film does not expect knowledge of or familiarity with these ancient sources. Indeed—and I like this example because it has been so thoroughly documented—for both of these possible uses of antiquity, the presence of the ancient world has been derived through intermediate (nonclassical) sources, namely, Edward Gibbon's *The Decline and Fall of the Roman Empire* and Joseph Campbell's *The Hero with a Thousand Faces*.[27] Knowledge of the ancient world may help the viewer but only indirectly; other, more recent sources are primary.

The next category is *envisioning*, in which the text uses the ancient world as part of its setting. Fidelity is not a concern here, as one expects (or at least should expect) the modern work to be shaped by its own time and its creators' own concerns. But because the imagined world engages directly with knowledge of the classics, at the point of reception a much broader base of knowledge becomes relevant for the reader. Films such as *Clash of the Titans* (either 1981 or 2010) and *Gladiator* (2000), comics such as *Age of Bronze* and *Asterix*, and even time-travel narratives such as *Bill and Ted's Excellent Adventure* (1989) and the *Doctor Who* episode "The Fires of Pompeii" (season 4, episode 3, first broadcast April 12, 2008; see Hobden 2009) all tend to operate at this level of engagement. Specific knowledge of the ancient world is beneficial and helps differentiate audiences. Some works may reward a classically informed reader or viewer, and others may simply annoy them. It may be that one can also identify specific intermediate texts that add to an appreciation of the modern source, as, for example, when the Cambridge Latin Course provides names for characters in the *Doctor Who* episode (although the significance of this does not really extend beyond the cosmetic). Envisioning brings the audience to a version of antiquity that may or may not be inspired by specific texts and that may contain anachronistic elements.

So far, only works in this third group are set in (a version of) antiquity. The picture of antiquity may be historical or mythical or simply fanciful; it may be informed by numerous specific classical sources, by a single text, or by a generalized undefined cultural literacy. Such imprecise cultural referents, not tied to any specific ancient or modern sources, may emerge

---

26. Kovacs (2015) explores how such cosmetic references, haphazardly applied, contributed and indirectly shaped the mythic world building of *Star Trek: The Original Series*.

27. See also Campbell (1988, 23–24, 177–181); and (targeted at children) Henderson (1997).

from Wikipedia, from memories of *I, Claudius*, or from even less specific elements of the ancient world as they are known (or "known") in wider popular culture. In spite of this, these first three groups remain relatively unproblematic. As conceptual categories, they remain distinct. One could, of course, argue that any piece of knowledge is mediated indirectly; conceding that is, I hope, sufficient to provide a rubric by which one can think helpfully in general terms about any modern point of reception. The next two categories are less straightforward, but I believe they remain useful to distinguish.

The fourth category, *revisioning*, defines itself by not presenting works set in the ancient world. There are many sites of reception that benefit from specific knowledge of the ancient world or of a specific ancient text. A number of different authorial activities make up this category. Here I would place retellings (envisionings) that do not use the ancient world as a setting. These include allegories, such as C. S. Lewis's *The Lion, the Witch, and the Wardrobe* (which is in part a revisioning of the Gospel narrative).[28] The recontextualizing of classical material in a new context exists here, too, as in the *Doctor Who* episode "The God Complex" (season 6, episode 11, broadcast September 17, 2011), which has a Minotaur wandering a labyrinthine hotel that is actually a spaceship prison. Knowledge of specific facts about the classical world is expected (leading us to see the Doctor as a Theseus embodiment), and lacking them may be seen to provide an inadequate or certainly partial reading of the text. This classification may also include counterfactual narratives, such as "Bread and Circuses," the 1968 *Star Trek* episode in which Rome never fell and is currently broadcasting gladiatorial contests on television with 1960s-era technology.[29] In all of these, audience members are expected to draw inferences from their knowledge of the classical world and apply it to something that is not antiquity. There are degrees of appreciation among members of any audience, but in this category, the effects begin to be more deeply felt because they shape interpretation more aggressively. Portions of the heterogeneous audience are able to perceive more than others, and a differentiated audience response is to be expected. Knowledge of specific classical texts may help, but it is not necessarily expected; however, the viewer who brings specific knowledge of the ancient world and applies it to the point of reception is rewarded.

The final category, *engagement*, is perhaps the most nebulous classification, in that it expects detailed knowledge of a specific ancient text and invites (and rewards) some degree of point-for-point comparison. Readers are expected to know a specific source text—which may or may not be named—and, as a regular part of the reading process, to associate it with its forerunners. This degree of reception has its origins in antiquity, such as when Euripides expects his audience to know Aeschylus' *Oresteia* to interpret his *Electra, Hecuba, Orestes*, or *Iphigenia* plays—a relationship that has sometimes been called palimpsestic, as if another text lies beneath the apparent one, ready to be read by those who know how.[30] It is the relationship that exists between Tom Stoppard's play *Rosencrantz and Guildenstern Are Dead* (1966)

---

28. Lewis himself denied that his tales were allegories (e.g., in a letter to schoolgirl Sophia Storr, December 24, 1959), preferring instead "supposals" or "imaginings" (I am grateful to Ian Storey for this reference). The distinction for my purposes is moot.

29. For a sustained reading of this episode, see Kovacs (2015).

30. See, e.g., Zeitlin (1980). The metaphor is imprecise because with a palimpsest, the "subtext" is completely independent of what one sees, whereas the relationship being posited is much more careful and deliberate.

or the film *Shakespeare in Love* (1998) and their respective Shakespearian source or between James Joyce's *Ulysses* and the *Odyssey*. Failure to recognize the classical model in works that offer engagement is to miss a crucial element at the point of reception. The audience that brings advanced knowledge of specific source texts possesses an essential hermeneutic tool for interpreting the work in question.

There is work for the classical scholar to do at all of these points on the continuum, and—this is important—nothing is being said about the quality of a given work based on where it may be placed in this typology; there will be good and bad in each class.[31] Indeed, there have even been some literary works in the history of the world that have not depended on reference to a classical source at all. One thing that does emerge, however, is that there is, at least in terms of the relationship to the ancient world, an increasing heterogeneity of audience response as one advances along the hierarchy; cosmetic reference does not differentiate audience response as much as engagement does. Further, there is a sense in which these build on one another, where each category may easily include elements of the ones prior to it. Within each category are many types of operation of classical reception that may be disentangled; doing so, however, would not, I feel, introduce new hierarchical levels of expected classical knowledge.[32] I have used a number of examples from science fiction because I want now to use this classification as a tool to understand the final issues of *The Infinite Horizon*.

IV

The discussion of the first four chapters of *The Infinite Horizon* (section II above) demonstrates that Duggan and Noto's comic *Odyssey* constitutes an attempt at *engagement* with the classical source. The work rewards the reader who possesses knowledge of the Trojan War through a knowledge of Homer in translation, and it expects its reader continually to measure the narrative against Homer's account. Many of the parallels are straightforward (*nostos*, the Trojan horse, and the Cyclops) and represent imaginative but still easily interpretable analogs—these are the qualities one would expect in a *revisioning*. There also exists enough *cosmetic reference* to encourage even an inattentive reader to pursue this line of thought. The name of the Captain's wife is Penelope, and that serves as a sufficient touchstone to authorize all other Homeric associations. Not all of the associations are so clean, however. As discussed, the supernatural apparatus in the comic manifests itself in at least three separate ways, from naturalistic explanations of geopolitics and the effects of nuclear weapons detonating in space, to the value of augury and folk wisdom, to an expected interpretation of a woman's body art. Similarly, the Cyclops' sheep become torture victims and ultimately serve as the agents of

31. All of the works studied in this book fall naturally into one of these five categories, and all categories are represented. Feel free to play at home.

32. To return to the classification of Keen (2006), his categories map variously onto the framework I discuss here: cosmetic reference (= allusion and some of his borrowing), envisioning (= retellings and interaction and some of his stealing), revisioning (= borrowing and appropriation), engagement (= some of his stealing). His ghosting ("stories where no direct influence of classical originals can be established, but where nevertheless there are strong hints of themes derived from antiquity") does not map clearly onto any category, but contains elements of my indirect reference and, potentially, engagement.

Polyphemus' curse, and the blurring of Circe with Calypso and Athena in the North African scenes confuses any straightforward assessment of the doctor's character, and she herself is only one of many redheads presented to the viewer in the series, each of whom serves as a doublet to Penelope.[33] These details expect a more specific degree of recognition from the reader, based on knowledge of the specific source. It is precisely because the interpretation of a given feature of the narrative is not straightforward that a more nuanced and sophisticated literary appreciation becomes possible.

Indeed, the example of North Africa can be pressed further. While he is recuperating, the Captain integrates himself into a band of child soldiers. He teaches them to fight, and ultimately this can be seen as a civilizing act: under his guidance and leadership, they become a more organized and disciplined militia; they also become an anchor to his new home. Chapters 4 and 5 show these children grow from young teenagers to young men (another sign of time passing), and there is no obvious Homeric correspondence for their identity. This is not a failure of the narrative, however, or merely an attempt to integrate the problem of real-world child soldiers in central Africa into the story. The Captain dreams of returning to Penelope, and this serves as an analog to Odysseus' underworld experiences in *Odyssey* 11; the two-page spread (4.18–19) is dark and heavily shadowed and is the only place in the series where the background behind the panels is completely black. Although there are no specific correspondences to mark the equivalence, the reader who knows the *Odyssey* makes the association because (a) it is what should be happening at roughly this point in Odysseus' homeward journey, (b) it appears to possess a supernatural resonance with what the reader knows (but the Captain does not) is happening in Upstate New York, which therefore suggests the otherworldly experience of the *katabasis*, and (c) it motivates the Captain to break from his inactivity.

The Captain's new life as a warlord is marred because of the broken leg he suffered in the plane crash. His existence stranded in Africa, a limping, deserted soldier wracked by pain, appears to the classically informed reader to evoke the hero of Sophocles' tragedy *Philoctetes* (409 BCE), and this is a reading that will be unavailable to most of the comic's audience. As readers, we should hesitate over insisting on this association, because it seems to draw us farther away from any close correspondence with Homer. Indeed, given that the Captain maintains some contact with a community and is not isolated and living in a cave, a closer analog may even be the lost Euripidean *Philoctetes* (431 BCE), known primarily through two works of Dio of Prusa (*Or.* 52 and 59). This is a problem, to which I shall return momentarily. Travel for the Captain is painful, but the doctor refuses to rebreak and set the Captain's leg because she lacks the antibiotics to do so safely. Following his nekuialgic dream, however, the Captain breaks his own leg and in so doing forces the doctor to act.[34] This is to be understood as a horrific act; yet as a means of rupturing the potential inaction, it signals the return of Odysseus.

---

33. The red-headed doctor is not a lover but an uneasy ally. Indeed, the associations with Circe and Calypso help to suggest a connection with a third female obstacle Odysseus encounters in Homer: Nausicaa. This is not explicit in *The Infinite Horizon*, but there is certainly enough to see the doctor as a plausible substitute for Penelope if the Captain were unable to leave North Africa. Compare the 1954 film *Ulysses* (dir. Mario Camerini), in which both Penelope and Circe (who is also assuming the narrative function of Calypso) are played by Silvana Mangano.

34. The Captain picks up a rock on 4.20, and in the first panel of 4.21, the reader is given the sound effect "THWAK THWAK THUK"; the repeated blows he inflicts on himself are clear, even if they are kept just off-panel.

I do not know that Duggan and Noto considered the story of Philoctetes, but ultimately it doesn't matter. My knowledge of that story imposes itself on a reading of issue 4, and the violence against the self is a brutal and unorthodox solution to a narrative problem and one that can be seen to resonate meaningfully with multiple classical texts. In this way, I suggest, we as classicists become better readers of *The Infinite Horizon* than many, because we can more easily see the way it engages with certain ancient sources. Because we recognize the comic engaging with specific features of the *Odyssey*, carefully and well, we are enjoined to pay more careful attention to those points when the correspondence is inexact or is lacking. Rather than a deficiency or failure, it is instead an invitation to consider the work more attentively. By transposing the *Odyssey* to a more familiar world, even one set in the near future, writer Duggan and artist Noto invite the reader to make judgments about the Iraq War based on Homeric values and to question the sorts of narratives that emerge from modern warfare generally. *The Infinite Horizon*, then, extends its compass from the world of Homer to today and demands to be read as a product of both.

Chapter 5 of *The Infinite Horizon* ("Red Sky at Night") presents an extended version of the Sirens episode in *Odyssey* 12: a female voice being broadcast over the radio promises hope and sanctuary to all who come unto them. The implied "sailor's delight" (from the rest of the weather rhyme in the chapter title) would apparently distance the reader from the more Homeric association that had been inferred from the title of chapter 2; we are moving away from rosy-fingered Dawn and a grounded, familiar story. When the Captain, the doctor, and one of the survivors from the Cyclops' island arrive, they find an old oil derrick and a tanker being made ready to sail to a promised land. It is a ruse, of course, and through the issue we see the workings of the society that has grown up on the beach around them and with which the angelic women maintain a parasitic relationship. The Captain reunites with a former crewman (Fortunatus, who serves as an antithesis to the Homeric Eurylochus), and together they disrupt the Sirens' operation and provide rescue and escape for a few, including the doctor, whose dyed purple-red hair has in chapter 5 washed out to brown, another sign of time passing. Perhaps unsurprisingly, all three of the Siren figures are also redheads. This creates a sense not only of replication—that the Captain's journey will extend out into infinity—but also of usurpation. When one of these women fires a pistol at point-blank range at the Captain (5.18, another splash page), the reader juxtaposes this with an imagined reunion with Penelope that has not yet happened. The emotional effect lies not in the violence or its immediate impact but in the continued absence of a proper homecoming. The narrative of the chapter engages with other tropes and themes present in contemporary science fiction (such as Paolo Bacigalupi's *Ship Breaker*, a young-adult novel published in 2010, between the publication of issues 4 and 5) and assigns a disproportionate weight within the narrative to Homer's Sirens. The effect of this prominence is to invite comparisons among the many women the Odysseus figure encounters on his journey. By the end of the issue, the Captain escapes, alone, on a small sailing vessel bound for home.

New themes are also introduced that may be seen as complementary to a reading or rewriting of the *Odyssey*, even if they do not emerge directly from it. Since each issue has included some presentation of the experiences of Penelope and her son, Terrence (Terry), it is possible to perceive time passing through seasonal change (issues 2 and 3 depict snow on the ground), and this suggests the passing of a year. Terry's growth is a more reliable marker, though, and one that more closely corresponds to the time passing for the Captain. Terrence begins as a child of maybe eight (a suitor offers to take him shooting with a .22 rifle at 1.11, and Penelope says he is

FIGURE 1.8 The Captain's homecoming. *The Infinite Horizon* 6.6 (Image, October 2011). Art by Phil Noto.

FIGURE 1.9 The Captain's homecoming. *The Infinite Horizon* 6.7 (Image, October 2011). Art by Phil Noto.

too young) and ends as one of perhaps fourteen (as seen on 6.10, when his mother hands him an automatic pistol to help repel the suitors). These two moments echo each other, but they also invite direct comparison between Terry and the Captain. Penelope's hostile reaction to Terry and the rifle comes only four pages after the Captain's demonstrated success as a sniper (1.7); the recapitulation of that moment comes on the page before Penelope hands him the gun (6.9). Terry proves very capable with the weapon (6.10), and the sequence serves as a reaffirmation of the Captain's marksmanship. Homer makes a similar juxtaposition, of course. Not only is Helen capable of identifying Telemachus' father at the mere sight of the son (*Od.* 4.138–146), but at the contest of the bow, the reader is told explicitly that—unlike the suitors—Telemachus does have the strength to string his father's bow and would have done so had Odysseus not signaled him not to (*Od.* 21.125–129). Odysseus' unique weapon is ready to be appropriated by his son, and Terry's precocious use of the pistol demonstrates a similar continuity.

The use of firearms in *The Infinite Horizon* is, ultimately, a false lead. Having invited the reader to update any archery associations in Homer with modern weaponry, the narrative again overdetermines how weaponry is to be understood. When the Captain does return, he demonstrates his marksmanship using a bow that has been hanging on Penelope's wall. In a tightly written sequence of ten long, thin, alternating panels over a two-page spread, the reader is presented with the actions of the Captain and of Penelope in parallel (6.6–7; see figures 1.8 and 1.9). The technique has a cinematic quality to it, as rapid cuts back and forth allow separate narratives to unfold at the same time. In the odd-numbered panels, outside at night, the reader sees the suitor figures come to realize that the Captain has returned. The first time an arrow is seen, it kills the oldest of the figures with an injury to the throat, evoking the death of Antinous in Homer (*Od.* 22.15–16):

> τὸν δ᾽ Ὀδυσεὺς κατὰ λαιμὸν ἐπισχόμενος βάλεν ἰῷ,
> ἀντικρὺ δ᾽ ἁπαλοῖο δι᾽ αὐχένος ἤλυθ᾽ ἀκωκή.

> And Odysseus, aiming, hit him with an arrow in the throat,
> And the point went right through the tender part of his neck.

At the same time, in the even-numbered panels, Penelope has a prophetic dream that her husband is finally home. The panel describing the dream shows her sense the Captain leaning over her and kissing her cheek. Or so she thinks. She wakes, and he is not there, and the attentive reader will note that it was a clean-shaven (and younger) Captain who bestowed the kiss. On awakening, she is at peace, reassured by the subconscious workings of her mind. Except that the dream was not just a dream. The dim outline of an unstrung bow can be seen on the bedroom wall, revealing where the paint has not been faded by the sun, which is seen burning into the bedroom in the same panel.

There is a tidy narrative sleight-of-hand at work, as Duggan and Noto introduce the absence of Odysseus' bow from their narrative at just the point when the bow is put to use. While not replicating the way they are used in Homer, the emblems of *anagnorisis*—the marriage bed, the bow—are redeployed here. For the reader, the emotional satisfaction only increases when one recognizes the derivation from the source text and the imaginative reuse for the new context. In this case, it is not adherence to the *Odyssey* that constitutes Duggan and Noto's creative success but the absences to which attention is drawn. This is reinforced by the serene presentation of Penelope throughout these pages: three of the five images of her here (every time her face is drawn) are at the same angle, occupying more or less the same part of the panel, and facing out. Her husband is home, and now it is time to get to work.

A similar absence can be noted on the previous page, when the Captain returns and is unrecognized, his hand sniffed by one of the dogs on his homestead (6.5, panel 4). For some readers, an implicit comparison is made between this scene and Odysseus' encounter with his old hunting dog Argus, who dies having awaited his master's return for twenty years (*Od.* 17.291–327). The dog sniffing the Captain is young, alert, and still very much alive. But its mere presence in the narrative has the ability to evoke the entire Argus narrative, even as the story eschews telling it. Readers who know Homer well may also recall that the silent acceptance by dogs is a sign for Odysseus of Telemachus' familiarity with Eumaeus the swineherd (*Od.* 16.4–10) and is part of the process of developing recognition sequences on Ithaca. This moment in *The Infinite Horizon* comes immediately after a woman has been hired by the suitors to pretend to be Penelope in a meeting with a judge. Another red-headed doppelgänger, this woman evokes the betrayal of Melantho in *Odyssey* 18. The dialogue for this panel has one of the suitors telling the Captain, "Get your homeless ass off my farm. This ain't a charity operation." The inset text, not in a speech balloon but representing the Captain's thoughts, says, "I smothered the urge to break his neck right on the spot. I stuck to the plan." The Captain's checked impulse also has Homeric precedent: Melanthius (Melantho's brother) kicks the disguised Odysseus, who is tempted to kill him in response (*Od.* 17.235–240); similarly, when boxing the beggar Irus, Odysseus stops himself from killing his opponent and is content with crushing his jaw (*Od.* 18.90–100). The single image of the comics panel evokes many different moments in *Odyssey* 16–18, and the engagement demands ongoing reevaluation by the reader about what meaning, if any, is primary. All of these associations, and more, are present, and Duggan and Noto create a paradigm that encourages the reader attuned to the Homeric influence to seek out such correspondences aggressively. Since there is no single moment of correspondence from which the panel's meaning may be conclusively derived, any associations that a reader might perceive (and there are more than I am describing here) are granted legitimacy, because the tendrils of association already extend seemingly so far.

Since the opening panel of the series (1.1; see figure 1.1 above), the moment of reunion between husband and wife has been anticipated. The reader knows how Homer accomplishes this encounter, with Penelope successfully tricking her husband with the story of their wedding bed. His angry outburst (*Od.* 23.183–205) serves as the final marker of his identity as her husband, and she finally relents (23.206–209). As in Homer, the reunion in *The Infinite Horizon* is circumspect and is notably at odds with the Homeric narrative. Instead of a final test from wife to husband, there is a tables-turned scenario in which all three family members are captured, on their knees, and surrounded by suitors who physically threaten them. "This isn't how I imagined our reunion," Penelope observes, suggesting that the mythic pattern has been violated (6.16, panel 1; see figure 1.10). The Captain is in the position of a captive, apparently begging for his life and that of his family, until Duggan and Noto have him reveal the extent of his activities before revealing himself in his home. The Captain has let surrounding homesteads know that he is back and is in control again by killing those who have undermined his home and family and stringing their bodies up from a highway overpass for all to see (6.18–19). This reestablishes a Homeric pattern: the

FIGURE 1.10 Family reunion in *The Infinite Horizon* 6.16 (Image, October 2011). Art by Phil Noto.

suitors are the last to know of the hero's return. When he declares, "Nobody's coming" (6.17, panel 3), the pseudonym from the Cyclops' cave becomes a nom de guerre.[35]

The Infinite Horizon never fully returns to the Homeric narrative. As its own creative work, it is much more concerned at this point to create the proper emotional context for the belated reunion of the Captain's family. The image with which the series began never comes. The suitors having been dealt with, peace is restored to the Captain's homestead, and he, Terrence, and Penelope put to rest the specters of lost comrades and lost time. Fortunatus' observation that the Captain had "never really put roots down" (5.19, panel 4) is recalled as the reunited family plants seeds in his memory (6.24–25). This departure from Homer, indeed, comes as a sort of relief. With no need to deal with repercussions from the suitors' families, domestic harmony is underlined. Nor is there any sense that this is just a waypoint on the Captain's journey. While Odysseus will need to continue his wanderings as he seeks to appease Poseidon (*Od.* 11.119–134), the Captain is finally home. The final image of a tree grown from the seeds planted (6.26) suggests instead a lasting return to domestic bliss, as the symbol of Odysseus' bedchamber is repurposed in the Captain's backyard.

Why, then, should we take notice of *The Infinite Horizon* when reading it as classicists? As an extended engagement with Homer, the work makes continued demands of the reader, requiring the development of an ongoing and evolving assessment of how Homer's story might inform a modern comic. Because it pursues a more complex relationship with Odysseus' story, the work challenges its readership continually to reassess the values expressed in the Greek epic. The science-fiction setting resonates closely enough with the modern world that we are encouraged also to consider the relevance of Homeric values to the modern world. That can only be effective as a literary technique when the values simultaneously resonate as authentic, as truly representing the Homeric source.

35. This panel serves as one end of a frame of the images showing what the Captain has accomplished (6.18–19). Immediately following, one of the suitors declares with an unconscious irony, "Nobody's leaving" (6.20, panel 1).

Comics Adaptations of Homer Cited

The *Iliad* and the Trojan War

Blum, Alex A. (a.), and "Homer" (w.). 1950. *Classics Illustrated* 77 [*The Iliad*] (November). New York: Gilberton.

Fontes, Justine (w.), Ron Fontes (w.), and Gordon Purcell (a.). 2007. *The Trojan Horse: The Fall of Troy*. Greek Myths and Legends. Minneapolis: Graphic Universe.

Maggin, Elliot (w.), and Yong Monaño (a.). 1977. *Marvel Classics Comics* 26 [*The Iliad*]. New York: Marvel Comics.

Messner-Loebs, William (w.), and Sam Keith (a.). 2003. "Helen's Boys," *Epicurus the Sage*, chapter 4 [unpaginated]. New York: Cliffhanger/DC Comics.

O'Connor, George. 2015. *Ares: Bringer of War*. Olympians 7. New York: First Second.

Pocket Classics. 1984. *The Iliad*. Westham, CT: Academic Industries.

Shanower, Eric (w./a.). 2001. *Age of Bronze*, Vol. 1: *A Thousand Ships*. Berkeley, CA: Image Comics. Originally *Age of Bronze* 1–9 (November 1988–December 2000).

Shanower, Eric (w./a.). 2004. *Age of Bronze*, Vol. 2: *Sacrifice*. Berkeley, CA: Image Comics. Originally *Age of Bronze* 10–19 (March 2001–March 2004).

Shanower, Eric (w./a.). 2007. *Age of Bronze*, Vol. 3A: *Betrayal Part One*. Berkeley, CA: Image Comics. Originally *Age of Bronze* 20–26 (June 2005–September 2007).

Shanower, Eric (w./a.). 2008–2012. *Age of Bronze*, Vol. 3B: *Betrayal Part Two*. Berkeley, CA: Image Comics. Originally. *Age of Bronze* 27–32 (July 2008–December 2012). Berkeley, CA: Image Comics. Also *Age of Bronze Special* 1 (June 1999) and *Age of Bronze: Behind the Scenes* 1 (May 2002).

Thomas, Roy (w.), and Miguel Sepulveda (a.). 2008. *The Iliad*. New York: Marvel Comics. Originally *The Iliad* 1–8 (February–September).

The *Odyssey* and the *Nostoi*

Caldwell, Ben (a.), Tim Mucci (w.), and Rick Lacy (a.). 2012. *The Odyssey*. New York: Sterling.

Chwast, Seymour (w./a.). 2012. *Homer: The Odyssey*. New York: Bloomsbury.

Duggan, Gerry (w.), and Phil Noto (a.). 2012. *The Infinite Horizon*. Berkeley, CA: Image Comics. Originally *The Infinite Horizon* 1–6 (December 2007–November 2011).

Gonick, Larry (w./a.). 1990. *The Cartoon History of the Universe*, Vol. 1–7. New York: Doubleday (see 224.1).

Grant, Steven (w.), and Scott Bieser (a.). 2009. *Odysseus the Rebel*. Round Rock, TX: Big Head.

Griffiths, Harley (a.)] and "Homer" (w.). 1951. *Classics Illustrated* 81: *The Odyssey* (March 1951). New York: Gilberton.

Hinds, Gareth (w./a.). 2010. *The Odyssey*. Somerville, MA: Candlewick.

Lob, Jacques (w.), and Georges Pichard (a.). 1974. *Ulysse*, Vol. 1. Paris: Dargaud Editions. Translated into English as *Ulysses* (2006) by Sean Kelly and Valerie Marchant.

Lob, Jacques (w.), and Georges Pichard (a.) 1975. *Ulysse*, Vol. 2. Paris: Dargaud Editions. *Non vidi*; also the combined edition in 1982.

Macdonald, Fiona (w.), and Li Sidong (a.). 2009. *The Odyssey*. Hauppauge, NY: Barron's Educational Series.

Mantlo, Bill (w.), and Jess Jodloman (a.). 1977. *Marvel Classics Comics* [*The Odyssey*]. New York: Marvel Comics.

Mazzucchelli, David (w./a.). 2009. *Asterios Polyp*. New York: Pantheon Books.

Navarro, Franco (w.), and Jose Saurí (a.) ["Saliri" on copyright page]. 2005. *The Odyssey*. Rockville Center, NY: Heavy Metal Classics. Originally *Heavy Metal* 1983.

O'Connor, George (w./a.). 2013. *Poseidon: Earth Shaker*. Olympians 5. New York: First Second (see 13–25).

Pocket Classics. 1984. *The Odyssey*. Westham, CT: Academic Industries.

Thomas, Roy (w.), and Greg Tocchini (a.). 2009. *The Odyssey*. New York: Marvel Comics. Originally *The Odyssey* 1–8 (November 2008–June 2009).

Thomas, Roy (w.), and Miguel Sepulveda (a.). 2009. *The Trojan War*. New York: Marvel Comics. Originally *The Trojan War* 1–5 (July–November).

2

Mythic Totality in *Age of Bronze*

George Kovacs

Age of Bronze is the ongoing project of Eric Shanower, intended to be a complete retelling of the Trojan War in comics format.[1] Shanower is not the first practitioner of the comics medium to tackle one of the best-known arcs of Greek myth, but his project speaks to an unparalleled ambition: the careful attention to detail and the creative policy of integration, rather than selection of narrative strands in the vast mythographic tradition, anticipate a final product of epic proportions.[2] Shanower incorporates ancient sources from the literary, historical, and material record as he constructs his narrative but also looks far beyond the Greco-Roman world of antiquity, appropriating images, characters, and story motifs from a wide range of modern sources in multiple media. Images from Greek vases, characters from Shakespeare, and story motifs from modern cinema are all comfortably juxtaposed; Shanower is incorporating not only literary texts of antiquity but the entirety of the classical tradition. My goal in this chapter is to demonstrate and analyze the position of *Age of Bronze* as one significant point in the (ongoing) mythographic tradition of the Trojan War and one that Shanower is specifically anxious to establish. As Hardie (1993, 1) notes, "The epic strives for totality and completion, yet is at the same time driven obsessively to repetition and reworking." Thus, like many epicizing projects before it, *Age of Bronze* attempts to encompass all earlier versions and media in which the myth was previously expressed, inducting them into a single, authoritative version.

Early versions of this chapter were delivered at annual meetings of the Classical Association of Canada (May 2009, Vancouver, British Columbia) and the Ontario Classical Association (October 2009, Stratford, Ontario).

1. The most recent issue published is number 33 (July 2013). Many individual issues of *Age of Bronze* are no longer in print, but all are available in multi-issue trade paperbacks. The four volumes—Vol. 1: *A Thousand Ships* (2001); Vol. 2: *Sacrifice* (2004); Vol. 3a: *Betrayal Part One* (2007); and Vol. 3b: *Betrayal Part Two* (2013)—are currently available either through the comic's website (www.age-of-bronze.com) or through conventional bookstore and comics shops. Issues 1–9 are collected as *A Thousand Ships* and include backstory to the initial gathering at Aulis. *Sacrifice* collects issues 10–19, which tell the stories of Telephus and Iphigenia. *Betrayal Part One* includes the story of Philoctetes' abandonment and the embassy of Menelaus and Odysseus to Troy, while *Betrayal Part Two* focuses on Troilus and Cressida. Neither page numbers nor issues are differentiated in the trade paperbacks, and counting is the only means of determining reference. I provide page numbers of the trade paperbacks, as they are more generally available to readers.

2. Shanower has plotted for approximately fourteen hundred pages spanning seven trade paperbacks. The most recent collection is referred to as Vol. 3b, suggesting that even Shanower's ambitious predictions are growing. Production has slowed considerably, however, and the project may never be complete.

I argue that Shanower's choice of the comics medium facilitates these efforts. Simultaneously, Shanower exposes preceding traditions to new readings and indeed to new readers; the student market and the pedagogical applications for *Age of Bronze* are explicitly included in Shanower's promotion of the series.

My access to this integrative process and the impact it may have on our understanding of the myth will be through a single but significant moment in the narrative arc of the war: the sacrifice of Iphigenia. Combining the unpalatable—yet morbidly captivating—motifs of kin slaying and human sacrifice, Iphigenia's death has inspired a long and varied tradition of reception within the larger context of the tradition of the Trojan War (including Aretz 1999 and Michelakis 2006b). The disturbing themes of the sacrifice make this event a useful point of reference in assessing an artist's approach toward ancient myth. The artist's treatment of broken taboos (ancient or modern), portrayal of the characters who break those taboos, and assimilation of previous treatments reveal much about the artist's agenda and self-positioning within the mythographic tradition. Shanower does not blink in the face of myth's gorier aspects, even if he does suspend other elements of ancient myth, including the supernatural.

Even in antiquity, a single undifferentiated narrative of the sacrifice of Iphigenia did not exist. The archaic poets appear to have either ignored the event (as in Homer) or to have mitigated it (Pseudo-Hesiod and the *Cypria*), usually through the substitution of the hind and the rescue of the maiden by Artemis, to whom the sacrifice is typically dedicated.[3] It was not until the humanist project of Greek tragedy, in which poets brought increased focus to human agency and the consequences of their actions, that poets began to declare Iphigenia unequivocally dead (so the *parodos* of *Agamemnon* and Pindar's *Pythian* 4).[4] It was Euripides who introduced the element of self-sacrifice on Iphigenia's part. By the end of the fifth century, the basic mythographic possibilities (sacrifice or self-sacrifice, with the possibility of divine rescue) were in place, and many popular adaptations, produced in different media, have developed (and combined elements of) these early versions. Today, in the era of mass media, most adaptations of the Trojan War, particularly those targeting a broad audience, have tended to avoid the sacrifice.[5] This is certainly true of previous comic-book adaptations of the Trojan War, though these projects have typically claimed only the *Iliad* as their exemplar and are thus bound more closely to those events depicted in the Homeric poem.

---

3. Homer mentions a still-living daughter, Iphianassa, at *Iliad* 9.145 (= 9.287), but this is unlikely the same figure; Gantz (1993, 582); but see Kullmann (1960, 189–190, 267–268); Dowden (1989, 12); Clark (1998, 21–22). The Pseudo-Hesiodic *Catalogue of Women* (fr. 23a.13–26 MW) and the *Cypria* both feature a last-minute salvation by Artemis. Stesichorus, who may also have made Iphigenia immortal, mitigated the sacrifice by giving Iphigenia an alternative lineage as the daughter of Theseus and Helen (Pausanias 2.22.6–7). On the reception of this narrative, through Euripides' *Iphigenia among the Taurians*, see Hall (2013).

4. See, for example, Hall (2010, 1–11). It is no coincidence that many Greek tragedies are set after the events of the Trojan War and so few during. While exceptional poems of the Archaic period (notably the *Iliad* and the *Odyssey*) bring sharp focus to the human emotional and psychological consequences of the war, poets of the Archaic period work in broader mythographic strokes. On the earliest appearances of Iphigenia's death, see Gantz (1993, 582–584).

5. Aside from Michael Cacoyannis's 1977 film, adapted directly from Euripides' *Iphigenia at Aulis*, the only mainstream film to depict or even acknowledge the death of Iphigenia is the 2003 miniseries *Helen of Troy*, produced for the USA Network.

As a Trojan War comic, *Age of Bronze* has several predecessors. Most notable are adaptations of the *Iliad* in the *Classics Illustrated* series (November 1950) and by Marvel Comics for its *Marvel Classics Comics* imprint (1978). Since the beginning of *Age of Bronze*, Marvel has released another adaptation under a newer, short-lived imprint *Marvel Illustrated* (collected 2009), along with an accompanying volume covering the events of the Epic Cycle. I have written on these before (Kovacs 2011), and they are all treated elsewhere in this volume (see chapter 1), so it will be sufficient here to include only a few key observations about these mainstream iterations. One is that all three were advertised as having some pedagogical value; in each case, school libraries were a target market. Second is that all three must make significant concessions to space; even covering only the *Iliad*, each adaptation must excise major characters or scenes. By the same token, all three have a rushed feeling (especially Roy Thomas's *Marvel Illustrated* series, despite comprising eight issues), as each tries to compress fifteen thousand lines of epic poetry (plus necessary backstory and a conclusion to the war) into a limited number of comic panels. As a synthesis of image and text, one comic panel may convey a significant amount of information, but the limits remain. Finally, in each case, the artistic presentation was affected by standards of the publishing house. Albert Kantor's *Classics Illustrated* had a strict house style (Versaci 2007, 187), while the recent Marvel versions are clearly designed to appeal to their key demographic: adolescent males reading superhero comics.

Although *Age of Bronze* demonstrates some debts to each of these incarnations, Shanower's primary inspiration came not from the comics tradition but from an audiotape version of Barbara Tuchman's *March of Folly: From Troy to Vietnam* in 1991 (Shanower 2011, 195). Issue number 1 appeared in 1998 under the publishing label of Image Comics. The label is significant: every creator publishing under Image has complete control, both creative and financial, over his or her own work.[6] Thus, Shanower avoids the censure and interference of larger, more financially motivated publishing houses. This freedom is to Shanower's benefit, since he is not writing a traditional superhero comic. Fighting is not a mainstay of each and every issue; in fact, the first battle on Trojan soil only occurred in issue 27 (July 2008), a decade after the series' inception. *Age of Bronze* is more carefully and deliberately paced than the mainstream American comic, which is expected to maintain (at least) a monthly schedule, and this helps with Shanower's inclusive mythographic agenda. One of *Age of Bronze*'s defining features is not fighting or violent action (though these do occur) but its treatment of the erotic; romantic and sexual relationships, both hetero- and homoerotic, are the underpinnings of the narrative (Sulprizio 2011).

Shanower's work reveals a much more carefully informed project and a very refined didactic agenda. The results are not always perfect. The deliberate pacing of the story sometimes stalls the narrative, starkly apparent in a medium that tends to favor swift action sequences to simulate substance and length in only twenty-two pages (the average length of a monthly comic book). Shanower's general policy of inclusion over selection of narrative traditions can

---

6. For much of comics' history, copyright to characters was owned by the publishing house. Writers and artists often had difficulty asserting creative control over their own creations or even achieving recognition for their efforts. In 1992, eight high-profile comics artists and creators left DC and Marvel in protest over ongoing rights issues (especially royalties in merchandizing) and formed Image Comics. The premise of Image was as an umbrella company, housing the studios of the individual creators. Image asserts no copyright over any material by member studios. See Khoury (2007).

be overwhelming. To any reader not closely familiar with the classical material, some of the characters and their roles in the narrative can be difficult to discern. In earlier issues, Shanower's realistic style did not always permit easy identification of characters (particularly the Trojans and the many sons of Priam), though Shanower has taken steps to address that issue, largely with more individualized costumes.[7]

Shanower is also keenly concerned with the scholarly validity of his work; he regularly attends academic conferences, selling *Age of Bronze* alongside other academic publishing houses. The first three trade paperbacks include seventeen pages of bibliography, with primary and secondary sources. For a comic book, this might seem excessive.[8] Shanower's careful research and his application of that research in his narrative and artwork produce a steady stream of references that will be understood only by the informed reader (though it should not significantly disturb the narrative for the lay reader). Agamemnon's appearance, for instance, is clearly modeled after Schliemann's famed Mask of Agamemnon found at Mycenae (Grave V). Clytemnestra wears a diadem also found at Mycenae (Grave III). Early in the second volume (issue 12), during the Greek attack on the Mysians, the reader finds a careful nod to the red-figure kalyx of the Sosias painter in which Achilles mends a wound of Patroclus (though Shanower is careful to change the armor; Petruso 2006; Shanower 2011). For archaeological inspiration, Shanower has eschewed the Minoan aesthetic that has stood in for Troy in the popular cinematic tradition.[9] Instead, he has looked to the Hittites for his Troy; Shanower himself credits a conversation with Manfred Korfman for this decision (Shanower 2011, 199–200). When one critic takes Shanower to task over the rounded crenellations of Troy's outer wall,[10] he demonstrates just how refined the discussion of accuracy in this comic can get; no other portrayal of Troy in modern popular culture can motivate discussion at this level of detail.

This meticulous effort at historical and mythographic detail restricts *Age of Bronze* to a niche market. It is too cerebral and involved for the average reader of the superhero genre (it sells better in Europe, where comics have traditionally enjoyed a much higher prestige and offered a wider range of narrative genres), and for the traditional academic, it is too easily conflated with the pulp material still produced for adolescents. Thomas's Trojan War miniseries for *Marvel Illustrated*, where the artists are particularly indulgent when it comes to the female form, validates these fears somewhat (see chapter 1 in this volume). For an informed or patient reader, *Age of Bronze* yields much. The story is coherently told and is complex enough to reward multiple readings.

The positive result of Shanower's academic bent is that *Age of Bronze* has great potential as a pedagogical tool, best suited for senior high school students and undergraduates. Each volume has detailed glossaries and genealogies. On the website for *Age of Bronze*, Shanower

7. Interview at http://www.ancientromerefocused.org/2011/08/interview-with-eric-shanower/, August 2008.

8. By comparison, Frank Miller's *300* lists four sources, of which only one (and not the first) is classical. In order, they are William Golding, "The Hot Gates" (a ten-page essay about the author's visit to the modern site); Herodotus, *The Histories*; Ernle Bradford, *Thermopylae: The Battle for the West*; and Victor Davis Hanson, *The Western Way of War*.

9. This is seen, for example, in *Helen of Troy* (Robert Wise, 1955) and *The Trojan Horse* (Giorgio Ferroni, 1961).

10. Petruso (2006) acknowledges the amount of detail and research put into these comics.

includes links to other sites, literary materials, and guides to the ancient world. He includes a "Free Features" area, where he lists works of ancient literature or modern research that readers might find interesting. These include the text of Theocritus' *Idyll* 18, Proclus' *Chrestomathy*, and the eleventh poem of the *Hellenics* by Walter Savage Landor in 1846, which describes the sacrifice of Iphigenia. This supplemental material also represents a conscious effort on the part of Shanower to position *Age of Bronze* in the ever-evolving classical tradition.

Shanower recognized the importance of the sacrifice as one of the key early moments in the Trojan War, with a rich tradition of reception in antiquity and beyond. He accordingly dedicated three full issues of the comic to telling the story (these are numbers 17–19, about one-third of the second collected volume). This story has presented a tempting crux for poets and writers since at least the fifth century, when the tragic poets fixated on the human consequences of the sacrifice. What exactly could motivate a father to knowingly sacrifice his first-born daughter? This inquiry began with Aeschylus' *Agamemnon* in 458 BCE, when the chorus describes in its opening song the portent of two eagles (Aeschylus' invention; Gantz 1993, 585) and Calchas' relaying of Artemis' demands (Aes., *Ag.* 104–159).[11] The chorus's description of her on the altar, bound and gagged like a sacrificial animal, clarify her status as innocent victim, the first treatment known to consider her emotional state (239–247) and the first to consider the human consequences of the sacrifice.

One of Shanower's particular strengths as a writer is his characterization, creating naturalistic characters who evolve in realistic ways as the narrative unfolds. In the closing pages of the Iphigenia arc, for instance, Odysseus reflects on his role in the sacrifice and in the entire expedition (*Sacrifice* 213-214). Back on Ithaca, he notes, Odysseus would never have assisted in the human sacrifice of Agamemnon's daughter, and he had used his tricks to avoid the war altogether. The early years of the Trojan expedition have taught him how much he enjoys manipulating men and their armies. "But now . . ." says the balding, middle-aged man. "Now I want to be here in the middle of it all, planning strategies, directing the moves of men, telling them what to do, how to act, how to think. Playing my tricks. I'm good at it. I like it" (*Sacrifice* 213.7). Odysseus' process of psychological self-discovery is largely foreign to the classical material but is indicative of Shanower's rationalistic integration of apparently conflicting mythological traditions. How does the figure who yoked an ox and a donkey to avoid the war become its most influential tactician?[12] In the classical period, the Greeks themselves would not have been bothered by such conflicting traditions. Shanower uses modern sensibilities of character development to unite these conflicting Odysseuses, though his is by no means the only approach to such a mythological paradox.

Even modern adaptations, with so many Odysseuses from which to choose, tend to portray a single type already developed: the wicked, self-serving manipulator (Christos

11. The portent of the eagles raises the very difficult question of moral culpability. If Agamemnon is on a mission from Zeus and responding to a portent from Artemis, is he ultimately culpable? Also, why does Artemis choose to wreak vengeance on a young woman, ostensibly under her protection as *parthenos*? The bibliography here is large, but see Lloyd-Jones (1982; 1983); Lesky (1966); Peradotto (1969).

12. No complete account of Odysseus' madness survives before Hyginus (at least second century CE), but the story must have been well known by the fifth century BCE, when Aeschylus, Sophocles, and Euripides all wrote tragedies depicting Odysseus' revenge on Palamedes for the exposure of his scheme.

Tsagas in Michael Cacoyannis's *Iphigenia*, 1977), the silly trickster (Kirk Douglas in Mario Camerini's *Ulysses*, 1954), the wise and knowing warrior (Sean Bean in Wolfgang Petersen's *Troy*, 2004). I use cinematic examples here but could as easily cite typical Odysseuses from other media—dramas such as Jean Racine's *Iphigénie* (1674) and Jean Giraudoux's *La guerre de Troi n'aura pas lieu* (1935) or novels such as Barry Unsworth's *The Songs of the Kings* (2002). Shanower's characters evolve, they grow and they change, and his epic takes on a very human credibility.

As a comic, *Age of Bronze* is a uniquely qualified inheritor of the disparate traditions of literary and artistic sources. As a hybrid descendant of many other media, comics may generate new meaning not available to other media. Sound, for instance, is represented iconically. This is a necessity of the medium: speech must be represented visually, most commonly in speech balloons (Carrier 2000, 27–46). In *Age of Bronze*, the wind itself is also represented visually. In the opening pages of issue 17 (*Sacrifice* 150; see figure 2.1), we see the wind rising, represented in the gutter between panels by letters that start small and then grow. This wind keeps blowing, through every panel on every page, for almost three full issues (fifty-two pages total), subsiding only when Iphigenia approaches the altar. In a film, this noise would drown out or interfere with other elements of sound design. This might explain the choice of director Cacoyannis, who has the Greeks trapped not in a windstorm but in an oppressive stillness. In a novel or a poem, the reader must be constantly and explicitly reminded of the weather. In *Age of Bronze*, however, the wind is a constant presence, intrusive and omnipresent but never interfering with the flow of the narrative.

Shanower models his Iphigenia story arc on the plot of Euripides' *Iphigenia at Aulis* (a play produced soon after the author's death, in 405 BCE; hereafter *IA*), and each episode of that tragedy is presented, though events from other versions (particularly the *parodos* of *Agamemnon*) frequently intrude. Euripides' tragedy is an ideal exemplar for Shanower in several ways. It is, for one thing, the earliest complete account of the sacrifice (even the chorus of *Agamemnon* looks away at *Ag.* 248 and so leave the actual moment of the killing undescribed), and as such it has informed (directly or otherwise) practically every major adaptation of the Iphigenia sacrifice in the intervening centuries. (see, for example, Hall 2005a and 2005b; Michelakis 2006a and 2006b). This is also the first time Iphigenia volunteers for the sacrifice, a motif that competes with the salvation story of the later mythographic tradition.[13]

A major motif of Euripides' tragedy is decision-making and character development—what motivates the decisions of key mortal characters and how these characters justify to others, and to themselves, some truly terrible and terrifying choices. The stress of the situation motivates such character building: "The stage action of the drama . . . focuses only on the moment in which Agamemnon must choose whether or not to proceed with the sacrifice of his daughter" (Sorum 1992, 530). Not only Agamemnon but also Menelaus, Iphigenia, Achilles, and, above all, Clytemnestra finish Euripides' play as different characters from when they began. The characters of *Iphigenia at Aulis* possess a psychological depth not seen elsewhere in Greek tragedy. The indecision of Agamemnon, the vanity of Achilles, and the self-centered criticisms

---

13. The motif of self-sacrifice is not new to Euripides, however. At least four other tragedies, composed over three decades, featured voluntary sacrifice from a youth: *Children of Heracles, Hecuba, Phoenician Women*, and *Erechtheus*. See O'Connor-Visser (1987) and Wilkins (1990).

FIGURE 2.1 Onomatopoetic text between the panels replaces wavy lines for wind in *Age of Bronze: Sacrifice* 150. Art by Eric Shanower.

of Menelaus are petty weaknesses not admitted in the tragic heroes of other playwrights of the fifth century. In this psychological realism, Shanower finds the templates for many of his own characterizations, even if some of these characterizations are mediated through later sources.

Although he uses it as the frame for his narrative structure, Shanower frequently deviates from Euripides' account. Some changes occur at the level of plot. Clytemnestra and Achilles work together to uncover the sacrifice plot with only minimal assistance from the old slave (here named Arcas after his appearance in Racine's 1674 play). More interesting are changes in characterization and the motivation for those changes. Although neither violence nor sexuality is taboo in Shanower's telling, new (anachronistic) moral principles of gender equality, ethnic tolerance, and other political correctnesses are now operating. Achilles, for instance, is far nobler than the young man only concerned about the honor of his name in Euripides. This may be another inheritance from Racine. Shanower's Achilles does not suggest, as his Euripidean counterpart does at *IA* 962–967, that he would have agreed to the marriage ruse had he been asked. But this nobler Achilles is also consistent with Shanower's positive portrayal of the homosexual relationship between Achilles and Patroclus. As for Iphigenia, when she accepts the sacrifice, she does not emphasize the importance of male lives over those of females (consider line 1394 of *IA*: "Better a single man should see the light than ten thousand women").[14] When Iphigenia tells her mother, "They'll kill me anyway once he's dead . . . let my death mean something!" (*Sacrifice* 199.2), she takes the pragmatic approach that at least some critics find in the Euripidean model. She asserts herself but without devaluing her position or gender.

Such nuanced characterization is part of the rationalizing approach to the myth, and this rationalization extends to the divine for both Shanower and Euripides. The role of the divine is important to any interpretive understanding of Euripides' original play. Euripides carefully distances the gods from the action. The prophecy of Calchas (*IA* 89–92) is supported by no inspiring omen that we hear of, even though previous versions provide several alternative narrative patterns. Agamemnon reports the prophecy of Calchas at second hand in a speech where he has little reason to be honest; he is, after all, attempting to vindicate his own actions. In the closing scene of the play, Clytemnestra is told by messenger that Artemis has substituted a deer for Iphigenia, thereby saving her life. Clytemnestra doubts the validity of the messenger's speech at *IA* 1616–1617: πῶς δ' οὐ φῶ παραμυθεῖσθαι τούσδε μάτην μύθους ("How can I say these stories are not idly told to reassure me?"). The *exodos* of Euripides' play, however, is one of the most textually dubious passages of Greek tragedy and is considered spurious by most modern critics (West 1981; Kovacs 2003). Here the textual tradition of the play aligns with thematic treatment of the divine: we have no way of knowing if Iphigenia is actually saved.

Shanower's comic is even more explicit in its suppression of the divine, and this feeds into a larger program to remove the supernatural from his telling of the war. Oracles, prophecies, and divine sightings are reduced to observable natural phenomena or filtered through human interpretation and memory. Thus, though the reader may infer a divine presence overseeing the affairs of the war, Shanower encourages a more secular interpretation. The prophecies of Calchas, for instance, may be no such thing but rather the ramblings of a desperate, paranoid

---

14. On Iphigenia's choice as reinforcement of a patriarchal value system, see especially Foley (1985); Loraux (1987); Rabinowitz (1993, 38–54); Wohl (1998, 71).

old man. We are given little privileged information regarding Calchas, what his motivations are or how he comes by his prophecies, and the divine framework is again destabilized.

Shanower validates Clytemnestra's misgivings by having the salvation of Iphigenia described not by a messenger but by Odysseus himself, in a scene perhaps borrowed from Racine's *Iphigénie*. In that play, Ulysse has a very different outcome to report: the voluntary death of Eriphile, a daughter of Helen and Theseus, whom Racine has found in Pausanias (see note 3). In *Age of Bronze*, Odysseus' tale of salvation immediately precedes his own self-revelation that he enjoys the manipulation of others. Clytemnestra's explosive response to Odysseus, with panels focusing on the face and eyes, closely recalls the performance of Irene Papas—and Cacoyannis's editing of that performance—in the film version of *Iphigenia* in 1977. Earlier scenes in the comic, including Clytemnestra throwing herself to the ground when Iphigenia is taken, also recall Papas's performance, a performance that many critics feel to be defining of the character in the modern era (critical responses are collected in Svendsen 1990, 62–64). Early scenes in which the invitation of marriage arrives in Mycenae (not Argos) are likely also inspired by Cacoyannis's film.

But Shanower's greatest deviation from or, more accurately, addition to the sacrifice story of Euripides is the reason provided for the sacrifice itself in the light of his attitude toward the divine. Euripides gives no reason for Calchas' prophecy, even though several mythographic choices are open to him in this regard (and he is always capable of further innovation). The tragic spectator can only speculate on the reason for the sacrifice and its validity. For many critics, this absence of clear signal deprives Iphigenia's sacrifice of meaning. But it must also be remembered that Euripides can make greater mythographic demands on his audience; they will have reasons in mind, if only from Euripides' own *Iphigenia among the Taurians* from the previous decade.[15]

By contrast, and in keeping with his integrative approach, Shanower includes four distinct reasons for the sacrifice, all with a classical legacy but always within his rational parameters. Late in issue 16, as the Telephus story arc is coming to a close in Aulis, Agamemnon shoots a deer in the woods (though we do not see him boast as he does in the *Cypria*). There is no sign of trouble until two pages later, when, as the deer is being carried through the camp, Calchas looks upon it with worry. The informed reader, familiar with the *Cypria*, expects trouble. In issue 17, we see a montage of the soldiers' activities at Aulis (*Sacrifice* 150; see figure 2.1): throwing discus, playing at draughts, Achilles racing a chariot, all scenes from the *parodos* of *Iphigenia at Aulis* (196–230). The wind picks up, literally arising between these panels. When Calchas is questioned by Agamemnon, Menelaus, and Odysseus, he reveals (1) that a sacrifice is demanded for the shooting of the deer, as per the *Cypria*, and (2) that Agamemnon is being punished for Atreus' failure to sacrifice his golden lamb for Artemis. The golden lamb is more commonly associated with Hermes, but Artemis' involvement is first seen in a fragment from Pherecydes[16] and recorded more completely with Calchas' involvement in Apollodorus.[17] Later in the same

15. It is likely that some in the audience also saw Aeschylus' *Oresteia* in performance in the 420s; see Marshall (2001, 62).

16. *FGrH* 3.133 = Schol. Eur. *Or.* 995.

17. *Ep.* 2.12, 3.21–22.

issue, the grumbling soldiers see (3) the omen of the twin eagles as they devour a pregnant hare; the different-colored tails, one white, one dark, are a clear reference to *Agamemnon* 115, our earliest source for this event. This omen leads Calchas to prophesy again, this time before the entire army, that (4) Agamemnon promised to sacrifice the most beautiful creature born on his estate fourteen years before, a vow first found at *Iphigenia among the Taurians* 15–25. Apollodorus combines Agamemnon's vow with Atreus' golden lamb, making the sacrifice doubly necessary. In *Age of Bronze*, the traditions are separated: readers may associate vow and lamb if they wish, but as the prophecy is presented, it is consistent with Iphigenia's own recollection of the events at Aulis in the prologue of Euripides' *Iphigenia among the Taurians* (6–30), where the foolish vow of sacrifice is made without mention of the lamb. Thus, the sacred deer, the golden lamb, the twin eagles, and Agamemnon's reckless vow are all presented by Shanower, all filtered through the divination of Calchas. The contradiction and duplicity of the sources that make up the mythic tradition are now incorporated into a single version of the story itself, and it is the reader of the comic who must now make the decisions of the mythographer.

The displacement of these mythographic decisions increases the demands made of the reader (and of Shanower himself, whose project of integration is much larger than adapting a single source). Not only is there more for the reader to read, but the level of competency in recognizing the various strands of myth also increases. Even a purely classically informed reader still needs to know his or her Shakespeare to recognize the Troilus and Cressida narrative. Modern mass-media adaptations tend to streamline Greek myth, often reducing mythic cycles to bare necessities. One could reduce the narrative requirements of the Trojan War to an attractive woman and a large wooden horse, and it would still be recognizable to the modern reader. Each such presentation, of course, enforces the necessity of those basic elements at the expense of others. The inclusion of multiple versions and almost all attested events in the mythic cycle in *Age of Bronze* will certainly be a challenge for those used to the pared-down approach of modern popular culture. Indeed, *Age of Bronze* is not always an easier read than its Homeric predecessors. As with most challenges, though, there are rewards. The reader is able to see, for instance, not only multiple versions of a given myth but also multiple versions happening simultaneously. Detailed annotations and footnotes would not be out of place.

In *Age of Bronze*, the sacrifice itself is presented across four pages, near the end of issue 19. There is little text, and most of the action is depicted in images. Iphigenia is gagged as in the *parodos* of *Agamemnon*, for fear of her curse, though her hands and feet remain unbound. At *Agamemnon* 243–247, the chorus of elders from Argos describe how as a young child, Iphigenia used to sing for the guests of Agamemnon. In the comic, this reminiscence is given to the elder statesman of the Greek army, Nestor. Agamemnon pulls a hood over his face, which refers to a tradition that appears to begin with a painting of Timanthes, sometimes thought to be reproduced in a famous fresco from the House of the Tragic Painter in Pompeii (probably Shanower's inspiration for the scene).[18]

The rarity of visualized sound on these pages—few speech balloons, and the interpanel text of the wind is now absent—emphasizes the silence of the scene. Here, more than ever, the reader is encouraged to see Iphigenia (compare *Agamemnon* 242, in which Iphigenia is

---

18. Both Pliny, *HN* 35.36.37, and Quintilian, *Inst.* 2.13.13, record the hooded Agamemnon in Timanthes' painting, an apotropaic gesture recognizing the evil that he is about to do.

"conspicuous as in a picture"). The first page of the scene is void of text, and the final image in the bottom corner is a close-up of the gagged Iphigenia. The following page has three panels focused on the Greek leaders watching the procession and contains the longest exchange of dialogue:

ODYSSEUS: Is the gag necessary?

PALAMEDES: If she could speak, she might curse us.

MENELAUS: Curse us? Not Iphigenia.

NESTOR: I remember when she sang for us once when I was a guest at Mycenae . . . a voice the gods might envy.

[Agamemnon says nothing but covers his face in silence.]

On the third page (figure 2.2), Achilles has arrived and shouts out to Iphigenia, should she desire rescue. Iphigenia kneels and removes her gag. Then, across five panels featuring Iphigenia, Calchas, Achilles, the sacrificial knife, and Iphigenia again, she delivers her final line: "Father . . . don't grieve . . . anymore . . . the ships . . . can sail." The words are quoted from the final line of Walter Savage Landor's *Hellenics* 11, written in 1846, and the scene also evokes Polyxena's words of acceptance at *Hecuba* 547–552. By stringing the words across five static images, Shanower slows the pacing of the sacrifice.[19] The fourth page (figure 2.3) is silent and shows images of the moon, in a shorthand allusion to Artemis, which probably explains why Shanower chose to make this a night scene. In four panels, the moon is full, then interrupted by a spurt of blood, full again, and then interrupted by approaching cloud cover—the rain and favorable wind that will allow the Greeks to sail.

The panel in which Iphigenia speaks her final words (on the third page of the sequence, figure 2.2) is also the final image we see of Iphigenia. Here she has raised her chin, in acceptance of the sacrifice. The image is in the same position (bottom right-hand corner) as that of the gagged Iphigenia two pages earlier. As one turns the page, the space occupied by the gagged Iphigenia is replaced by that of the speaking Iphigenia. Even the moon over Iphigenia's shoulder is replaced by her speech balloon, " . . . can sail." Ancient and especially tragic depictions of sacrifice are frequently concerned with the voice of the sacrificial victim, which is tied to notions of consent. In antiquity, at least by the fifth century, sacrifice even of an animal must appear to be consensual to be considered successful, and that practice typically extends to the humans sacrificed in Greek tragedy (Kirk 1981; Henrichs 2000). Aeschylus' Agamemnon gags his daughter for fear of refusal; Euripides in *Iphigenia at Aulis* allows Iphigenia to confirm her sacrifice. Shanower leaves little doubt that the sacrifice occurs, although, as with the chorus at *Agamemnon* 248, the reader's point of view turns away so that we do not see the knife fall. We then may almost believe Odysseus when he tries to convince Clytemnestra that Iphigenia was saved (*Sacrifice* 212-213).

Shanower's *Age of Bronze* strives for Hardie's mythic totality. If it is completed, *Age of Bronze* will be one of the largest single accounts of the Trojan War since Homer himself. Shanower adapts and reworks a vast tradition that came before it. But does *Age of Bronze*

---

19. For more on the ability of the comic artist to manipulate time, see McCloud (1993, 94–117).

FIGURE 2.2 The sacrifice of Iphigenia in *Age of Bronze: Sacrifice* 208. Art by Eric Shanower.

FIGURE 2.3 The sacrifice of Iphigenia in *Age of Bronze: Sacrifice* 209. Art by Eric Shanower.

demand its own reworking? Does it open up new avenues of mythographic interpretation and enable new traditions in new media? Perhaps. Modern popular culture, particularly the comics and cinema, is particularly prone to repetition and reworking, more so even than Greek myth. Shanower has said his series is going to end before the *nostoi*; he expects to be exhausted by then.

3

Classical Symbolism in *Asterios Polyp*

ABRAM FOX AND HYOSIL SUZY HWANG-ESCHELBACHER

It's my version. Besides, all the great artists revisit the classics.
WILLY ILIUM, *Asterios Polyp*

David Mazzucchelli's 2009 magnum opus, *Asterios Polyp*,[1] opens with panels of ominous dark purple rain clouds from which jagged lightning bolts erupt. The next few pages depict a disheveled apartment where the graphic novel's namesake protagonist resides. An Olympian clap of thunder jostles Asterios Polyp out of bed (figure 3.1), and a lightning strike sets his apartment complex ablaze. Asterios frantically searches his bedroom for several keepsakes, the only possessions he elects to save before fleeing down the building's staircase. The brief first chapter concludes with yellow and purple flames slowly engulfing the apartment and all it contains (*Asterios Polyp* 1–13).

Already by the close of the first passage, the reader is confronted with conspicuous graphic aspects, such as the use of a limited color palette, which constantly reinforce the text's formal qualities. Mazzucchelli's use of multilayered visual references forces a reconsideration of each panel in search of deeper significance, further complicated by the text's reliance on classical references for plot and character development. While allusions to classical myth are not overt at first, the author-illustrator interweaves classics into the storyline with increasing emphasis as his novel unfolds, their allusions remaining crucial to the narrative and offering a more complex interpretation than what simple words and images can convey alone.

As the reader follows Asterios on his journey, prominent classical resonances, such as Greek and Roman temple architecture, the five Platonic solids, and myths and epics such as the *Odyssey* and the tale of Orpheus and Eurydice, propel the story forward and lead to enhanced

We would like to thank George Kovacs and C. W. Marshall for their patience and guidance in helping us prepare this chapter for publication. Their insightful comments, and those of the anonymous reviewers, encouraged us to strengthen our arguments and improve the organization and style better than we could have on our own. We would also like to thank Marjorie S. Venit from the Department of Art History and Archaeology at the University of Maryland, College Park, for drawing our attention to the call for papers and *demanding* that we submit a proposal. We dedicate this chapter to her and all of her years serving as our adviser, mentor, professor, and friend.

1. David Mazzucchelli (w./a.), *Asterios Polyp* (Pantheon Books, 2009).

FIGURE 3.1 Lightning illuminates Asterios Polyp's apartment. *Asterios Polyp* 7 (Pantheon, 2009). Art by David Mazucchelli.

awareness of antique referents throughout the novel. The lightning bolts that open the comic, first understood as simple acts of nature, become divine attributes of Zeus, and the bedraggled fate of Asterios at the close of the first chapter serves as demonstration of the effect of the whims of the gods on the lives of humans. At times, knowledge of these classically inspired themes is necessary to fully grasp the author's intentions. This chapter examines the Greek and Roman elements of *Asterios Polyp*, exploring the ways in which both the art and the ideas of antiquity can provide meaningful resonance in contemporary comics.

The text represents a new direction in the career of Mazzucchelli, who first achieved fame as a mainstream superhero illustrator on titles such as *Batman* and *Daredevil* in the 1980s, and for his 1994 coadaptation with Paul Karasik of Paul Auster's novella *City of Glass*. *Asterios Polyp* is Mazzucchelli's first graphic novel, and it operates as a unified whole; rather than first appearing serially in another venue, it was published as a single 344-page hardback volume, divided into twenty-two chapters labeled not by numbers but by "introductory" images that reflect some content contained within each section. Nor are the pages numbered, placing additional responsibility on the reader to pace the story.

Although introduced in the first pages of the book, Mazzucchelli's protagonist is not identified until the second chapter. Brilliant from an early age, Asterios Polyp excelled in school and earned tenure at an unidentified university in Ithaca, New York,[2] on the strength of "his renown as a 'paper architect'. . . . an esteemed architect whose reputation rested on his designs, rather than on the buildings constructed from them. In fact, none of his designs had ever been built" (17.3). Although the narrator claims that Asterios "taught because he enjoyed the intellectual environment," Mazzucchelli juxtaposes those words with a reverse view of a half-robed Kallipygian-type Venus, suggesting Asterios's womanizing proclivities, which reveal his true interest within the ivory tower (18.1). No connection is made between his past and the forlorn individual he has become by the present day of the book, set in the second half of 2000, and early passages contain content that unlocks meaning only through reading later sections of the text. Just as Homer's *Odyssey* "insists on the complexity of its own narrative structure and thereby draws attention to the very process . . . of generating and regenerating epic song" (Slatkin 1996, 268), so, too, does Mazzucchelli's *Asterios Polyp* become "a craftily self-reflexive artist's book about art" (Hatfield 2010) and the process of creating an intricate storyline in a comic.

Mazzucchelli brings direct attention to the mechanical process of comics creation through repeated deconstruction thereof, and the reader need not go farther than the cover of *Asterios Polyp* itself to see Mazzucchelli's experimentation in disassembling the typical structures of the medium. The dust jacket only covers a portion of the book, leaving two layers exposed underneath: a solid protective binding around the spine of the book and, along the edges, its softer cardboard interior. Upon opening *Asterios Polyp*, the reader encounters more of Mazzucchelli's deconstructions of form, line, color, and the printing process in this visual tour de force, which maintains a meandering narrative throughout.

2. Mazzucchelli's treatment of the school's campus and its atmosphere makes it clear that it is Cornell University or its fictional equivalent. For the purposes of *Asterios Polyp*, the name of the city is far more important than the name of the school.

Paramount to navigating the twists and turns of Mazzucchelli's storyline is recognition of the author's knowledge of the classics and determining whether his usage of ancient texts reflects serious engagement with works from antiquity or a thin Homeric patina covering a contemporary story. While it is impossible to assess Mazzucchelli's knowledge of classics that are not referred to in *Asterios Polyp*, his use of various facets of works such as the *Odyssey*, Virgil's *Georgics*, and Plato's *Symposium* demonstrate a strong theoretical awareness of the texts and references he does incorporate into his novel, as will be discussed throughout the remainder of this chapter.

What's in a Name? Eponyms, Agnomens, and Pseudonyms

Asterios is an unusual name, which begs to be deciphered. Asterios's heritage is Greek and Italian, but the word *asterios* itself is not native to any language. It does, however, possess the Greek root ἀστήρ, which can refer to a star, any luminous body, or a meteor.[3] A related English term is *asterism*, which refers to a recognizable, nonconstellation grouping of stars.[4] Perhaps the best-known asterism is the Big Dipper, part of the larger constellation Ursa Major, which Calypso directs Odysseus to use as a guide home to Ithaca (*Od.* 5.276–277). Likewise, a character in the novel, Ursula Major, helps to guide Asterios mentally, spiritually, and physically "home."

Additional etymological information about the protagonist's surname is provided by the narrator, who notes that it was cut in half by an "exasperated Ellis Island official" when Asterios's upper-class father, Dr. Eugenios ("well born" in Greek) Polyp, and lower-class mother, Aglia Olio (a play on *aglio e olio*, or "garlic and oil," a traditional Italian pasta dressing), emigrated to the United States (20.2). The result of the bisection, *polyp*, is etymologically a "many-footed creature," a term with roots in zoology.[5] While seemingly irrelevant at first, the name derives significance when the reader is informed that Asterios had a stillborn twin brother named Ignazio. Asterios, left to carry on the family name, retained the truncated appellation, while Ignazio, like the latter half of the family's surname, did not survive. Even though the second half of the name is unidentified, the remainder summons two connections to the *Odyssey*. The first and most obvious is Polyphemus, the one-eyed giant who captured Odysseus and his men on the island of the Cyclopes in Book 9.[6]

---

3. ἀστήρ is also the root of the name of the ancient Cretan king Asterion/Asterius, the stepfather of the demigod King Minos, and the name of the offspring of Minos' wife Pasiphaë and the Cretan bull, the monster more popularly known as the Minotaur. See Pausanias, *Description of Greece* 2.31.1. Although another connection to Greek mythology would be tempting, the authors are unable to find any reference to the Minotaur or the Cretan king in *Asterios Polyp*.

4. *Asterism* and *constellation* are often used synonymously in nonscientific contexts. In 1922, the International Astronomical Union defined eighty-eight official constellations; all other recognizable groupings of stars are asterisms. See International Astronomical Union, "The Constellations." http://www.iau.org/public/constellations/. Another definition of *asterism* applies to modern printing, where it describes a grouping of three asterisks in a triangle, used in typography to draw attention to a particular section of a text.

5. *Polyp* has other meanings in zoology and pathology, but this definition is the most pertinent to our discussion.

6. See Mondi (1983) for an explanation of the giant's one-eyed nature and a possible solution for the discrepancies between Homer's Polyphemus and "traditional" Cyclopes.

Like a Cyclops, Asterios has a restricted view of the world. He sees things as binaries and believes in an inherent "truthfulness" that renders one aspect superior to its opposite. Mazzucchelli's depictions of Asterios—almost always in profile such that only one eye is visible to the reader—reinforce the protagonist's limited scope. Asterios's loss of an eye at the end of the book cements his Cyclopean association, although it becomes reversed; not until his vision becomes literally monocular does he break out of his binary mindset.

The second connection between the *Odyssey* and Asterios's last name is *polytropos*, the first adjective Homer uses to describe Odysseus (*Od.* 1.1). Meaning "well traveled" or "turning many ways" or, in other words, crafty, both definitions of the word are applicable to Asterios throughout the comic. His romantic flings with multiple women further liken him to the Greek hero,[7] and in an early scene, he is even rendered as Odysseus tied to the mast of his ship, shouting, "Sing sweet, O Siren!" while halfheartedly attempting to ward off a student's inappropriate advances (39.4). Like his "well-traveled" counterpart, Asterios's journey takes him far away from Ithaca. Having previously left the university there and moved to Manhattan, Asterios witnesses his apartment's destruction and then takes the subway to a Greyhound bus terminal and uses most of his cash to purchase a bus ticket, requesting the most distant destination his money can buy (31.4). He ends up in the fictional town of Apogee, which appropriately means "the highest or most distant point."[8] Apogee appears to be in the American South or Southwest, and it is the spiritual opposite of Asterios's home in Manhattan. In this small town, Asterios undergoes a transformation into a new man more understanding of the complexities of life.

Other characters possess names that reveal essential truths of their beliefs and personalities. The aforementioned deceased twin brother of Asterios, Ignazio, serves as the book's disembodied narrator, and the significance of his name as it relates to the word *ignatius*, meaning "ardent" or "burning" in Latin, is discussed at length below. On Asterios's first day in Apogee, he encounters a man obsessed with asteroids hitting the Earth: Steven "Spotty" Drizzle (72–75), a character from an earlier Mazzucchelli short story.[9] Another character is Kalvin Kohoutek, a musician composing the score for a theatrical production, *Orpheus (Underground)*, which factors into the second half of the story. Upon meeting Kohoutek, an elderly African American man, Asterios wonders about the name's provenance (218.1). A common Czech surname, Kohoutek is also the name of a comet discovered in 1973 and predicted to be the "comet of the century."[10] The comet failed to deliver in brilliance, however, and the shared name with the

---

7. See Finkelberg (1995) for a discussion of the type of hero embodied by Odysseus. In contrast to heroes of the *Iliad*, who bravely meet death on the battlefield, the hero of the *Odyssey* is willing to face suffering and various ordeals in life—not unlike Mazzucchelli's eponymous "hero."

8. *Apogee* is also the astronomical term for the point in a heavenly body's orbit in which it is farthest from the Earth, derived from the Greek *apogaios*, "away from the Earth."

9. Drizzle first appeared in the short story "Near Miss" in *Rubber Blanket* 1, published in 1991. *Rubber Blanket* was a self-published comics anthology by Mazzucchelli and his wife, Richmond Lewis, published in three issues in 1991, 1992, and 1993. *Asterios Polyp* was originally planned to appear in a fourth issue of *Rubber Blanket*, before Mazzucchelli decided to give it the full-length graphic-novel treatment. In "Near Miss," a man named Steven abandons his home and family after learning of an asteroid passing close to the Earth and ventures into the desert to set up a telescope and keep a vigilant watch. David Mazzucchelli, "Near Miss," reprinted in *An Anthology of Graphic Fiction, Cartoons and True Stories*, edited by Ivan Brunetti, Vol. 2 (New Haven, CT: Yale University Press, 2008).

10. "Special Report: Kohoutek: Comet of the Century," *Time Magazine*, December 17, 1973. http://www.time.com/time/magazine/article/0,9171,908347-1,00.html.

composer alludes to the notion that Kohoutek's efforts as a musician will also lead to imminent failure.[11]

Less direct but nonetheless revealing is the name of Asterios's ex-wife, Hana Sonnenschein, who is seen primarily in flashback scenes. Hana is a creative yet timid art professor and a perfectionist afraid of the spotlight, whose gentle demeanor and proclivity for natural forms in art act as a foil to Asterios's cynicism and preference for symmetry and structure. Hana's name reflects the ethnic heritages of her German-American father, Ernst Sonnenschein, and her mother, Mitsuko, a Japanese woman who met Sonnenschein when he was stationed in Japan after World War II. The Sonnenscheins gave their only daughter a name fitting for her personality: *hana* means "flower" in Japanese, while *sonnenschein* is German for "sunshine." The disparate outlooks of Hana and Asterios are bridged in part by their cat, Noguchi, named after the Japanese-American artist and landscape architect Isamu Noguchi, whose mass-produced furniture also appears in the apartment shared by the couple. Noguchi's aesthetic, incorporating both the organic and the geometric, demonstrates that the distinct styles of Hana and Asterios are not mutually exclusive.

Strong connections to the *Odyssey* are again forged through the name of Asterios's nominal nemesis, Willy Ilium. Introduced in flashbacks in the second half of the book, Willy is the wedge that drives Asterios and Hana apart, leading to their divorce. His last name is an alias for Troy, the home of the adversaries of the Greeks and Odysseus in particular. As the Trojan War preceded Odysseus' journey home, so, too, do the exchanges among Asterios, Hana, and Willy predate the present-day narrative of Asterios's journey. The name is further significant since in human anatomy, the ilium (or ilion) is the largest bone in the pelvis; coupled with his praenomen, Willy, the full name affirms the character's prick-like nature.[12] Yet while Willy Ilium is a prick, he is no villain. He bears no ill will toward Asterios—in what is perhaps the ultimate insult to Asterios, he seems simply to ignore him—and his turpitude is limited to inadvertently instigating situations in which Asterios demonstrates his own failings as a supportive husband. Willy is introduced as a postmodern artistic pantomime, combining existing dances to create new works and contributing nothing himself except the new arrangement of old material. This alchemy, characterized by the narrator in a negative light, in fact mirrors the same approach taken by the sympathetic Hana in her own art making, linking the two more closely, with Asterios as their antithesis.[13]

Understanding the full significance of names reveals an additional layer of motivations and relationships among the graphic novel's characters that enriches the narrative and provides further insight into Mazzucchelli's overall design. Many of these names in *Asterios Polyp* are rooted in classical sources, which privileges readers familiar with the great texts of antiquity,

11. Also noteworthy is that David Berg, the founder of the Children of God, incorrectly predicted that Comet Kohoutek would signal the apocalypse of the United States in January 1974. "Religion: Children of Doom," *Time Magazine*, February 18, 1974. http://www.time.com/time/magazine/article/0,9171,942791,00.html.

12. Willy's name is also the most malleable of any of the character names in *Asterios Polyp*, as it is a self-given pseudonym. Previously, he was identified on theatrical posters as Willy Iridium, Willy Illuminato, Willy the Hip, and Willy Gilgamesh; see *Asterios Polyp* 184. Asterios gives him another identity, privately calling his rival Willy Chimera.

13. One can argue that Mazzucchelli's own graphic novel, which mixes classic stories and ancient sources, is a similar form of postmodern amalgamation.

particularly Homer's *Odyssey*. Recognizing the juxtaposition of the comic with the epic poem reveals to the reader not only a fuller comprehension of characters but also themes from the *Odyssey* that loom large in *Asterios Polyp*.

Calling on the Classics

In the *Odyssey*, Homer repeatedly stresses the Greek concept of *xenia*, or hospitality toward those who are far from home. Similarly, Mazzucchelli bases the relationship between Asterios and the couple he lodges with in Apogee—Stiff and Ursula Major (figure 3.2)—on this guest friendship. When Asterios first arrives in Apogee, he sees a "Help Wanted" sign outside Major Auto Repair and approaches the proprietor, Stiff, about a job, room, and board. Stiff sees through Asterios's lie about possessing prior car-repair experience but nonetheless offers the stranger employment and lodging (52). Ursula later reveals to Asterios that "when you first showed up at his shop with, like, nothing but the clothes on your back, he [Stiff] thought you'd just got out of prison" (178.1). Nonetheless, Stiff trusted his ability to sense the true nature of people and welcomed Asterios as a guest.

The Majors' hospitality fits the Greek model of guest friendship outlined through the interactions of Odysseus and Telemachus with others in the *Odyssey*. At the end of Book 15, after hearing all the news Menelaus has to offer about Odysseus' whereabouts, Telemachus asks to return home. As an exemplary host, Menelaus replies, "I'd never detain you here too long, Telemachus, not if your heart is set on going home. I'd find fault with another host, I'm sure, too warm to his guests, too pressing or too cold. Balance is best in all things. It's bad either

FIGURE 3.2 Asterios prepares to leave Apogee. *Asterios Polyp* 306.1 (Pantheon, 2009). Art by David Mazucchelli.

way, spurring the stranger home who wants to linger, holding the one who longs to leave" (*Od.* 15.74–80). Menelaus not only fulfills Telemachus' wish to leave his palace, but he also bestows on him lavish gifts and a bountiful farewell feast. Likewise, the Majors support Asterios's decision to leave Apogee and even assist with repairing a car in order to do so. In this way, the Majors resemble those in the *Odyssey* who are fit models of guest friendship, including Menelaus and Helen, Nestor, and particularly Phaeacian King Alkinous and Queen Arete of Scheria.

Books 9 through 12 of the *Odyssey*, collectively known as the *apologoi*, feature Odysseus' encounter with the Phaeacians and describe his adventures to that point.[14] The Phaeacians in the *Odyssey* are the examples of *xenia* par excellence,[15] and although Asterios does not rehash his past to the Majors as Odysseus relates to his hosts, chapters that flash back to earlier moments in his life fulfill the same function. Thus, just as Schein (1996, 17) identifies the Phaeacians as "institutionally and symbolically, a halfway house between the surreality or unreality of the people and places Odysseus tells of in his first-person narrative of his adventures (Books 9–12) and the reality of Ithaca," the Majors of Apogee behave in a similar fashion for Asterios. As "Odysseus achieves his *nostos*, his 'return home,' not so much by physical prowess and warrior heroism . . . as through mental toughness" (Schein 1996, 8), Asterios returns to Hana only as a result of the mental change he undergoes in the Majors' home.

Just as the relationship between Asterios and the Majors positions the former in the guise of Odysseus, demonstrations of hubris also unite the Greek epic hero and the paper architect. Odysseus cannot help but reveal his true identity to Polyphemus as he sails away in Book 9, even though his pseudonym, "Nobody," has fooled the Cyclops and allowed him and his men to escape the giant's island. This mistake allows Polyphemus to exact revenge on Odysseus, since he is able to tell his father, Poseidon, who blinded him. Poseidon's wrath results in the deaths of more of Odysseus' shipmates and costs Odysseus additional time away from his homeland.[16] In *Asterios Polyp*, Ignazio introduces the concept of hubris to the reader in an early discussion of Aristophanes from Plato's *Symposium*, the textual description accompanied by a visual of a sixteen-year-old Asterios being turned down for a date by a classmate (78). Rejections aside, Asterios grows up to be arrogant about his abilities as an architect, his overall intelligence, and his interactions with women. In fact, most of the storyline of the graphic novel revolves around Asterios's hubris and the destructive effect it has on his life.

Yet despite their hubris, Odysseus and Asterios both subscribe to the belief that the gods control one's fate. For each individual, higher powers remind them that no one is invincible and one's fate can change in an instant. The *Odyssey* illustrates this concept clearly, as even the

---

14. Most (1989) believes that the *apologoi* are designed to exemplify proper *xenia* by illustrating its opposite. Odysseus' reminiscences of the Lotus Eaters, Scylla, Circe, and others are meant to show how proper hosts should *not* act.

15. Segal (1994, 202–215) explains the *xenia* of the Phaeacians in contrast to the inhospitable and brutish Cyclopes. Broeniman (1996) presents a contrary notion that the Phaeacians should not be considered polite hosts but rather "are more akin to the fantastic world of Odysseus' wanderings." See also Cook (1992), who reads the Phaeacians as belonging to the underworld and Scheria as a metaphor for Hades/Elysium. Despite these theories, Scheria is the last stop Odysseus makes before reaching Ithaca, and the Phaeacian ships are the vessels that finally bring the epic hero home. Furthermore, in contrast to the Laestrygonians, the Cyclopes, the Lotus Eaters, or others Odysseus and his men encounter on their journey, the Phaeacians are unrivaled in their generous hospitality.

16. See Friedrich (1991) for a discussion of Odysseus' *hubris*, particularly in the *Cyclopeia*.

hospitable Phaeacians cannot escape punishment from the gods. For helping Odysseus reach home, Poseidon turns the Phaeacian ship to stone, which sinks and blocks their sea route from any further travel (*Od.* 13.155–164). *Asterios Polyp* opens with bolts of lightning setting fire to the protagonist's apartment, and a meteor soars through the sky toward Asterios and Hana when he reconciles with his ex-wife at the end of the novel—both random, natural phenomena that can be interpreted as divine actions with profound effects on the human world. The major change for Asterios is the eventual realization that he is not the hero of his story but rather an insignificant character in a larger universe. And as Vidal-Naquet (1996, 38–39) suggests, "the *Odyssey* as a whole is in one sense the story of Odysseus' return to normality, of his deliberate acceptance of the human condition." Likewise, Mazzucchelli's novel replicates that acceptance through Asterios's cognizance of his true relationship to the world around him.

One of the most provocative chapters late in *Asterios Polyp* (245–265) is devoid of dialogue. It is striking not only because of its wordless narrative but also for its scratchy, expressive style, a departure from the hard lines and smooth contours that characterize the rest of the book. Whereas all the first sixteen chapters of the novel feature purple ink accompanied by generous application of the primary printer's colors of cyan, magenta, and yellow, the seventeenth chapter is presented almost entirely in a dark violet tone, emphasizing its surreal setting. Asterios acts out the tragic story of Orpheus and Eurydice, with himself and Hana playing the starring roles. Initially, the context of the passage is unclear, but Asterios's encounter with Cerberus evokes classical myth. As with its classical counterpart, this dog's three heads are calmed when Asterios plays his lyre, rendered as a stringed architect's T-square. Having assuaged Cerberus, Asterios enters a modern-day version of Hades: the New York City subway. He descends a long flight of stairs and goes through a turnstile, retracing his journey away from his burning apartment at the book's beginning. Instead of crossing the River Styx in Charon's ferry, Asterios boards an empty subway car that floats him along a watery train tunnel to his destination (246–249).

In his descent to the underworld, Asterios passes the shades of deceased family members and other minor characters he previously encountered in New York City at the start of the book.[17] He then enters a theater, where he again strums his architect's lyre, this time as accompaniment to two masked silhouettes acting out a play. The performance, executed across eight panels on one page, is that of Orpheus and Eurydice, and Asterios's mourning the loss of his love is mirrored by the masked silhouette's sorrow (255). The part of Hades is played by Willy Ilium (in his only sympathetic role in the novel), who haughtily procures another chance for Asterios/Orpheus and his Eurydice—Hana—to be reunited (figure 3.3). Yet, like his Greek counterpart, Asterios/Orpheus is unable to resist temptation, and one glance back at his former lover separates the two again for eternity. She is not merely returned to the Underworld, as in the classical myth. Hana/Eurydice disappears behind a wall of fire that begins to engulf Asterios/Orpheus, even as he droops his head in defeat. Meanwhile, a bolt of lightning cuts across the rainy-sky backdrop, recalling the dramatic opening of the book once again (264–265).

---

17. This episode also recalls Book 11 of the *Odyssey*, when Odysseus meets the shades of the deceased.

FIGURE 3.3 **Asterios/Orpheus ascends from the Underworld.** *Asterios Polyp* 261 (Pantheon, 2009). Art by David Mazucchelli.

The panels illustrating Asterios's song present Hana/Eurydice's death as a result of a snake bite, recalling Virgil's version of the myth in which Eurydice is bitten while fleeing from the unwanted advances of the demigod Aristaeus.[18] The choice to refer to Virgil's version of the tale comments further on the tenor of Asterios and Hana's relationship. Eurydice shunned Aristaeus to remain faithful to Orpheus, just as Hana refused Willy's advances. The fidelity of both women, however, still produced a marred fate. The snake's venom forever separated Orpheus and Eurydice, while Asterios's jealousy and cynical reaction to Willy's charismatic personality poisoned his marriage.

Although Mazzucchelli specifically evokes Virgil's account of Orpheus and Eurydice, the classical narrative also appears in texts of other ancient authors. Ovid, in one version of the myth, mentions that Orpheus' melody deeply moved other characters in Hades (*Met.* 10.1–85). Tantalus stopped reaching for water, the Danaids rested by their urns, and Sisyphus paused in his eternal task of pushing a boulder up a hill to listen. In the chapter in *Asterios Polyp* immediately following the Orpheus passage, lyrics to a song heard over a radio refer to Sisyphus: "still goin' 'round tho' it's very old/The greatest story ever told/How's a dead man gonna move that boulder?"[19] The effect for the reader well versed in the classics is a multidimensional reading and close-looking experience marked by esoteric themes and messages that deny a direct storyline and simple characters. Instead, clues such as the mention of gods, heroes, and ancient sources signal the reader to pay closer attention to all parts of the novel.

Reading Alternative Narratives through a Classical Lens

While Willy Ilium seems like the obvious antagonist of the graphic novel, and Asterios certainly perceives him as such, knowledge of the *Odyssey* and other classics unlocks a subnarrative in which Asterios's adversary is his twin brother, Ignazio. Having been stillborn, Ignazio functions as the narrator of the comic and only appears in person in dream sequences with Asterios. Narrowly missing a birthdate under the astrological sign Gemini (May 21–June 21), the twins were born on June 22 after a thirty-three-hour labor (20.2), emphasizing in an abstract manner how losing his identical twin affected Asterios's life and character. Instead of a Gemini, he is a Cancer, a fitting state considering the pathological implications of his last name. The allusion to Gemini also triggers another classical reference: Castor and Pollux (or Polydeuces), together known as the Dioscuri. Upon their death, Castor and Pollux became the two brightest stars in the constellation Gemini, and the likening of the Polyp twins to the mythological brothers affirms a celestial undercurrent to the story.[20]

18. Virgil, *Georgics* 4.453–527. This adds yet another layer to the story of Asterios and Hana; the "death" of Asterios and Hana's marriage is a direct result of Asterios's poor reactions to Willy's unwanted advances toward Hana. See Guthrie (1996, 31).

19. *Asterios Polyp* 268.2–3. See Ovid, *Met.* 10.44.

20. Pindar, *Nemean Ode* 10, offers the tale of the immortal Pollux begging his father, Zeus, to save his mortal brother, Castor (born by the same mother, Leda, but by a different father, King Tyndareus), from death. Zeus turned the twins into two stars of the Gemini constellation on the condition that they would alternate days between Mount Olympus and Hades, or immortality and death. This quality of the mythological twins moving between worlds finds some resonance in Asterios and Ignazio in *Asterios Polyp*, but a direct parallel is difficult to draw. Moreover, other ancient authors give differing accounts of the Dioscuri, and the account of the twins in the graphic novel does not clearly map onto any one textual account of the Dioscuri.

Acting as direct counterparts, Asterios and Ignazio complete each other's persona even as they oppose each other. Mazzucchelli inserts design details throughout their encounters to affirm this: he positions them as the two halves of a yin-yang when discussing their birth (21); Asterios is left-handed, Ignazio right-handed; Asterios's preferred style of architecture is modernism struck by functionality, symmetry, and parallelism, while Ignazio's style is that of the deconstructivist Frank Gehry (in fact, he seems to take on the role of the "starchitect" himself), which disregards form following function.

A glimpse of adolescent Asterios's room reveals an obsession with twins and dualities. Two books, *The Prince and Pauper* and *The Man in the Iron Mask*, are prominently displayed on a desk, and the young Asterios has adorned his walls with posters of Romulus and Remus and Tweedle-Dee and Tweedle-Dum. The black and white chess pieces on a board and the DNA double helices adorning his bedspread further insist on his preoccupation with dichotomies (figure 3.4). He remains intrigued by the idea of the dual into adulthood, and imagery and subtle references to dyads throughout the book affirm this major theme. Asterios lectures a college class about opposing design principles such as linear versus plastic and factual versus fictional (114), tells a student "there are two ways you can approach design: through line or through form" (37.1), and praises the Twin Towers for their brilliance in that "there are *two* of them" (118.2).

Even in this discussion of dualities, the novel filters the dialogue through a classical lens. Early in the text, Ignazio provides the reader a brief description of Aristophanes' explanation of humankind's original condition (78–79). This account is recorded in Plato's *Symposium*, where Aristophanes states that humans once had double sets of each body part—four arms, four legs,

FIGURE 3.4 **Young Asterios Polyp.** *Asterios Polyp* **20.1 (Pantheon, 2009). Art by David Mazucchelli.**

two heads, and so on—and each human possessed two sets of female genitalia, two sets of male genitalia, or one male and one female. Jealous and suspicious that they would overthrow the gods, Zeus bisected these humans, and humanity's present condition is to seek a partner and restore the equilibrium (Pl., *Symp.* 189d–193e).

Mazzucchelli refers to this episode several times throughout *Asterios Polyp*, and it remains his protagonist's goal to find his other half. This search doomed Asterios in his earlier life and drives his new life after the apartment fire. Yet the fulfillment Asterios had been looking for in the opposite sex he already had in Ignazio: another human being to complete him. The merging, however, was unsatisfactory; Ignazio exists only in Asterios's mind, after all. Only when Asterios leaves Ignazio (rendered as an outline of a human form) behind at the subway platform and embarks on his voyage to Apogee in the second chapter (28.3) is Ignazio disassociated from his host and Asterios given the possibility of success.

Ignazio will not let go of Asterios so easily, though, and careful reading of the text reveals that Ignazio plays a larger role in the narrative than it first appears. Asterios senses a presence as he explains to Hana that he has always "expected to see someone" over his shoulder even when alone (124.4). When he learned as a teenager that he had a brother in the womb, he became haunted by the notion that he was the surviving twin. Wondering what his brother's life would have been like, Asterios places video cameras throughout his apartment and claims that having his "own video doppelgänger" comforts him. This doppelgänger is given a physical presence with the library of row upon row of neatly ordered and labeled VHS tapes that Asterios stores in his living quarters but never watches, each consisting of one day's worth of recording.[21]

It seems that Asterios's paranoia is well founded, for even though Ignazio is not a living human, he nonetheless appears frequently in another material form. His name, a variation of Ignatius, has a fiery connotation in Latin, which finds visual references in the frequency of fire imagery in the comic. In the novel's beginning, Mazzucchelli devotes a full page to fire consuming Asterios's video library, and the conflagration seems to free his recorded doppelgänger from its video confines (13). As Asterios flees his burning apartment, he grabs three keepsakes: a watch, a pocketknife, and a broken lighter, the last item a gift from his father which he later gives to his seatmate on the bus to Apogee (9.2, 50.8). The same lighter, in working condition, appears in dream sequences, flashbacks, and later in the storyline, when the erstwhile seatmate reappears in a bar and drunkenly smashes a beer bottle across Asterios's face (272.7–8). The etymology of Ignazio's name and the numerous visual references to flames indicate an equation of any imagery of fire with Ignazio. Read this way, Ignazio is more prominent in the novel than at first blush.

The recurrence of fire recalls another narrative, that of Prometheus.[22] Like Prometheus, Asterios is punished by Zeus (as the lightning bolt from the beginning of the novel illustrates),

21. Asterios tells Hana that he never watches the tapes, but Mazzucchelli depicts Asterios watching videotapes in the first chapter. While the reader assumes from the suggestive dialogue that Asterios is watching a pornographic tape, it is later revealed that the protagonist was watching a scene of himself and Hana dining together early in their courtship.

22. The story of Prometheus is captured by Hesiod in his *Theogony* (starting at 507) and *Works and Days* (starting at 42) and by Aeschylus, though any companion plays to *Prometheus Bound* have been lost, and the authorship is questioned.

and his offering the lighter to his seatmate on the bus can be interpreted as a modern-day "bringing fire to man." Interestingly, Prometheus had a brother, Epimetheus, and their names describe the qualities they embodied, "foresight" and "hindsight," respectively. Asterios, the modernist theoretician and paper architect, has the ability to conceive of the future, while Ignazio is an afterthought, only existing in physical form as video recordings of past events or as fiery imagery.

Only in the dream sequences does Ignazio take on human form. In the last of six dream encounters between the twins (289–297), Asterios attacks Ignazio with a lug wrench after becoming enraged that Ignazio is posing as him and recounting the events of Asterios's life as if they were his own. After the attack, Ignazio no longer appears in the book, and his narration also ceases. This is further complicated by the speech bubbles and fonts emanating from Ignazio in this scene, which gradually shift from his own unique style into that which normally characterizes Asterios. Through this technique, Mazzucchelli affirms the converging identities of the two brothers, and the final words from Asterios—"STOP IT!"—are encased in Asterios's normal speech bubble with the font typically ascribed to Ignazio (297.3).

The following chapter opens with Asterios waking up in the hospital, where he learns of the loss of his left eye (299.3–4). While the brawl at the bar caused him the physical damage, the missing eye and the eye patch Asterios he wears symbolize the absence of Ignazio in the physical world after Asterios's subconscious murder of his brother. Feeling freed from Ignazio, Asterios wakes invigorated and quickly begins to prepare a solar-powered car for his journey to reunite with Hana. During his efforts, Ursula offers Asterios a bottle of beer, which he accidentally drops and breaks. As an explanation, Asterios tells Ursula, "I'm still getting used to the lack of parallax" (302.5). By having him use the technical term *parallax* rather than the more common *depth perception*, Mazzucchelli reinforces a direct connection between his novel and James Joyce's canonical work, *Ulysses*.[23] *Parallax* is defined as a "difference or change in the apparent position or direction of an object as seen from two different points . . . such a difference or change in the position of a celestial object as seen from different points on the earth's surface."[24] In *Ulysses*, the protagonist, Leopold Bloom, frequently thinks about astronomical implications of parallax, and the entire novel is an example of narrative parallax: several different, simultaneous observations of Dublin at the same place and time (Kenner 1980).

Asterios's "lack of parallax" is a boon to him. Now that Ignazio is no longer a shadowy presence watching over his shoulder and interacting with him in his dreams, Asterios feels free to honestly pursue his true love. Unfortunately for Asterios, who finally realizes that he is merely "a supporting character in the larger story" (282), Ignazio refuses to accept this schism and returns in the penultimate chapter of the novel in a literal recombination of *Asterios* and *Ignazio*, a *fiery asteroid*.

23. Mazzucchelli's desire to have *Asterios Polyp* mirror a traditional novel also manifests in the physical structure of the comic. The work is broken into chapters, is published as a hardback, and on the whole appears more like a novel than a conventional comic.

24. *Oxford English Dictionary Online*. Oxford University Press, March 2015.

Ratios, Forms, and Sequences

Like the reader who would find this graphic novel most rewarding, Asterios is well versed in antiquity. For all of his prize-winning architectural designs, he is less a modernist architect than a classicizing philosopher working in the mold of his ancient Greek predecessors. His obsession with the Platonic solids is first glimpsed in the fourth chapter, when abstract forms—presumably the subject of his oration—are shown floating above a wire-frame model of him mid-lecture (36). The forms serve as visual representations of Asterios's "construction of the world." The five shapes—tetrahedron, cube, octahedron, dodecahedron, icosahedron—reappear as shorthand for the beauty Asterios finds in the ideal world. As Ignazio tells us: "Abstractions have always appealed to my brother—especially systems and sequences that are governed by their own internal logic" (figure 3.5). When the Platonic solids resurface at the end of the novel in Hana's studio (323.1), they represent Asterios's impact on Hana and his success in altering her perception of art and the universe to align more closely with his own.

The influence of the Platonic solids on art and architecture is familiar to scholars of antiquity, the Renaissance, and the modern era.[25] Plato, in his dialogue *Timaeus*, speculates on the nature of human beings and the physical world through the voice of his title character. In order to make sense of the universe, Plato states that the creator ordered the world into four elements: fire, earth, air, and water. Each of these elements had a minute particle of a particular shape: tetrahedron, cube, octahedron, and icosahedron, respectively. As for the dodecahedron, Plato remarks that the creator had used it for placing the constellations in the heavens. Following in the footsteps of Renaissance artists such as Leonardo da Vinci and Paolo Uccello (Emmer 1982), Asterios applies geometrical shapes to his own designs. Mazzucchelli's inclusion of the Platonic solids in this narrative is even more intricate, for in the early seventeenth century, Johannes Kepler discussed how the solids were formed:

> from different classes: the males, the cubes and the dodecahedron, among the primary;
> the females, the octahedron and the icosahedron, among the secondary, to which is added
> one, as it were, bachelor or hermaphrodite, the tetrahedron, because it is inscribed in itself,
> just as those female solids are inscribed in the males and are, as it were, subject to them, and
> have the signs of the feminine sex, opposite the masculine, namely, angles opposite planes.
> (Kepler 1952, 1011)

Although Kepler does not mention it directly, the dialogue regarding male, female, and hermaphrodite genders evokes Aristophanes' discussion about the condition of humans from Plato's *Symposium*. Thus, the Platonic solids that our protagonist is so fond of bespeak another reference to the dual nature of humankind.

Furthermore, Plato's analysis of the solids prompts another topic crucial to art and architecture through the centuries: the golden ratio, or golden mean.[26] A formula for creating aesthetically pleasing works characterized by symmetry, balance, and harmony, the golden

25. See Emmer (1982). By incorporating the Platonic solids into his graphic novel, Mazzucchelli is, in a way, assimilating the genre of comics into the realm of "high art."

26. Euclid, in his *Elements* (c. 300 BCE), Book 6, Proposition 30, gives the first recorded definition of the Golden Ratio and refers to it as ἄκρος καὶ μέσος λόγος, or "extreme and mean ratio," but Plato's Timaeus implies the proportion in his dialogue (Pl., *Ti.* 31c–32a).

FIGURE 3.5 The importance of sequences. *Asterios Polyp* 112 (Pantheon, 2009). Art by David Mazucchelli.

ratio has figured into the design of countless buildings, sculptures, paintings, and drawings throughout history. Some propose that the Parthenon is composed of golden rectangles (Padovan 1999, 80–98), and the first dream sequence with Asterios and Ignazio takes place inside the fifth-century BCE temple (*Asterios Polyp* 44–45). In modern times, the Swiss architect Le Corbusier was fond of the golden ratio (Le Corbusier 2000), and it is unsurprising that Asterios decorated his Manhattan apartment with furniture in the style of Le Corbusier.[27]

Closely related to this ratio is the Fibonacci sequence,[28] which also appears in *Asterios Polyp* in a variety of forms. In the second chapter, which begins with Ignazio's statement, "Abstractions have always appealed to my brother," Mazzucchelli illustrates the digits of the sequence and the Fibonacci spiral (figure 3.5).[29] More subtle references include plant forms that exhibit the golden ratio and Fibonacci sequence: the daisy, Asterios's pet name for Hana (80.1–2); the sunflower, which figures prominently when Ignazio places some in the car in place of its engine in the last scene he appears in (295); and the pine cone, which shows up as a slide during Asterios's lecture on his book, *The Seeds of Design*, and also in a flashback as Hana's evidence of nature's perfection (182.2, 80.3–4). The two former lovers also serve as conduits through which Mazzucchelli expresses his proclivity toward Platonic solids and the golden ratio, which make up the underlying structure of the universe and provide the proportions for creating the most aesthetically pleasing works of art.

Conclusion

Knowledge of the classics—the plot of the *Odyssey* along with its themes and characters, Plato's works and theories, classical myths, and Greek and Latin vocabulary—reveals the endless complexity of Mazzucchelli's narrative and questions analysis of the graphic novel as a "clichéd, tedious, poorly imagined, ruthlessly uninsightful story" (Berlatsky 2010). Utilizing the pictorial language of comics, *Asterios Polyp* privileges subtle implications about a character's nature, the complexity of a conflict, or the tenderness of a relationship more than pure words alone can convey. Yet the strength of the comic relies on the classics to bridge storyline gaps, enhance character strengths and flaws, and represent specific philosophies. Appropriating the legends and traditions of antiquity, Mazzucchelli presents his work as a case study for the possibilities of comics in the twenty-first century. His text remains an innovative and elegant demonstration of a graphic novel's ability to support complex narratives.

As the deconstructed nature of the book and its meandering storyline attest, *Asterios Polyp* challenges convention but rewards its meticulous reader for acknowledging its deliberate design and piecing together its puzzles. The key to unlocking the full storyline with all of its intricacies, however, belongs to the reader knowledgeable in classical literature, philosophy, language, and theory, capable of deciphering the work's images, words, and subnarratives.

---

27. *Asterios Polyp* 4.2. The aesthetics Asterios favors in his architectural designs are also reminiscent of Le Corbusier's style.

28. A sequence of numbers beginning with 0 and 1, in which each subsequent number is the sum of the previous two. The sequence is detailed by Leonardo Pisano (called Fibonacci) in *Liber Abaci* (Fibonacci 2002).

29. The Fibonacci spiral is created by drawing circular arcs connecting opposite corners of squares that have sides measuring the length of the Fibonacci sequence numbers. *Asterios Polyp* 182.2, 80.3–4.

PART TWO

East's Wests

4

Mecha in Olympus

Shirow Masamune's *Appleseed*

GIDEON NISBET

This chapter examines *Appleseed*, a manga by Shirow Masamune, known mostly in the West for *Ghost in the Shell* (1989–2003). The author's first major work, this epic science-fiction saga ran to four complete volumes of approximately two hundred pages apiece (1985–1989). Unusually among manga, these received first publication not as serials in a weekly, biweekly, or monthly omnibus but as individual books, graphic novels in a true sense, each telling a complete and self-contained story while collectively building into a larger narrative, which was sadly never completed. A preliminary episode of a possible fifth volume appeared alongside supplementary material in the two-volume *Appleseed Databook* (1990, reissued in 2007 as *Appleseed ID*), but *Appleseed Hypernotes* (2007) recategorized it as a short story, and the story is unlikely to be continued in manga form (*Hypernotes* 5). The world of *Appleseed* has inspired several anime adaptations and two video games. English-language translations of the four main volumes were published between 1988 and 1992.

Again unusually, and marking a radical step up from the superficial application of names from miscellaneous mythologies in Shirow's semiprofessional debut, *Black Magic* (1983), *Appleseed* invokes Greek mythology extensively and thoughtfully as a source of characters and motifs—some well known, others relatively obscure. These add nuance to its exploration of the hidden costs of a utopian future society in the aftermath of global war.

In this chapter, I examine *Appleseed* as a site of classical reception, exploring its use of myth and relation to sources. I begin by locating it within a separate and distinctively modern reception history, that of manga in English-language translation, rebranded for Western consumption as comics and graphic novels. My engagement in this chapter is solely with the English-language translations, to which all citations refer. Sidestepping the cogent methodological concerns raised by Theisen (2011, 67–71), my main focus is not on how *Appleseed* has historically been received by constituencies of readers in its native Japan. Instead, I consider how *Appleseed* repackages and "teaches" Greek myth, both in its storytelling and through the introjection of a didactic authorial voice in marginal notes and explanatory supplements.[1]

---

1. I regret that constraints of space preclude analysis of the sporadic but intriguing elaborations on Shirow's Olympian mythos within the ongoing anime franchise.

Its twofold exegesis will be experienced very differently by Western readers of manga and by Shirow's fellow Japanese, because these are our classics, not theirs.

One might imagine that translating a manga version of "our" myths back into English (as into other Western languages; I know of German, French, and Spanish versions) would deliver myths made strange and new again by their sojourn in Japan's eschatological imaginaire. *Appleseed* thus has the potential to stimulate a partial revision of Theisen's observation that manga engages only occasionally with Greece and Rome, and then typically at the most superficial level. Japan has no ongoing classical reception history in Western terms, whether in popular or literary culture; it has classics of its own to service (Theisen 2011, 59, 62). As we will see, Shirow's Hellenophiliac magnum opus actually confirms Theisen's argument through its marked atypicality as manga. This atypicality is in turn to be explained in terms of the author's familiarity with classic Western science fiction, a popular genre whose use of Greek mythic tropes lies at the critical heart of the *Appleseed* universe.

Introducing *Appleseed*

Appleseed (a title with no obvious classical referentiality) is set in the early twenty-second century, in the aftermath of a nonnuclear world war. Devastated nation-states have been supplanted by new, transnational organizations, including the high-tech Poseidon, a sea-based commercial power based around old Japan and specializing in the export of high technology to anyone with the money to pay for it, including terrorist groups (*Appleseed* 3.129). Its classical-sounding name is belatedly glossed by Shirow as perhaps merely a coincidental corruption of *Nippon Seihin*, "Made in Japan" (3.82). This feeble retcon aims at retrospectively underscoring the trademark neo-Hellenic branding of the new global superpower and self-appointed global policeman: Olympus, an ecologically perfected utopia, which the *Databook* reveals to be an artificial island off the coast of North Africa, close to the mouth of the Mediterranean (*Databook* 1.2). For fans of classical culture, this location evokes the Atlantis of Plato's *Timaeus* and *Critias*, lying as it does just beyond the Pillars of Hercules.

Starting from a blank slate like the ideal city-state of Plato's *Republic*, Olympus has fashioned itself into a utopia of peace and stability. As in Plato's scenario, communal autarky comes at the cost of curtailed individualism, but its mechanism of social engineering is appropriately futuristic: Olympus is largely populated by "bioroids," vat-grown, hybrid clones based on carefully selected and edited human DNA. Through a combination of genetic manipulation and childhood conditioning, these artificial people are unchained from humanity's inborn propensity for aggression, selfishness and greed (*Appleseed* 1.104–105): "The age of the bioroids. . . . This will be the age when 'homo sapiens' takes on its true meaning . . . 'man of wisdom' " (2.180).

They already constitute eighty percent of the population (1.104–105, 112), and their seven Elders constitute a deliberative council that runs the Legislature and thus guides the city's long-term policy, a role that recalls that of Plato's philosopher-kings. While regarding themselves as humanity's helpers and servants, even their slaves (2.82, 3.192–193), bioroids share a further advantage over "natural" humans: they will outlive them all. Bioroid physiology is sterile but also effectively immortal, provided that a regular schedule of antiaging treatments is maintained.

An enthusiastic police recruiter assures the newly arrived Briareos that "Olympus is leading the world to a brighter future. We *need* a lot of them" (1.105), but not every human agrees with his view of bioroids as a necessary good. The tipping of the balance toward benevolent bioroid hegemony and the dawning realization that unmodified humanity may have no long-term future outside of a managed conservation program (2.49–53) lead to social tension among the remaining "natural" human inhabitants of the city, many of whom are first-generation immigrants brought in from the badlands left by the war. Their combat skills are necessary to police Olympus and protect it from external threats but also threaten to destabilize the social and technological progress that continues to be made as the story progresses—a conundrum that goes back all the way to the *Republic* (375b–e). The primary narrative strand follows the adventures of two such outsiders: Deunan Knute, a hotheaded young female soldier, and her cyborg partner, Briareos. (As prosthetically modified natural humans, cyborgs are distinct from the genetic enhancements that characterize bioroid physiology.) In the service of the elite police unit ESWAT and equipped with sophisticated suits of powered armor called Landmates (a human-scaled and technologically plausible variant of the science-fiction manga trope of the giant warrior robot, or *mecha*), they handle cases of cyborg crime and terrorism in Olympus and (in later volumes) farther afield.

Appleseed had a pivotal role to play in the history of translating manga for Western readers. In the late 1980s and early 1990s, its critical and commercial success helped open up a significant American market for manga, both translated and later home-grown, which in turn encouraged American comics creators to look across the Pacific for influence. The English translation was the work of Toren Smith's Studio Proteus, a small, self-described manga "packager" based in San Francisco. Smith, an experienced comics writer fluent in Japanese, identified titles with Western commercial potential, bought the rights, and sold his compellingly terse translations to established American comics publishers as camera-ready finished products.[2] *Appleseed* was identified as an ideal prospect because its dark science-fiction themes resonated with contemporary tropes popularized by films such as *Blade Runner* (1982) and in literary SF by the cyberpunk movement, of which William Gibson, author of *Neuromancer* (1984), remains the most famous exponent. Shirow's gritty detail, ultrarealistic mechanical designs, and visually dense storytelling—features that, as Smith has reflected in interview, are actually atypical of manga (quoted in Schodt 1996, 319–320)—responded to and complemented cyberpunk's aesthetic of tightly controlled prose and viscerally credible near-future environments, in addition to making his pages more conventionally palatable to American comics fans.[3]

One of Studio Proteus's first translations, *Appleseed* was initially picked up by the now-defunct independent comics publisher Eclipse Comics. Best remembered today for its role

---

2. On *Appleseed* and Studio Proteus, see Schodt (1996, 318–321). *Appleseed* was translated by Smith and his colleague Dana Lewis.

3. The "bible" of cyberpunk stylistics is the "Turkey City Lexicon," current version at http://www.flashfictiononline.com/docs/Turkey_City_Lexicon_Primer.pdf.

in publishing Alan Moore and Neil Gaiman's much-litigated *Miracleman*, Eclipse at its peak under editor-in-chief Cat Yronwode was known for progressive innovation in areas including creator's rights and positive depictions of homosexual characters (e.g., in Scott McCloud's *Zot!*). It also had an eye for new commercial niches within the established comics retail market, including the first nonsports trading cards. Eclipse was at the time based in California, a state whose economy looks outward to its neighbors around the Pacific Rim, most of which (South Korea, Taiwan, the Philippines, Hong Kong, and, of course, Japan) are major producers and consumers of manga or manga-influenced media, much the same reason Studio Proteus was itself already California-based (Lee and Shaw 2006). Accordingly, Eclipse was one of the first publishers to invest in manga in translation. Following the collapse of Eclipse in the early 1990s, the books were picked up by another ambitious independent, Oregon-based Dark Horse. They remain in print to this day as a modern manga classic, in the West as in Japan, where the series' initial publication was honored in 1986 with a prestigious annual Seiun ("Nebula") award for science fiction in comics form.

Appleseed is one of a kind in populating its fictional world with figures derived from and alluding to ancient Greek mythology. This is more than a mere inclusion of Greek or Greek-sounding names, itself an extremely rare feature but one that Theisen (2011, 62–63) is able to illustrate with reference to the eccentric *sentai* ("team") manga, Masami Kuramada's *Saint Seiya*, also known as *Knights of the Zodiac* (1986–1991).[4] Even there, however, Theisen observes that the names are mere window dressing, attached to characters that "only vaguely resemble their namesakes" in Western myth. They contribute nothing to the story, which remains predicated on the familiar thematic, visual, and character tropes of *sentai*. But for its exotically foreign names, *Saint Seiya* might as well be *Battle of the Planets* (1978–1985, adapting the anime *Science Ninja Team Gatchaman*, 1972–1974) or any of a hundred similar *sentai* manga franchises. *Appleseed* goes further. It delivers classically derived characterizations, which in turn selectively evoke classical themes.

What is more, the author's own paratextual interventions, in the *Databook* and in marginalia to the panels of the continuing story, make the classical connection explicit. *Appleseed* may not expect its "home" audience to bring *to* the text even a rudimentary familiarity with Greek mythology, but an attentive reader may come *away* from it having acquired a fair approximation of that body of knowledge, at least as regards several important and connected myths. Shirow even steers his Japanese readers toward some further reading: "If you're wondering why the Artemis of Greek mythology would be related to a cat, please refer to the section on Typhon in Volume 1 of the book on Greek mythology published by Kinokuniya Books" (*Databook* 1.16). His postapocalyptic, cyberpunk epic thus becomes an unlikely yet effective primer on Greek mythology, introducing the reader, whether Japanese or Western, to some impressively obscure ancient stories, while stimulating further independent learning and information exchange among fans.[5]

---

4. *Sentai* manga depict the adventures of a uniformed task force, military unit, or superhero team.

5. Internet searches turn up numerous examples, e.g., a Shirow fan on myth, http://www.reocities.com/Tokyo/towers/1073/apple.htm; a mythology fan on *Appleseed*, http://www.animenewsnetwork.co.uk/bbs/phpBB2/viewtopic.php?t=15134.

The New Olympus

The bioroids of Olympus have drawn a line under the military-industrial past by looking far back beyond it, to a time before the emergence of the nation-state. Hitomi, Deunan's and Briareos's bioroid host when they first come to the city, introduces their new home through Aesopian fable and later fills in the background with a learned allusion to the myth of Aphrodite's birth (*Appleseed* 1.46, 3.87):

> [They started it] years ago, before wartime. Everyone thought they were crazy . . . Didn't take them seriously. Now everyone worldside is rebuilding their cities on our model. Like the tortoise and the hare.
>
> Back in the beginning they called bioroids *aphros*, you know, "creatures of foam," like in the myth. Not that we really come from foam! Anyway, they've been using Greek names for things ever since.

Deunan has just raised a query about the name of the new supermaterial, Hermes (on which see below), and Hitomi has expressed surprise that her former guest is now such a keen student of Greek mythology. Deunan retorts that sojourning in Olympus has turned her into a classical scholar so that she can keep track of what is going on around her: "Well, I've been hearing names like that ever since I got here, so I've been studying a bit" (3.86) By modeling their utopia on an idealized classical *polis* and putting the figures of classical myth at the center of the public discourse that articulates both its civic identity and its global mission, the bioroids of Olympus have come full circle, looking to ancient abstractions as a template for building a concrete future. They have additionally expropriated a second level of myth making: the ideology by which the nation-states of the developed world had formerly claimed the amassed cultural capital of "the glory that was Greece" as their shared origin story. These former Titans had leveraged their Eurocentric heritage to assert entitlement to power and privilege, but their mutual immolation has conclusively discredited all such claims; now rendered obsolete, they are in the process of being supplanted by a new race of political gods, the enlightened Olympians. None of this is articulated explicitly; instead, the pattern built by Shirow's names and themes invites the reader to put the pieces together. Whatever its sources, this is impressive use of classical subtext.

Tellingly, there is no Zeus in this new Olympian pantheon—no stern father god to punish the hubris of humanity and deny them fire—and correspondingly no Hera. The prime minister, or Permanent Secretary, of Olympus is instead the wise and devious Athena, as resolute in pursuing the welfare of her favored humans as was her divine namesake, the Greek goddess of technology; her loyal and inseparable Home Secretary is Nike. (These and other personal names, including the series title, *Appurushiido* and those of individual volumes, are original to the Japanese version, a fidelity that cannot be taken for granted when reading manga in translation; a literal appleseed becomes at one point a crucial plot device.) This paired reference far exceeds *Saint Seiya*-style window dressing; it evokes a real and close ancient cult relationship, centered around the Athenian Acropolis, while also reminding readers of the important plot point that these classically named characters are able to take the long view that comes with effective immortality (the *Permanent* part of Athena's job title could well be literal truth).

Athena and Nike head the Administration, responsible for Olympus's day-to-day operation. The Administration, Legislature, and Ministry of Justice fall under the governmental umbrella of the Central Management Bureau, familiarly referred to in conversation among characters as Aegis, in an obvious reference to the protective aegis of Athena in myth. Its policy is guided by a powerful artificial intelligence, Gaia, which, in dialogue with the Seven Elders, safeguards the intentions of Olympus's founders. A second specialized supercomputer, Tartarus, handles bioroid production. The reader is never told why it's called Tartarus, and no apposite mythic connection is evident, but Gaia's name[1] directly evokes the primal Earth goddess of the Greeks by way of the "Gaia hypothesis" of James Lovelock, the former NASA engineer whose *Gaia: A New Look at Life on Earth* (1979) and its sequels became foundational texts of the international green movement.

Lovelock's neo-Stoic perception of a radically interconnected planetary biosphere—the Earth as a single, living and breathing organism—feeds into Shirow's authorial persona, as expressed through expository paratext in addition to visual storytelling.[6] Both the cover image of book 1 and its expository pretitle page show the Earth from space as a whole entity, visually alluding to the cover designs of Lovelock's books, which predominantly feature the same image. At the close of book 2 (p. 183), Shirow revisits this gods'-eye perspective to deliver satisfying closure to books 1 and 2 as a matched pair, following a climactic and thematically crucial sequence (2.170–178) in which Deunan's actions finally give concrete form to the initially gnomic series title, *Appleseed*. The Gaian ecological vision is also evident in Athena's application of green metaphors to the philosophy of *polis* management—"Is a tree an accurate model of a forest?" (2.22)—and in the sustainable and holistic infrastructure of their carefully planned garden city. Complex technologies (biotech and cybernetics) have been used to create a truly humane urban environment. Hitomi explains:

> The factories are underground, half the powergrid's in orbit . . . so few cars you can count them . . .
>
> "Functional simplicity, structural complexity: the best life for all." That's the maxim the city planners gave our managers. Even the arcology blocks are designed to minimize shadows in the winter. Optical fibers bring natural sunlight inside. (1.47, 1.57–58; see 2.109)

The title of each volume of *Appleseed* uses overt mythology to conjure large philosophical issues, relating to Olympus's juggling act between human freedom and social progress: *The Promethean Challenge, Prometheus Unbound, The Scales of Prometheus*, and *The Promethean Balance*. There is no Prometheus in the story, whether as a character or an institution; his presence in concrete form would break the metaphor, since it was against the "new" (and tyrannical) god Zeus that Prometheus rebelled, not against the old order of the Titans. This makes

---

6. E.g., *Databook* 1.11: "Earth's resources are finite." Shirow's *Dominion Tank Police* (1985), a seriocomic graphic novella undertaken as a side project while writing *Appleseed*, explores ecological themes in a polluted future Japan and includes a scientific hero named Jim E. Lovelock (the real Lovelock's middle name is Ephraim).

it all the more striking that Shirow places him at front and center in a figurative role as the unifying motif of the series. By repeatedly evoking *The Modern Prometheus*, the famous subtitle of Mary Shelley's *Frankenstein*, these thematic titles declare *Appleseed*'s generic affiliation to the Western science-fiction tradition. More particularly, they speak to the ambiguous gift of the new technologies introduced as the story develops, particularly Hermes, a magnetic field that (appropriate for the winged god) unshackles its users from the pull of gravity and thus changes the rules of combat even as it fulfills its intended aim of revolutionizing transport. Like Victor Frankenstein in Shelley's foundational science-fiction novel, the "modern Prometheus" bringing the fire of artificial life from the heavens to mankind, the bioroid philosopher-kings of Olympus can never be sure how "natural" humans will use their gifts or what risks they may incur themselves.

Recurring characters are similarly representative of large philosophical issues. The catlike rogue bioroid Artemis Alpeia, whose pursuit is a major plot element of book 3, *The Scales of Prometheus*, was genetically coded by Gaia to introduce an element of the wild nature of "original" humanity into bioroid society and thus preserve its stability from stagnation: "*Artemis* was a Greek goddess who protected the things of nature, a virgin huntress associated with the moon. She showered a hail of arrows on her enemies . . . She holds the key to solving Gaia's problems? You think she can preserve and protect the wild side of human nature?" (3.196).

This theme is foreshadowed a book earlier, where members of Aegis worry over "the domestication effect" (2.38),[7] and even in book 1, a human immigrant from worldside, rejecting Deunan's perception that Olympus is a utopia, denounces it as a "zoo for those weird animals that build their own cages and hide inside of them" (1.98, responding to Deunan at 1.96). The introduction of Artemis Alpeia in book 3 thus reifies what we already know to be an overarching concern for both human and bioroid inhabitants of Olympus. Manga frequently introduce stereotyped characters who embody "Other" (typically foreign) behavioral traits through reductive abstraction, but *Appleseed*'s Greek mythological framework transcends simple stereotyping to deliver something more akin to classical personification. Shirow's application of abstraction is thus made uniquely exotic (for Japanese readers) and resonant (for readers with a European cultural heritage).

Sometimes these allusions are impressively recondite. Calling Artemis "Alpheia" is one example. Some lay readers in the West, and a few in Japan, will have heard of Artemis, but very few outside of academia will be familiar with this limited cult name. The small glitch in the orthography—*Alpeia* for *Alpheia*—results from the cult epithet having been transliterated into Japanese and then back into English, but the level of detail is impressive for what from the point of view of the Western cultural mainstream is merely an action-themed, science-fiction comic book. (An explanatory marginal note in the *Databook* [1.22] clarifies while introducing additional complication: Artemis is actually the name of her model of bioroid, Alpeia is her personal name, and her three feisty infants are Artemis-Telon, Artemis-Selene, and Artemis-Hecate.) Similarly, the heads of Olympus's FBI are Arges, Brontes, and Steropes. Like Alpheia's, their names are mangled by having jumped the language barrier twice—Arges becomes Arugess, Steropes becomes Strepos—but these are the three stubborn Cyclopes who, in Hesiod (*Theog.*

---

7. This page's dialogue also flags Scipio on how successful societies always contain the seeds of their own systems failure; see 2.60 on how the "domestication" of humanity could result in "the social destruction of a social animal."

139–146), forged Zeus' thunderbolts. The motif is both recondite and apt, given the characters' role in tracking down terrorist threats to Olympus.

Deunan's combat partner, mentor, and lover ("Hey! You *sleep* with that guy?! That's *mega*! He's gotta weigh a *ton*"; *Appleseed* 3.30; see 3.92–93) is the cyborg Briareos Hecatonchires. The Briareos of myth was one of the Hecatonchires, one of the hundred-handed giants who sided with Zeus against the old order of the Titans, again a tale from Hesiod (*Theog.* 147–156, 617–735). Thematically, the naming of *Appleseed*'s Briareos plays to his ongoing role in the plot: he watches Deunan's back as she straps into her battle armor to defend the new posthuman order. It is additionally specific to his rebuilt identity as a cyborg, following serious trauma in which his human body was left unsalvageable. His patched and augmented brainstem can operate numerous weapons and devices at once, making him "hundred-handed" through prosthesis. He can just keep on plugging in more figurative hands (guns, sensors, etc.) and multitask among them, as the dialogue of a cornered hostage taker in book 3 makes explicit: "All those attachments . . . You must be a Hecatonchires. Yeah, I heard all about you guys . . . Keep adding on terminals and you can run a goddamn aircraft carrier by yourselves. The monster with the octopus brainstem . . . Son of a bitch probably has an augmented brain . . . [to his fellow hostage takers] They've got a Hecatonchires. I'm gonna scrap him" (3.139).

Shirow and his Sources

Shirow's use of these mythic motifs may be all the more imaginative because he comes to Greek mythology as an interested general reader and draws his information from a very limited range of sources. He comes close to naming a particular secondary source in the *Databook*, as quoted earlier, where "the book on Greek mythology published by Kinokuniya Books" is clearly a nonscholarly reference source in two volumes (or more). Internal evidence pins this down to a Japanese-language version of Robert Graves's classic popular treatment in two volumes, *The Greek Myths*. Shirow explicitly name-drops Graves in a marginal note when the FBI discuss Alpeia's relation to the Artemis myth in the main text: "Alpeia was a 'white goddess' (c.F. [*sic*] Graves, et al.). Also known as Alpina and by many other names" (3.196). The "et al." suggests at least one additional fount of information, but in fact, the first volume of *The Greek Myths* stands as a sufficient source for absolutely all the mythological detail in *Appleseed*, including Aphrodite's birth from foam, the three Hecatonchires, and the three Cyclopes (Graves 1960, 31, 49). Artemis Alpeia's catlike appearance, explained by Shirow with reference not to her own myth but to that of Typhon, is straight out of Graves: "When [Typhon] came rushing towards Olympus, the gods fled in terror to Egypt, where they disguised themselves as animals: Zeus becoming a ram; Apollo, a crow; Dionysus, a goat; Hera, a white cow; *Artemis, a cat* . . . Athene alone stood her ground" (Graves 1960, 134; emphasis added).

Shirow is not a particularly attentive reader of Graves—perhaps just as well for him, given the latter's eccentric insistence on reading all these ancient stories as aftereffects of his own poetically conceived theology. For instance, Artemis Alpheia is not *a* white goddess in *The Greek Myths*; her classical cult is instead a confused echo of *the* White Goddess, the triune Maiden, Mother, and Crone of Graves's imagined primal matriarchy (Graves 1960, 86). Rather than buying into this idiosyncratic package, Shirow raids the text opportunistically for names and stories relevant to his own thematic intent. He has not even gotten very far with Graves; all the classical references in the manga come from the first third of volume 1 (chapters 1 through 39 of 104). However, this need not be understood as laziness. These opening chapters are wholly sufficient and apt for his purpose: the mythification of an epochal transition from convulsed chaos (the war) to an enlightened new order (Olympian hegemony). Appropriately, the very last chapter alluded to (chapter 39) is titled "Atlas and Prometheus" and ends with the release of Hope from Pandora's box.

In *Appleseed*, this becomes the Hope Plan, a secret strategy of Olympus's city founders to secure humanity a long-term future, initially safeguarded by Gaia, in which Athena and Nike suspect that even they may be pawns on a larger board, as may be the city of Olympus itself (1.179–180, 2.179, 3.83–84). Shirow gives the Hope Plan an explicitly classical gloss, in a marginal note that neatly ties it to *Appleseed*'s story of building a better future following global war: "*Hope*: in the myth of Pandora's Box. Hope was the last creature left in the box after all the ills of the world had already escaped" (2.45).

A short passage from Graves's third chapter neatly illustrates Shirow's pattern of borrowing:

> [Gaia's] first children of semi-human form were the hundred-handed giants Briareus, Gyges, and Cottus. Next appeared the three wild, one-eyed Cyclopes, builders of gigantic walls and master-smiths, formerly of Thrace, afterwards of Crete and Lycia, whose sons Odysseus encountered in Sicily. Their names were Brontes, Steropes, and Arges, and their ghosts have dwelt in the caverns of the volcano Aetna since Apollo killed them in revenge for the death of Asclepius. (Graves 1960, 31)

We have already met hundred-handed Briareos and Olympus's triad of latter-day Cyclopes. Through the same double transliteration that turned Arges into Arugess, Gyges becomes Guges, the agile, anthropomorphic model of Landmate power armor worn by Deunan and other ESWAT officers in the line of duty. Hitomi's human boyfriend, Yoshi, is a mechanic at Akechi Motors, where the Landmates are sold and serviced, and is an enthusiastic exponent of the new technology: "The linear lock control prevents power loss, and this little beauty comes in at under 1.5 tons!" (1.65). Cottus becomes Kotus, a prototype police robot encountered in book two (2.6–11). The model lacks the flexibility of judgment to be relied on in a tight spot and is later reprogrammed by Gaia to turn on Deunan and Briareos. Gunning it down, and for reasons that will shortly become apparent, Briareos quips: "Dr. Asimov must be rolling over in his grave!" (2.166).

Graves's three hundred-handed giants thus become, in the world of *Appleseed*, emblematic of the three distinct ways in which human form and cybernetic technology may come together: the cyborg, part man and part machine (Briareos); the prosthetic exoskeleton (Guges); and the robotic simulacrum (Kotus). This use of the Hecatonchires as philosophical abstractions is characteristically mangaesque and completely ignores the speculative exegeses that follow each chapter in Graves's *The Greek Myths*. Graves's idée fixe of tying every myth to a single cultic etiology, lost in the mists of Greek prehistory but recoverable through modern

poetic divination, pays homage to James Frazer's protoanthropological *The Golden Bough* (originally published in 1890). The three Hecatonchires are glossed as follows:

> Gyges ("earth-born") has another form, *gigas* ("giant"), and giants are associated in myth
> with the mountains of Northern Greece. Briareos ("strong") was also called Aegaeon
> (*Iliad* i. 403), and his people may therefore be Libyo-Thracians, whose Goat-goddess
> Aegis (see 8.1) gave her name to the Aegean Sea. Cottus was the eponymous
> (name-giving) ancestor of the Cottians who worshipped the orgiastic Cottyo. . . .
> These tribes are described as "hundred-handed," perhaps because their priestesses were
> organized in colleges of fifty, like the Danaids and Nereids; perhaps because the men
> were organized in war-bands of one hundred, like the early Romans. (Graves 1960, 32)

Be it ever so improbable, divining a connection between Gyges and northern Greece is important to Graves because placing him there will turn the myth into an echo in folk memory of the
prehistoric Hellenic "invasion" of northern Greece, which caused a "clash between the patriarchal and matriarchal principles"—a theme dear to Graves's heart—and which the myth of
the marriage of Ouranos and Gaia faithfully if unknowingly "records" (Graves 1960, 32). No
subsequent scholar has been inspired by Graves to think about Greek myth in this way, with the
cautionary exception of the anything-goes historical conspiracy theory of Martin Bernal's three
Black Athena volumes (1987–2006), but *Appleseed* does not take a side on the merits of Frazer's
latter-day progeny; it simply does not find Graves's commentary worth engaging with. The
whole point is to transpose the essence of these mythical figures into a science-fiction universe,
so that their defining traits can lend the narrative allegorical weight. Factoids such as "The
Cyclopes seem to have been a guild of Early Helladic bronzesmiths" (Graves 1960, 32) can
contribute nothing to this aim, with which they are irreconcilable. Instead, they are already
part of a separate science-fictional universe, the universe that Graves himself mythopoetically
wrote into being and that he chose to situate in prehistory, as recalled through (his imaginative
reading of) subsequent Greek collective memory.

Appleseed and Asimov

The world of *Appleseed* successfully melds a 1980s cyberpunk sensibility with the grand utopian themes of SF's early- to mid-twentieth-century golden age, when the trope of the uto-
pian/dystopian future society still loomed large in its repertoire. Shirow's cloned bioroids find
their obvious literary origin in the Hatcheries and Conditioning Centres that spawn the docile
population of Aldous Huxley's *Brave New World* (1932), another communitarian idyll coun-
terpointed by harsh badlands (Savage Reservations) and which in turn scores points against the
liberty-denying ideal *polis* of Plato's *Republic*.

Similarly, Briareos's pithy aside—"Dr. Asimov must be rolling over in his grave!"—is an
in-joke, delivering additional value for the manga reader who is also a fan of classic science
fiction. It invokes a fan's knowledge of the Three Laws of Robotics, a defining plot conceit
of Isaac Asimov's *Robot* series, which commenced with the short story "Runaround" (1942).
The much-quoted First Law is: "A robot may not injure a human being or, through inaction,

allow a human being to come to harm." In later years, Asimov retrospectively merged his *Robot* series into the universe of his best-known work, the *Foundation* series, originally a trilogy (1951–1953) but sporadically expanded in later novels (1981–1993). Set in a distant future, this sequence of novels chronicles the slow but inevitable fall of the Galactic Empire, a theme directly if loosely inspired by Edward Gibbon's monument of historiography, *The Decline and Fall of the Roman Empire* (1776–1789). (Asimov also wrote young-adult ancient history of Gibbonian sweep, *The Roman Empire* [1967] and *The Roman Republic* [1973], which together cover Rome's history from 1000 BCE to 493 CE.)

The *Foundation* series' great hero, Hari Seldon, is the inventor of "psychohistory," a new science that enables him accurately to predict the course of human history. The Foundation is his attempt to shorten the violent Dark Ages that will inevitably follow the Empire's fall: a privileged stronghold of great minds who will accelerate the rebirth of technological civilization and thus return peace and stability to the Galaxy. *Appleseed*'s overarching narrative pays obvious homage to *Foundation*, as does the plot device of the Hope Plan, introduced above. This echoes the secret Seldon Plan, which successive generations of the Foundation strive to fulfill, while wrestling with the awareness that they can never really know their part in it.

In addition to Roman histories, Asimov also wrote *The Greeks: A Great Adventure* (1965) and, even more germanely, a Greek mythological primer, *Words from the Myths* (1969), perhaps the "et al." of Shirow's note on sources, cited earlier, as it features many of the same names and basic stories as Graves. Moreover, Asimov was himself familiar with the work of Graves, whose secular humanist sympathies he shared. The title of his short-story collection *I, Robot* evokes Graves's *I, Claudius*, and while Gibbon's grand sweep underlies the *Foundation* sequence, a more immediate influence was Asimov's recent reading of Graves's *Count Belisarius* (1938).

In Graves, Hope is emphatically "Deceitful Hope." This is reflected in *Appleseed*'s plot: Athena and Nike consider the founders' Hope Plan ultimately unknowable, and even the far-sighted Elders do not realize its limitations (2.44–45, 179–180). However, the more immediate influence may well be Asimov. In *Foundation*, the Seldon Plan is similarly tricky; the members of the Foundation do not realize for a long time that Seldon has gone behind their backs and set up a rival Second Foundation along entirely different lines, focusing on the mental sciences. Delivering closure relevant to this chapter's topic, a prequel novel published shortly before *Appleseed*'s run, Asimov's *Foundation's Edge* (1982) introduces a planet called Gaia (its story is continued in *Foundation and Earth* [1986]). Under the influence of psionically gifted "Mentalics" from this mysterious and devious Second Foundation, the planet and its biosphere have become a single self-aware entity, the Gaia hypothesis made real and quite likely the place where Shirow first encountered Lovelock's radical ecological vision.

Conclusion

Shirow's evocation of Greek myth demands to be read against his engagement with the masterworks of Western science fiction, a literary genre that since its inception has engaged fluently and imaginatively with classical mythic motifs. In part, this comes with the territory: tales of galactic exploration and struggle (so-called space opera, on which Asimov's *Foundation* is a variant) are part of the furniture of the genre, and the heavenly bodies against which they play out are typically and suggestively named after Greek mythological figures. In part, too, classical name-dropping at the level of plot and title has served to assert the literary credentials of a genre that (like comics) was until recently written off sight-unseen by the critical mainstream as subliterary trash and to which (unlike comics) classical reception scholars have not yet begun to pay sufficient attention. Science fiction's use of Greco-Roman materials is often far from superficial and calls for its own equivalent of the *Classics and Comics* volumes.[8] By invoking an SF-literate readership, *Appleseed* escapes the strictures identified by Theisen and solicits the attention of an established international fan base that is already primed for classical mythic subtext.

Judged by the standards of Western SF, Shirow's cyberpunk utopia is a sophisticated response to an apt portion of ancient Greek theogonic myth. He turns the overthrow of the old order of Titans and the institution of a more enlightened age into an allegorical mirror for a future society that must find its own path between wild nature and sterile science, between utopia and anarchy. Touted initially by Hitomi as a panacea for the ills of the old social order, the ancient myths turn out in practice to be merely helpful for working the issues through. The Seldon Plan of *Foundation* was always a creaky plot device, and as an expert reader of SF, Shirow knows this all too well. At the conclusion to book 2, Deunan explicitly disengages from all such grand designs: "Whether Gaia's right or wrong . . . I can't let her destroy this city. The city where *you* live, Bri" . . . "With you, Deunan" (2.178). Much as in Xenophon's *Oikonomikos*, and in rebuttal of Platonic *polis* opera, Shirow's utopia made real can only thrive when the family ties of the *oikos* are placed at its heart.

---

8. Rogers and Stevens (2015) appeared as this volume was going to press.

5

(Un)reading the *Odyssey* in *Nausicaä of the Valley of the Wind*

NICHOLAS THEISEN

Naushika Is Not Nausicaa

Miyazaki Hayao's *Kaze no tani no Naushika* (*Nausicaä of the Valley of the Wind*, hereafter *Naushika*) was originally serialized in fifty-nine chapters that appeared in the magazine *Animage* beginning in February 1982 and ending in March 1994. It took just more than twelve years for *Naushika* to appear in its final form, largely because Miyazaki took four long hiatuses to direct and complete production on the animated films for which he is mostly known both in Japan and in the West: just more than a year to work on the *Naushika* film in 1983–1984, a year and a half for *Tenkū no shiro Rapyuta* (*Laputa: Castle in the Sky*) in 1985–1986, nearly three years (June 1987–March 1990) for *Tonari no Totoro* (*My Neighbor Totoro*) and *Mahō takkyūbin* (*Kiki's Delivery Service*), and almost two years for *Aka no buta* (*Porco Rosso*) in 1991–1993. The manga now appears (in Japanese) in both a seven-volume paperback set and a two-volume hardcover one. The manga's English translation, from Viz Media, was published first in a four-volume "perfect collection" from 1995 to 1997, which mirror-reverses the pages in order to read more like an English-language comic; later, a seven-volume edition was published beginning in 2004, which more clearly reflects both the breakdown and the page orientation of the currently available Japanese edition.

Unfortunately, because neither the volume breakdown nor Miyazaki's breaks in working on the manga (with one notable exception to be discussed at length in this chapter) correspond well to the roughly three narrative arcs in the story, it is difficult to treat this 1,060-page epic as anything but a single unit, even though its publication history would make it out to be no such thing. The three arcs—and these are by no means standard—are as follows. The story opens with Naushika[1] landing her glider at the edge of the Sea of Corruption (*fukai*), a massive forest that engulfs most of the world's landmass and releases toxic spores into the air, where she encounters both the giant insect Ohmu and Lord Yupa, a close friend. When they

---

1. Because of the nature of my argument, I refer to Miyazaki's character (and the works that bear her name) as Naushika, using the Japanese transliteration so as to interrupt, if only momentarily, an easy association of Naushika with the Nausicaa of the *Odyssey*.

return to the Valley of the Wind, they are confronted with a Torumekian army led by a warrior maiden named Kushana. Naushika and some of the men from the valley are conscripted
into fighting for Kushana and the Torumekians against Pejite, a small city where a god-warrior
(*kyoshinhei*) from the legendary Seven Days of Fire has been unearthed. In a time long before
the events of the manga, there was an "abrupt and violent decline. The cities burned, welling
up as clouds of poison in the war remembered as the Seven Days of Fire" (*Naushika*, inside
cover). Until the seventh volume, it is unclear exactly what purpose these god-warriors served,
but the terror with which the characters of the text regard them makes clear that the purpose
could not have been terribly noble. The people of Pejite eventually capture a baby Ohmu that
they use to incite a stampede of its larger brethren but are thwarted when Naushika intervenes
and calms the giant insects. The second arc, the longest by far, begins two-thirds of the way
through the second volume and ends, so to speak, along with the sixth. It recounts the long
war, along with various divergent episodes, between the Torumekian Kingdom and the Dorok
Holy Empire. Throughout, Naushika finds herself on both sides of the conflict, which ends
only when the Dorok emperor uses a mutant mold to cause a massive Ohmu stampede that
spreads the toxic spores of the Sea of Corruption over most of the remaining inhabitable
land and in the process almost wipes out both the Torumekian and Dorok armies. While
this is going on, Naushika meets Selm, one of the people who have adapted to living deep
within the Sea of Corruption, who shows her the land beyond the toxic forest where the
world has, presumably, been purified. In the final arc, which corresponds to the final volume,
the god-warrior discovered near the beginning of the text, whose "cocoon" has been passed
around throughout the story, is finally activated and begins to wreak havoc. Naushika subdues
it but only after it identifies her as its mother. With the god warrior in tow, she travels to the
crypt of Shuwa to confront its master, which has slowly been revealed to be the source of many
of her world's current crises.

The vastness of this text and its relationship to the animated film of the same name, which
corresponds roughly to the first narrative arc above, have lent it to a variety of thematic treatments[2] yet, oddly, never a comparison with the *Odyssey*, even though its title character is clearly
named after the Phaeacian princess Odysseus encounters in Book 6. One presumes this is partly
a result of the introduction Miyazaki composed for the collected edition:

> I have been fascinated by [Nausicaa] ever since I read about her in [a Japanese
> translation of Bernard Evslin's] small dictionary of Greek mythology. Later, when
> I actually read *The Odyssey*, I was disappointed not to find the same splendor in her
> there as I had found in Evslin's book. So, as far as I am concerned, Nausicaa is still the
> girl Evslin described at length in his paperback. (*Naushika* 7.134)[3]

2. For treatments of the film, see especially McCarthy (1999), Napier (2005), and LaMarre (2009), but the vast
majority fall into the category of comparison and contrast of manga and film: Osmond (1998) and Paik (2010)
in English; Ōtsuka (1988), Inaba (1996), and Kumi (2004) in Japanese. Ōtsuka in particular uses *Naushika* as
ground for considering the structural differences between comics and animation.

3. All references are to the seven-volume edition of *Kaze no tani no Naushika* (Tokyo: Tokuma Shoten, 1994) and
correspond precisely to the seven-volume English version, translated by Matt Thorn (San Francisco: Viz
Media, 2004).

The lack of focused attention on the manga's relationship to the *Odyssey* has led to a great deal of critical repetition in the form of critics making remarkably similar arguments[4] and also failing to sufficiently examine Miyazaki's problematic pronouncements on his own work, this despite his claim in an interview with *Comic Box* that finishing *Naushika* (the manga) was difficult precisely because he did not feel he understood it anymore.[5] In fact, taking Miyazaki's word for so much of what should be the purview of scholarly inquiry has led to a pervasive critical blindness to the relationship between *Naushika* and the *Odyssey*. Critics' dismissal of the *Odyssey* as a relevant source seems to echo Miyazaki's own. *Dismissal* is perhaps not even the right word, as more often than not, the possibility of there being a relationship between *Naushika* and the *Odyssey* is never even broached.

The girl Evslin (1975) describes is, in fact, quite different from the Nausicaa one encounters in the *Odyssey*. He claims that she, not Demodokos, is the one to make Odysseus weep by singing of the Trojan War, and he even goes so far as to suggest that Homer merely stitched together an epic poem from episodes he had heard her sing. A full three pages are given to her entry in *Gods, Demigods, and Demons*, more than any other mythological personage and three times longer than Odysseus' own entry. For Evslin, Nausicaa is the quintessential poet and world traveler, two things that have no real basis in the Homeric text: "One legend says she never married, but became the first woman minstrel, traveling from court to court singing hero songs" (Evslin 1975, 147). Yet it should be clear from even a cursory read of Miyazaki's text that his adolescent warrior and ersatz messiah is a far cry from the princess of the epic poem and Evslin's wandering bard. She is at times aggressive and violent, as when she attacks Kushana and her men upon their first entering the valley (*Naushika* 1.54–64), and at times a serene mystic, as when she calms the angry Ohmu in the culmination of the Torumekians' battle with the people of Pejite (2.77–79). From the very beginning of the manga, she could hardly be considered "the girl Evslin described at length in his paperback."

Just as Evslin profoundly revises Nausicaa's character, I argue that Miyazaki's *Naushika* revises not only certain aspects of the *Odyssey* but also the sense of a tradition that undergirds it, in which what we do now, be it literary or otherwise, is irrevocably indebted to the past and to the texts that record it. This revision ultimately seeks to undo that tradition, or at least the burden it imposes, and also to unread the texts that make it up, in Naushika's case by annihilating them. Because *Naushika* revises the *Odyssey* and as such reenvisions it, the manga does not necessarily resemble the Homeric text, and where it does, it is only as if through a glass darkly. For the difficulty in identifying *Naushika*'s correspondences to the *Odyssey* stems from their being inversions of episodes and of characters rather than easy transpositions, such as the visual and thematic similarities of the giant insect Ohmu to the sandworms of Frank Herbert's *Dune*, the analogy of Naushika (the character) to George Bernard Shaw's Saint Joan, or the relationship between the film/manga and Brian Aldiss's *Hothouse*, which Miyazaki is known to have read prior to working on *Naushika*. As Osmond (1998, 63) has already noted, "both [*Naushika*

---

4. Cavallaro (2006) is an excellent example of this tendency in how it largely seems to repeat McCarthy (1999).

5. This is perhaps an inference on my part. In the interview with Saitani Ryō, Miyazaki says, "It wasn't that I had forgotten most of what I had written, but rather, that I had *tried* to forget. It was scary. What had I written? [laughs] It was painful. Really! I still wondered if this was the right conclusion for [*Naushika*], but I didn't know. Even now I'm not sure" (Miyazaki 1995).

and *Hothouse*] centre on revelation, which the humans receive via superintelligent terrestrials (the fungal morel in *Hothouse*, the insect *Ohmu* in *Nausicaä*)."

However, I would argue that *Naushika* cannot be understood outside of its inversion of habitual, symbolic associations with its various figures: the Sea of Corruption being, in fact, what purifies the world; the light from the master of the crypt of Shuwa being a shadow cast over the land; and the Ohmu, who for so much of the manga seem to embody nature itself, being merely part of an elaborate ecological engineering project designed to prepare the world for the reemergence of a more peaceful contingent of the human population who preceded the Seven Days of Fire. The most important of these inversions occurs in the final volume (and narrative arc) of the manga, an inversion of the comic narrative itself and a most obvious turn *toward* the *Odyssey*, so it is there that I wish to begin, with what I refer to as Naushika's *nekuia*, after the ancient necromantic ritual by whose name the eleventh book of the *Odyssey* is commonly known. There the complex politics of a world at war are broken down into Naushika's relatively straightforward journey into the West and her confrontation with the ineluctable presence that has loomed over the entire story but has remained, for the most part, unacknowledged.

As noted above, the final volume recounts the awakening of the last god-warrior. Its maturation, marked most notably by its gradual shift from childish/robotlike speech to archaic Japanese,[6] plays out against Naushika's manipulation of the god-warrior into accompanying her to Shuwa, where she plans to use it to destroy the crypt located there. She arrives there, having been separated from the god-warrior, and is confronted at first with a vision of the specters of the past, who explain that the world is being remade and that the long cycle of purification will soon end. Naushika rejects this vision as an illusion, which brings forward the master of the crypt, the sentience that embodies the massive sphere at the crypt's heart. He/it overturns much of what the characters have taken for granted so far about what is happening to the world and confirms all of what Naushika had deduced about the nature of the land beyond the end of the Sea of Corruption (that it is uninhabitable for human beings in their present state). He/it offers to remake humanity so that it might survive the purification, but Naushika refuses. Instead, she commands the god-warrior to destroy itself and the crypt in one last destructive blast and conspires with Selm to deceive everyone about what has transpired.

By assuming that *Naushika*'s relationship to the *Odyssey* is one of inversion, we encounter a uniquely difficult challenge in trying to determine what in Odysseus' own sojourn to the land of the dead corresponds to Naushika's journey to the crypt, because any obvious point of comparison is likely to be misleading. For example, the land of the dead is for Odysseus a point of departure. Once Circe has instructed Odysseus how to invoke the shades of the dead, she says that Tiresias "will tell you the way to go, the stages of your voyage,/how you can cross the swarming sea and reach home at last" (*Od.* 10.539–540; trans. Fagles 1997, 247). The invocation of Odysseus' *nostos* or homecoming at the beginning of line 540 is key to establishing the land of the dead as a point of departure. Odysseus goes there to acquire the special knowledge

---

6. The god-warrior begins its life "speaking" entirely in *katakana*, a syllabic script used to represent nonstandard language of various sorts (e.g., foreign words, words being emphasized, onomatopoeia, etc.), which develops into a mix with some *kanji* (Chinese characters) and eventually into full-blown classical Japanese. Its "birth" recalls the first words of another anthropomorphic machine, Astro Boy, who also initially speaks simply and in *katakana*.

that he will need to return home. Naushika's journey to the crypt, however, inverts most of the key points of Odysseus' *nekuia*. For her, the crypt is a destination and her journey a homegoing (if that is a word) rather than a homecoming. She goes to the crypt not to acquire its secret knowledge but to prevent it from ever getting out again. In many ways, Odysseus and Naushika represent two different kinds of readers: one patiently receptive of what he sees and hears, the other impatiently dismissive. This Naushika, the Naushika of the final volume, does not even square well with what the reader had seen so far just prior to Miyazaki's last two-year hiatus. Unlike the hero she seems to be when confronting the Dorok emperor, she looks anxious and burdened both by what she has come to know and by what she knows she must do. At the end of the sixth volume, when the god-warrior reappears for the final time, it remains to be seen how Naushika would develop and how in her encounter with the master of the crypt at Shuwa she would become the perfect counterpoint to Evslin's characterization of Nausicaa as a poet: Naushika as the ultimate—and most horrific—reader.

Both Osmond (1998) and Paik (2010) have attempted to account for this radical shift, but Osmond's reliance on easy correspondences causes his reading of the manga's climax to perhaps oversimplify what is at stake:

> Nausicaä declares it is "for the planet to decide" if man will endure. When she is accused of "nihilism, nothingness," she shouts, "The sympathy and love of the Ohmu was born from nothingness!," suggesting the world always throws up creatures with appreciably human qualities and values. While this is the premise of much popular sf . . . its centrality demotes *Nausicaä*'s end to a fable. (Osmond 1998, 74)

If it is merely a fable, though, it is hard to see what the moral ought to be. This is, in part, the fault of the translation on which Osmond relies and particularly how it glosses over several key subtleties in how things are said, especially the ambivalent conditional that ends the dialogue being rendered as an unambiguous imperative, "we must live." In Japanese, Naushika ends her telepathic conversation with Selm and says to the crowd of refugees gathering around her, "*sā minna shuppatsu shimashō. donna ni kurushiku tomo ikineba . . . .*" (*Naushika* 7.223), or "so, everyone let us depart. No matter how painfully, if we do not live" followed by two long ellipses. The ellipses are important, because they indicate not only that something should follow the protasis of the conditional (*naranai, naranu*, or something to that effect) but that something really should follow in the narrative to justify or at least explain Naushika's deception of humanity on a massive scale. However, the epilogue straightaway prevents that from happening: "There is much that remains untold, but let us end our story here" (7.223).

Exhortations in Japanese can be expressed directly through the use of the sentence-terminal particle *beki* but are just as commonly expressed though negative conditional statements, something to the effect of (in clumsy English) "It is wrong, if we do not live." Subsequently, it is also not uncommon to express such exhortations with only the protasis of the conditional, "if we do not live," because the rest can be readily assumed by one's interlocutor. Thus, the translation as it appears in Viz's edition is not out of line but rather glosses over a subtle point that is key to understanding why the manga ends as it does: what remains unsaid is, in many ways, more important than what is said.

Osmond's claim (1998, 65) that "Miyazaki's *Nausicaä* is effectively Evslin's character" is only justified so long as one assumes that like must correspond to like, that Naushika corresponds to Nausicaa, be she Evslin's or the *Odyssey*'s. What is much harder to see and more key to understanding the comic's narrative, especially the final volume, is how Naushika, Miyazaki's Naushika, is an inversion of Odysseus and, thus, how her *nekuia* in the manga is a revision of his. It is important, then, when considering the relevance of the *Odyssey* to *Naushika* to look past obvious similarities toward complementary, supplementary, even contradictory points of correspondence.

Where Odysseus' journey is one from "away" to home, Naushika begins in her home, the Valley of the Wind, and over the course of the narrative moves farther and farther away, never to return. Each has a divine companion: Odysseus has Athena, and Naushika has the god-warrior (*kyoshinhei*), the only one to survive the Seven Days of Fire it was originally designed to perpetrate. However, where Odysseus' divine companion is a goddess possessed of her own will and her own concerns, the god-warrior begins its existence as a rash, immature thing whose coming of age in the final volume is facilitated by its identification of Naushika as its mother. Last, and perhaps most important, both Odysseus and Naushika are liars, but where Odysseus might be forgiven his constant recourse to deceit as a necessary survival mechanism, Naushika's grand deception at the close of the story may, in fact, doom to extinction the people she ostensibly wishes to save.

"Never Again" Is to Never Remember

The climax of the final volume centers around what turns out to be the true source of all the problems plaguing Naushika's world, both political and natural: the crypt at Shuwa and its master. Her final encounter with the master, though, is presaged first by a stop at what initially appears from overhead to be ruins. Outside these ruins, Naushika buries the fox squirrel Teto, who was her constant companion and who has died as a result of the radiation or "light" that the god-warrior gives off. This act draws the attention and sudden appearance of a herder or gardener,[7] who, failing to introduce him-/herself in any way, invites Naushika to come rest when the god-warrior suddenly collapses. Now bereft of her only means of transportation, Naushika is brought by the herder deep into the ruins, which are revealed to be an illusion hiding a large estate populated by sentient goats. She falls asleep and awakens to find herself floating in a large bathtub next to one of these goats, who gives her a towel and fresh clothes. Sitting down for a meal, Naushika quickly notices something amiss: "This fruit . . . these children . . . the trees and plants . . . these are all species that became extinct ages ago" (7.105).[8] How Naushika knows this is never made clear. She tries to remember why and how she has come to this place, but her attention is suddenly drawn by distant music.

7. It is not clear at all at first glance just who or what. Only much later is it revealed that the "herder" is the guardian of a repository of ancient knowledge, technology, and plantlife.

8. The translation is, perhaps, misleading. Naushika means animal offspring, not human, when she says "children," offspring.

Naushika passes through an arcade into an enormous library, where the sons of the Torumekian emperor sit playing a piano. As she approaches, unable to recall who the two men are, one of the sons says to her, "This room is a treasure trove of music and literature that was supposed to have been lost long ago! All the music mankind ever produced escaped the Seven Days of Fire and has been preserved here!" (7.107). As the two men play, Naushika's mind drifts from where she is, and as her grief over Teto hits her once again, the spell of the place is broken. At once, the entire herd of goats appears in an attempt to keep her there, but she manages to escape through a series of acrobatic feats that carry her across the rooftops of the estate. Eventually, she is confronted again with the herder/guardian, who tries to ease her back into submission by appearing in the guise of her mother. Naushika resists, and thus begins the long revelation of the true nature of the crypt.

The guardian tells Naushika of the first person to use the technologies of the past in an effort to save humanity and the world. He failed, overcome by his own inability to convince his people of the necessity of his utopian goals, and began a cycle of parasitic relationships between humanity and the master of the crypt at Shuwa that persists into Naushika's present. What the guardian offers Naushika instead is something like a Buddhist withdrawal from the world: "Everyone believes they alone will not err. Yet none can escape from the cycle wherein karma gives birth to karma, sorrow gives birth to sorrow. This garden is the place where all chains can be severed" (7.122). The garden, then, functions as a stand-in for the Western Paradise of Pure Land Buddhism, where one might find respite from the endless cycle of karmic transmigration that plagues an unenlightened human being. Naushika begins to lose her resolve, but Selm comes to her telepathically to bolster her against the spiritual and intellectual assault of the guardian. Standing firm together, Naushika and Selm are confronted with the revelatory, intratextual inversions that will come to color the entire narrative and culminate in Naushika's confrontation of the master of the crypt.

The climax of Selm and Naushika's confrontation with the guardian of the garden repository is crucial, precisely because in it the true nature of the world is revealed to them even before Naushika enters the crypt. The guardian says to Selm at the top of the page, "Surely you and your people have discovered the meaning of the Sea of Corruption . . . why it is that humans cannot live in the place where the forest ends . . . and the fact that you are all doomed to die the day the forest has fulfilled its role" (7.128). Selm tries to protect Naushika from the truth, but the guardian moves in closer to add more pointedly (at the bottom of the page): "Child of the forest, long ago your people sent scouts to the place where the forest ends . . . several times. But not one of them ever came back. Every one of them vomited blood and died. Now it is considered to be a holy and forbidden place. Why do your people go on deceiving themselves that a place that can only be visited in spirit somehow represents *hope*?" (7.128).

Selm tries to protect her, but Naushika wants to know the whole truth, no matter where it might lead. She even begins to piece it all together on her own, saying to the guardian, "You said that although we may long for a purified world, we could never survive there—that the human body is different from what it once was. But it's not a tolerance that developed naturally, is it? Human beings changed themselves of their own will, didn't they?" (7.130). With that, the guardian ceases his/her mental assault, leaving Naushika feeling "strangely, almost frighteningly serene" (7.131).

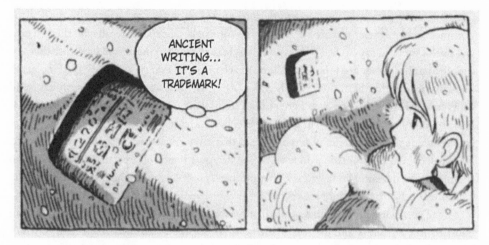

FIGURE 5.1 Naushika inspecting the hallmark on the side of the god-warrior. *Nausicaä of the Valley of the Wind*
7.22. Art by Miyazaki Hayao.

The garden is the true repository of what survives the Seven Days of Fire. As the guardian
says, it "contains the only things human beings were able to create that are worth passing on to
the next world" (7.134). The crypt and its master, then, must be something else, as Naushika
continues the guardian's thought in the following panel: "There is something else built into the
heart of Shuwa. There is technology leaking from the crypt that has allowed men to manipulate
life" (7.134). The guardian can say nothing to justify the crypt's existence, and so Naushika
finally takes her leave.

Naushika's stay with the guardian is, in many ways, analogous to the *Odyssey* episode with
the Lotus Eaters; the pleasant spell cast over her causes her to forget why she is there in the first
place, just as the lotus causes Odysseus' men to forget their *nostos*, and as a result, Naushika is
delayed from reaching Shuwa, while the god-warrior has pressed on ahead of her. However,
she is immediately inserted back into the ongoing chaos of the fallout from the Torumekians'
defeat of the Dorok emperor and of the god-warrior's assault on the crypt, which she observes
from afar as a mushroom cloud rises in the distance (7.153). The confrontation with the gar-
dener/guardian and the later confrontation with the master only approach history and historical understanding from a broad, nearly theoretical perspective, but the comic is also inscribed
with Japan's own particular history, specifically the nuclear holocaust of Hiroshima and
Nagasaki. By this point in the narrative, there have been more and less obvious clues that the
god-warrior is an embodied nuclear weapon. Its "light" keeps making Naushika more and more
sick, and the god-warrior is stamped with a recognizably Japanese hallmark: 東京工広 (7.22;
see figure 5.1).[9] 東京 is clearly Tokyo, but 工広 is more difficult to parse, as it is not a word in
Japanese and likely an abbreviation, although it could mean something like "construction yard."
工 clearly indicates industry or an industrial facility, but 広 is a more complicated matter. The

9. While the first three characters in the second line of the stamp are perfectly legible, the fourth is not, and as
such, this is at least partially a conjecture on my part given the context. The English translation makes no attempt
to render this.

character by itself simply means "wide" or "broad," as in a wide open space (thus, the "yard" above), but it is also the first character used to write Hiroshima, 広島.[10] With the invocation of the atom bomb with the mushroom cloud (figure 5.2) and more subtly with the hallmark, it is difficult to say what any abrogation of the past might mean for the nuclear devastation wrought on Japan at the end of the World War II, for it may amount to Miyazaki's most controversial (implicit) claim in the text of *Naushika*: that the bombings of Hiroshima and Nagasaki also fall into the category of that which is to be willfully disregarded.

How Naushika (and Miyazaki) arrive at this willful disregard comes out most clearly once she finally arrives in Shuwa and encounters the master of the crypt. The master is an enormous sphere at the crypt's core, seemingly alive, on which an elaborate and complicated text appears one line at a time, twice per year on every winter and summer solstice. Around it, scholar-priests labor away at each single line (figure 5.3) in an attempt to decipher it and develop new technologies from what they learn, new technologies to keep themselves alive and to offer each new emerging hegemonic power in exchange for protection. As one of the priests explains to the Torumekian emperor, "The text is not finished. We have as much work ahead of us as we do behind us. We require the cooperation of an outside force" (7.191). *Naushika* has rendered as manipulation what in the *Odyssey* is a noble service to the dead. The first shade Odysseus encounters at 11.51 is Elpenor, his own crew member, who died having fallen off the roof of Circe's house. He makes one final request of Odysseus:

> Don't sail off
> and desert me, left behind unwept, unburied, don't
> or my curse may draw god's fury on your head.
> No, burn me in full armor, all my harness,
> heap my mound by the churning gray surf—
> a man whose luck ran out—
> so even men to come will learn my story. (*Od.* 11.72–76, trans. Fagles 1997, 251)

Even though Odysseus is also threatened, his duty to Elpenor is a personal and ethical obligation, whereas the kind of service to the dead that the master proposes in *Naushika* is a simple quid pro quo. What *Naushika* emphasizes is how impersonal this laboring away at a text truly is, in stark contrast to what we see in Odysseus' reception of the dead, many of whom he knew in their lifetimes.

Once Naushika touches the sphere's surface, the master finally appears to her and to the Torumekian emperor as a vision in their minds: "We speak to you as representatives of the great many who died meaningless deaths because of their own folly. You are living in the long period of purification" (*Naushika* 7.195). On the following page, the "great many" conduct a variation on Naushika's encounter with the guardian/gardener. "Read the words that appear on our body, and pass on the technology you find there. When the text at long last appears in its

---

10. It is common practice in Japanese to use the first character of a word or place name as a form of abbreviation. For example, *Nagoya daigaku* 名古屋大学 (Nagoya University) is often referred to as *Mei-dai* 名大, where *Mei* is an alternative reading of *Na* 名, the first syllable in Nagoya, and *dai* 大 is the first syllable in *daigaku* ("university"). As such, 広 could easily stand for Hiroshima, 広島.

FIGURE 5.2 The mushroom cloud resulting from the god-warrior's weapon. *Nausicaä of the Valley of the Wind* 7.153. Art by Miyazaki Hayao.

FIGURE 5.3 The text on the surface of the master of the crypt. *Nausicaä of the Valley of the Wind* 7.191. Art by Miyazaki Hayao.

entirety, then that day shall come . . . the day the suffering ends" (7.196). Because of her earlier
encounter with the guardian, Naushika recognizes the deceit for what it is and rejects the offer
of the "great many." "Why do you not speak the truth!? The truth about your plan to completely replace the polluted land and all living things?" (7.197). With this, the master finally
appears by possessing the jester who accompanies the Torumekian emperor.

> Which truth? [. . .] Have you ever tried to imagine the degree of hate and despair that
> filled the world in those days? It was a world in which tens of billions of human beings
> would do anything to survive . . . Our choices were limited. We had no time. We decided
> to entrust everything to the future. This is the grave marker of the old world, but it is
> also the hope for a new world. (7.199)

Naushika is strong enough now to fend off the verbal and mental assault of the master, but it
remains for the Torumekian emperor to say what is implicit in Naushika's argument with the
master: "We shall not serve you!! We shall decide our fate for ourselves" (7.202).

What the master fails to realize is that the collusion of the past with the future always
excludes the present, and it is the present—how humanity has evolved on its own, outside the
plan the people of the ancient past laid out for the future—in the form of Naushika's assertion
of leaving life to be as it will, no matter what, that threatens the grand schemes of history or the
past. Her confrontation with the master of the crypt is not only an attempt to deal with and ultimately annihilate its polluting influence on the politics of her present day but also an allegory
of the inexplicable and unwanted burden that the past places on the present and of the possibility that the only means to truly progress as a civilization or species is to sever ties permanently
with history and thus with the past. This is the endgame of Miyazaki's inversions—Naushika
of Odysseus, of light as a source of terror and death (i.e., the god-warrior's light), of pollution
as purification. The "doom" of humanity in Naushika's refusal to allow the master to remake
the human body so that it can survive the purification of the world turns out to be its last hope.
For the hope, in this context, is for a world where present humanity, adapted as it is to present
conditions, can choose for itself, rather than as a function of or reaction to the established dic-
tates of the past. Of course, the paradox of this hope lies in the potential for choice only being
revealed by Naushika's denial of that choice to the very people she champions. This is, perhaps,
the problematic result of trying to embody such a radical stance in a messianic figure. It is hard
to make the claim that humanity should not be saved with a character whose apparent function
is to "save" humanity from itself.

There is another, less grandly philosophical aspect to Naushika's encounter with the
master—less grand but perhaps more profoundly unsettling. The master of the crypt is, first
and foremost, a *text*, meaning that Naushika's rejection of the mandate of the past is also a rejection of the text that chronicles it, in the form of the sphere that reveals itself line by line to the
attendant priests. What is so unnerving about this depiction of priests laboring away at a text is
that its analog is not a cloister of Buddhist monks droning away at a sutra (though that image,
to a certain extent, is invoked) but philologists laboring away at a line of Homer or some other
overworked text, as if the master of the crypt were akin to Riese's edition of Catullus (1884),
where only one or two lines are revealed at a time or per page so that the rest of the time or the

page might be filled with copious commentary on it. The very nature of the master invites interpretation of this kind, as it only reveals two lines per year, which further means that Naushika's rejection of him/them/it is also a rejection of historical or literary analysis of any kind. For Naushika, living—or surviving, rather—demands that the past and the texts that manifest it be discarded wholesale. The master is one such text, the gardener's repository another, and the god-warrior yet another. Naushika abandons all of them. For to live with them is to become like the priests of the crypt or the Dorok emperor, hideously deformed, with rotting bodies kept barely alive by the technologies of the crypt. They live in this place, this mausoleum of the past, because theirs is an animated death.

Naushika recognizes that texts (and their problems) are perpetuated (and perpetrated) by readers, not authors, and that the true power of a reader lies in negation, refusing to listen to "the voice of the text"—a metaphor rendered very literal in the manga—and, in Naushika's case, annihilating it. Naushika seems to understand implicitly what Vernant (1996, 61) says of the relationship between the "beautiful death" of epic renown and the meaningless death of the unremarkable many on display in the *Odyssey*'s *nekuia*:

> The only values that exist are the values of life, the only reality that of the living. If Achilles chooses to die young, it is not that he values death above life. On the contrary, he cannot accept sinking, like just anybody, into the obscurity of oblivion, merging into the indistinct mass of "nameless ones." He wants to continue forever in the world of the living, to survive in their midst, within them, and remain there as himself, distinct from any other, through the indestructible memory of his name and renown.

What Naushika realizes is that the "memory of his name and renown" is perfectly destructible, for the burden of establishing the relationship between "a dead individual and a community of living people" (56) falls entirely on the reader, the living, the present.

History Takes Its Revenge on the Present

What the master, Hiroshima (or any memorial project), and Odysseus have in common is the palpable fear of forgetting and being forgotten: for the master, forgetting the world before the Seven Days of Fire; for Hiroshima, forgetting the horrors of the atom bomb; and for Odysseus, forgetting the *nostos* that is the goal of his journey. The invocation of Hiroshima in the context of *Nausicaä* and the *Odyssey* may at first seem odd, but it is there to drive home the point that what is at stake in Miyazaki's text is an undermining not just of a classical tradition and inheritance but of history and tradition writ large. For in this context, Hiroshima, too, is a land of the dead, and the pilgrimage to it that legions of Japanese students are compelled to undergo every year is a kind of *nekuia* wherein the lessons and knowledge of the past are inscribed on monuments, dioramas, and video presentations rather than the apparitions of the dead. As with various Holocaust memorials around the world, "never again" underlies each particular object on display and renders the entire project of remembrance a noble imperative. So what possible good could come of undermining this, too? For that, we must turn to the *Odyssey*'s second *nekuia*, in Book 24, and the revenge that the suitors' families plot against Odysseus and his household.

The *Odyssey's* own conclusion brings to light the potential negative consequences of historical awareness, how knowledge of the past can fuel a desire for further revenge (e.g., Telemachus' revenge on the unfaithful servants) just as easily as a failure to remember. In Book 11, Agamemnon's story of how he was betrayed by Clytemnestra and murdered by Aegisthus (lines 405–434), serves as the "never again" for Odysseus, a model of what could go wrong and should not be repeated. It is no coincidence, then, that he should appear again to listen to the story of how Amphimedon, one of the suitors, was killed by Odysseus.

> So we died,
> Agamemnon . . . our bodies lie untended even now,
> strewn in Odysseus' palace. They know nothing yet,
> the kin in our houses who might wash our wounds
> of clotted gore and lay us out and mourn us.
> These are the solemn honors owed the dead.
>   "Happy Odysseus!"
> Agamemnon's ghost cried out. "Son of old Laertes—
> mastermind—what a fine, faithful wife you won!" (24.186–193, trans. Fagles
>   1997, 474)

Agamemnon sees Amphimedon's account of the slaughter only from the perspective of the conquering hero, one that vindicates his own feelings of betrayal, even though Amphimedon ends on the point of disrespect shown to the bodies of the suitors that at that moment lie unburied and unmourned. The end of his tale recalls Elpenor's encounter with Odysseus in Book 11 and his request that Odysseus bury and remember him. Bringing to mind that other *nekuia* also perhaps puts into play Elpenor's curse, which never comes to pass, because Odysseus buries the man as he asks. The gods' fury there becomes in Book 24 the revenge of the suitors' families, who organize against Odysseus after having been convinced by Antinous' father Eupeithes, starting at line 426. Because Agamemnon only understands Amphimedon's story in one way, he fails to see how the revenge he himself perhaps wishes he could undertake plays out in the present, that is, the political situation on Ithaca and the open warfare that nearly breaks out between Odysseus' family and those of the suitors. Odysseus has his *nostos* in the way he and, as Zeus notes, Athena (479–480) envision, yet he never accounts for the problems that may ensue.

Only through forgetting does the *Odyssey* come to a peaceful conclusion: "let both sides seal their pacts that [Odysseus] shall reign for life,/and let us purge their memories of the bloody slaughter/of their brothers and their sons" (483–484, trans. Fagles 1997, 483). Zeus' compulsory forgetting of the very reason for the families' revenge is not without precedent, for in Book 4, Helen mixes a drug (*pharmakon*; line 220) into the wine that brings a forgetfulness of pain, even if one's mother or father were lying dead before him (224). The sense in these two disparate moments is that there is a burden placed on one's present by the memory of the past and that the only cure for it is to forget. Miyazaki's *Naushika* takes what is a psychological problem in the *Odyssey* and turns it into a sociohistorical one, where history as memory (and the record thereof in the form of the master) burdens Naushika's present with a design on the future that it may neither want nor need. Naushika's lie, then, to the whole of humanity is both a personal and a social willingness to forget, to use the past to annihilate itself, both in how Miyazaki appropriates the *Odyssey* so as to undermine it and in how Naushika uses that special weapon of the past, the god-warrior, to destroy both the crypt and the weapon itself. However, this leaves one question unanswered in Miyazaki's text. It is easier to see why Naushika might reject the designs that the crypt of Shuwa and its master have on the present day, but it is less easy to see why one might abandon the lessons of Hiroshima. Is the memorial project that Hiroshima represents merely collateral damage in the absolute abrogation of the past? Is its invocation in the text a subtle reminder of the ramifications of Naushika's inversion of Odysseus' *nostos*? *Naushika* simply does not say.

6

Xerxes, Lost City in the Desert

Classical Allusions in *Fullmetal Alchemist*

SARA RAUP JOHNSON

As Theisen (2011, 59) observes, Western "classical" allusions—references to the ancient Mediterranean world of Greece and Rome, as opposed to references to Japanese classical literature and lore from the period before 1600 CE—carry a different significance in Japanese popular culture from what they might carry in America or Europe.[1] Rather than bearing the venerable weight of centuries of tradition and resonating with immediate recognition, they represent a set of stories and concepts more likely to be experienced by the reader as exotic and unfamiliar. It is precisely this exotic quality that makes allusions to Greco-Roman history and mythology attractive to writers in the fantasy/science-fiction genre when they set out to create fantastic otherworlds. In this chapter, I examine a work that is particularly rich in Western classical allusions, the manga 鋼の錬金術師 (*Hagane no Renkinjutsushi*, "Alchemist of Steel," translated into English as *Fullmetal Alchemist*).[2]

The world of *Fullmetal Alchemist* (*FMA*) is far from being exclusively classical in its inspiration. The primary mythos of the series is a form of magical alchemy loosely based on the practice of alchemy in medieval Europe; the primary inspiration for the technological and social setting is steampunk, infused with elements from nineteenth- and early-twentieth-century England and Germany.[3] Just as medieval alchemy drew on many classical terms and concepts,[4] however, *FMA* makes extensive use of classical allusions for the purpose of both world building and plot development.

1. All further references to "classical" are to the Western classical tradition unless otherwise stated.

2. For Japanese citations, I give the original script first, followed by a transcription into the Roman alphabet and a translation. All translations of Japanese, Greek, and Latin are mine unless otherwise noted.

3. Arakawa (2006, 100–105) contains an interview in which the *mangaka* (author/artist, creator of a manga, in this case Arakawa Hiromu) discusses some of the sources of her inspiration. See also Wong (2006).

4. For this reason, I will not attempt to highlight or discuss in detail classical terms that properly belong more to the tradition of medieval alchemy, such as *homunculi* and the Philosopher's Stone, both of which play a major role in the narrative. (On *Harry Potter and the Philosopher's Stone*, see note 24 below.) For a brief discussion of the alchemical traditions underlying the fictional world of *FMA*, see Arakawa (2006, 76–81, 138–140); for an exhaustive treatment of the subject of alchemy itself, see Pritchard (1981). Pritchard's work was updated with a CD-ROM and online edition in 2008, but according to a review of the updated edition, it disclaims any coverage of fictional alchemy, specifically including *FMA*; see Kahn (2008, 830).

In this chapter, I examine three modes of allusion that are employed, often interchange-ably: allusions that are highly eclectic, used primarily to create an exotic impression, with little or no regard for their original meaning and context; allusions that begin by making reference to classical lore in its original sense, only to alter the classical concept to suit the manga; and, finally, classical motifs that are cited with a full understanding of their traditional significance, though not always in perfect harmony with the details of the original context.

Throughout the discussion, I concentrate on the original manga version of *FMA*.[5] Those who are chiefly familiar with the first anime adaptation (*Fullmetal Alchemist*, 2003–2004) should be aware that its storyline diverges significantly from the manga about halfway through; the second anime adaptation (*Fullmetal Alchemist: Brotherhood*, 2009–2010) hews much more closely to the manga storyline.

FMA is set in a fantasy world (loosely resembling our world in some respects but not oth-ers) in which magical alchemy is widely recognized and practiced. It is the story of two brothers, Edward and Alphonse Elric,[6] who made a forbidden attempt to perform human transmutation in order to bring their dead mother back to life, with disastrous consequences: eleven-year-old Edward (Ed) lost his right arm and left leg, while ten-year-old Alphonse (Al) survives as a dis-embodied soul, housed in a giant suit of armor.

Contrary to expectations,[7] the Fullmetal Alchemist of the title is not the robotic Alphonse but Edward, who was given "automail" prostheses of solid steel to replace his lost limbs and who subsequently passed the test to become a state alchemist employed by the military. "Fullmetal" is his alchemist alias. The two brothers (now ages fifteen and fourteen; Arakawa 2006, 13, 19) embark on a journey to discover a way to restore their original bodies. In the course of their journey, they stumble upon a conspiracy rooted in the deepest levels of the military govern-ment, one that (in typical *shounen*[8] manga style) threatens the very existence of the world in which they live.

5. Japanese edition: 荒川・弘 (w./a. Arakawa Hiromu), 鋼の錬金術師 (*Hagane no Renkinjutsushi*), vols. 1–27 (Square Enix, 2002–2010). English edition: Hiromu Arakawa (w./a.), Akira Watanabe (trans.), *Fullmetal Alchemist* (Viz, 2005–2011). The manga was serialized in Japan in the magazine *Monthly Shounen Gangan*, pub-lished by Square Enix, and it ran from July 12, 2001, to June 11, 2010. The 108 chapters were collected into twenty-seven *tankoubon*, or graphic-novel volumes, the last being released in November 2010. The English version, released by Viz Manga, was likewise collected into twenty-seven volumes, with the same pagination and orienta-tion, and appeared from 2005 through 2011, the final volume being released on December 20, 2011. In subsequent citations, I give volume number, followed by chapter number(s) (for larger sections) or page and frame number(s) (for precise citations), citing both Japanese text and English translation wherever possible. Volume, chapter, page, and frame numbers are the same in both Japanese and English. The English translation is not "flipped," as earlier translations of manga into English sometimes were. This avoids the complications that can result from the mirror-ing of images, such as those discussed by Theisen (2011, 70–71).

6. It seems probable that the Elric surname is an evocation of Elric of Melniboné, the albino king-sorcerer who is the hero of many fantasy stories by Michael Moorcock, but no direct influence is evident.

7. It is a running joke in the series that when introduced to the brothers, people routinely mistakenly think that Alphonse is the "Fullmetal" alchemist. Al, although younger and a less powerful alchemist than his brother, appears in his armor to be a much more imposing figure than the diminutive Ed. Ed, who is smaller than normal for his age, is particularly sensitive about his short stature.

8. The target audience of Japanese manga is determined by the magazine in which chapters were originally serial-ized. *Shounen* (meaning "young boy") manga is serialized in magazines originally aimed at an audience of adoles-cent boys, although the actual readership may be much larger, both in Japan and in other countries.

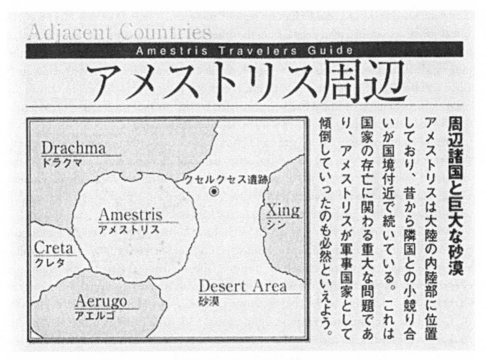

FIGURE 6.1 *Fullmetal Alchemist Perfect Guidebook* 2 (Japanese). Art by Arakawa Hiromu.

The peculiar geography of the Elric brothers' fantasy world contains the most idiosyncratic classical allusions in the series. Overall, the geography of the world bears some resemblance to our own world. The Elric brothers' home, and the center of most of the plot, is the country of Amestris (figure 6.1). Far to the east, beyond vast expanses of desert, is the empire of Xing,[9] which recalls China in many respects (e.g. the clothing worn by the characters from that region and the alchemy they practice, which is based on a flow of energy resembling chi).[10] Amestris itself is divided into a number of regions, the most important of which for the plot is Ishbal (to which we will return). Its northern border, which is snowbound and bitterly cold, borders on the country of Drachma (which, despite its name, seems to resemble Russia much more closely than it resembles Greece at any period); to the southwest is Creta (of which nothing more is said, at least not in the manga, but the resemblance of the name to Crete has not gone unnoticed).[11]

Of greatest interest, both to the plot of the manga and for the purposes of this chapter, is the country of Amestris. The region of Ishbal, in the southeastern corner of the country, seems

9. First introduced at vol. 8, 91.2–4; see the crude map at 115.5.

10. For chi (sometimes called in the *FMA* world the "dragon's flow"), see vol. 8, 159.3, and vol. 11, 140.5–6. See also the *FMA* wiki, s.v. "Xing" and "Alkahestry." The names of the most important Xingese characters in the story are Ling Yao (リン・ヤオ, *Lin Yao*) and May Chang (メイ・チャン, *Mei Chan*).

11. Drachma and Creta are first mentioned at vol. 8, 117.4–5. For lively English-language fan speculation about the culture and identification of the various regions in the *FMA* world, see the *FMA* wiki, s.v. "Amestris," "Creta," "Drachma," and "Xing."

clearly intended to evoke a Middle Eastern region[12] on several counts. Ethnically, the people of Ishbal are darker-skinned than people from the other regions of Amestris; they are also said to have red eyes (vol. 2, 122). The Ishbalans are said to be deeply religious, even fanatical, worshipping a god[13] named Ishbala, a name that vaguely recalls a combination of the Assyrian divinities Ishtar and Bel/Baal.[14] Following the outbreak of civil war thirteen years before the time of the main story, the region of Ishbal had been occupied by the military government of Amestris, which subdued it in a long and bitter war and all but exterminated its people.[15] A very small number of Ishbalans survive as refugees, and references are made throughout the narrative to the fear of Ishbalan terrorist attacks. Several main characters in the narrative are veterans of the Ishbalan War and suffer from pangs of conscience with regard to the acts they committed there. During the flashback to the details of the Ishbalan War, related by Lt. Hawkeye to Ed, the parallels with the US campaign in Iraq that began in 2003 are unmistakable.[16]

While the parallels with the Iraq War might be of more interest to a reader looking for political allusions in popular Japanese culture, operating simultaneously are more rarefied allusions to the ancient empire of Persia. If the names of Ishbal and its god seem to evoke the names of two ancient Assyrian deities, the name of the kingdom of Amestris itself and the lost city of Xerxes are direct allusions to the king who invaded Greece in 480 BCE, Xerxes (r. 486–465 BCE), and his wife, Amestris. Historically, of course, both names refer to people, not places. Arakawa confirmed in an interview that the names were intended as an homage to historical characters she admired. One website calls the allusion an "Easter egg,"[17] not an inappropriate

12. The most common candidates proposed by fans are Iraq (in modern political terms, the Iraq War; for a Western classically trained reader, Mesopotamia, in particular the Assyrian and Babylonian kingdoms), and Israel/Palestine; see further below. See also below on the associations of the kingdom of Xerxes with ancient Persia (modern Iran).

13. Whether the divinity is male or female is never made clear, since Japanese rarely uses gendered pronouns, and we never see a visual representation.

14. Both the name of the country and the name of the divinity raise some difficulties with transliteration, although less extreme than in the case of Xerxes, to be examined later. In Japanese, the character Scar is first introduced as a "citizen of Ishbal" (イシュヴァールの民, Ishuvaaru no tami, vol. 2, 122.6). As it uses a syllabic alphabet to pronounce foreign words, Japanese has difficulty transliterating clusters of consonants, such as *shb*, and must insert extra vowels (here, *shu*, a single syllable in Japanese). In *katakana*, the script used for transliterating foreign words, *va* may represent either the sound "va" or "ba" in the original non-Japanese word, and the "r" and "l" sounds in Japanese are interchangeable (in this case, the final *ru* represents a final "l" sound). Early volumes of the manga used the transliteration *Ishval* or *Ishvarlan* (in vol. 2, 122.6, the Viz translation has "He's an Ishvarlan"), but later volumes consistently use *Ishbal*, which is a more likely reading.

15. The Ishbalan War is first mentioned in vol. 2, 122–133. The detailed flashback to the events of the war is found at vol. 14, chap. 57, and vol. 15, chaps. 59–60.

16. So, for instance, Thompson (2007, 115). As one might expect, the similarities are more generic in vol. 2 (Japan 2002, US 2005; I see no indication that the English translator's knowledge of events since 2002 made any material difference in the translation) and become more striking when the reader learns more details about the war in vols. 14–15 (both Japan 2006, US 2007). However, I would hasten to add that any attempt to enforce a strict one-on-one correspondence with places in our world is unwise. A contemporary analogy that seems self-evident to one fan may be hotly disputed by another. Ishbal has also been identified by North American fans as representing variously Palestinians, Jews during the Holocaust, Native Americans, and the Ainu (Arakawa is a native of Hokkaido in northern Japan). Discussion is spread widely across many threads on many different boards. Arakawa has disclaimed any particular reference to real-world places or events (Wong 2006), save as a loose source of inspiration, and it is left to readers to draw their own comparisons.

17. *FMA* wiki, s.v. "Xerxes," under "Trivia."

characterization. An Easter egg is a whimsical image or reference inserted by a programmer, who knows that the vast majority of readers/users/viewers will never discover the hidden joke. In the same way, the names of Xerxes and Amestris retain little or none of their original significance in the narrative[18] but might draw a smile of recognition from the rare Japanese reader who might recognize the allusion to the Persian Wars.

Although apparently used for little more than exotic coloring and as an in-joke to fellow lovers of Herodotus, the name of Xerxes is particularly interesting, both for the role it plays in the narrative and for the problems it raises in translation. It is worth noting that both Xerxes and Amestris are transliterated from their Greek forms (not the original old Persian or English). Amestris is the name given to Xerxes' wife in the Greek sources.[19] The appearance of the name in Japanese is relatively uncomplicated (アメストリス, *Amesutorisu*) and was readily recognized by the translator, who correctly rendered it as Amestris.[20] The name of Xerxes, however, was another matter. It first appears in vol. 8, 115.5 and 116.2–3, when Ed and Al first meet Ling Yao of the empire of Xing. Ling tells them that he crossed the desert from Xing, passing through the ruins of the ancient city of "Cselkcess." The Japanese *katakana* spelling is クセルクセス (*ku-se-ru-ku-se-su*). Not surprisingly, this seems to have caused the translator some difficulty, and the name was rendered as an unrecognizable "fantasy place" called Cselkcess (*ku-se* = *cse; ru* = *l; ku* = *k; se-su* = *cess*). In fact, however, this is precisely the correct *katakana* spelling of the original Greek—not the English—pronunciation of Xerxes (Ξέρξης) when rendered in the Japanese syllabic alphabet (*ku-se* = *kse* (*xe*); *ru* = *r; ku-se* = *kse* (*xe*); *su* = *s*).[21] The missed reference caused not inconsiderable hilarity among English-speaking fans of the manga when the Viz translation of volume 8 first appeared in July 2006.[22] Whether out of stubbornness or a regard for consistency, however, the word continued to be spelled *Cselkcess* throughout subsequent volumes of the Viz translation.[23]

18. On the most basic level, they have ceased to be individual historical personalities and become kingdoms. It is debatable whether any of the literary significance that a Western classically trained reader might attach to the names is carried over. In Greek tradition and particularly Herodotus, Xerxes is depicted as the model of a lawless tyrant and Amestris as the scheming, bloodthirsty queen of the harem. For Greek attitudes toward Persia in general and the Persian court in particular, see Llewellyn-Jones (2010, 24–30, 45–55, and the references cited there, esp. 45 n. 122). It would require a fairly advanced degree of Western classical training to make the connection between (orientalist) Greek ideas of Persian tyranny and cruelty and the ruthlessness of the unnamed king of Xerxes in *FMA*, who is willing to commit mass human sacrifice in exchange for immortality—but see discussion of Herodotus' anecdote about the aged Amestris later in this chapter.

19. Hdt. 7.61.2; 7.114.2; 9.108–113; Ctesias, *Persica* §34, 39, 42–46; Pl., *Alc.* 123c; Plut., *Alc.* 23.4, 27.4.

20. Vol. 8, 89.1, and subsequently throughout.

21. See, for example, the Japanese Wikipedia entry for the Persian king Xerxes I (http://ja.wikipedia.org/wiki/クセルクセス1世), which is titled クセルクセス1世 (the last two characters are read as *issei* and mean "generation one"). That the generally accepted Japanese transliteration of the name is based originally on the Greek rather than the English pronunciation can be seen in the rendering of the initial *xe* as *kse*, not *ze*.

22. For a few examples of North American fans' bewildered reactions, see the following threads on the Fullmetal Alchemist Discussion Board: "Vol. 8" (June 2006), "Vol. 10" (November 2006), and "Xerxes/cselkcess?" (November 2009).

23. Perhaps not a regard for consistency, since other names (Ling Yao/Lin Yao, Ishval/Ishbal, etc.) are often spelled inconsistently. The problems with consistent transliteration merit a mention on the TV Tropes website, s.v. "Fullmetal Alchemist," subpoint "Spell My Name with an S," where we find "Xerxes/Cselkcess(!)" (emphasis theirs). Cselkcess was similarly transliterated in some early Japanese factbooks about the manga and in the 2003

Why Viz adhered throughout to the spelling of Cselkcess, despite the fact that it is demonstrably incorrect, is an open question. It may, however, be at least partly because of the role played by Xerxes in the narrative. Amestris, the homeland of the Elric brothers (and the wife of Xerxes), is not a well-known name to English readers; a very few, to be sure, might recognize the reference, but for most it would go unnoticed, and thus cause no confusion. By contrast, Xerxes is a much better-known name (not least, in recent years, due to the popularity of the movie *300* (2006)), and it is very possible that some English readers might have been confused by the use of a relatively well-known king as the name for a ruined city.

Xerxes (Cselkcess) comes to play a pivotal role in the narrative. At first we know only that it is a ruined and abandoned city that lies in the desert between Amestris and Xing (vol. 8, 115.5) and that, according to legend, it was destroyed in a single night (116.3). Later, however, we learn that the entire population of the city, "one million souls," had been sacrificed hundreds of years before in a monstrous attempt to create the coveted "philosopher's stone."[24] Given the importance of its role in the narrative and the need to create a fantastical-sounding ancient ruined city to play that role, it is possible that the exotic-sounding "Cselkcess" in English comes closer to reproducing (for an English-speaking audience) the effect of "Kuserukusesu" on a Japanese audience, a significant majority of whom would not know who Xerxes was.

The Japanese are far from being the only ones to use more or less garbled versions of unfamiliar names from another culture to create an exotic effect:

"My name is Ozymandias, king of kings:
Look on my works, ye Mighty, and despair!"
Nothing beside remains.[25]

Appropriately enough, the exotic-sounding name of Ozymandias in Shelley's famous sonnet comes from the attempt of a Greek author, Diodorus Siculus,[26] to render the throne name of Ramses II of Egypt. The allusion and the identification with Ramses were first suggested by Griffiths (1948), who pointed out that while hieroglyphics had not yet been deciphered at the

anime, but it was correctly changed to Xerxes in the 2009 anime (*FMA* wiki, s.v. "Xerxes," under "Trivia"; *Fullmetal Alchemist: Brotherhood*, episode 15).

24. Especially vol. 19, chap. 75, and vol. 20, chap. 80. In the world of *FMA*, the philosopher's stone (賢者の石, *kenja no ishi*, literally "stone of a philosopher") is believed to be a myth but is coveted by alchemists for its legendary power to enhance alchemical transmutation; as it turns out, it is quite real, a liquid/crystalline substance (its form varies) that can be used directly to amplify an alchemist's power or can be absorbed by the body to create a homunculus (a humanoid figure with supernatural powers). The standard phrase *kenja no ishi* as a translation for the alchemical term *philosopher's stone* predates the translation of the first Harry Potter novel into Japanese in 1999—UK: *Harry Potter and the Philosopher's Stone*; US: *Harry Potter and the Sorcerer's Stone*; Japan: ハリー・ポッターと賢者の石 (*Harii Pottaa to Kenja no Ishi*)—but no doubt the appearance of the translated Harry Potter series not long before *FMA* began serialization in 2001 made the concept more popularly accessible. However, to my knowledge, no reference is made to Harry Potter in any *FMA* fanbook or interview, Japanese or English.

25. Percy Bysshe Shelley, "Ozymandias," lines 10–12.

26. Diod. Sic., *Bibliotheca* 1.47.4: ἐπιγεγράφθαι δ' ἐπ' αὐτοῦ "βασιλεὺς βασιλέων Ὀσυμανδύας εἰμί. εἰ δέ τις εἰδέναι βούλεται πηλίκος εἰμὶ καὶ ποῦ κεῖμαι, νικάτω τι τῶν ἐμῶν ἔργων. "Written upon it was: 'King of kings, Osymandyas, am I. If anyone wishes to know how great I am and where I lie, let him surpass one of my works.'"

time of the poem's writing (and so the poet could hardly have learned of the inscription from "a traveller from an antique land" (line 1), as he claims), Shelley was in the habit of reading and translating classical texts.[27]

In a curious footnote, Herodotus (7.114.2) writes of Amestris that in her old age, she "buried twice seven sons of eminent Persian men as an exchange-offering on her own behalf to the god who is said to be beneath the earth" (Ἄμηστριν τὴν Ξέρξεω γυναῖκα πυνθάνομαι γηράσασαν δὶς ἑπτὰ Περσέων παῖδας ἐόντων ἐπιφανέων ἀνδρῶν ὑπὲρ ἑωυτῆς τῷ ὑπὸ γῆν λεγομένῳ εἶναι θεῷ ἀντιχαρίζεσθαι κατορύσσουσαν). The alleged human sacrifice of fourteen Persian nobles (no historical evidence exists to support this practice or to substantiate the incident) in exchange for the prolongation of one human life is eerily reminiscent of the fate of the city of Xerxes in *FMA*, which was supposedly sacrificed by the king (unnamed) of that country in an effort to make himself immortal. However, lacking explicit confirmation, there is no way to be certain that Herodotus' story about Amestris was a direct inspiration for the events of the manga.

Passing from the first type of classical allusion (names used primarily for exotic effect, with little regard for their original meaning) to the second (use of recognizably classical images or motifs but in a manner significantly different from that found in the classical context), a good example of the latter may be found in the role played throughout the narrative by creatures called Chimeras.

In classical mythology, the Chimera (χιμαῖρα, "she-goat") was a mythological creature with a hybrid body, most commonly composed of the head of a goat (which was pictured as sprouting from the back), the body (or, more precisely, the fore parts) of a lioness, and the tail of a snake. In Homer's *Iliad*, it is described as

ἡ δ' ἄρ' ἔην θεῖον γένος οὐδ' ἀνθρώπων,
πρόσθε λέων, ὄπιθεν δὲ δράκων, μέσση δὲ χίμαιρα,
δεινὸν ἀποπνείουσα πυρὸς μένος αἰθομένοιο.[28]

It was slain by Bellerophon, with the help of Pegasus. Like any of the female monsters in Greek mythology (the Chimera is always said to be female), it served as a symbol of the forces of disorder needing to be tamed by civilization and of the monstrous feminine needing to be subdued by the male hero.[29]

---

27. The circumstances that lay behind the poem's composition were further elucidated by Davenport (1978), describing how the poem was inspired by a conversation and friendly competition with a fellow poet, Horace Smith, who was reading Diodorus at the time. Smith submitted his Ozymandias poem (rather painfully titled "On a Stupendous Leg of Granite, Discovered Standing by Itself in the Deserts of Egypt, with the Inscription Inserted Below") to the *Examiner* a month after Shelley's was published.

28. *Il.* 6.179–182: "a divine being, not born of men, a lion in front, a snake behind, and in the middle a goat, breathing forth the terrible might of blazing fire." Similar descriptions may be found in Hesiod (*Theog.* 319–325), Pseudo-Apollodorus (*Bibliotheca* 2.3.1), and Ovid (*Met.* 6.339, 9.648).

29. On the (Greek) conception of the feminine as a monstrous force needing to be tamed by civilization and the male hero, see especially Zeitlin (1996); on the concept of the monstrous feminine more generally, see Creed (1986), drawing on the work of Julia Kristeva.

FIGURE 6.2 Few chimeras resemble their Greek models in *Fullmetal Alchemist*, vol. 1, 48.1. Art by Arakawa Hiromu.

In *FMA*, too, a chimera is a hybrid (and monstrous) creature but of a rather different sort. In the first chapter, a chimera appears (summoned by Father Cornello, discussed in more detail below) that comes closest to resembling the Greek monster. It has a lion's body and the tail of a snake, although the goat's head is nowhere in evidence (figure 6.2). It soon becomes clear, however, that Arakawa has a significantly different conception of the Chimera in mind.

Early in the narrative (vol. 2, 7–50), the Elric brothers come to military headquarters in Central City, in search of more information about bio-alchemy (to help them in their quest to regain their original bodies). Ed's superior, Colonel Roy Mustang—a snarky rival but ultimately a sympathetic ally and one of the heroes of the narrative—suggests that he seek out a "chimera researcher" named Shou Tucker.[30] The subject of Tucker's research is given in Japanese as 合成獣錬成, with the pronunciation marked in *furigana* as キメラれんせい (*kimera-rensei*; literally, "chimera-transmutation"). The phrase 合成獣, which would ordinarily be pronounced *gousei-juu*, means "synthetic beast" but has been glossed as "chimera," a common use of *furigana*[31] to indicate not only how a word should be pronounced but also how it should be

30. On the Tucker episode, see also Gallacher (2011, 459–463), who is particularly interested in manga as a representational medium.

31. *Furigana* are small letters placed above a word, normally in *hiragana* (the native Japanese script), but sometimes in *katakana* (the script used to render foreign words), used to indicate the pronunciation of a *kanji*

understood. Conveniently for our purposes, Mustang reads from his notes a definition of the word: "Chimera: an artificial fusion created by alchemically 'marrying' two genetically dissimilar life forms."[32] In this case, it seems that the concept of the chimera invokes not only the Greek mythological creature from which it was named but also the use of the word in the biological sciences; if one removes "alchemically marrying" from the definition, it is almost identical to the definition of a biological chimera as listed in Japanese medical-scientific dictionaries.[33]

Mustang explains that Tucker gained his certification as a state alchemist two years before, when he created a chimera with the power to speak and understand human speech. "But all it said was . . . 'I want to die'" (figure 6.3).[34] It then refused to eat and eventually died.[35] When the brothers meet Tucker, they learn that he has been raising his daughter, Nina, alone since his wife left him two years earlier (13.3, 23.1). He spends most days immersed in his work, since he is anxious about his inability to reproduce his first successful experiment (22–23). Nina, an affectionate and happy child, spends most of her time with her beloved dog, Alexander, and quickly bonds with the Elric brothers, who decide to stay for a few days to do research in Tucker's library. Nina hails Ed as "big brother" (18.7)[36] and is delighted to have someone to play with her.

But one day, when the Elric brothers come to the library, Nina and Alexander are nowhere to be found. Tucker proudly introduces them to his newest creation: another doglike chimera

---

compound. It is used routinely in texts aimed at younger persons, who might not yet have mastered quite all of the two-thousand-odd "educational *kanji*" required for adult literacy in Japan, and may be used in texts aimed at adults when a particular *kanji* is rare or likely to cause confusion. Since *FMA* is aimed at an audience of adolescent boys, *furigana* are used as a matter of course on nearly all words, but in some cases, as here, it also serves as a kind of interpretive gloss. In this case, 合成獣, "synthetic beast," is labeled not with its normal pronunciation but (in *katakana*, as befits a foreign word) as *kimera* ("chimera"), while 錬成 (*rensei*, "transmutation") is labeled in *hiragana* with its normal reading.

32. Vol. 2, 10.3 (Viz translation). Japanese: 遺伝的に異なる二種以上の生物を代価とする人為的合成 (*identeki ni kotonaru nishu-ijou no seibutsu wo daika to suru jin'i-teki gousei*). The words might more literally be translated: "Chimera: an artificial synthesis which uses as its cost (i.e., is made from) two or more creatures that differ genetically." *FMA* has a recurring emphasis on the cost to be paid in exchange for performing alchemy, an emphasis that, interestingly, is lost in translation in this particular instance.

33. For instance, Oda (1998), s.v. "chimera": 遺伝子型の異なる細胞をもつ個体 (*idenshigata no kotonaru saihou wo motsu kotai*: "an individual that possesses cells of differing genotypes"). The biological use of the term in this sense (in English scientific literature and presumably hence in Japanese) goes back at least to the 1950s. Mustang's use of the terminology, when taken alongside the appearance of the chimera summoned by Cornello, shows that Arakawa was fully aware of both the mythological and biological definitions.

34. Vol. 2, 11.2–3 (Viz translation). Japanese: ただ一言「死にたい」と (*tada hitokoto "shinitai" to*).

35. Shades, perhaps, of Petronius' Sibyl? (Petron., *Sat.* 48, spoken by Trimalchio: *Nam Sibyllam quidem Cumis ego ipse oculis meis vidi in ampulla pendere, et cum illi pueri dicerent:* Σίβυλλα τί θέλεις; *respondebat illa:* ἀποθανεῖν θέλω.) The phrase was famously quoted by T. S. Eliot as a preface to *The Waste Land*: "For with my own eyes I saw the Sibyl at Cumae hanging in a bottle, and when the boys said to her, 'Sibyl, what do you want?,' she replied, 'I want to die.'" The phrase "I want to die" is as stark in the Japanese as in the Greek, and the context would be appropriate to the broader themes of the manga (the Sibyl was cursed with immortality without youth, because of a bad bargain made with the god Apollo; Von Hohenheim in the manga is similarly cursed, against his will, with immortality, although his appearance does not age), but perhaps the echo is only a coincidence. If the allusion is intentional, it is most likely an allusion to Eliot's poem rather than to Petronius directly.

36. She picks up the form of address from Al, who always addresses his brother as 兄さん (*nii-san*, "big brother"). At first (18.7), Nina, like Al, uses *nii-san*, but she quickly (19.3) switches to the more childlike and affectionate お兄ちゃん (*oniichan*), which she then uses consistently.

FIGURE 6.3 A chimera that can speak. *Fullmetal Alchemist*, vol. 2, 11.2–3. Art by Arakawa Hiromu.

that can speak and understand human speech (28.1). But when the creature addresses Ed as "big brother" (29.5),[37] Ed realizes the horrifying truth: Tucker had created his first chimera by using the body of his wife and has now created the second one from the bodies of Nina and Alexander (32.3–4; see figures 6.4 and 6.5).

Tucker is defiant; the progress of science, he says, requires experimentation, and when Ed charges him with playing with people's lives, he replies that Ed is no different, since he attempted human transmutation in spite of the fact that it was forbidden (34–35). Ed attacks Tucker but stops short of killing him (he evinces extreme reluctance to kill throughout the series). Al apologizes to the chimera because they don't have the power to change her back (38–39), but all the creature says is "Wanna play" (38.2–3).[38] Tucker and his creation, the Nina-chimera, are destroyed not long afterward by the Ishbalan Scar, who is pursuing a vendetta against state alchemists.

Although the story of Nina is only a single chapter and at first seems only marginally relevant, it is in fact programmatic for the entire manga. It foreshadows the use of human sacrifice as an ingredient in alchemy, which will become one of the main threads of the story. It highlights Ed's deep guilt over his own failed experiment in human transmutation,[39] and toward the very end of the manga, he refers to Nina when he is reflecting on his own inability to help

37. お…にい…ちゃ…(*o…nii…cha…*).The creature speaks haltingly and in a slightly altered font that suggests its voice is not quite normal, but it is clearly attempting to address Ed as *oniichan*.

38. あそぼうよ, *asobou yo*, repeated several times.

39. A theme further developed by Ashby (2009, 98).

FIGURES 6.4 The truth behind the chimera. *Fullmetal Alchemist*, vol. 2, 28 and 29.4–6. Art by Arakawa Hiromu.

FIGURE 6.5 The truth behind the chimera. *Fullmetal Alchemist*, vol. 2, 28 and 29.4–6. Art by Arakawa Hiromu.

people with his alchemy (vol. 27, 127.4).[40] It also foreshadows the ambivalent role of Scar, who will later become a reluctant ally and something of a redeemed figure. Scar appears destructive and vindictive, murdering alchemists without pity, but his words to the chimera are compassionate. He says that he only wants to put her out of her misery, since there is no way to change her back (vol. 2, 48–49).

The introduction of the alchemical chimera, then, is essential to the plot, and in fact we will meet other, more monstrous, human chimeras later in the story, the product of secret military experiments that Tucker knew nothing of.[41] The concept of the chimera is clearly rooted in the classical conception, but it is fundamentally altered both in substance and in significance. On the most obvious level, none of the chimeras is a winged or goat-headed creature

40. 合成獣（キメラ）にされた女の子ひとり助けられない小さい人間だ (*kimera ni sareta onna no ko hitori tasukerarenai chiisai ningen da*: "I'm just a small human being who couldn't help one little girl who was turned into a chimera." The phrase "small human being" (which Viz renders as "hopeless human being") is particularly poignant coming from Ed, who is sensitive about his height and prone to violent rages when he even thinks someone has called him small.

41. Like Nina, they are usually humans fused with animals, though produced via a much more sophisticated process. In vol. 7 (chaps. 26–27, especially pp. 51–55), we meet four chimeras who were created in a military lab and

that breathes fire. Only the first to appear even vaguely resembles a lion-snake hybrid. As the monstrous product of an illegal crossing of species, they share with the Greek Chimera only their hybrid nature.[42] The element of the monstrous feminine is lost. Although both of Tucker's chimeras were technically female, the other chimeras that the brothers meet later are mostly male. And though monstrous in a sense, the chimeras themselves inspire more pity than horror in the onlooker. The real monster in this scenario is the creator of the chimeras.[43] Rather than symbolizing chaos that must be subdued and civilized, the chimeras represent the danger inherent in an alchemist's misuse of power and the fine ethical line that Ed himself must walk.[44]

Directly related to this overarching theme, the dangers of alchemy, is the most obvious and fully realized classical analogy in the series: the comparison of the Elric brothers to Daedalus and Icarus. Like the chimera incident, it occurs early (vol. 1, chaps. 1–2), and like the story of Nina, it at first appears to be in the context of a passing adventure that later turns out to be tied into the story at a much deeper level.[45] In this story, too, themes are introduced that are key to the entire series: human transmutation, the philosopher's stone, and, above all, the risks of alchemy.

In the course of their journey, Ed and Al come to a town called Reole, in which the dominant religion is the cult of the sun god Leto. The name of the god raises a side issue deserving brief discussion. Leto is another example of a classical allusion that only partially maps onto its referent. The leader of the cult is Father Cornello, who acts more like a Catholic priest than a pagan one. Leto, of course, was not the sun god but the mother of Apollo (sometimes a sun god) and Artemis. Moreover, when we do see a statue of Leto, it is bearded and unmistakably male (vol. 1, 17.3) and looks more like a cross between Zeus and Helios (figure 6.6).[46]

Exactly why Leto is depicted as male is uncertain. It is not likely to be through ignorance, since the name of Apollo's mother was surely not chosen by coincidence, and anyone who knew her name would not likely mistake her gender. More likely, this is a case of the deliberate use of unfamiliar mythological allusions for exotic effect. Arakawa has definitively stated that Father Cornello and his god are fictional inventions, not meant to represent any particular world faith (Western readers, of course, have been quick to see the parallels with Christianity).[47] To that

who are now working for the maverick homunculus Greed; although enemies, they are relatively sympathetic and die a sympathetic death (vol. 8, 19–29). In vol. 18, chaps. 71–73, the brothers encounter even more monstrous chimeras who are working for President Bradley, but they, too, end up becoming sympathetic allies.

42. In discussing monstrosity in *FMA*, Gallacher (2011, 458) notes that Ed and his brother are themselves monstrous hybrids, created as the result of an illegal experiment—Ed with his automail limbs, Al as a soul bound by alchemy to a suit of armor. Al's plight as a soul without a body has probably attracted more discussion than any other aspect of the series; see, e.g., Michaud (2010).

43. Perhaps surprisingly to the Western reader, no reference (explicit or implied) is made to the tale of Frankenstein and his creation, although a Japanese reader familiar with the story might certainly make the connection.

44. The theme of the danger of alchemy mirrors another common theme in manga and anime: the dangers of technology. See Ashby (2009, 91) on the use of this theme within *FMA*, and Napier (2005, 84–102; 2007) on the theme generally. Wittkower (2010) approaches the dangers of alchemy in *FMA* from a different angle, seeing it as a metaphor for capitalism.

45. In this case, the role later played by Rosé and the town of Reole are not relevant to the classical analogy in question, so I will pass over it here.

46. The sun rays around the head are particularly associated with Helios (*LIMC*, "Helios/Sol," 4.2 pl. 366–385), but Helios is more often depicted as a beardless youth, not a mature bearded male (*LIMC*, "Zeus," 8.2 pl. 218–242).

47. *FMA* wiki, "Christianity," "Leto."

FIGURE 6.6 The Leto of *Fullmetal Alchemist*, vol. 1, 17.2–3. Art by Arakawa Hiromu.

end, elements both from Christianity and from pagan Greek mythology have been drawn on as needed to create the image of a god who is associated with the sun, all-powerful, male, and foreign (not clearly associated with any Japanese deity or indeed with Chinese tradition).

There might be another parallel with the case of Xerxes in this respect. I argued above that the name would be unfamiliar to many Japanese readers, while English readers would be more likely to recognize the reference; Xerxes thus fails as an exotic marker in English. For the image of an exotic patriarchal figure associated with the sun, Arakawa could have invoked Apollo or Helios directly, but those names would somewhat more likely be recognized by Japanese readers. By contrast, the name of Leto would be much less familiar to a Japanese reader who has not made a special study of Greek mythology.[48] Thus, the name Leto is more likely to produce the desired exotic, alien effect. Alternatively, Arakawa could have followed Greek tradition and made her Leto female, but to a Japanese reader, this would immediately recall the female sun goddess Amaterasu, who is at the very center of the Shinto pantheon. The image of a female sun goddess would therefore be less likely to produce the desired exotic, non-Japanese effect.[49]

In Reole, the brothers meet a young girl named Rosé, who is a faithful follower of Father Cornello because he has promised her that he can restore her dead boyfriend (*koibito*) to life. The promise, as it turns out, is a lie, and the philosopher's stone that Cornello claims to have is a fake (vol. 1, 87–89); Cornello himself is a tool of the homunculi, who bear the names and natures of the seven deadly sins. However, it is in the course of the confrontation with Cornello that Ed first reveals to the reader his own disastrous experiment with human transmutation,[50] and the narrative accompanying the flashback clearly invokes the myth of Icarus.

Ed first invokes the story in a conversation with Rosé, when he says that alchemists are scientists who don't believe in God, but ironically, their powers bring them closer to God than most people. "It's like that myth about the hero . . . He made wings out of wax so he could fly . . . But when he got too close to the sun . . . to God . . . the wax melted and he crashed to the ground."[51] Icarus is never named,[52] but the reference is quite clear. (Daedalus is not named, either, perhaps because Ed is both Daedalus and Icarus, engineer and victim of his own

---

48. By way of a rough measure, a Google search on アポロ (Apollo, also picking up the alternative Japanese spelling アポローン) produces more than nine million results, while レートー (Leto) produces just more than ten thousand hits.

49. To be fair, one should not overanalyze the creative process. Perhaps Arakawa just liked the sound of the name Leto.

50. Apart from a brief and cryptic sequence on the very first page of the manga, this is the first account the reader is given of how Ed and Al came to be the way they are (vol. 1, 54–65, 74–77). Later, there are more extensive flashback accounts that give further details (particularly vol. 5, chap. 21, and vol. 6, chaps. 22–24).

51. Viz translation, vol. 1, 23.2–3: そういやどっかの神話にあったっけな。「太陽（カミサマ）に近づきすぎた英雄は蠟で固めた翼をもがれ地に墜とされる」...ってな (*sou iya, dokka no shinwa ni atta kke na. "taiyou (kamasama) ni chikazukisugita eiyuu wa rou de katameta tsubasa wo mogare chi ni otosareru . . ." tte na*). The literal translation is a little vaguer than the Viz translation would imply: "That's right, I heard it happened in a myth from somewhere." The glossing of the *kanji* word normally pronounced "taiyou" ("sun") with the *furigana* reading (in *katakana*) *kamisama* ("god") is another example of *furigana* being used as an interpretive gloss rather than a simple pronunciation guide.

52. In the manga, at least. Icarus is named in a "Trivia" section of Arakawa (2006, 106). For the widespread occurrence of the Icarus motif in popular culture generally, including anime and manga, see TV Tropes, s.v. "Icarus Allusion."

downfall.)[53] Like Ed, the Japanese reader might or might not recall the name of the hero in the story, but it is clear that Ed expects the story to be a familiar one that Rosé (and the reader) may recognize. It soon becomes evident that not only the details of the myth but also the moral behind it are being deliberately invoked. The words are echoed at the start of the flashback to Ed and Al's failed experiment (vol. 1, 61.2), and although neither Daedalus nor Icarus is mentioned by name, the moral is explicit: by attempting forbidden human transmutation, the Elric brothers attempted to fly too high—to become like gods—and were punished accordingly.[54] The story is a warning to Rosé not to make the mistake of traveling down the same path.

When it comes to the use of classical allusions in Japanese manga, it would be unwise to push the parallels or to enforce them too rigidly. From the examples I have explored, it is clear that the invocation of classical elements can range from the casual to the elaborately detailed and that fidelity to the classical model is followed only insofar as it serves the narrative and no further. Some parallels, indeed, may exist only in the mind of the classically trained reader, accidental rather than deliberate echoes. It is, however, also clear that at least some Japanese *mangaka* such as Arakawa have a knowledge of European classical lore that extends beyond the trite (the example of Icarus is arguably a cliché) to the obscure (how many people in the West, let alone Japan, can correctly name Xerxes' wife?). Very few Western artists could boast an equal knowledge of Japanese classical history and mythological lore. Like elements from traditional Japanese lore, elements of Western classical tradition are employed by manga artists with remarkable inventiveness and creativity. A few elements might be head-scratching for a classically trained reader (why is Leto male?), but at its best, the creative use of classical elements carries the potential for profound resonance within the context of the Japanese work. It is one of the rare areas in which the classically trained Western reader has the opportunity to perceive references that might well escape the average Japanese reader.

---

53. Ed himself can, of course, be understood as a mythic hero in a broader sense, a theme explored by Chandler (2010).

54. Indeed, although the flashback to Ed's words about the "hero" in the fight with Cornello appears to be in a thought bubble, not spoken aloud (61.2), Cornello invokes the same metaphor to describe the brothers' transgression: "You fools are the ones who came too close to God and fell to earth" (67.1, Viz translation): (神に近づきすぎ地に墜とされたおろか者どもめ: *kami ni chikazukisugi chi ni otosareta oroka-mono-domo-me*). The words *chikazukisugi chi ni otosareta* are very nearly a direct quote of Ed's earlier words (*chikazukisugita . . . chi ni otosareru*).

PART THREE

All Gaul

7

Reinventing the Barbarian

Classical Ethnographic Perceptions in *Astérix*

Eran Almagor

All the ethnographic perceptions concerning the ancient Celts come from classical Greek and Roman literature and art. All of them? Well, not entirely. There is also the French comic book *Astérix*.[1] In more than one way, this popular series has a place of honor alongside the great works of classical literature, whose proud descendant it should be considered.[2] Not only is the imaginary world of these unlikely heroes firmly rooted in Greek and Latin descriptions, especially the ethnographic passages and digressions explicitly dealing with the Celts or Gauls, but also the medium that conveys the story, the francophone *bande dessinée* (henceforth BD) as it developed in the latter half of the twentieth century, supplements and completes the form, purpose, and ingenuity of these ancient texts.[3] It might be said that *Astérix* essentially provides its French readers with amusing references to current items by anachronistically planting them in the historical times of Roman Gaul.[4] Yet can *Astérix* only be understood in terms of its modern French connection?[5] It would

1. An earlier version of this chapter was presented at Lampeter, and I am thankful for all the comments that helped me improve it. I shall treat here only the twenty-four first albums that were the fruit of the joint collaboration between René Goscinny and Albert Uderzo and not the following ten albums continued solely by Uderzo. The discussion here is therefore only up to the last album after the untimely death of Goscinny in 1977, i.e., *Astérix chez les Belges* (1979). Henceforth the names of the albums are given in French. See the appendix for the English titles. References to the albums include page and panel numbers.

2. The first attempts to find truthful details in *Astérix* are those of Manson (1966), Vals (1966), and Lentz (1967). See Stoll (1974); Brenne (1999); and the studies in Brodersen (2001).

3. On the BD, see Fresnault-Deruelle (1972); Sadoul (1976, esp. 64–69); Masson (1985); the studies in Forsdick, Grove, and McQuillan (2005); Miller (2008, 75–146). On ancient ethnography, see the papers in Almagor and Skinner (2013).

4. Pinet (1980); Nye (1980, 184–185, 191–192); Steel (2005, 205, 214); Dandridge (2008, 3); Dinter (2011, 186).

5. *Astérix*'s portrayal of the struggle against the Romans in Gaul is sometimes made to hint at the French Resistance against the then-recent German occupation of France; Nye (1980, 190); Chante (1982, 423); Clark (2004). Rouviere (2006, 150) shows the complexity of this allusion and also the play on collaborative guilt. Stoll (1974, 161–165) stresses an anti-American allegory, while others point at the the crisis of French imperialism; see Miller (2008, 154–155). See Pellegrin (2013). Resistance to the Romans can also be seen as a struggle against the French Empire and imperial concepts, or at least the Roman element in the French imperial identity; see Dietler (1994, 588). It is the Gauls and the Belgians who defeat Caesar, portrayed as Napoleon, facing his Waterloo (*Astérix chez*

seem that this interpretation does not address all the facets of *Astérix*, in particular its very setting or the role of classical allusions in it. For a new myth, so to speak, has been created in this comic strip, almost inseparable from the format in which it came to life.[6] It is comics, with its combination of text and image, that enabled the author (or *scénariste*) René Goscinny and the artist (or *dessinateur*) Albert Uderzo—the new "mythographers," as it were—to produce a strong fantasy story that brings antiquity closer to modern readership at the price of superseding history.[7] So great is the success of the strip that today the character of Asterix has unseated the figure of the Gaulish warrior Vercingetorix, who is largely forgotten or even "devoured" by the fictional hero.[8] Instead of being associated with real historical Celts, Gaul is popularly linked with a detached dreamland set in the timeless year of 50 BCE. In this respect, Goscinny and Uderzo should be seen as latter-day ethnographers, following in the footsteps of their classical predecessors in creating a world but conceptually recasting the Celts or Gauls in a completely new textual and graphic garb.

The Gauls in *Astérix*'s village may not be subdued by Romans, yet they succumb to two other forces pulling this BD series in different directions. One is the tradition of the ancient classical sources of which the prejudices of Greek and Roman authors are part and parcel.[9] The other is the unique significance of the Gauls in French cultural and ethnic identity and historiography. It is no coincidence that *Astérix* echoes ancient texts. In later interviews, Goscinny admitted to being influenced in the series by two written texts: Julius Caesar's *Commentarii de Bello Gallico* (*Commentaries on the Gallic War*), a firsthand account of his nine years of war in Gaul against local tribes during the 50s BCE, and *La vie quotidienne à Rome* by French historian Jérôme Carcopino (1939).[10] It would seem that Goscinny was also inspired by *La vie quotidienne en Gaule* by Paul-Marie Duval (1952), which was found in his personal library[11] and which appears to have been valuable in conveying the images of other Greek and Latin works.[12] While the impact of these sources is indeed discernible throughout the comic strip, this inspiration is effected with a twist, caused by the importance attributed to the Gauls in the French notion of self-presentation. An ethnic dimension in the perception of class division in France was already suggested at the beginning of the eighteenth century.[13] The aristocracy

les Belges 39.8–45.8); see King (2001, 113). Some suggest allusions to Fifth Republic internal political divisions (Rouviere 2006, 138–140; Miller 2008, 156–157) echoed by caricatures of leading politicians (Giscard d'Estaing, Jacques Chirac).

6. On comics and mythology, see McCloud (1993, 188). On the myth of *Astérix*, see Stoll (1974, 146) on the *Trivialepos Frankreichs*, where the series is seen as a parody of orthodox mythology. See also the collection *Ils sont fous . . . d'Astérix!* (1996), subtitled *Un mythe contemporain*. See Baur (2004).

7. See Kovacs (2011, 12–13, and see 6, 10, on mythography and iconography). For the reasons for *Astérix*'s worldwide success, see Dandridge (2008).

8. King (2001). See Nye (1980, 183); Dietler (1994, 593).

9. Sherwin-White (1967, 6–32); Balsdon (1979, 65–66); Dauge (1981, 93–95, 415, 661); Isaac (2004, 411–425); Almagor (2005); Riggsby (2006, 47–71), to name but a few.

10. See du Chatenet and Marmonnier (2005, 269).

11. Note also several others, such as L. Krabbe's *Histoire de Danemark* (Paris, 1950), apparently used in *Astérix et les Normands* (1967). See du Chatenet and Marmonnier (2005, 174).

12. Another popular textbook in those days was Pernoud (1957).

13. It goes back to the writings in Comte de Boulainvilliers's *Histoire de l'ancien gouvernement de la France* (1727).

of the Ancien Régime was associated with the Franks, while the lower stratum of society, the so-called third estate, was linked with the peasant Gauls, thought to predate proper French history.[14] Yet from the great revolution onward, a new significance was given to the third estate in France, and consequently to the Gauls, in its national story. The beginning of France was not dated henceforth to Clovis the Frank but rather marked by an appeal to antiquity, whereby *Nos ancêtres les Gaulois* had a role to play in official ideology, elementary-school curriculum, history books, and popular culture.[15] So the tables were turned, and a completely different perspective from that of the classical sources was adopted: the Gauls were no longer the "others" of Greco-Roman literature, a passive external object to the Greek and Roman gaze, but the heroes of a story told from their own perspective, the story of the French national community.[16] It should be stressed, however, that though regarded as ancestors, the Gauls were still imagined as a separate group in the collective portrayal; their heroism, for instance, was set as an ideal for contemporary France.

On his way to becoming a national hero, Asterix had to overcome, as it were, several internal Gallic opponents. There were earlier attempts to present Roman Gauls in a BD format, all very different from one another and all but one appearing for a very short period. The first attempt was made by Uderzo himself, in a peculiar short-lived strip called *Arys Buck* (1946–1948) for the magazine *OK*. Toying with several drawing styles and techniques, this strip showed a fantasy world whose main figure was a markedly strong prince of the American superhero type, with a short, grotesquely drawn Gallic companion called Cascagnace, with a big nose, a mustache, and a winged helmet—a graphic forerunner of the later drawing style (including the *gros nez*) and of Asterix himself (at this stage as a sidekick only).[17] The second was *Tototrix*, created by Jaboune (the alias of television presenter Jean Nohain) with illustrations by Poleon (the alias of Louis Lampereur). These adventures (1947–1950), rather caricaturistic in type, were published in the feuilleton *Le Petit Canard Illustré*.

From 1948, the popular strip *Alix*, created by Jacques Martin, appeared in the Belgian comics magazine *Tintin*.[18] This hero had an interesting multilayered identity. Of Gaulish descent yet adopted by a rich Roman noble, Alix was later given his freedom and Roman citizenship (as "Alix Gracchus"). One may wonder whether Asterix did not begin as a pun on Astorix, the Gallic chieftain and father of Alix,[19] in an attempt to present the new character as an antihero of sorts. Drawn in the *ligne claire* (clear line) style and encompassing complex

14. Dietler (1994, 586–587); Collis (2003, 199).

15. Of special importance is the *Histoire de France* (1833–1836) of Henri Martin and Paul Lacroix. See Leerssen (2006, 204–218). See also Nye (1980, 191, 195 n. 24); Dietler (1994, 590–593). This trend coexisted alongside a tendency to stress the importance of the victory of Roman civilization.

16. Chapman (1992); Olivier (1997). One of the heights of this movement was the erection of the monumental bronze statue of Vercingetorix by Millet in 1865 at the request of Napoleon III on the site of the battlefield of Alésia. See Dietler (1994, 589).

17. Few images of this strip appear to survive and none of sufficient quality to reprint here. One image of Arys Buck with Cascagnace can be found here: http://www.arretetonchar.fr/ok-arys-buck/.

18. Chante (1982); Dinter (2011, 184). The series appeared for approximately thirty years.

19. See the first album of Alix, *Alix l'Intrepide* (1948), 35.16, 36.1–2; and the second album, *Le sphinx d'Or* (1949), 3.2.

storylines in different locations within the Roman Mediterranean at the time of Julius Caesar (and beyond it), *Alix* was an impressive comic strip but did not make full use of the new medium's potential in terms of its textual and visual features.[20] For one thing, these adventure stories portrayed the protagonists as archaic heroes excelling in skill and courage and exemplary models; there was hardly any caricature involved or tongue-in-cheek references to their role as moral paradigms.[21] The same might be said about another effort, namely, the adventures of *Aviorix le Gaulois*, created by Marcel Moniquet. This short-lived Flemish strip (1955–1956) appeared in the *Héroïc Albums* of Fernand Cheneval.

Why did Asterix succeed where the others had failed? What was his secret weapon? Though not as realistically drawn as *Alix*, the new BD series *Astérix* was closer to the original ancient texts by way of parody. It introduced complexity and humor to the image of Gauls and their relations to the French of today on the one hand and to the Roman texts on the other.[22] In fact, humor, wit, and irony were not lacking among the ancient Gauls, as the classical sources tell us.[23]

One feature of comics that Goscinny and Uderzo utilized in their BD series was precisely the flexibility of viewpoint it enables, facilitating an objectification of the heroes, in correspondence to a portrayal made by outside groups (e.g., the Greeks and Romans), side by side with a narration of a tale focalized through the eyes of the protagonists. As the reader's involvement in comics was enhanced to the point of identification with the cartoon images,[24] the Gaulic heroes were no longer regarded as complete "others." An earlier joint collaboration of the two authors, the stories of *Oumpah-pah le Peau-Rouge* (*Oumpah-pah the Redskin*), can be considered a precursor to this subtle combination of perspectives. Following its first format in 1951 (which was put on hold), the shape that *Oumpah-pah* took when it was commissioned in 1958 for the *Tintin* magazine made the Native American warrior a scout for the French during the eighteenth-century colonization in America, thus presenting the story from both a colonial viewpoint (through the hero's French officer friend, Hubert de la Pâte Feuilletée) and a local one (Oumpah-pah's indomitable village, as it were).[25] Pressured by an imminent deadline set for their contribution to the inaugural issue of their new French magazine *Pilote* (October 29, 1959), which was aimed at adults and a sophisticated audience, Goscinny and Uderzo came up with the idea for a story taking place in Roman Gaul.[26] It was not the one

20. *Ligne claire*: McCloud (1993, 42). Yet see the analysis of *Alix* in Fresnault-Deruelle (1972, 45–48).

21. Chante (1982, 426); see Dinter (2011, 184). *Tintin* was basically aimed at children and adolescents.

22. For the absence of this sort of humor in the Belgian BD to that point, see Ory (2007, 84). See also Feuerhahn (1996).

23. Cato, *Orig.* fr. 34 (Peter): "Most of Gaul engages in two things: military matters and witty discourse [*argute loqui*]." See also Diod. Sic. 5.31; Juv. 7.147.

24. See McCloud (1993, 31, 36–37, 42, 59).

25. On the perspective shift: Nye (1980, 184). Five thirty-plate albums were made of *Oumpah-pah* between the years 1958 and 1962. See Gaumer and Moliterni (1994, 475–476).

26. On the deadline, see Nye (1980, 184). On *Pilote*, see Michallat (2005). In France of those days, Roman Gaul was in the air, at least on the airwaves. The popular Henri Salvador and Boris Vian tune "Faut rigoler" ("One Has to Laugh"), known also as the "Cha-cha Gaulois," promoted hilarity as practiced by "Nos ancêtres les Gaulois," to prevent "the sky from falling" ("Pour empêcher le ciel de tomber").

they originally planned, and it was chosen only after they discovered that their initial idea had already been taken.[27] From when *Astérix* was placed on the back cover of *Pilote* in issue 92 and appearing in individual albums from 1961, *Astérix*'s success gradually became a phenomenon.[28] Admittedly, Gaul was a more nuanced and highly charged topic. Yet it allowed a far greater scope in combining two viewpoints: that of the Gauls as "others," with the overriding authority of the ancient texts taken into consideration; and that of the Gauls with their own voice. The effect of this dual perspective was to yield some baffling and enjoyable results with respect to identity and perspective. A sophisticated plot went along with another trait of the comic strip's form, namely, the remarkable relation of words and images, where none gets precedence.[29] The medium perfectly suited the notion of *Astérix*, as the words that formed the very basis of the series, in themselves influenced by ancient texts, were actually put side by side with the graphic dimension that aimed to subvert their Greco-Roman-centered perspective.

Astérix is linked to the ancient ethnographic discourse in form and content. First, like ethnographic writing, comics share in the mental construction of a world, which has a "timeless present" as its dominant feature.[30] While ethnography aims to construct something close to a Weberian *Idealtypus* (ideal type), that is, an abstract notion, which aims to describe the common features of phenomena, especially regularities in a particular society,[31] in BD this effect is caused by the spatial layout of the panels (*mise en page*), so that a panel appears alongside other images and simultaneously with them.[32] In both media, occurrences within the "world" have an existence utterly detached from the time frame of the observer/reader and have a perfectly iterative trait.[33] Moreover, an ethnographic depiction, either within a narrative (as a digression) or on its own, involves an entry to a different world, a satellite structure or a peripheral world.[34] In BD, this peripheral world appears to be central, as its boundaries (the "peritext") are clearly marked. The main differences are that in comics, the metaphor of "world" becomes visual and concrete; and by including a story, the BD in fact becomes a hybrid between the satellite structure (i.e., digression) and the narrative.

Second, the ethnological descriptions of the ancients are employed in creating the particular imagery of *Astérix*. The comic strip clearly revolves around the classical accounts depicting

27. Hence the two moved from *Roman de Renart* to Roman Gaul. The decision came after running through the major periods in French history in chronological order. Later, Uderzo commented that fortunately, they were unaware of *Tororix* and *Aviorix*: "Le seul Gaulois que nous avions en mémoire était Vercingétorix" ("The only Gaul we had in memory was Vercingetorix"). See Guillaume (1987, 51–52); Gaumer and Moliterni (1994, 29).

28. See Gurgand (1966).

29. Bridgeman (2005, 131–132). In comics, the reader's eye constantly shifts between the graphic and the textual. Eisner (1985, 124–127); McCloud (1993, 72, 97, 101, 104); Miller (2008, 97–101).

30. On construction of a world, see Bridgeman (2005, 115–118). On the timeless present, see McCloud (1993, 103); see also Bridgeman (2005, 128): "Perpetually shifting *present*."

31. Hammersley and Atkinson (1983, 195–197).

32. Miller (2008, 82–83); Peeters (1991, 15).

33. In this respect, comics are closest to the visual medium of the frieze, which also has this specific timeless iterativity of occurrences. See McCloud (1993, 15) and Petersen (2011, 15) on Trajan's Column as a forerunner of the comic strip itself. Yet BD is far more developed in the ways it enables separate series of images to appear together.

34. Ryan (1992, 543–544).

Celts or Gauls, above all the five ancient portrayals of this ethnic group found in surviving texts: Diodorus (5.25–32), Strabo (4.4.2–6), Caesar (*De Bello Gallico* 6.11–28), Athenaeus (4.151e–152f, 154a–c), and Ammianus Marcellinus (15.9)—two Roman authors and three Greek imperial writers.[35] *Astérix* maintains many features of the ancient ethnographic portrayals of the Celts/Gauls, which may be regarded as the backbone of this fantasy world. For instance, the figures of the bard Assurancetourix (Cacofonix) and the Druid Panoramix (Getafix), among the first to be introduced to the series, are found in classical sources describing the Celtic society as divided into these classes of people.[36] A passage from Pliny the Elder (*HN* 16.95.251) may be read not only as providing the idea for the entire second album, *La serpe d'or* (1962), but indeed as the inspiration for the celebrated magic potion itself:

> *nihil habent Druidae—ita suos appellant magos—uisco et arbore, in qua gignatur, si modo sit robur, sacratius . . . sacerdos candida ueste cultus arborem scandit, falce aurea demetit, candido id excipitur sago . . . fecunditatem eo poto dari cuicumque animalium sterili arbitrantur, contra uenena esse omnia remedio.*

> The Druids—for that is the name they give to their magicians—held nothing more sacred than the mistletoe and the tree that bears it, supposing always that tree to be the oak. . . . Clad in a white robe the priest ascends the tree, and cuts the mistletoe with a golden sickle, which is received by others in a white cloak. . . . It is the belief with them that the mistletoe, taken in drink, will impart fecundity to all animals that are barren, and that it is an antidote for all poisons.[37]

Another detail from Caesar (*BG* 6.13), that the Druids assemble from everywhere at a certain time of the year, sets the scene for the album *Astérix et les Goths* (5.2–13.4).[38] The ancient sources specify the colorful (striped) clothes and horned helmets of the Gauls[39] and even their physical appearance—images that found their way to the BD series. One passage from Diodorus (5.28.3) about the mustache of the Gauls is extremely vivid; in fact, it is such a lively picture that it almost seems to require a graphic representation in the form of comics:

> οἱ δ' εὐγενεῖς τὰς μὲν παρειὰς ἀπολειαίνουσι, τὰς δ' ὑπήνας ἀνειμένας ἐῶσιν, ὥστε τὰ στόματα αὐτῶν ἐπικαλύπτεσθαι. διόπερ ἐσθιόντων μὲν αὐτῶν ἐμπλέκονται ταῖς τροφαῖς, πινόντων δὲ καθαπερεὶ διά τινος ἡθμοῦ φέρεται τὸ πόμα.

---

35. The historian and philosopher Posidonius was an important figure in expounding these descriptions. See Edelstein-Kidd frs. 53, 57, 64, 67, 68, 73, 75, 274; Tierney (1960); Nash (1976); Malitz (1983, 169–198); Kidd (1988, 308). On the ethnography of the Celts, see Kremer (1994, esp. 202–219, 266–273, 304–315).

36. The third group, that of the diviners, is represented only in the album *Le devin*. Strabo (4.4.4) claims that Druids and bards are held in exceptional honor; see Diod. Sic. 5.31.2; Athen. 6.246c; Caesar, *BG* 6.13. Pernoud (1957, 51–75).

37. On other practices of Druids to ward off diseases and dangers, see Plin. *HN* 24.103–104, 29.52. On the Druids, see Piggott (1968, 119–127); Rankin (1987, 270–281).

38. Kessler (1995, 29).

39. Caesar, *BG* 7.88; Diod. Sic. 5.30.2; Strabo 4.4.3.

the nobles shave their cheeks, but they let the mustache grow until it covers the mouth. Consequently, when they are eating, their mustaches become entangled in the food, and when they are drinking, the beverage passes, as it were, through a kind of a strainer.

The ancients were fascinated by the hair of the Gauls,[40] and in fact, the northern part of the country, farthest from Italy, was called by the Romans *Gallia Comata*, "Hairy Gaul." In the series, too, the hair and mustache are distinctive features of the Gaulish outward appearance.[41] Albeit in different media, both the ancient writers and the authors of *Astérix* aim at the pleasure of their respective readerships and share in the means of achieving enjoyment from outlandish images. Note that in this case, both Diodorus and the iconography of *Astérix* present iterative phenomena.

The large dinner party at the end of each album also has its origin in classical texts. Athenaeus (4.152a) describes the impressive banquets of the Celts, in which they "sit in a ring with the mightiest in the middle, like a chorus leader." The ring element is maintained (especially in the first albums of *Astérix*), though the socially unequal component mentioned by Athenaeus is not preserved, presumably for both artistic and ideological reasons in making Roman Gaul relevant for contemporary readership.[42] To be sure, the Gauls are all equally prone toward fighting with one another, a running gag and an indispensable part in the series, which also comes from the classical authors. Diodorus (5.28.5) characterizes them as querulous: "And it is their custom, even during the course of the meal, to seize upon any trivial matter as an occasion for keen disputation and then to challenge one another to single combat."[43] Concerning the argumentative feature of the Gauls, our sources have no argument. Strabo (4.4.6) agrees: "all Celts are given to strife."[44] And Ammianus (15.12.1) portrays the Gauls as "fond of quarrelling" (*auidi iurgiorum*). It is the graphic element in comics closely linked to the grotesque[45] that lends itself to present the ridiculous and the incredible mentioned in the textual sources and to complement them.

The fact that our heroes resort to aggression rather than persuasion and reasoning as a means to settle disputes is in accordance with the usual ethnographic portrayals of northern nations (from Arist., *Pol.* 7.1327b18–33 onward) as courageous but lacking in sense or

40. Strabo (4.4.3): The Gallic people "let their hair grow long, and wear tight breeches." See Livy 38.17 on lengthy hair and other features that betray softness and Gaulish weakness. The hair and mustache are echoed in the artistic portrayals of "the dying Gaul" and "the dying couple," originally part of a group in Pergamum. See Rankin (1987, 208). Translations of ancient passages are from the Loeb Classical Library.

41. In the first album (*Astérix le Gaulois* 11.2–20.3), the Roman soldier chosen to infiltrate the village (Caligula Minus) is careful to put on his false hair and mustache. The same gag appears in *Le bouclier Arverne* 25.7–27.2.

42. On an ideology of solidarity and community in the strip, see Miller (2008, 157). But see Goscinny's interview in *L'Express*, July 27–28, 1974, pp. 9–60; see also Nye (1980, 188), Dandridge (2008, 80).

43. εἰώθασι δὲ καὶ παρὰ τὸ δεῖπνον ἐκ τῶν τυχόντων πρὸς τὴν διὰ τῶν λόγων ἅμιλλαν καταστάντες, ἐκ προκλήσεως μονομαχεῖν πρὸς ἀλλήλους. The single combat features as the subject of an entire album, *Le combat des chefs* (6.8).

44. ὅτι πάντες Κελτοὶ φιλόνεικοί (v.l. ἡδόνεικοί) τέ εἰσι.

45. Petersen (2011, 30–35).

wisdom.[46] Undeniably, the characters, except for the Druid and Asterix himself, are not depicted as particularly bright.[47] An image that highlights this trait and is used throughout the series (as another running gag) ultimately originated in Ptolemy's account and is found in Strabo's depiction (7.3.8). It tells of a group of Celts that encountered Alexander near the Danube and responded to his question that they feared nothing at all, not even the Macedonian king, except the sky falling on their heads:

φησὶ δὲ Πτολεμαῖος ὁ Λάγου κατὰ ταύτην τὴν στρατείαν συμμῖξαι τῷ Ἀλεξάνδρῳ Κελτοὺς τοὺς περὶ τὸν Ἀδρίαν φιλίας καὶ ξενίας χάριν, δεξάμενον δὲ αὐτοὺς φιλοφρόνως τὸν βασιλέα ἐρέσθαι ... τί μάλιστα εἴη ὃ φοβοῖντο, νομίζοντα αὐτὸν ἐρεῖν: αὐτοὺς δ᾽ ἀποκρίνασθαι ὅτι οὐδὲν πλὴν εἰ ἄρα μὴ ὁ οὐρανὸς αὐτοῖς ἐπιπέσοι

Ptolemy, the son of Lagus, says that on this expedition the Celti who lived about the Adriatic joined Alexander for the sake of establishing friendship and hospitality, and that the king received them kindly and asked them ... what it was that they most feared, thinking they would say himself, but that they replied they feared no one, unless it were that Heaven might fall on them[48]

It is interesting that just as in the original classical context, it is the Gauls in *Astérix* who are generally seen as describing this anxiety in their own voice. The chief exponent in displaying this fear is the chief himself. The custom of raising Abraracourcix (= Vitalstatistix) on a shield goes back to a depiction of Tacitus (*Hist.* 4.15) as part of a German coronation ceremony,[49] although it may be the case that the direct influence on the authors was the appearance of the custom in depictions of the Frankish kings and Napoleon I (and a caricature by Honoré Daumier).[50] In presenting the quarrelsome Gallic habits, the ancients sometimes turn to the bizarre, thereby laying the basis for a graphic presentation. Ammianus speaks of a woman fighting better than a man (15.12):

Nec enim eorum quemquam adhibita uxore rixantem, multo fortiore et glauca, peregrinorum ferre poterit globus, tum maxime cum illa inflata ceruice suffrendens

46. As opposed to people of the eastern nations, who are wise but are effeminate cowards. See *Airs, Waters, and Places* 22.

47. As observed by Derrrick de Kerckhove during the Celtic Consciousness Symposium in February 1978 in Toronto and quoted in Clark (2004). See Hampton (2001, 34). See Strabo 4.4.2: "otherwise [they are] simple" (ἄλλως δὲ ἁπλοῦν); also 4.4.5.

48. See also Arr., *Anab.* 1.4.7. See Hampton (2001, 2–6, 33). This passage may be the result of a misunderstanding of a proverbial phrase to express the eternal length of a fulfillment of a vow or of a rule, i.e., as long as heaven would not fall and the earth would not open; see Piggott (1968, 126–127) and Jackson (1964).

49. Concerning Brinno, chief of the Cananefates: *igitur ipso rebellis familiae nomine placuit impositusque scuto more gentis et sustinentium umeris uibratus dux deligitur* ("His very name, the name of a family of rebels, made him popular. Raised aloft on a shield after the national fashion, and balanced on the shoulders of the bearers, he was chosen general"). See Ammianus 20.4.17 on Julian.

50. See Teitler (2002, 501–502), who dwells on Abraracourcix in an article devoted to the practice. See also Stoll (1974, 87).

ponderansque niueas ulnas et uastas admixtis calcibus emittere coeperit pugnos ut catapultas tortilibus neruis excussas.

A whole band of foreigners will be unable to cope with one of them in a fight, if he calls in his wife, stronger than he by far and with flashing eyes; then [= *tum*], especially when she swells her neck and gnashes her teeth, and poising her huge white arms, proceeds to rain punches mingled with kicks, like shots discharged by the twisted cords of a catapult.[51]

Principally, this passage has many components of comics:[52] it is not only the caricaturistic depiction[53] but also the elements of sequence and intervals (fight with a Gaul/description of the wife, description of her way of fighting). Note the *tum*, which may function as the gutter, the space visible between the frames, which both separates and connects closely related scenes.[54] The description necessitates a filling of this gap analogous to the one involved in the reading of comics (i.e., the transition from a fight with a Gaul to a fight with his wife). It also calls for a visual closure, which is already given in the graphic medium.[55] Its ethnographic-iterative aspect is close to the "timeless present" of comics mentioned above.

The transition from a textual form into a graphic construct can be seen as a reversal of media comparable to the one occurring in an *ekphrasis* depiction.[56] The visual trait latent in the texts is realized in the ostensible presentation of pictures. Yet while the ancients meant to scoff at the objects of the scenes, that is, the barbarians, Goscinny and Uderzo have an additional element of mocking the texts and images of ancient Greco-Roman literature themselves, by representing certain motifs as absurd, such as the Gauls' physical appearance. A consensus among ancient writers depicts them as beautiful and immensely elevated or big. Diodorus (5.28.1) claims that "the Gauls are tall of body,"[57] and Strabo (4.4.2) asserts that "as for their might, it arises partly from their large physique,"[58] while Ammianus (15.12.1) maintains that "almost all the Gauls are of tall stature and fair."[59] This representation of the Gauls' huge dimensions is not discarded through the figure of Obelix but is made to be literally adopted from the ancients

51. See also Diod. Sic. 5.32.2: αἱ δὲ γυναῖκες τῶν Γαλατῶν οὐ μόνον τοῖς μεγέθεσι παραπλήσιοι τοῖς ἀνδράσιν εἰσίν, ἀλλὰ καὶ ταῖς ἀλκαῖς ἐνάμιλλοι ("The women of the Gauls ... are a match for them in courage as well"). See Strabo 4.4.3 on the exchange of roles between men and women. On the bravery of Celtic women, see Paus. 10.23.7–8. See Rankin (1987, 245–258).

52. In fact, this particular theme of women fighting was a picture picked up for *Astérix* in the album *Le devin* (43.8–44.3).

53. Isaac (2004, 425): "this reads like a caricature."

54. Eisner (1985, 47).

55. McCloud (1993, 63, 68, 73, 82, 89).

56. For instance, the prologue to Longus' *Daphnis and Chloe*, where the narrator describes a painting adorned with a story of love and his decision to relate it. See also the picture described in Lucian's *Hercules*, in a Celtic context. Goscinny and Uderzo sometimes include reliefs of a frieze in several panels, which spell a return to a form of sequential art current in the days of our heroes. In one of these reliefs, the authors appear subduing a bull (presumably insinuating the Herculean task involved in creating *Astérix*; see Kessler 1995, 24) and respectively expressing the negative Greek words *despotes* and *tyrannos* (*Astérix aux Jeux olympiques* 29.10).

57. οἱ δὲ Γαλάται τοῖς μὲν σώμασίν εἰσιν εὐμήκεις.

58. τῆς δὲ βίας τὸ μὲν ἐκ τῶν σωμάτων ἐστὶ μεγάλων ὄντων; see also Polyb. 2.15.7.

59. *celsioris staturae et candidi paene Galli sunt omnes.*

and ridiculed, by distancing the large physique from being a symbol of beauty and casting it oftentimes as ludicrous.[60] Notwithstanding the derivation of his name from the typographical symbol or critical mark *obelisk*, corresponding to *Astérix/asterisk*, the name is also a play on the mighty pillar, and these features are surely not accidental.[61]

The adventures are focalized from the perspective of the Gauls and not from that of the Romans, in contradistinction with the actual Celts, who barely gave us evidence of their outlook and left us no examples of their "voice" regarding their clash with Roman might.[62] This fact opens the floor for an important transformation, which a medium like comics can achieve. In *Astérix*, Roman customs and notions such as military maneuvers or other Latin concepts are not immediately self-understood and have to be clarified explicitly to the audience by the narrator (or a delegated narrator) in the box of the *récitatif* or by the figures themselves.[63] Utilizing the juxtaposition of text and picture, Goscinny and Uderzo insert well-known Latin phrases in a manner that gives them an esoteric status. In the very first images of the series (later in the album *Astérix le Gaulois* 5.10; see figure 7.1), one of Roman soldiers bashed by Asterix says the words *uae uictis* ("woe to the vanquished"), which are claimed to have been first uttered not by a Roman but by Brennus, chieftain of the Gallic tribe the Senones during the Gallic sack of Rome (Livy 5.48). Although they still refer to a humiliation to Romans caused by a Gaul, the circumstances are different. In the same panel, an allusion to Naevius' famous epitaph that the Romans will forget how to speak Latin[64] is attributed to the harshness of Asterix's bashing. The presence of these allusions cannot be denied and is not accidental. Not only does the new text of *Astérix* absorb earlier textual references and expressions, but an entirely new world is invented as their context. A recurrent use of this device is seen in the sayings of the old pirate Triple Patte (Pegleg), much to the dismay of the captain (e.g., *Astérix et Cléopâtre* 10.7; *La zizanie* 11.4–5; *La grande traversée* 13.3–4). Here the very relevance of these Latin citations to the situation at hand (or indeed of Latin to everyday life) is put into question.[65]

---

60. In this way also adopting the aesthetic taste of the Gauls while distancing this figure from his ancient ancestors, for Strabo claims explicitly (4.4.6, from Ephorus): "they endeavor not to grow fat or pot-bellied and any young man who exceeds the standard measure of the girdle is punished" (ἀσκεῖν γὰρ αὐτοὺς μὴ παχεῖς εἶναι μηδὲ προγάστορας, τὸν δ᾽ ὑπερβαλλόμενον τῶν νέων τὸ τῆς ζώνης μέτρον ζημιοῦσθαι).

61. In *Astérix et Cléopâtre* (26.6, 48.7), Obelix even wishes to bring home an obelisk. The play is even more insightful, when we recall that in ancient Greek, ὀβελός (*obelos*) means "roasting spit" (LSJ, s.v., A.1), quite in character with the gluttonous desires of this figure.

62. For Celtic inscriptions, see Lambert (1994, 20–21, 71–79, 122–125, 150–172).

63. On Roman concepts, e.g., in *Astérix et Cléopâtre* 39.4, and *Astérix et les Normands* 27.4, see Nye (1980, 190–191). On the *récitatif* and delegated narrator, see Peeters (1991, 86); Miller (2008, 97, 100, 108, 120). Amusingly, when Gallic customs, such as the single battle of chieftains (*Le combat des chefs* 6.8), are expounded, it is because the perspective momentarily changed from that of the Gauls to that of Romano-Gauls, in an album where a sense of belonging is constantly in flux.

64. Gell., *NA* 1.24.2: *Immortales mortales si foret fas flere flerent donc Camenae Naeuium poetam. Itaque postquamst Orchi tradius thesauro, obliti sunt Romae loquier lingua latina* ("If it were right for the immortal ones to mourn for mortals, then for the poet Naevius would mourn the Goddesses of Song. And so when unto Death's own treasure-house he was delivered, Romans no longer did remember how to speak the Latin tongue"). The allusion is not preserved in the English translation shown here.

65. Dinter (2011, 187). This figure, like all the pirate characters in *Astérix*, is in fact a parody of another comic strip appearing in *Pilote, Barbe-Rouge* (*Redbeard*) by Jean-Michel Charlier and Victor Hubinon. The original figure

FIGURE 7.1 Latin phrases recontextualized in *Asterix the Gaul* 5.10 (1961). Art by Albert Uderzo.

Ils sont fous ces Romains ("These Romans are crazy"), Obelix's celebrated expression repeated throughout the series, testifies to the fact that the Gauls are providing the norm, by supplying the criteria to judge the Romans.[66] Occasionally, it is accompanied by a graphic presentation of a metalepsis (or a violation of narrative levels) in the form of a breach of the fourth wall, in a direct address of one figure to the readers—a breach that is consistent with the type of break that BD series display from the ancient texts.[67] The Gauls are also seen as tourists in other lands, holding a key position in evaluating other ethnic groups, which are presented as *fous*.[68] The reversal of viewpoint from that of the classical texts is evident in the fact that the Gauls are not explicitly presented as barbarians.[69] This category is relegated in the comic strip to others, particularly the Goths, who are depicted in an unflattering manner (*Astérix et les Goths* 35.4). Interestingly enough, like Caesar, who, for his own reasons, draws a boundary between Romans, Gauls, and Germans,[70] *Astérix* adopts this unique three-way ethnography from its very first panels (*Astérix le Gaulois* 5.3). Moreover, while ironically applying the very criteria that Greek authors used to portray the Celts, the Gauls deem themselves even better than the Hellenes, as when chief Abraracourcix/Vitalstatistix asks his men not to mock the Greeks, who unfortunately *n'ont pas notre passé glorieux et notre culture* ("do not have our glorious past and cultural heritage," *Astérix aux Jeux olympiques* 22.1). Goscinny and Uderzo's play with

in the other strip was that of Redbeard's right-hand man, who utters scholarly remarks. For instance, see the first album, *Le démon des Caraïbes* (1959), 19.5. See Gaumer and Moliterni (1994, 43–44).

66. The phrase appears for the first time in *Astérix Gladiateur* 28.7.

67. On the metaleptic breach of the diegetic world in BD, see Miller (2008, 134–138).

68. For instance, *Astérix et Cléopâtre* 15.10; *Astérix aux Jeux olympiques* 44.7; *Astérix chez les Belges* 19.9. The Gauls themselves are described this way; e.g., *La grande traversée* 26.12, 38.11; see Stoll (1974, 88–91).

69. Even though there is solidarity among the non-Romans. see *Le domaine des dieux* 19.8–20.8, 25.3–9. A celebration of the "anniversary of the battle of Gergovia" is an occasion that provides an opportunity for a reunion of all the "others," that is, all the rebellious groups in other countries, such as Britain, Spain, Helvetia, and others (*Astérix en Corse* 9.1–16.2); Clark (2004).

70. Riggsby (2006, 50–51, 65–67).

Greco-Roman precepts and views thus essentially involves the preservation of the content of the ancient texts with a complete transformation of its context and perspective along with the medium that conveys it. Yet this applies to the very reversal of perspective itself. We should note in particular the description of Diodorus (5.31.1) that the Gauls are arrogant with respect to other groups:

πολλὰ δὲ λέγοντες ἐν ὑπερβολαῖς ἐπ᾽ αὐξήσει μὲν ἑαυτῶν, μειώσει δὲ τῶν ἄλλων.

they like to talk in superlatives, to the end that they may extol themselves and depreciate all other men.[71]

So what seems to be subversive turns out to be traditional after all and perfectly in tune with ancient sources ... or is it?

Corresponding to the way the Gauls defy the Roman army within the series, Goscinny and Uderzo themselves struggle to challenge the authority of the classical texts both in the graphic layout and in the plot and storyline.[72] The childlike stature of Asterix is a case in point. In contrast to the dimensions of Obelix, Asterix's image appears to deliberately subvert the Greek and Latin picture of the Gauls as huge.[73] Contrary to the depiction of promiscuous and public displays of sexual intercourse among the Gauls,[74] Asterix and Obelix do not share their lives with women.[75] In the BD series, human sacrifice and cruel ceremonies, which according to classical writers were practiced by the Celts,[76] are said to be relevant to either the Romans (the gladiatorial games, e.g., *Astérix Gladiateur* 40.8–9; *Astérix le Gaulois* 48; *Les lauriers de César* 36.9–40.8), the Goths (*Astérix et les Goths* 39.3), the Vikings (*La grande traversée* 44.2), or the Egyptians (*Astérix et Cléopâtre* 13.3, 29.7); although the threat is made, it is never carried out in actual fact.[77] Surely, it is no accident that the latter three groups habitually have a different style of script in their speech bubbles (e.g., Gothic or hieroglyphics), denoting their utter "otherness."[78] Similarly, it is the Normans who drink from skulls (*Astérix et les Normands* 10.3, 16.1) and not the Gauls, as the ancients would have them.[79] One may even speak of a mirror image (if not a Bizarro World) that *Astérix* sets up against the ancient texts. As the story of the

71. See also Diod. 5.32.4: they "regard all men with contempt" (καταφρονεῖν ἁπάντων).

72. This is clearly seen in the visual side, when well-known Greek and Roman works of art are grotesquely caricatured; e.g., "Diana on the hunt" (*Astérix chez les Bretons* 25.4).

73. For Goscinny's insistence on this portrayal, see du Chatenet et al. (2003, 116).

74. Diod. Sic. 5.32.7; Caesar *BG* 5.14.

75. Except for the infatuation that Asterix and Obelix experience in *Astérix Legionnaire* (2.2, 7.8, 11.9–12, 12.1–4, 48.6–7) or *Le devin* (20.3). This feature has probably more to do with the 1949 French law governing children's literature, especially article 2. See Dandridge (2008, 18–21) and Goscinny's interview in Manson (1966).

76. For example, Diodorus (5.31.3) claims: "they devote to death a human being and plunge a dagger into him . . . when the stricken victim has fallen they read the future from the manner of his fall and from the twitching of his limbs." See also Caesar *BG* 6.16; Athen. 4.160e; Luc. 1.444–446. See Rankin (1987, 264–265, 285).

77. Nye (1980, 187).

78. Kessler (1995, 79–81). See also Miller (2008, 99) on the function of non-Roman script in BD.

79. See Livy 23.24 on the head of the Roman general Postumius. On head trophies collected by Gauls, see Strabo 4.4.5.

first album unfolds, the Druid Panoramix dupes the Romans into believing that the brew they obtain by deceit is the magic potion, while in effect he provides them with a false one, which causes them not to be stronger but rather to grow hair instantly and continuously. In the new Gallia Comata, it is the Romans who have become hairy barbarians.

Meanwhile, something happens to Caesar in the transition from being the writer of an authoritative classical text to being a character in the fictional world based on it, a process that makes him a pivotal figure in the representation of the status of classical sources in *Astérix*. His supreme authority is largely accepted, making him appear as a presidential figure in the comic strip,[80] almost a fatherly figure. He is mocked[81] but never really hated by the Gauls. Nevertheless, his attempt to conquer the insubordinate village is denied. One would assume that he is acknowledged as a text but resisted as a figure. An example for this is the famous assertion of Caesar, at the beginning of the *De Bello Gallico* (1.1), that the ethnic group of Belgians is the bravest (*horum omnium fortissimi sunt Belgae*; see also 8.54 and Strabo 4.4.3). The Gauls' response is to initiate clashes with the Roman soldiers, an activity shared by both them and the Belgians, and invite Caesar himself to act as referee to determine which group is braver (*Astérix chez les Belges* 36.8–37.4). Here the authority of Caesar's description in creating images and attitudes by his words is accepted, but his specific portrayal is challenged. The megalomania of this figure is seen either in his metaleptic self-reference to his works (the *commentarii*) or to his commentator position as ostensibly overriding the framing story of the series (a case of *mise en abyme*).[82] His effort to set up a standard, with variations to his own aphorisms (e.g., *ueni, uedi, uici*, *Astérix chez les Belges* 30.8–9; *Le bouclier Arverne* 47.4; *Astérix Gladiateur* 42.1), often results in undermining his own authority as a text.

Caesar provides a point in which the comic strip may even interchange with the original classical text. In *La zizanie* (6.6), he declares that the Gauls could not be bought off, because *L'or n'intéresse pas ces barbares. Sinon, ça fait longtemps que la potion serait dans le commerce!* ("These barbarians are not interested in money. If they were, the magic potion would have been on the market long ago!"). But in fact, in the special section on Gauls in *De Bello Gallico* (6.24), the *real* Caesar actually has quite the opposite claim: *Gallis autem prouinciarum propinquitas et transmarinarum rerum notitia multa ad copiam atque usus largitur, paulatim adsuefacti superari multisque uicti proeliis ne se quidem ipsi cum illis uirtute comparant* ("Upon the Gauls, however, the neighborhood of our provinces and acquaintance with overseas commodities lavishes many articles of use or luxury; little by little they have grown accustomed to defeat, and after being conquered in many battles they do not even compare themselves in point of valor with the Germans").[83] In this passage, Caesar actually views the Gauls as corruptible and weak because of the effect of the Romans. A reader would have expected him to

---

80. Woolf (2007, 177). Yet see Clark (2004) for an interpretation that the stories reflect the French dislike for authority figures.

81. *Ces Gaulois me ridiculisent* (*Obélix et Compagnie*, 12.2).

82. *Le domaine des dieux* 5.1. On *mise en abyme* in BD, see Miller (2008, 139–141).

83. Strabo 4.1.11, 4.4.2, on the difference between Germans and Gauls because of Roman influence and conquest. On Gauls as great lovers of money, see Diod. Sic. 5.27, Polyb. 2.7.5.

voice quite a different depiction in Book 6, corresponding to his other statements in which he extols his enemies and therefore himself as a military leader,[84] while not portraying Roman civilization as a corrupting force.[85] Conversely, *Astérix* consistently presents a recurrent theme of Roman decadence sweeping Latinized Gauls (*Obélix et Compagnie* 13.1–4; *Les lauriers de César* 8.5–9, 9.1–10; *Le combat des chefs* 5.1–4, 7.3–6, 8.1–5). An entire album has as its theme an attempt to show how a plan close to the real Caesar's depiction in this passage is implemented and almost succeeds in corrupting the Gauls (*Obélix et Compagnie*, especially 12.5–8, 33.2–3). Thus, it is as if the two passages of *Astérix* and of the text of Julius Caesar have traded places.

The medium of comics, placed between the written and the graphic and defined by the special relations between word and image,[86] can be described as a liminal art that depicts liminal heroes and is in some sense located at the thresholds of several worlds. As such, it perfectly matches the ancient ethnographic imagery of Gauls as transformed in the series. By possessing extraordinary powers that assist them in their insubordination toward the Romans, the Gauls only confirm the impression of the ancient authors that the barbarians step outside mankind. The temporary superhuman strength of the Gauls makes them nonhuman, in a sense. As the ancients compared the Celts to wild beasts,[87] there is a very thin line between the two groups of nonhuman entities.[88] The existence of the magical potion of the Gauls only corroborates the Romans' fears of the power exerted by the Druids, a belief that eventually led to abolishing their form of religion from Augustus to Claudius.[89] Moreover, the Gauls reside on the shore, which is a place of geographical marginality, almost at the end of the known world; this is another theme that recurs in ancient ethnography depicting the barbarians at the margins.[90] In some respects, the Armorican village is in another space, between the land and the sea. For the Romans, it is a land beyond their political and cultural reach, signaling a passage to another

84. Extolling his enemies, for example, on the *Nervii*: *BG* 2.15.5 (*hominess feri magnaeque uirtutis*, "savage men of great courage/virtue"), 2.27.5 (*tantae uirtutis hominis*, "of the greatest courage/virtue"; *quae facilia ex difficillimis animi magnitude redegerat*, "with a greatness of heart they rendered difficult things easy"). See Rankin (1987, 132). On an appraisal of the Gauls' discipline and fight for freedom, see 3.8.4, 7.4.10, 7.5.1, 7.89. See, however, 7.42.2. Roman civilization is said to be preferred to Gaulish barbarism at 7.77. On the different tone in the "formal ethnologia" of *BG* 6, see Sherwin-White (1967, 25–29). The boundary between Gauls and Germans is not always clear-cut (*BG* 4.3.3). See Schadee (2008, 169, 176–178).

85. See Riggsby (2006) on the manner in which Caesar shows the Gauls' success to depend only on their ability to imitate the Romans and fight the Roman way (96–100, 125) and on the Gauls' aptitude to assimilate (68–69).

86. See McCloud (1993, 46–47, 92, 96–97, 138–161) on the language of comics as composed of pictures and words, both "showing" and "telling." see also Fresnault-Deruelle (1972, 41–48); Eisner (1985, 10–24, 26–27); Masson (1985, 50–110, esp. 83–95).

87. Diod. Sic. (5.29.5) writes: "to continue to fight against one of our own race, after he is dead, is to descend to the level of beasts" (τὸ πολεμεῖν τὸ ὁμόφυλον τετελευτηκὸς θηριῶδες). See also Dion. Hal., *Exc.* 14.10.1.17, 2.18; and Wiedemann (1986).

88. Wiedemann (1986, 190, 196).

89. Pliny, *HN* 30.13.4; Suet. *Claud.* 25. See Piggott (1968, 127–130).

90. See Wiedemann (1986, 190). Surprisingly, there is not so much on this in Romm (1992, 12–13), but see 156–171 on the western horizon as an area most distanced from Rome: a new world or a ground for an escapist flight. The choice of place for *Astérix* was deliberate: either echoing Uderzo's own escape to Brittany during the war or a location from which the characters could travel by sea; see Kessler (1995, 11).

sphere. Indeed, in one of the adventures, Asterix and Obelix are traveling beyond the boundaries of the known world, to America, where no Romans can be found (*La grande traversée* 24.5, 27.9). The Gauls thus act as a bridge to the "other" world and partially belong to it.

Paradoxically, the protagonists of the story belong to the Roman world in their very defiance of it. For instance, the only way our heroes could participate in the Olympic Games and spite a Roman soldier is by acknowledging that they are Romans (*Astérix aux Jeux olympiques* 13.8–9, 14.1–9). If the Romans, in their self-presentation, can pretend to be associated with the Greeks and so participate in the sacred games, why could the Gauls not act as if they were Romans? The inclusion of the Romans in the games was in fact grounded in their power over the Greeks. Why could this power not include the Gauls and so ultimately beat the Romans at their own game? Romanization was never that much fun! An implicit clever allusion, which is spelled out in the translations, appears at the beginning of the album *La serpe d'or* (5.3). The bard is seen teaching some children at school. His question "Into how many parts is Gaul divided?" sets a context for his math class and the writing on the rock ("III + I = IV").[91] It is supposed to allude to the famous beginning of the *De Bello Gallico*, and enlarge on it, to the effect that Gaul is essentially divided into four parts (figure 7.2). The assertion both accepts Caesar's dictum (*Gallia est omnis diuisa in partes tres*) and is disharmonious with the original text through an addition, implying that the fourth part is the famous village, impenetrable by Caesar (the figure within the series). In adopting both perspectives at once, Assurancetourix (or Cacofonix) is being multivoiced (or polyphonic).

From the very second panel on the first page of *Astérix* and the very first gag, in which the defeated Vercingetorix lays his arms "on" and not "at" Caesar's feet (*Astérix le Gaulois* 5.2), it is clear that while still moving within the framework of classical texts and connotations, the world of the BD series gives an intentionally distorted image of the ancient outlook. *Astérix* requires the ancient Greek and Roman sources as a premise for the construction of its world and, as we have seen, remarkably follows them on many points of content. Yet in the format of comics, these texts undergo a transformation that not only visualizes them but also turns the classical expressions into speech bubbles, takes them out of their original context, and alters them. The imaginary world of Roman Gaul in *Astérix* is built as a juncture of two viewpoints: classical literature, in which Gauls are depicted as representing the barbaric way of life, and a reverse position, in which the Gauls have a voice and treat Romans and various ethnic groups as "others." The meeting ground is the ethnographic plane. Goscinny and Uderzo both defy and accept the classical tradition and in so doing introduce a completely new ethnographic portrayal of the Gauls. Rather than merely perceiving of the Gauls as barbarians, the characters are depicted in a way that effects an intensified identification with them from the readers. This portrayal generates a new type of Gauls in *Astérix*, in which the notion of otherness is harder to pin down. This fact may account for the universal appeal of the series, across nations, races and age groups, and may also provide a sense of continuity between the historic Gauls and modern BD readers. Thus, ethnography or ethnographic depictions as developed by ancient authors and transformed by the format of BD provide one of the possible links between comics and classics.

---

91. See Miller (2008, 158) on the bafflement of the schoolchildren in the scene.

FIGURE 7.2 Caesar's geography is skewed in *Asterix and the Golden Sickle* 5.3 (1962). Art by Albert Uderzo.

Appendix: *Astérix* Albums (1961–1979)

Asterix the Gaul (*Astérix le Gaulois*), 1961.

Asterix and the Golden Sickle (*La serpe d'or*), 1962.

Asterix and the Goths (*Astérix et les Goths*), 1963.

Asterix the Gladiator (*Astérix Gladiateur*), 1964.

Asterix and the Banquet (*Le tour de Gaule d'Astérix*), 1965.

Asterix and Cleopatra (*Astérix et Cléopâtre*), 1965.

Asterix and the Big Fight (*Le combat des chefs*), 1966.

Asterix in Britain (*Astérix chez les Bretons*), 1966.

Asterix and the Normans (*Astérix et les Normands*), 1966.

Asterix the Legionary (*Astérix Légionnaire*), 1967.

Asterix and the Chieftain's Shield (*Le bouclier Arverne*), 1968.

Asterix at the Olympic Games (*Astérix aux Jeux olympiques*), 1968.

Asterix and the Cauldron (*Astérix et le chaudron*), 1969.

Asterix in Spain (*Astérix en Hispanie*), 1969.

Asterix and the Roman Agent (*La zizanie*), 1970.

Asterix in Switzerland (*Astérix chez les Helvètes*), 1970.

The Mansions of the Gods (*Le domaine des dieux*), 1971.

Asterix and the Laurel Wreath (*Les lauriers de César*), 1972.

Asterix and the Soothsayer (*Le devin*), 1972.

Asterix in Corsica (*Astérix en Corse*), 1973.

Asterix and Caesar's Gift (*Le cadeau de César*), 1974.

Asterix and the Great Crossing (*La grande traversée*), 1975.

Asterix Conquers Rome (*Les 12 travaux d'Asterix*), 1976 (usually excluded from the canonical list of *Astérix* volumes).

Obelix and Co. (*Obélix et Compagnie*), 1976.

Asterix in Belgium (*Astérix chez les Belges*), 1979.

8

Astérix and the Dream of Autochthony

Stuart Barnett

Truth to tell, the best weapon against myth is perhaps to mythify it in its turn, and to produce an artificial myth: and this reconstituted myth will in fact be a mythology. Since myth robs language of something, why not rob myth?
ROLAND BARTHES, *Mythologies*

To discuss *Astérix* in the anglophone world by necessity requires a certain amount of introduction and contextualization. While *Astérix* has achieved a certain amount of popularity in the United Kingdom, the series remains virtually unknown in the United States. This is all the more remarkable in that the authors of the series, René Goscinny and Albert Uderzo, are, thanks to *Astérix*, France's best-selling authors outside of France (Shirbon 2009). While this topic deserves its own separate treatment, it is noted here to explain what might strike those readers more familiar with *Astérix* as self-evident.

Astérix written by Goscinny and illustrated by Uderzo, is in the medium of the *bande dessinée*, a distinct comic art form very popular in Europe. Each volume is a continuous narrative, typically around fifty pages in length and in a larger format than US-style comics (usually, in paperback, 28.6 cm x 21.6 cm, or 11¼ x 8½ in.). The series began with *Asterix the Gaul* (1961; English 1969) and was an instant hit. Each book outsold the previous one in ever-increasing numbers (to eventually sell altogether more than 325 million copies), so that by 1966, the cover of *L'Express* could herald "le phénomène Astérix." Together, Goscinny and Uderzo published twenty-five volumes from 1961 to 1977, managing two volumes a year at their peak. (Following the death of Goscinny in 1977, Uderzo continued the series on his own, producing eight volumes in addition to two volumes of short stories.) The *Astérix* comics clearly touched a cultural nerve, with stories of plucky resistance to all-but-total domination. The reason for the hunger for something like *Astérix* in France is explained in part by the fact that before *Astérix*, the field of French comics was dominated by comics imported from the United States

I dedicate this essay to the memory of my mother, Regina Prestel (a native Bavarian, she would take me to Germany to visit family; thanks to her, I experienced the height of the *Astérix* craze in Germany in the 1970s). And to Hermann Steinhauser, my own Majestix.

and the French-speaking part of Belgium. As a result, there was no truly successful indigenous French comic—and certainly not one capable of being successfully exported. Thus, *Astérix* quickly became a point of French pride, an act of cultural reappropriation and repatriation of the medium of comics that, moreover, struck a chord internationally, with translation into more than one hundred languages.[1]

The basic context of the *Astérix* series is fairly straightforward and is established with an opening page that is reproduced in each volume. This page informs us: "The year is 50 B.C. Gaul is entirely occupied by the Romans. Well, not entirely . . . One small village of indomitable Gauls still holds out against the invaders." This small village on the coast of Brittany in France is able to hold out against the Romans because their Druid Getafix is able to brew a magic potion that temporarily bestows superhuman strength. The diminutive eponymous hero of the series, Asterix, defends the village by means of cunning and the magic potion. His constant companion in the series is Obelix, who, while certainly not characterized by anything remotely resembling cunning, is endowed permanently with superhuman powers as a result of falling into the magic potion as a baby.

One of the key reasons for the great appeal of *Astérix* is the notion of a small group being able to resist domination by an extremely powerful foreign people. As such, *Astérix* engages with what I term the myth of the origin of the pure native. By this I mean a point in the past when a people was characterized by a purity uncontaminated by influence from any other group or people—in other words, the point of origin of an autochthonous people. The desire to make distinctions, to demarcate one people from another, has been in full evidence in Europe since the breakup of the Soviet Union. And the more there are mechanisms such as the European Union to create such transnational entities as "the European," the more there will be counter-reactions insisting on the pure native. Indeed, the greater the perceived threat of the nonnative, the stronger the recourse to the concept of the pure native. As it is so difficult to deny the hybrid nature of any people in a contemporary context, the notion of the pure native usually is pushed into the distant past. This same myth of purity and distinction is all too eagerly seized upon as the sole meaning of *Astérix*. It holds forth the dream—despite the opposition of an overwhelming might—of an autochthonous people. Thus, *Astérix* can function as the model of resistance to anything with perceived imperial ambitions such as the United States or the European Union.[2] Following the logic of the origin, moreover, *Astérix* is taken to encourage the belief in a native purity untainted by what it denounces as nonnative.

Before proceeding with an analysis of how these ideas are worked out within *Asterix*, a brief consideration of the notion of autochthony itself will be useful. Autochthony has a long conceptual history, from the ancient Athenians to the work of Martin Heidegger. While the present study concerns itself with the Romans portrayed in *Astérix*, it is worth noting the vital role the notion played in Greek antiquity. Autochthony (literally, "born of the earth or soil") was crucial to the self-understanding of the Athenians. Other city-states, it was argued, were

---

1. See Miller (2008); McKinney (2008); and the marvelous reception study specific to *Astérix* by Dandridge (2008).

2. See Wall (2005) for a nuanced exploration of the relation of *Astérix* to globalization. For a discussion of Asterix, globalization, and Franco-American relations, see Vines (2010). Also intriguing is Ehrhart (2000), which is a quite serious policy paper examining France's relation to NATO that frames its presentation in terms of Asterix's "quarrel with the Roman Empire."

the result of conquest or immigration and intermingling. The Athenians, by contrast, were a people born from the soil and thus a more authentic and pure people best suited both to self-govern and to govern.[3] Remarkably, the very same vocabulary and argumentation associated with the term *autochthony* are in evidence in contemporary political struggles, particularly in Africa (notably in Rwanda, the Democratic Republic of the Congo, and the Ivory Coast). Even more remarkably, similar patterns of thought surface in European rightist anti-immigration parties (Geschiere 2009). Indeed, globalization would seem to be the generative force behind autochthony—which, in turn, forms as an inverse and necessary response to interaction with the Other. The present examination of these stories of an indomitable Gallic village seeks to outline how *Astérix* participates in and furthers the traditional notions of autochthony by resisting and, paradoxically, colluding with the invading forces.

Even Better Than the Real Thing

Despite the series being placed in a specific historical context, it would seem that what is at stake in *Astérix* is not a verifiable cultural and historical past but the assemblage of received ideas about this cultural and historical past that exist and are at work in the present.[4] This is an important distinction. In their unusual apology to the English in *Asterix in Britain* (1966; English 1970), Goscinny and Uderzo reveal something very profound about the entire series: "when it comes to presenting this skit on the British to the British, we feel we owe them a word or two of explanation. Our little cartoon stories do not make fun of the real thing, but the ideas of the real thing that people get into their heads, i.e., clichés" (*Asterix in Britain* 2). This is a crucial point if one wants to understand the entire series: *Astérix* is not about the "real thing." It is not about any specific people or historical events. It is about the ideas we have about these things. This strategy broaches what Roland Barthes defined as mythology. Goscinny and Uderzo are interacting with the contemporary ideological significance of stories about the past and with the political work that the past is made to do. *Astérix* thereby constitutes, particularly in the French context, a cultural Rorschach test that reveals a culture's political and cultural self-understanding via the past. *Astérix* is a cultural phenomenon that paradoxically exists uncoupled from any point of empirical origin and a cultural artifact that insists on the difference that origins, even the very myth of the origin, make within culture.

Asterix: Ready for His Close-Up

Astérix presents a reimagining of Roman antiquity in a way that interacts with contemporary attempts at cultural and political self-definition. It is this reimagining, moreover, that has interlocked so successfully with contemporary political sensibilities. The cultural appropriation of *Astérix* has taken the central idea of the series—the indomitable resistance to a mighty empire—and made it its own self-sustaining myth. Thus, the reception of *Astérix* is, to a great

---

3. For discussion of the notion of autochthony in Athens, see Detienne (2003); Loraux (1994); Loraux (2000); Rosivach (1987).

4. Indeed, there are entire studies devoted to this. See Brodersen (2001) and van Royen and van der Vegt (1997).

extent, a reenactment of what is taken to be the basic storyline of the comic. It is very much about French, if not European, resistance to the political and cultural hegemony of what Barber (1996) termed "McWorld," the US-driven movement of economic and cultural globaliza-tion. In other words, today's Roman Empire. Accordingly, the plots of *Astérix* are allegories of French, or European, resistance to an American political and cultural empire.

This transposable allegory of resistance explains the broad appeal of *Astérix* that extends beyond the comics themselves. *Astérix* has been reconfigured into games, video games, ani-mated films, live-action films, and a theme park. The live-action films are the most significant in this regard. The *Astérix* films have grown to be serious undertakings, drawing the talents of such major French film stars as Gérard Depardieu and Catherine Deneuve. The success of the *Astérix* films has become a matter of national importance in France, with the French film industry itself at stake. It has been a long-standing concern of the French government to preserve French cul-ture and prevent it from being swamped by non-French imports (Hayward 2005). To that end, the French government imposes quotas on the ratio of French and non-French product in film, TV, and radio. It has a particular interest in film and subsidizes French film production in order to protect the French film industry. Yet the overwhelming success of 1997's *Titanic*—specifically, its success in drawing French filmgoers away from French-made films—was a shock to these ambitions. Faced with such cultural imperialism, the French turned to that indomitable Gaul Asterix and produced *Astérix et Obélix contre César* (1999). As the *Economist* (1999) succinctly put it: "A culture is threatened by an invasion from the most powerful nation on earth, and the only resistance comes from a pocket of indomitable Gauls. This is the plot of 'Astérix,' the most expensive French film ever made. It is also the story of the European film industry." The gamble paid off: it was the biggest-grossing film in France in 1999. And Asterix has continued to save the day. *Astérix & Obélix: Mission Cléopâtre* (2002) became the second-most-attended French film in France ever, earning more than twice its production cost ($50 million) and drawing more viewers than that year's Harry Potter film (*Economist* 2002). In 2008, France had a record year of film-ticket sales, the second highest in twenty-four years. Moreover, for the second time since 1986, the market share for French films exceeded that of US films. The film *Astérix aux Jeux olympiques* (2008) was one of the two films that made that achievement possible (Prot 2009). According to *Variety*, as of 2010, *Astérix* is Europe's biggest movie franchise, and thus, it is the cornerstone of the French battle against US cultural imperialism (Keslassy 2010).

The clear parallels between the basic story of *Astérix* and the larger stakes of trying to counter the encroachment of Hollywood films with French-produced *Astérix* films were not lost on those reporting the events. As the *Wall Street Journal* reported on the publicity cam-paign for *Astérix et Obélix contre César*:

> The French have drafted new soldiers for their tireless war against American cultural imperialism: Asterix and Obelix of ancient Gaul. . . . [The film] is being hailed as France's riposte to *Titanic*. The American blockbuster swamped French box offices last year, drawing 21 million viewers out of a population of 59 million. It also caused the domestic market share of French movies to drop to 27% from a healthy 34.5% in 1997. "We've got to sink *Titanic* with this film, in the name of French pride," Asterix's co-creator, Albert Uderzo, told the French newspaper *Journal du Dimanche*. And the

newspaper *Le Monde* called the movie "a national affair of the highest importance." The media's common theme—little France taking on big bully Hollywood—reflects the plot of the film itself. (Barrett 1999)

What is striking here is the full self-awareness on the part of all the participants; everyone is aware that this is a strangely self-referential story. The comic adventures of the indomitable Gauls are being repeated on a scale of enormous proportions. What is at stake now is French national pride and the French film industry itself in the face of US cultural imperialism—an imperialism that, with its Hollywood blockbusters, is busy invading and dominating the box-office returns of many nations. The success of the *Astérix* films thus constitutes an emotionally charged (albeit partial) victory against US cultural imperialism.

The success of the *Astérix* films often appears to be less about the story of *Astérix* than about the recontextualization of that story into a contemporary struggle to resist cultural domination. Yet that recontextualization reveals something paradoxical about the attendant appropriation of the notion of resistance. This recontextualization dreams of small-scale, popular resistance; in actuality, however, it assumes large, corporate forms. It assumes that the only effective resistance to cultural imperial hegemony is by means that look suspiciously like the imperial culture it seeks to counter. The *Astérix* movie franchise is itself a venture that requires significant capital and corporate investment, a far cry from *Pilote*, the shoestring magazine in which *Astérix* first appeared. In point of fact, the reception and appropriation of *Astérix* which tends to emphasize the intractable resistance of the Gauls against the Romans, only furthers the myth of the autochthonous, pure native by insisting on the noncontamination of the Gauls by the Romans. The appropriation of *Astérix* therefore also appropriates this notion of native purity that was projected onto *Astérix* in the first place.[5] Thus, while worth considering if only in order to gauge the power of this myth, to embrace this reductive assessment of *Astérix* is to fail to escape the mythology about origins that *Astérix* is, in fact, questioning and to become part of what *Astérix* is resisting. And to find out what exactly is being resisted (which may turn out to be the notion of *Astérix* embodying indomitable resistance), it is necessary to consider the stories themselves.[6]

The Dream of Autochthony

What, then, is actually going on in the *Astérix* comics themselves? *Astérix* is, first of all, not the retelling of a classical myth or narrative from antiquity. Admittedly, there are points of contact with classical sources. One such story is *Asterix and the Chieftain's Shield* (1968; English 1977).

5. No clearer statement against the notion of purity and noncontamination can be found than that in a brief piece that Goscinny and Uderzo wrote mocking the French attempt to keep English words out of the French language. They present some villagers unconsciously using a string of words of Latin origin. Getafix urges them not to pollute their language with Latin but can only offer substitutions that require at least half a dozen words for one Latin word (*Asterix and the Class Act*; 2003; English 2004, 47–48).

6. I am mainly considering here the *Astérix* stories that both Goscinny and Uderzo produced, even though volumes written and drawn by Uderzo support the argument presented here. (See especially *Asterix and Son*, where Caesar promises to rebuild the village after Roman bombardment and then holds a banquet on Cleopatra's barge as a reward for having saved his son.) My argument is very much based on narrative as opposed to graphic presentation. Thus, it seems fitting to focus on Goscinny's *Astérix*.

The entire narrative presents itself as a forgotten footnote to known history and is sprinkled with references to Vercingetorix and the battle of Alesia. The story begins with the surrender of Vercingetorix to Caesar (familiar to the French more from Plutarch's vivid account than from Caesar's own *De Bello Gallico*), with the slight twist that instead of throwing his armor *at* Caesar's feet, he throws it *on* Caesar's feet.[7] Following this opening, however, the shield of Vercingetorix passes unrecognized from hand to hand so that its whereabouts are unknown. Thus, when Caesar decides to do a triumphal march in Gaul and to make prominent symbolic use of Vercingetorix's appropriated shield in order to remind the Gauls of his dominance, it clearly must be found. After much searching on the part of both the Romans and Asterix, it turns out that the shield has belonged to Vitalstatistix, the chief of Asterix's village, all along.

On the penultimate page of the story, Asterix organizes an attempt to wrest the political significance of the shield from Caesar. A triumphal march, with Obelix holding Vitalstatistix aloft on the shield, parades in front of all the citizens of Gergovia in addition to Caesar and the local Roman garrison. This does indeed shock Caesar, who decides that no one must know that this symbolic defiance happened in his presence, and so he exiles the garrison commander and his troops to Numidia, essentially erasing it from history. While the triumphal march appears to be a successful appropriation of the shield that wrests its political significance from Caesar, much suggests an ambiguity about it. To begin with, all of the just-described action takes place on the penultimate page; the actual "triumphal" march is confined to one paltry panel. Atop the shield, a weak, emaciated, post-spa Vitalstatistix is borne aloft solely by Obelix. Indeed, the entire "triumph" consists of Asterix, Obelix, and Vitalstatistix; the citizens of Gergovia are merely spectators. Furthermore, Caesar's exile of the garrison ensures that this Gallic victory will not go down in history and will thus be forgotten. Finally, as if to drive home the notion of the shield's impotence, the very last panel depicts Vitalstatistix shouting in fear as his wife, Impedimenta, prepares to hit him with this symbol of defiance.

Thus, while Caesar is prevented from exploiting the symbolic significance of the shield, the shield's symbolic capital does not seem to carry over into the village of the Gauls.[8] It is tempting to imagine that possession of the shield of Vercingetorix would ratify Vitalstatistix as his successor, as the next leader of Gallic resistance. Yet Vitalstatistix could never be mistaken for a heroic leader. (Indeed, much of the narrative depicts a sickly Vitalstatistix having to go to a spa to cure his liver of the effects of consuming too much rich food and beer.) Rather, the shield has become a comic prop that ultimately resists political symbolization. Shield bearers lug Vitalstatistix about on it, usually for no ostensible purpose other than to provide comic relief when they misunderstand his instructions, causing him to topple from his station. Interestingly, in the stories that follow this one, Vitalstatistix often falls down from his shield. In fact, in *Asterix and Caesar's Gift* (1974; English 1977), in which Vitalstatistix's rule over the

7. As Plutarch (27.10) writes: "Caesar was sitting there, and Vercingetorix circled him three times on horseback, leapt down, threw off his armour, and sat quietly at Caesar's feet"; trans. Pelling 2012, 97.

8. Unless otherwise specified, I use the term *the Gauls* to refer to the inhabitants of Asterix's village, which is never given a name in the series. This is common practice and actually works to further the myth I am examining. To use *the Gauls* in this way is akin to constantly referring to the amazing inhabitants of a small town in Nebraska as "the Americans." Such catachresis subtly allows a transposition of the amazing qualities of the villagers to all Gauls and thus to their descendants.

village is openly challenged by a significant contingent of the village, Vitalstatistix falls off his shield three times (pp. 10, 13, 22). Indeed, his vexed relationship with his shield forms one of the many running visual gags of the series. For instance, we see Vitalstatistix as he conducts the chores of many a long-suffering and disempowered husband—fetching water for his wife's laundry and carrying her bags and baskets during shopping—all atop his symbol of "authority," the shield of Vercingetorix. Thus, a known historical artifact of clear, politically symbolic importance is stripped of its symbolism and reduced to a prop. There could be no clearer way to get across that these Gauls do not embody another Vercingetorix; if there was such a thing as a "pure Gaul" ready to resist and fight the Romans in this series, he died with Vercingetorix.[9]

As can be seen in an examination of just this one story, *Astérix* seems to be up to more than either just faithfully elaborating on classical sources or offering up a glorious depiction of the indomitable resistance of the Gallic ancestors of the French. As already suggested, the true origin that *Astérix* refers to is the mythological use made of the notion of the pure native in contemporary culture, the dream of autochthony. It should come as no surprise, then, that there is an unsettling complexity and ambiguity wrapped around the notion of indomitable resistance that is not considered in its mythic appropriation. The Gauls' attitude toward the Romans can indeed be characterized as one of defiance—an impression fortified by the regular fights between the Gauls and the Romans, fights as predictable as the banquet that ends every adventure. Yet a more careful consideration of the stories suggests a far more nuanced relationship. While the Gauls often do fight the Romans and resist any Roman attempt to assert authority over the village, that does not necessarily make them "resistance fighters." It is hard to argue that the Gauls are rebels, setting out to undermine and topple the Roman Empire. They do not conduct campaigns against the Romans. They simply beat up Romans who get in their way. This is a crucial distinction, so much so that the ultimate point of the resistance of the villagers would seem to be coexistence. Granted, from Caesar's perspective, the refusal to be conquered is tantamount to open defiance. Yet the attitude of the four Roman camps surrounding the village gets across the point that if the Romans just stay out of the way of the villagers, there isn't all that big of a problem. Rebellion or resistance does not exist in any real political sense.

The tone of this strange form of defiant nonrebellion is established in the first *Astérix* story published, *Asterix the Gaul*. Most of the story is concerned with preventing the magic potion from falling into the hands of the Romans, in particular, Crismus Bonus, who dreams of using it to become ruler of Rome. Asterix and Getafix manage to prevent the potion from falling into the wrong hands, even though it entails capture. When Caesar appears at the end of the story, they inform him of Crismus Bonus' plot. Caesar is grateful for the information and graciously frees them, reminding them that while this interchange was a draw, they will meet again. Unlike Crismus Bonus, Caesar has no thought of getting his hands on the potion himself. He is powerful enough without it. Indeed, it is actually in Caesar's interest to keep the magic potion safely in the confines of Asterix's village, for then it is out of the hands of both the other Gauls and his political rivals. Thus, the foundational story of the *Astérix* series depicts the

9. I differ from some notable assessments of the role of Vercingetorix in *Astérix*; see Kovacs (2011, 13). King (2001) goes into great detail on this issue. For an excellent contextualization of these questions of national identity, see Pomian (1996); Rouvière (2008). I also differ from more general sociopolitical readings of *Astérix*; see Stoll (1974; 1978); Duhamel (1985); Miller (2008).

relationship between the Gauls and the Romans as somewhat complicitous. In the final analysis, Asterix has identified a political threat to Caesar and has also helped him in his quest for power by confining the magic potion to his village. It is too dangerous for use by those outside the village, and its containment ensures Caesar's continued rule over the rest of Gaul.

The inaugural story of the *Astérix* series draws attention to the fact that the villagers keep the magic potion to themselves and essentially only use it on an as-needed basis. If they are such rebellious, proud Gauls, why do they not share the potion with other Gauls? They could easily organize an unstoppable rebellion. In the one story in which they do share their magic potion in order to help others resist the expansion of Roman power, *Asterix in Britain*, the ultimate point seems to be that it's more trouble than it's worth. The potion never makes it to the village it was intended for and, in fact, narrowly escapes falling into the hands of the Romans. Furthermore, as indicated in *Asterix and the Goths* (1963; English 1975), the magic potion is a dangerous substance that irresistibly entices people to exploit it for self-gain and power. (Perhaps this is the true resistance in *Astérix*, the ability to resist exploiting the magic potion.) When the potion is distributed to others—as in *Asterix and Cleopatra* (1965; English 1969) or *Asterix and the Mansions of the Gods* (1971; English 1973)—it is done in a controlled manner and with the objective of thwarting a particular action of the Romans. Thus, while the magic potion clearly makes possible the resistance of the Gauls, it is, shall we say, a "controlled substance." For the most part, the magic potion is used for self-defense. Hence it is not really possible to claim that the Gauls are rebels. They simply resist the extension of Roman power to themselves.

Veni, Vidi, Wiki: Caesar and the Power of Collaboration

The focal point in the series of the relationship between the Gauls and the Romans is Caesar; he appears as a significant character in fourteen of the twenty-five volumes produced by Goscinny and Uderzo and in five of the eight volumes produced by Uderzo alone. Clearly, Caesar, the conqueror of Gaul, is cast as the recurring antagonist. Yet even here, the same complex approach to the myth of the pure native holds. For that myth would require a rigid distinction and opposition between Caesar and the pure Gaul. However, closer examination of the stories reveals a complexity to this apparently antagonistic relationship that complicates the notion of indomitable resistance.

For instance, for all the "enmity" between Caesar and the Gauls, it is worth noting that on five occasions, Caesar releases and frees Asterix and Obelix when they are essentially at his mercy. This occurs in *Asterix the Gaul, Asterix the Gladiator* (1964; English 1969), *Asterix the Legionary* (1967; English 1970), *Asterix and Son* (1983; English 1983), and *Asterix and the Actress* (2001; English 2001).[10] In *Asterix the Legionary*, the desire to get to Africa quickly in order to rescue Panacea's betrothed, Tragicomix (who has been press-ganged into joining Caesar's forces being arrayed against Scipio), motivates Asterix and Obelix to join the Roman

---

10. In *Asterix in Belgium* (1979; English 1980), the Gauls actually have Caesar in their power and let him go. In *Asterix and Cleopatra*, Caesar technically lets them go, but this is at the express mandate of Cleopatra.

army, which, by itself, is unusual for supposedly sworn enemies. Once in Africa as Roman legionnaires, they cause endless confusion between the camps of Caesar and Scipio—to Caesar's distinct advantage, enabling him to win the battle of Thapsus. Once again, Asterix and Obelix meet with Caesar, who thanks them for their help and allows them to return to Gaul with Tragicomix.

Likewise, in *Asterix the Gladiator*, Asterix and Obelix travel to Rome to rescue the village bard, Cacofonix. They discover that the simplest way to gain access to Cacofonix is as gladiators, because he is to be thrown to the lions in the Circus Maximus. When they finally all meet at the Circus in the presence of Caesar, Cacofonix's singing drives the lions out of the amphitheater, and the gladiators simply do not fight. Incensed at this failure of an entertaining spectacle, Caesar orders his best legionnaires into the amphitheater to massacre the Gauls. Of course, Asterix and Obelix decimate the legionnaires, much to the delight of the attendant crowd. This is the "bread and circuses" for which they have been waiting. Both Caesar and the Gauls are hailed with enthusiastic shouts of "Long live Caesar!" and "Long live the Gauls!" (p. 45). In a move typical for the series, Asterix has managed to thwart Caesar by handing him a victory. And since all has ended well, Caesar grants all the Gauls their freedom. In both of these instances, then, Caesar releases Asterix and Obelix and allows them to achieve their objective, fully aware that they are the key figures in the Gallic village that is a permanent thorn in his side. Yet in both instances, the Gauls for their part have done Caesar a great service; they have helped bring about a military victory and the "bread and circuses" that the citizens of Rome expect. Caesar could not have more useful enemies.

There is, then, an element of "live and let live" between Caesar and the Gauls, to their mutual benefit. This is not to suggest that Caesar never attempts to conquer the Gauls. He does. Yet it is the form that these attempts take that is noteworthy. Caesar does not attempt to conquer them the way he conquered the rest of Gaul.[11] Instead, in four instances, Caesar launches various schemes to undermine the Gauls in hopes of thereby bringing about such disunity that they can no longer function as a threat. As these are the few instances of sustained conflict between Caesar and the Gauls, these stories merit closer inspection. The stories divide into two distinct categories. Two stories turn on issues of group psychology and self-governance, and two turn on the socioeconomic life of the village.

The schemes that address group psychology and self-governance are surprisingly simple to initiate. In *Asterix and the Roman Agent* (1970; English 1972), Tortuous Convolvulus, who is known to be able to start arguments between people effortlessly, is sent by Caesar to the village to wreak havoc. This he does by giving Asterix a vase, as he is, in the words of Convolvulus, the most important man in the village. This immediately triggers jealousy and suspicion. (Some even wonder if Asterix and Getafix have given the recipe for the magic potion to the Romans.) So much acrimony results that Getafix refuses to distribute the potion to the villagers. Together with Asterix, Getafix pretends to leave the village in order to teach them a lesson. This in turn prompts the Romans to launch a full-scale assault on the assumption that they are defenseless. However, Getafix returns in time to provide the potion to the villagers, who are thus able to

---

11. Since I am focusing on Goscinny stories, I am not discussing Caesar's attempt to send female legionnaires to do battle with the villagers in the Uderzo-written *Asterix and the Secret Weapon* (1991). In any case, a cohort of female legionnaires immediately becoming distracted by clothing sales hardly constitutes a serious military engagement.

repulse the joint attack by all four garrisons. The battle is depicted, in a rare gesture for the series, in a panel that takes up an entire page, which establishes clearly the scale and magnitude of the threat and also the danger that discord represents. In the end, order is reestablished, and Asterix convinces the Romans that Convolvulus has betrayed them, thus ensuring that he is never a problem again.

In *Asterix and Caesar's Gift*, Caesar has given the land of the village as a joke retirement gift to a drunken legionnaire by the name of Tremensdelirius. Tremensdelirius, however, sells it to an innkeeper, Orthopaedix, who in turn packs up and travels to the village to lay claim to his property. Orthopaedix is scoffed at but then invited to live in the village. He then decides to run for chief of the village and is indeed able to attract a faction. Soon the village is acrimoniously divided, so much so that Getafix refuses to distribute any more magic potion. Meanwhile, Tremensdelirius resurfaces. Unable to acquire his deed back from Orthopaedix, he convinces the nearby Roman garrison to defend his claim and attack the village. Having learned that the villagers do not have the magic potion, they prepare for this with siege towers and catapults. Thus, once again, the threat to the village is dire and real. Yet as long as there is division in the village, Getafix refuses to make any magic potion available, even after the catapult assault has begun. It is only when it is clear that the factionalism is over—as evidenced by Vitalstatistix asking for magic potion not for himself but for his political rival Orthopaedix—that Getafix provides the potion, and the villagers are able to repel the Roman attack.

In both stories, dissension presents the greatest danger to the Gauls. It is the one circumstance that makes Getafix refuse to provide magic potion, despite the great peril this poses to the village. From this, we can see that the real point of the magic potion is not to beat up Romans but to protect a way of life. If that way of life did not exist anymore, then there would be no reason for the magic potion. A close-knit, supportive community devoted to remaining self-sufficient constitutes that way of life. Moreover, it is characterized by simple needs and wants. And this seems to be a key point: fighting the Romans is easy, but truly not needing or wanting anything the imperial culture can provide is much harder. This is why mutual support and cooperation are absolutely essential; they guarantee collective self-sufficiency. And it is precisely this issue that is the focus of the other stories within which Caesar figures prominently.

The other two stories concerned with Caesar's schemes against the Gauls focus on socioeconomic issues. In *Asterix and the Mansions of the Gods*, Caesar has decided that if the Gauls do not embrace Roman civilization, then Roman civilization must be brought to them. This takes form in the construction of a luxury apartment complex. Once the Romans move in, they commence to shop at the village of the Gauls. What they mainly buy are fish from Unhygienix (because they are so much cheaper than the prices they are used to) and "antiques" from the blacksmith Fulliautomatix. Before long, the entire village is engaged in the selling of either fish or antiques. As a result, the economic system of the village is utterly disrupted, hijacked from the notion of a self-sustaining and self-sufficient economy. Fortunately, Asterix and Getafix arrange a ruse that unifies the village to attack and destroy the apartment building, thus bringing an end to Caesar's plot.

Caesar launches his most ambitious socioeconomic scheme in *Obelix and Co.* (1976; English 1978) under the advice of Preposterus, a young upstart who has studied economic theory. With Caesar's backing, Preposterus arranges an encounter with Obelix, buying all the menhirs he can produce at inflated prices. As Preposterus demands more menhirs than Obelix himself can produce, Obelix hires workers to help him produce more. Once Obelix is working so much, he does not have time to hunt for wild boar, so he hires people to hunt for his food. Soon more and more people are working for Obelix. Preposterus convinces him that as a successful man of business, he needs to start to spend some of his growing wealth. Obelix does indeed do this, an act that in turn triggers the envy and jealousy of the other villagers. Meanwhile, Caesar is annoyed at having purchased so many menhirs. So Preposterus launches a massive advertising campaign in Rome in order to sell them. They sell so well that more and more people enter the menhir business, both Romans and foreigners. Menhirs flood the market. This causes a price war, which ends up making the menhirs worthless and causing something akin to a stock-market crash. So the effort to destroy the Gauls by economic means wreaks havoc on the Roman economy, and all the money in the pockets of the Gauls is essentially worthless.

These two stories focusing on socioeconomics get at the heart of what makes the villagers distinct. They do not want to topple the Roman Empire; to do so would essentially require that they become an empire themselves. They seek no social or governmental entity larger than their own village. And they have what they need: they are by the sea and next to a forest full of wild game (though their fish, thanks to Unhygienix, come from Lutetia, Gallic Paris, which is why the fish smell and so often cause arguments, perhaps an ongoing reminder of the dangers of not being self-sufficient). The Romans, by contrast, are characterized by consumption and never-sated desire.

Moreover, examination of the interaction between the villagers and the Romans reveals the myth of the pure native as an origin point for a contemporary people to be precisely that, a myth. There is absolutely no ethnic basis for what distinguishes the villagers from other Gauls. And Goscinny and Uderzo do not hesitate to show other Gauls—as in *Asterix and the Cauldron* (1969; English 1976) and *Asterix and the Big Fight* (1966; English 1971)—easily adopting Roman ways. Neither can the notion of culture be used to distinguish the villagers, as they share this with other Gauls. Only the notion of a microculture in the broadest anthropological sense distinguishes the villagers. This microculture is defined by a commitment to group autonomy and self-sufficiency—and the cooperation necessary to make those things possible. It is a commitment to a certain mental outlook and modes of behavior. These are precisely the factors that are overlooked in the hasty appropriation of *Astérix* to celebrate both the sense of a contemporary people's distinction and its valiant resistance of its version of the Roman Empire.

These last two stories draw clear parallels between the Romans and contemporary Europe and America—with the building of suburban luxury condominiums, the unionization of workers, and the manipulation of the market through advertising. And such parallels are not confined to these two stories. These parallels make for good comedy, but they should give us pause in our all-too-easy identification with the indomitable Gauls. For it is clear that we are more like these Romans than the Gauls. Despite the admiration for plucky people who resist large, threatening entities, most readers have little desire to live in self-sufficient communes—which is what Asterix's village essentially is—or to reject the finer goods and services of civilization. If this is the case, it raises troubling questions about our identification with this mythical pure native that could function as one's own origin. We want to believe that there is a genealogical connection between ourselves and the pure native. Yet this mythical origin might have a different purpose. Instead of residing in the past, this origin might be an ever-recurring moment in the present whose function is to reframe palliatively our complicitous relations with power. Thus, the very concept of the origin serves to disavow the ideological work that is being done in the present by means of it.

The myth of the origin, essentially, is a way of refusing to admit to ourselves what we have become. Perhaps this is the true secret message of *Astérix*, that there is only one answer to the question of who today are the Romans: *c'est nous*. We live in a world of myth, consumerism, and never-sated desire. And if we claim to take inspiration from *Astérix*, we usually do so only to transform ourselves into new Romans despite our intentions. (Once you spend $50 million on a film, you're no longer outside the culture industry.) Our task is not to tap into the mythological pure native but to resist what we have become, to think about Asterix and his village and admit that it has no relation to how we choose to live. This might be the uncomfortable explanation for why Asterix and Obelix end up helping Caesar so much: the delusional belief that we are connected to the pure native makes it easier to be a Roman; it functions as guilt-reducing disavowal. So just as Asterix helps Caesar, our hasty interpretations of *Astérix* help us maintain a life decidedly more Roman than like Asterix's village. The true site of indomitable resistance is the volumes produced by Goscinny and Uderzo. There is something in them that resists appropriation, that works to undermine the myths that we are only all too happy to keep employing—employing, sadly, in the name of *Astérix*. And it is only in reading them that we come to the uncomfortable conclusion: *nous sommes fous*.

9

We're Not in Gaul Anymore

The Global Translation of *Astérix*

Siobhán McElduff

A good scribe must speak all the modern languages: Latin, Greek, Celtic . . .
Asterix and Cleopatra

If a good scribe speaks three modern languages, then Astérix[1] surely qualifies as a superscribe: the Gallic hero currently speaks 107 languages and dialects ranging from Arabic to Korean to Welsh.[2] (This figure includes several bootleg translations in Chinese and Vietnamese). International success on this scale[3] tends to naturalize that success. Why shouldn't this comic-book series about Astérix the Gaul, his chubby menhir-selling comrade Obélix, their tree-loving dog Idéfix (English Dogmatix), and the last free village in Roman Gaul be so phenomenally successful? By all the laws of marketing and cultural insularity, *Astérix* should not be as globally translatable as it has proven to be, especially given the relative weakness of France as a producer of popular

Many thanks to Justin Choi for translating and providing commentary on the Korean translations of *Astérix*, Maya Yazigi for the Arabic, Chris Rea for help with the Mandarin, and the volume's editors for their comments and advice.

1. Throughout this chapter, "Astérix" refers to the character, "*Astérix*" to the series. When listing titles for the first time, I give the title of the French source and the original date of publication; thereafter, I give the English title only.

2. For a total of 1,456 albums at the date of writing; "Asterix around the World" (http://www.asterix-obelix. nl/) is the best place to track the languages of *Astérix*. The languages include Latin, ancient (Attic) Greek, and Esperanto; the dialects include Cretan and Cypriot Greek, Alsatian, Gents, Occitan, Picard, and no fewer than twenty-nine German dialects. The large number of German dialects testifies to the series' massive popularity in Germany, *Astérix*'s second-largest market outside France.

3. However, no translation has replicated the phenomenal level of the French sales figures. In 2005, *Asterix and the Falling Sky* (*Le ciel lui tombe sur la tête*) sold 1,305,300 copies, outselling the French translation of *Harry Potter and the Half-Blood Prince*. In 2002, *Asterix and the Class Act* (*Astérix et la rentrée gauloise*) was the second-best-selling book—*Harry Potter and the Order of the Phoenix* won that battle—selling 865,900 copies. In 2001, *Asterix and the Actress* (*Astérix et Latraviata*) sold 2,288,065. (All figures are taken from Grove 2010, 165–166.) These figures are a huge jump from the initial print run of 6,000 for the first album, *Asterix the Gaul* (*Astérix le Gaulois*, 1961); the second album, *Asterix and the Golden Sickle* (*La serpe d'or*, 1962), had a run of 20,000, while the 1963 *Asterix and the Goths* (*Astérix chez les Goths*) doubled that to 40,000.

culture in comparison with the United States, South Korea,[4] or the United Kingdom. Not only does a considerable amount of the original's humor rely on puns, wordplay, and some arcane (to an international audience) French cultural referents, but the series as a whole is explicitly and repeatedly tied in with French and European history and identity, rather than global ones. The originals even contain Latin quotations, and, although it pains me to write this, Latin is not precisely a language that universally shrieks fun.

In translation, the series makes few concessions in shape, size, or imagery to norms outside the French *bande dessinée*; in all official translations, Astérix always appears as he was originally drawn by Albert Uderzo (with the exception of some bootleg versions; see below) and is not redrawn to fit different comic or cultural conventions. He is astonishingly and remarkably stable as an icon within comics; the languages he speaks change, but he remains resolutely the same.[5] *Astérix* is issued in the French album format, an A4-size format of forty-eight to sixty-four pages, usually in full color.[6] This is true no matter what formats local comic books are issued in (see below); some translations stress the source's foreignness by incorporating both the original French and the target language on the cover, as the Japanese translations do. Such strategies show *Astérix*'s heritage and may aim for an exotic appeal to counteract the foreignness of the product (unsuccessfully in the case of the Japanese translations, which only ran to three albums, all issued in 1974).[7]

Some of the *Astérix* series' success in translation should be credited to careful planning on the part of the authors and publishers, along with other factors such as the skill of the translators. It is common for the first book translated into a language to be one with a connection to the target language and culture. Thus, *Astérix in Corsica* (*Astérix en Corse*, 1973) was the first album translated into Corsican/Corsu, in 1993. Not surprisingly, given that album's depiction of the Corsicans as touchy, work-shy, chauvinistic, sexist, and obsessively keen on vendettas, it did not prove very successful. It was eleven years before the next album, *Asterix and the Actress*, was translated; none has been translated since then. In 2007, *Asterix and the Magic Carpet* (*Astérix chez Rahazade*, 1987) was the first album to be simultaneously translated into Arabic and Hebrew; this proved successful enough to be followed by a Hebrew (but not Arabic) translation of *Asterix and the Black Gold* (*L'odyssée d'Astérix*, 1981) in 2008. The most successful version of this strategy has been in the United Kingdom, where the appeal of *Astérix* was initially lost on the many English publishers who passed on the chance to pick up the rights to the series, until Brockhampton Press purchased them (the volumes have subsequently been

4. Since the beginning of the Hallyu (Korean) Wave of the 1990s, Korean popular culture has been hugely influential in Asia; Keun Kim (2010) is a good introduction to this phenomenon.

5. Our heroes' names are nearly always retained: Astérix may lose his accent mark, but he is always Asterix; the same for Obélix. One exception is the Mandarin Chinese translation of *Asterix the Gaul* (*Yali Lixianji*, 1986), where he is called Yali and Obélix is Oubi. *Yali* means literally "the power [*li*] of Asia [*Ya*]"; *Oubi* combines "to compare" (*bi*) and "Europe" (*Ou*). The primary appeal of their new names probably lies in their symmetry, with Asia and Europe matching each other.

6. Most comics translated into French are reformatted into this format; when Alan Moore's *Watchmen* was translated into French, it was released in six albums with new covers, despite the fact that this altered the graphic proportions and narrative thrust of the original (Zanettin 2008, 17).

7. *Asuterikkusu no bôken* (*Asterix the Gaul*); *Ôgon no kama* (*Asterix and the Golden Sickle*); *Asuterikkusu to gôtozoku* (*Asterix and the Goths*). All were published by Futubasha.

issued by several publishers). The first English-language translation, by the celebrated team of Anthea Bell and Derek Hockridge, came in 1970; not surprisingly, it was *Asterix in Britain* (*Astérix chez les Bretons*, 1966);[8] this came with an apologia by Goscinny and Uderzo for their gentle mockery of English culture and obsessions, such as a fondness for breaking off fighting the Romans for a spot of hot water and milk (*Asterix in Corsica* did not get such an apology, although it could have done with one). However, while the series' European appeal may at least be explained by the shared cultural appeal of Roman conquest and aided by the fact that many of the adventures occur around Europe,[9] it cannot explain why the series has been so successful in other, more distant markets, such as Indonesia, where thirty albums have been translated. The Indonesian translator, Rahartati Bambang, is popular enough to be a minor celebrity (sometimes called Mrs. Astérix)[10] and interviewed Uderzo for the popular Indonesian magazine *Tempo*.[11] Nor does it explain why the series has been so popular in Korea, where all the albums have been translated and the animated series still occasionally appears on television.[12]

No single chapter could possibly address all the complex ways *Astérix* has traveled from medium to medium and culture to culture, and I will not attempt such a Sisyphean task. Nor does this chapter address the other forms of translation that *Astérix* has experienced, such as animated and live-action feature films,[13] advertisements (including one particularly controversial 2010 campaign for McDonald's, which featured billboards showing the characters banqueting inside a McDonald's with only the bard and Idéfix remaining outside),[14] computer

8. For similar reasons, *Asterix and the Great Crossing* (*La grande traversée*, 1975), which is set in America, was the first of the series to be given a US English translation, in 1984; it was followed by *Asterix the Legionary* (*Astérix légionnaire*, 1967) and *Asterix and the Olympic Games* (*Astérix aux Jeux olympiques*, 1968), in 1992. The American publications came with extra ancillary material written by Goscinny and illustrated by Uderzo but still did not prove successful enough to warrant being continued for long; the last US English translations were published in 1995. There is not space here to explore the differences between the UK and US translations, unfortunately, beyond a few comments. Places names are different: Baboarum, one of the Roman camps in the French original, is Totorum in the UK translation and Opprobrium in the US. Names are also different: for example, UK Getafix is US Magigimmix (magic gimmicks), and UK Cacofonix is US Malacoustix. The US translations also provide more explanatory footnotes than the UK ones and use different slang and language. For further comparison, see the "Asterix Annotations" website (http://asterix.openscroll.org/), which has a downloadable file covering all the books in their English translations.

9. A number of the later albums wander farther afield: *Asterix and the Great Crossing* is set in America, *Asterix and the Black Gold* in the Middle East, *Asterix and the Magic Carpet* in India.

10. http://www.telegraph.co.uk/expat/expatnews/6345931/Half-a-century-on-Asterix-retains-his-magic.html.

11. An English version of the interview can be found at http://web.archive.org/web/20110130180744/http://majalah.tempointeraktif.com/id/arsip/2000/10/09/LYR/mbm.20001009.LYR99320.id.html.

12. Korean interest in *Astérix* may be aided by a general interest in Greek and Roman mythology, evidenced by the animated movies and series *Olympos Guardian*.

13. The live-action films include *Astérix et Obélix contre Cesar* (1999), *Astérix et Obélix: Mission Cléopâtre* (2002), *Astérix aux Jeux Olympiques* (2008), and the forthcoming *Astérix et Obélix: Au service de Sa Majesté*, each starring Gérard Depardieu as Obélix. There are a remarkable number of fansubs of these films available, testifying to a popularity in languages where authorized translations are rare or nonexistent, such as Thai and Vietnamese. (Fansubs are unauthorized subtitles produced and timed by fans, rather than by studios or authorized sources. Rewards generally come in the form of cyberpopularity or thanks; for this reason, people tend to provide subtitles for films that will generate the most thanks and reaction.)

14. It was not the first time that Astérix had appeared in a McDonald's campaign: he replaced Ronald McDonald as the French spokesperson in 2001, in a tie-in with the release of *Astérix et Obélix: Mission Cléopâtre*. The slogan

games, and a theme park. Instead, I set my sights much lower: first, I will situate the translation of
the *Astérix* series within theories of translations of comics and graphic novels; then I will briefly discuss some of the less well-known translations (primarily Korean and Arabic) and touch on the far
better-documented UK English translations; I will end with a brief discussion of why the *Astérix*
series has proven to be so translatable and why it struggles to gain footholds in certain cultures.

Theories of Translation and Translation of Comics

Types of translation are often rather crudely divided into two broad categories: domesticating
or foreignizing. While both categories trace their lineage to Friedrich Schleiermacher's seminal essay "On the Different Methods of Translation" (1813), they gain much of their contemporary currency from their use by Laurence Venuti in his much-cited and controversial work
The Translator's Invisibility (1995). Briefly, in domesticating translations, the translated text
is brought closer to the reader by a process of adaptation to the norms of the target (translating) culture;[15] in a foreignizing translation, fewer concessions are made to the reader, who is
expected to move toward the source text. In the domesticating form, the translating process and
translators tend to be invisible; in foreignizing translations, the translator, or at least the work's
status as a translation, is far more visible.[16]

Problematically, these categories—and a great deal of ancillary theorizations of translation and translation strategies—arose to discuss and deal with textual translation and often
have a difficult time accounting for hybrid forms of translation that involve image *and* text
or speech, let alone the complex format of comics, where text is only one component of an
intensely visual complex medium. Hence translation of comics presents a problem for translation studies and sits uneasily within its established theoretical categories. First, translations of
comics are affected by certain pressures that are unique to their form: no matter how much a
translator wants to foreignize or domesticate a comic, he or she is constrained by the fact that
the visuals usually cannot be changed, as redrawing is very expensive and normally occurs only
within bootleg translations, as in the 1993 Vietnamese translation of *Asterix the Gaul* (*Chang
Axtêrix nguoi Gô loa*) from the publisher Phụ nu (figure 9.1). Like subtitlers working with
films, translators of comics have to make certain that what they are translating matches what
the readers see before them.

For this reason, Bell and Hockridge work on the principle that their translations must fit the
expressions on the faces of the characters and must be about the same length as the original (Kessler
1995, 60).[17] However, emotions are not always expressed in the same way across all comic-book

---

for the 2010 campaign was *Venez comme vous êtes* ("Come as you are"), cleverly playing off the stability of Astérix
as French icon.

15. Sometimes by such drastic measures as reordering the narrative to fit within the target culture's expectations,
as occurred in the first English translation of Milan Kundera's *The Unbearable Lightness of Being*.

16. Foreignizing translations tend not to be very popular: they are less accessible, are often deliberately challenging, and frequently employ language that is nonstandard and difficult. A good example of a foreignizing translation
is the Zukofskys' (1969) version of Catullus; a good example of a domesticating translation is almost every other
English translation of Catullus.

17. The Korean translator, on the other hand, will increase font size to fill out a bubble if necessary (see the Korean
translation of *Asterix and Cleopatra* 11.6).

FIGURE 9.1 *Astérix* in Vietnam. Cover artist unknown.

traditions; for example, Japanese manga and Korean manhwa have a very different visual palette for showing emotions compared with Western comics. If additional images are drawn around a speech bubble in a comic, the translator is further limited, as in panels where the bubble is surrounded by flowers (indicating flattery) or musical notes (indicating that the contents are sung) or some other metanarrative or extranarrative element that the reader must process. For these reasons, comics translations are often described as a form of constrained translation.[18]

However, because they are trained in theories of textual translation, those who study translations in comics focus primarily and problematically on text, assuming that images are a universal language that will be understood in the same way across multiple cultures. But text—or, rather, lettering—is only a small portion of what comics deal in; the reader must interpret not only images but a welter of other information: sounds, placement of speech bubbles, color, and so on.[19] However, despite all the complex elements involved when we read a

18. One form of constraint is specific to *Astérix*. Uderzo has compiled lists of puns and the cultural jokes in the stories that are given to translators (Kessler 1995, 59), which will necessarily affect their translations. It is not clear how much control this exerts over translators; although it ensures that they are aware that a pun or a joke has been made, they may not choose to translate that joke or pun.

19. On the complex messages sent by representations of sound in comics, see Marshall (2012).

comic, publications on translating *Astérix* almost exclusively examine issues such as the translations of names, puns, accents; how the translators struggle to fit certain text within speech bubbles; how they make their text match the image,[20] and so forth, taking the universal meaning of the images for granted. But, "like verbal communication, visual communication relies on shared cultural assumptions" (Zanettin 2008, 22): images are *not* a universal language. Comics have their own sets of conventions, which vary widely from culture to culture; as we read a comic, we read on both the textual and the visual level, and the shape, the colors, the images—everything that populates a page of a comic—all have meaning and affect our reading. Take the flowers mentioned above that indicate flattery in *Astérix*; even their meaning is not stable across cultures. In manga and manhwa, flowers, especially blossoming flowers, indicate consensual sexual activity.[21]

What a comic is and how we read it are heavily influenced by the form that comics take within our own culture, what types of stories they tell, and how widespread and valued they are as a literary medium (Celotti 2008, 35). Take the signals sent by the traditional album size of the series:[22] in cultures that do not produce comics in those sizes, the shape signals *Astérix's* foreign origin even before the text is opened. For a Korean used to manhwa or a Japanese reader primarily familiar with manga, both of which are produced in paperback-sized volumes, the size is strange and unwieldy (figure 9.2).[23] This is also true of Italy, where indigenous comics are usually issued in the *bonelli* format, which has about one hundred pages in each black-and-white volume of six by eight inches. Size matters: when you are expecting a small but fat paperback, a slim but larger album requires you to reevaluate your expectations.

There are also the visual elements of lettering and typeface to consider, none of which is unmarked for comics readers (Kannenberg 2001, 168). There are considerably different conventions of imagery and lettering in different comics traditions; in Germany, comic books generally use machine lettering for both German and translated comics (Zenettin 2008, 13), and the first translations of *Astérix* used such lettering (more current translations use a machine lettering that evokes hand lettering).[24] To those used to different conventions, this can appear unpleasing or overly formal,[25] creating a disjuncture between the narrative and the typeface,

20. For example, on names, see Delesse (2008), Gay (2001), Embleton (1991); on puns and compensation, see Harvey (1995); on accents, see Delesse (2004). Many of these discussions are concerned with assessing whether these changes are an improvement on the source or not; Embleton, in particular, has harsh words for those who (in her eyes) do not improve on or match the wit of the original, a criticism that ignores that some cultures may not find the same things amusing or witty as the French or English do.

21. On the visual language of manga, see Cohn (2010).

22. The only *official* exception to the retention of this structure is a series of *Astérix* books published in A5 (8.3 x 5.8 in.) size in 1971 in the United Kingdom by Knight Books. These have redrawn covers, focusing almost totally on Astérix.

23. A good introduction to manga is Johnson-Woods (2010). There is almost nothing published in English on manhwa, which is often folded into discussions of manga, although it is *not* a subgenre of manga but an independent development.

24. On German translations of *Astérix*, see Penndorf (2001).

25. Chris Sims's railing against the speech bubbles and lettering used in the manga of the popular young-adult series *Twilight* shows what happens when readers—even experienced comics readers—are faced with conventions that they feel are inappropriate ("The Twilight Graphic Novel Review," http://www.comicsalliance.com/2010/03/18/twilight-manga-review/). Sims was particularly uncomfortable with elements that are typical of manga, finding them confusing and inappropriate. On comics text and lettering and their effects, see Kannenberg (2001).

R.GOSCINNY **Astérix** A.UDERZO

2

글 **르네 고시니**
그림 **알베르 우데르조**

오영주 · 성기완 옮김

아스테릭스,
클레오파트라를
만나다

문 학 과 지 성 사

FIGURE 9.2 Cover of the Korean translation of *Asterix and Cleopatra* (1965, translation 2001). Original art by Albert Uderzo.

even encouraging them to read it as a "serious" comic. This is an issue with the first Latin translations of *Astérix* from the Dutch/Belgian publisher Elsevier (these were later published by
Delta Verlag), which used machine lettering in the German tradition. As these are intended to
be used also by English and French readers, the more formal tone introduced by the typeface
became an extranarrative problem: given that these translations were marketed as a useful book
for teaching children, the formal tone signaled by machine lettering to French, English, US,
and other readers was unintentionally inappropriate.[26] Perhaps as a result, later Latin translations, such as the 2007 translation of *Asterix and the Falling Sky* (*Le ciel lui tombe sur la tête*),
use fonts that resemble hand lettering.[27]

Astérix also presents particular problems in lettering and typeface for translators, especially
those working in languages that do not use the Roman alphabet, as it marks some languages
and ethnicities by using different scripts for their speech. In the original albums, Goths speak
in Gothic script, Norsemen use *ø* rather than *o*, Greeks speak in squared lettering, Egyptians
speak in pictures (hieroglyphs), and so on; all these scripts mark ethnic identities, informing
us of a character's background without needing to say anything. The "hieroglyphic" nature
of Egyptian speech allows Goscinny and Uderzo the chance to play with ideas of language,
power, and translatability in ways that can (but do not automatically) translate. In *Asterix and
Cleopatra* (*Astérix et Cléopâtre*, 1965, one of the most frequently translated albums), the story
opens not in Astérix's village but with Caesar and Cleopatra in mid-argument about whether
the Egyptians are only suitable to live in slavery. In the original, this argument is in French; in
translations, it is in the language of the target culture. On the first panel of the next page (6.1),
we see Cleopatra enthroned majestically and speaking in hieroglyphs as an Egyptian cowers
before her. The switch in speech not only places us in an exotic environment but also cleverly
matches Cleopatra's relative power status, as she shifts from client queen to pharaoh when we
flip the page. This shift can translate but only if the language of translation is associated with
power and authority; one can see that this might not work in the Creole translations, for example, originating as they do in a culture where French is the language associated with political
and cultural power. Goscinny follows up the impressive first appearance of the hieroglyphics
in the story with a note stating that from now on, Egyptian speech will be dubbed for the ease
of the reader; the additional comment that the speech bubbles will not match the speakers' lip
movements points to the failure of translations to ever absolutely mimic the original language.

This is not the only place in the story where the authors play with issues of language and
translation. At 21.7, faced with a recalcitrant Egyptian who will not tell them what has happened to the stone needed to build a magnificent palace for Caesar, Obélix asks the Egyptian
scribe how to say *talk* in Egyptian. The scribe's answer is given in the form of a perfectly
well-drawn hieroglyph. Obélix repeats the word, but his hieroglyph is shakily drawn, showing

---

26. The Latin translations contain glossaries in several languages and are advertised as useful teaching tools.
Some other translations, such as the Polish ones issued by Egmont, initially also came with a small lexicon, signaling their straddling of the educational and entertainment categories. The various Creole translations also have
small Creole-French glossaries in the back, a feature promoted by the official website (http://www.asterix.com/
the-collection/translations/asterix-in-reunion-creole.html).

27. This translation, however, is an anomaly; it did not use the German translator of the other volumes (Karl-Heinz
Graf Rothenburg) and was published by Editions Albert René.

his poor accent. Such scenes may invite us to reflect on translation and its limitations, until we realize that Goscinny is not actually translating anything at all from Egyptian but is inventing the language as he goes along. That Goscinny and Uderzo get to speak for the Egyptians, dubbing over their voices in French, raises some disturbing postcolonial issues of who gets to speak for whom, reinforced by a story in which the Gallic heroes are there to save Cleopatra and her architect from shaming themselves before the imperial power of Rome.

While the hieroglyphic connection with ancient Egypt is strong enough to require no explanation and the images can be represented in any target language (although they may evoke different responses in different languages), other scripts may not translate so well or even be possible to transfer into a non-Roman alphabet. The Arabic translation of *Asterix the Gaul*[28] uses a slightly different script for Gothic speech[29] but cannot and does not attempt to replicate the cultural meaning of Gothic script for European readers, for whom Gothic script is tied in with the Germany of Bismarck and World War I (a link that is stressed by the fact that the Goths of *Astérix* wear World War I–era German helmets from time to time).[30] In the Arabic translation, all of this is unavoidably lost; although we know the Germans speak differently, that difference is not tied in with a specific cultural meaning.

As previously mentioned, there are other metatextual elements in comics that play an important role in influencing the reader, some of which may not be translatable in traditional textual forms. While skulls and other symbols to symbolize swearing can be effective across many cultures, colors may present problems. One good example of this is in *Asterix and the Roman Agent* (*La zizanie*, 1970), where a green tinge in a speech bubble shows that the character has been affected by the malign influence of the Roman agent sent to turn the villagers against one another. This works in translations for cultures where green is associated with envy but not quite as neatly in those where green has primarily positive connotations, such as Korea or Arab countries (it is also a problem, of course, for publishers that print volumes partially in black-and-white).

Finally, the shape of the original speech bubbles may look foreign or just plain wrong in some target cultures such as Korea and Japan, where speech bubbles in manhwa and manga frequently take up far more space on the page than in Western comics, and readers are familiar with bubbles that are imposed over characters' forms, either partially obscuring them or fading into transparency over their figures.[31] Thus, the neat and small speech bubbles of *Astérix* present text to a Japanese or Korean reader in a highly unfamiliar (and perhaps unattractive) way, and readers process that unfamiliarity simultaneously as they read the narrative. The lack of success of the Japanese translations of *Astérix* may be because issues like these gave readers too much of a feeling of cultural disjuncture and proved too big a hurdle to overcome. Given the success of the series in other Asian countries, I suspect that such factors had far more impact than cultural issues with understanding the narrative or "failures" in the translation.

28. The date of 1961 on the translation seems impossibly early and may simply be transferred from the source.

29. See 6.3, showing the Goths surrendering to the Romans.

30. Because of the 1941 Nazi ban on Gothic script, it has largely avoided association with Nazism, instead evoking a less troubling and earlier form of German nationalism.

31. See http://sundaycomicsdebt.blogspot.com/2010/07/here-have-balloon.html for a discussion of manga speech bubbles and how unnatural Western conventions of text boxes can feel for someone raised on Japanese and Korean comics.

The success of the Korean translations, on the other hand, is probably a result not just of skillful translation but also of the fact that the *Astérix* series had a considerable impact on the Korean genre of educational comic books. This genre was pioneered by Rhee Won-Bok, himself inspired by *Astérix*, a series he encountered while studying in Europe.[32] As a result, Won-Bok's cartoons are drawn in a manner that fits more closely with European norms of comics drawing than with manhwa; familiarity with these surely made it easier for *Astérix* to penetrate the Korean comics system.

Translator Strategies for *Astérix*

Anthea Bell, one of the celebrated team responsible for the UK English *Astérix* translation, has described herself as "an unrepentant, reconstructed adherent of the school of invisible translation" (Bell 2004, 14).[33] In line with this philosophy, the English translations do their best to obscure their status as translations, being published without the translators' names anywhere on the front cover, suggesting that they are the unfiltered work of Goscinny and Uderzo (or Uderzo alone for later albums). Bell and Hockridge's translation strategy is to make the translations read as smoothly as possible, adapting the source material considerably; one consequence is that around 88 percent of the specific French references in *Astérix* (to songs, French food, French bureaucracy, and so forth) are changed to English (Gay 2001, 148). One extended example of such adaptation occurs on page 31 of *Asterix and Caesar's Gift* (*Le cadeau de César*, 1974), where quotations from Shakespeare (specifically, from the climactic duel in *Hamlet*) replace the source's dialogue, which comes from Rostand's *Cyrano de Bergerac* (see further Gay 2001, 23–24); high, but familiar, literature has been replaced with a comparable English author.

Bell admits that such strategies have resulted in some believing that the English translation is in fact the original; she mentions a secondary-school headmistress who didn't realize that the source was French, although Bell felt that the series had "THIS IS FRENCH" (her capitals) all over it (Bell 2004, 10). Such interventions—and the success of those interventions in masking the foreign nature of the source—would offend translation scholars who prefer foreignizing strategies. However, any such criticism ignores one important feature of comics that distorts their reception in translation and can help them to appear as if they were originally written in a target language. When we open a comic book and gaze on the characters, it seems as if we eavesdrop on them as they speak; the characters appear to speak directly to us and in our own voices, creating a particularly intimate relationship between reader and text, promoting a sense an unfiltered access to the material (Khordoc 2001, 160). That intimate relationship is a particular feature of comics, and it ensures that we are particularly primed to approach comics translations as if they spoke to us directly in their authors' words. This relationship may encourage domesticating translations or ensure that foreignizing translation strategies break down when faced with our sense of accessing the world of the comic directly.

32. His name is also transliterated as Yi Won-bok and Rhie Won-bok. *Korea Unmasked* (2002) is his most available title in English. The Korean translations of *Astérix* contain an afterword by Won-Bok discussing his debt to the series and their influence on his work.

33. Invisible and domesticating translations are one and the same.

46   ◦ 세계 최초로 산업 혁명이 일어난 영국은 오랫동안 골해로 유명했다. 템스 강의 오염된 강물은 악명 높았다. 지금은 템스 강을 정화하려는 노력으로 비교적 맑은 물이 흐르고 있다.

FIGURE 9.3 The consequences of dropping magic potion in the river. Korean translation of *Asterix in Britain* (1966), with explanatory footnote. Art by Albert Uderzo.

Naturally, that intimate relationship between comic and reader may break down in traditions with vastly different comic-book conventions, where the translator cannot disguise the translated nature of the text. In these systems, translators may feel empowered to adopt strategies that explicitly mark the text as foreign. In the Korean translations, the iconic opening map of Gaul with Astérix's village in the corner is shown with the French names in Roman script and a Korean transliteration above. The album is also footnoted extensively throughout, which is most likely an influence from Korean educational comics. The Latin phrases, for example, are translated into Korean in the panels but come with footnotes that give a Korean transliteration of the Latin, the Latin in the Roman alphabet, plus information on the author of the phrase.[34] The Korean translations also make considerable use of footnotes to supply historical and cultural information not strictly required for understanding the flow of the narrative or a joke. On page 46 of *Asüteriksu hyeonggog-e gada* (*Asterix in Britain*), which shows the barrel of magic potion the Gauls have brought to Britain falling into the Thames, a footnote informs the reader that the Thames has been dirty for a long time but is cleaner now than it has been for a while (figure 9.3).[35] Additionally, each volume contains a translator's afterword containing a brief summary of the historical background to the story. These ensure that the series is framed

34. The Indonesian translations adopt a middle strategy, supplying the Latin and then translating it in parentheses immediately following.

35. It is not clear if the translator is implying that "a long time" extends as far back as Astérix and Obélix or not. Similar footnotes are found on pp. 31 (historical background on the Tower of London), 39 (explanation of the outfits of the Caledonian bards), and 47 (explanation that French food has far more garlic than English cuisine).

not just as a window into a comic, imagined European past but as one into current European history and culture.

The Arabic translation of *Asterix the Gaul* adopts a very different strategy. The opening map is entirely labeled in Arabic and changes the names of the camps to Sasuum, Babooum, Najooum, and Ahuum. This retains the *-um* ending of the original (and makes for a nice rhyming effect), but unlike in the source text, where the names have humorous meanings, the translator uses names that have no particular meaning in Arabic, humorous or otherwise. Unlike the English and Korean translations, this Arabic translation gives no special notice to the Latin phrases that pepper its source, either translating the Latin literally or substituting different dialogue as necessary. At 5.9, the original "Vae victo, vae victis" uttered by a Roman legionary unfortunate enough to run into Astérix while on patrol (see figure 7.1) is translated as "Pity us." Puns in the original Roman names are simply ignored; names are either transliterated or completely ignored and dropped from the text. Interestingly, this Arabic translation refuses to conform to local cultural norms in other ways, leaving in elements that might offend local culture, such as magic, pigs (the wild boar are clearly labeled as wild pigs throughout, and our heroes are shown feasting on them), and extremely uncovered female bodies. This contrasts with translations of Disney comics into Arabic, which rigorously cut out elements that might be offensive to Arab culture, drawing in clothes on women and even deleting entire pages if necessary (Zitawi 2008). The tactics of the Arabic translator of *Asterix the Gaul* thus do not fit within neat categories of domesticating or foreignizing; while leaving the original Latin unmarked by translating it into Arabic without comment might be seen as domesticating, having the heroes eat wild pigs shows that the text originates in a foreign world. The title chosen for the translation encapsulates that: *Asterix the Gaul* is now *Asteriks Batal al Abtal,* that is, *Asterix the Hero of Heroes*; although Astérix keeps his name, the extended title casts him in the role of a traditional Arab hero.

Translation in *Astérix*

Astérix also has much to say about our ability to understand and misunderstand one another and comments on translation and its limits. On the one hand, the books give us the fixity of Astérix as never changing, never affected by the world around him,[36] both within the series and as a translated object. This is, after all, Astérix the *Gaul,* the hero of a series that specifically evokes French school texts and is "in a real sense a re-view of a cultural experience common to all French, part of each one's childhood and a recollection of his or her first consciousness of their heritage" (Nye 1980, 192). The series cannot help but point French readers to a fixed past, even if it is a past that only exists in nostalgic memory and is stripped of its more unpleasant moments.

The series does more than that, however; it reorients the world and fixes its axis on one small village in northern Gaul (not even near Paris). Everyone comes to Astérix for help and asks for it in French—even the English, who speak French "English style" with the adjective before the noun.[37] Astérix's village is a unique source of help against the imperial power

36. Perhaps best shown in *Asterix and the Roman Agent*, where Astérix and Getafix (Panoramix in French) are the only two Gauls who remain unaffected by the Roman agent who sows disharmony throughout their village.

37. The English translation deals with this by placing stereotypical English expressions such as "What" at the ends of sentences; the Korean translation has the English speak an invented Korean dialect. Other translators make

of Rome; alone (or almost so), they stand against the threatening forces of imperialism and English. The Spaniards, the English, and the Indians—even Edifis (French Numérobis), the Egyptian architect, speaks Gaulish and is a friend of Getafix (and has a scribe who speaks all the modern languages including Gaulish).

Everything revolves around this tiny village, much as the Romans might like to think Rome is the center of the earth; we can easily see how Rome can be switched with America or any other cultural behemoth that threatens minority cultures and languages. *Astérix* shows a world where cultural power and creative influence still remain with the Gauls. In *Asterix in Britain*, Astérix creates tea by adding herbs to the hot water the English drink; in *Asterix in Spain*, he invents bullfighting. The French (or their ancestors, at least) create key components of national identity, while their own needs no such interventions.

Our heroes inhabit an ancient but invented world, where the periphery has an unnatural impact on the center and considerable power over the narrative of history and culture. In the never-identified village in Gaul—a region that no longer exists and can thus escape identification with the colonial past of France—*Astérix* shows how those on the fringes can still have significant impact and resist the great centers of culture and power. This anonymous village sits both at the periphery of an empire and at the center of the narrative, wielding enormous cultural power without seeking also to wield political or military power. Further, the series allows other countries to share in that fantasy, by having several albums (such as *Asterix in Britain* and *Asterix in Spain*) show how repeatable—and endlessly translated—is the conceit of the one small village holding out against the Romans. The series imagines the world as spinning on a Gaulish axis, perhaps best encapsulated by Obélix's refrain of "These Romans are crazy" when faced with something he doesn't understand; as readers, we are invited to share Obélix's perspective and identify with the Gallic, Asterixian definition of what is and isn't normal behavior.

Where *Astérix* does not translate in Europe is in regions with complicated and fraught relationships with the French center of power, where the narrative of a heroic French resistance against imperial power cannot help but sit very uncomfortably. There are, for example, only three translations of *Astérix* into Breton,[38] which surely has less to do with the fact that Breton speakers also speak French than that Bretons are uncomfortable with their story—as Celtic holdouts against an imperial culture on the edge of France—being co-opted as a French national tale.[39] Likewise, the series has gained little traction in Corsica, another region with a troubled relationship with its mother country of France.

---

clever use of dialect in ways that are not possible in their source; in the 2008 Antillean Creole translation of *Asterix and the Great Divide* (*Grand kannal la*), an album whose plot revolves around a divided village and a Romeo and Juliet story, the divided village speaks Guadeloupe Creole on the right-hand side and Martinique Creole on the left. Astérix's village, however, speaks a mixture of both dialects, showing its unified nature (http://www.asterix.com/the-collection/translations/asterix-in-creole.html).

38. The Breton translations are of *Asterix in Britain*, *Asterix and the Big Fight*, and *Asterix and the Actress*. The first translation came one year before the creation of Diwan, the league of schools that teaches Breton through immersion.

39. *Astérix* has had variable success in Celtic languages, which is surprising, as it seems it would be an obvious children's book to translate, especially because the village is clearly located in Brittany and there is interest in the Gauls on the part of many modern Celtic-language speakers. There are eight Welsh translations, one Scottish Gaelic translation (of *Asterix the Gaul*), and no Irish Gaelic translation.

Conclusion

Explaining the continuing appeal of Astérix as a French cultural touchstone, Steel (2005, 214) writes that he is "reassuring (as opposed to disturbing), he is Mr. Clean, fairly conformist, predictable, straight, patriotic, non-ideological, a rallying point or a unifier through military exploits and above all someone who evolves in a non-contentious period of French history." From time to time, *Astérix* may play with the potential for Astérix to change, as in *Asterix the Legionary*, where Astérix and Obélix go undercover and enroll as legionaries to rescue a conscripted Gaulish youth. But even then, they sow chaos by remaining indisputably themselves, never becoming Romanized. And this points to the complexity of Astérix: he may stay the same, refuse to be translated, but he is a figure of narrative order that creates disorder. Like its hero, the series is both flexible and inflexible at the same time; the stories nearly always begin in the village, and they always end up there, with a rousing banquet toasting the success of the Gauls. Astérix may move, but the move is never permanent; he is fluid while still remaining fixed. In a global culture where different Romes always seem to win, gobbling up villages and local cultures as they expand, Astérix can come to the rescue.

Appendix: List of Translations

The following is a list of translations (other than the UK English) that are specifically referred to in this chapter. The names are those of the translators, if known.

Arabic

Losienne. 1961. *Asteriks Batal al Abtal* (*Asterix Hero of Heroes* = *Asterix the Gaul*). Cairo: Dar el Maaref.

Breton

Kervella, Divi. 1976. *Asteriks e Breizh* (*Asterix in Britain*). Paris: Dargaud.
Kervella, Divi. 1977. *Asteriks hag Emgann ar Pennoú* (*Asterix and the Big Fight*). Paris: Dargaud.
Kervella, Divi. 2004 *Astérix hag an Distro* (*Asterix and the Actress*). Paris: Albert René.

Chinese (Mandarin)

1968. *Yali Lixianji* (*Asterix's Adventures* = *Asterix the Gaul*). Beijing: Chaohua Arts Publishing House.

Corsican/Corsu

Albertini, François. 1993. *Astérix in Corsica*. Paris: Dargaud Editeur.
Albertini, François. 2004. *Astérix gira è volta . . . à a scola*. Paris: Albert René.

Creole

(Antillean) Poulet, Hector, and Jean-Marc Rosier. 2008. *Grand kannal la* (*Astérix and the Great Divide*). Paris: Caraibéditions.
(Réunion) Saint Omer, François. 2008. *Astérix la Kaz Razade* (*Asterix and the Magic Carpet*). Paris: Caraibéditions.

Japanese

Watanabe, Kazuo, and Nishimoto, Koji. 1974. *Asuterikkusu no bôken* (*Asterix the Gaul*). Tokyo: Futabasha.
Watanabe, Kazuo, and Nishimoto, Koji. 1974. *Asuterikkusu to gôtozoku* (*Asterix and the Goths*). Tokyo: Futabasha.
Watanabe, Kazuo, and Nishimoto, Koji. 1974. *Ôgon no kama* (*Asterix and the Golden Sickle*). Tokyo: Futabasha.

Korean

Yŏng-ju O and Ki-Wan Sŏng. 2001. *Asûteriksû Kûlleopatûra-rûl mannada (Asterix and Cleopatra)*. Seoul: Munhak kwa Chisŏngsa.

Latin

Collognat, Anna. 2007. *Caelum in caput ejus cadit (Asterix and the Falling Sky)*. Paris: Editions Albert René.

Scottish Gaelic

Morgan, Peadar. 1989. *Asterix an Ceilteach (Asterix the Gaul)*. Skye: Taigh na Teud.

US English

Caron, Robert Steven. 1984. *Asterix and the Great Crossing.* Greenwich, CT: Dargaud International.

Caron, Robert Steven. 1992. *Asterix the Legionary.* Greenwich, CT: Dargaud International.

Caron, Robert Steven. 1992. *Asterix at the Olympic Games.* Greenwich, CT: Dargaud International.

Caron, Robert Steven. 1995. *Asterix in Britain.* Greenwich, CT: Dargaud International.

Caron, Robert Steven. 1995. *Asterix and Cleopatra.* Greenwich, CT: Dargaud International.

Vietnamese

1993. *Chang Axtêrix nguoi Gô loa. (Asterix the Gaul)*. Phụ nữ.

PART FOUR

Modern Classics

10

Classical Allusion in Modern British Political Cartoons

Ian Runacres and Michael K. Mackenzie

It is unsurprising that cartoonists passing comment on the Greek debt crisis of 2011 draw on imagery from the art, literature, and history of ancient Greece. Given that Greece's own Olympics opening ceremony pageant in 2004 leaped straight from Alexander the Great to the Greek War of Independence, with a brief interlude for some scenes derived from Byzantine art, it is reasonable to say that Greece has not produced a significant cache of images internationally identifiable as Greek since the Roman conquest of the second century BCE. Steve Bell in the *Guardian*, for example, depicted an antiausterity protester as the Discobolus statue, his mouth masked, hurling a euro coin instead of a discus at a line of riot police.[1] A few days earlier, he had satirized Germany's and France's insistence that every EU country assist in any bailout of Greece by altering the image of Europa and the Bull on the obverse of the Greek two-euro coin to depict a bovine Nicolas Sarkozy abducting Angela Merkel, her middle finger raised to the reader (figure 10.1).

To a viewer with no classical education or knowledge that Europa and the Bull are in fact depicted on the Greek two-euro coin, the cartoon can work as political commentary. Merkel appears to behave imperiously, supported by or crushing Sarkozy, the Greek flag in the background suggesting that Greece is the root of her dominance. A rudimentary knowledge of classics might be rewarded with a deeper, more satisfying interpretation: Merkel, the de facto leader of the eurozone countries as head of its biggest economy, is depicted as Europa, representing Europe. Her obscene gesture and lordly riding of France symbolize her power to make the other European countries participate in the Greek bailout; their rude takeover of the Greek coin is analogous to the EU riding roughshod over the Greek economy with the imposition of austerity measures.

So far, so good. But an educated classicist prone to literal overanalysis might make this interpretation: Sarkozy is Zeus. He has forcibly abducted Europa in order to rape her. Merkel is the intended victim of this rape, implying that France, the bearer of more Greek debt than Germany, wishes to screw the German economy for its own benefit against the

---

1. *Guardian*, June 29, 2011. www.guardian.co.uk/commentisfree/cartoon/2011/jun/29/euro-euro.

FIGURE 10.1 Two-euro coin with Nicolas Sarkozy abducting Angela Merkel. Art by Steve Bell, *The Guardian*, June 17, 2011, © Steve Bell. Used by permission of the artist.

background of the Greek crisis. The rape of Europa is a foundation myth for Europe; she is not "Europe" already. The forced union between Germany and France might therefore be interpreted as the birth of a new European order. Merkel's obscene gesture could, in this context, be a modern reception of the version whereby Europa was a willing victim of Zeus' bull: Germany's assumption of power in exchange for fiscal rape by France as a parallel to Europa's gain of womanhood over her virginal friends abandoned to their girlish ball games on the shore.[2]

This interpretation is palpably wrong. The political commentary in this cartoon relies on a shallow and basic awareness of the classical material, and any deeper "reception studies" will lead one away from its obvious meaning. Unfortunately, this means that the wealth of literary source material for this cartoon—be it Herodotus, Ovid, Moschus, or another—appears to be at best a distraction and at worst irrelevant. Better, perhaps, to console oneself with the fact that the image is clearly derived from a long history of Attic vase painters, sculptors, and Roman fresco artists to the extent that it has become iconic, even if the meanings behind it have been lost—although it could also simply have been lifted from the modern coinage. This chapter explores the extent to which images derived from classical sources in modern political cartoons have become divorced from their sources and diluted by history and what this means

2. See Moschus, *Europa* 101–105; see also Eaton (2003, 162–164) on Titian's portrayal of Europa as complicit in her abduction.

for our understanding of how the classics continue to be perceived and represented in everyday political discourse.

Bell did not invent the idea of commenting on recent events using the image of Europa; she has a long history in the annals of caricature. John Tenniel used her in *Punch* in December 1863 in a cartoon captioned "Europa carried off by the (John) Bull," depicting the Bull, England, abducting Europa from the shore where Napoleon III offers a general congress, reflecting how the rest of Europe followed Britain's lead in rejecting Napoleon's overtures (Tenniel 1870, pl. 16). This is a standard use of the myth: a powerful figure snatches a weak one. Modern Europa cartoons are similar. Sometimes the Europa character represents Europe, as in the Tenniel prototype: as Georges Pompidou being carried off by Edward Heath upon Britain's entry into the common market in 1971, or as distressed European currencies being abducted by the Bull of Recession in 1992.[3] But other times, confusingly, it is the bull that represents Europe, as the EEC budget carrying off a defiant Margaret Thatcher in 1979, or as the European Exchange Rate Mechanism carrying off an older, more terrified Thatcher as her backstabbing cabinet colleagues joyfully wave her off from the shore in 1990.[4] Even with these examples, then, we are drawn to the conclusion that the classical myth is only of the vaguest importance: the image is deployed when someone is being swept away by a force beyond his or her control, when either of them have something to do with Europe. The peripheries of the story are irrelevant.

It is almost invariably the case that any one classical allusion is not confined to a single cartoon but rather is repeated very often by different cartoonists over a long period of time.[5] The classically themed cartoons that appear regularly in today's newspapers constitute, with few exceptions, what we would describe as a toolbox of convenient allegorical clichés, images generally unwedded to any one particular account of the myth and generally familiar enough to the average reader to form a visual opinion column. Hercules facing the Hydra often depicts a politician facing a multiplying, undefeatable (and therefore typically political) problem; Odysseus with the Sirens shows a politician trying to resist some course or other; Nero fiddling

---

3. Nicholas Garland, *Daily Telegraph*, October 29, 1971; September 12, 1992.

4. Nicholas Garland, *Sunday Telegraph*, September 29, 1979; Garland, *Independent*, October 9, 1990. Thatcher's colleagues are later Prime Minister John Major, former Chancellor Nigel Lawson, Commons Leader Geoffrey Howe, and European Competition Commissioner (former Trade Secretary) Leon Brittan. Arguably, this subverts the classical myth of Europa's friends lamenting her abduction on the shore, but the image of internal enemies condoning Thatcher's rape for their own benefit is powerful without this knowledge.

5. The chief source for research into British political cartoons is the British Cartoon Archive at the University of Kent. Its website (www.cartoons.ac.uk) allows researchers to find cartoons from a large number of publications from the twentieth century and before by searching keywords. We discovered the vast majority of our examples by trying every classical keyword and character we could think of. While the collection itself is not exhaustive owing to rights restrictions, this method quickly and simply gives a broad sample of relevant cartoons from an impressively vast database, and it is for this reason that this chapter focuses on British cartoons. The Association of American Editorial Cartoonists archive was also used (http://editorialcartoonists.com), although this is less comprehensive than the British archive. Bell's website (www.belltoons.co.uk) also permits searches by keyword. More recent cartoons were discovered by clicking backward through the *Guardian, Independent,* and *Telegraph* websites' cartoon archives. Older cartoons not in the British Cartoon Archive were chiefly sourced from collected volumes of *Punch* and the separate collections of Tenniel cited in the footnotes.

FIGURE 10.2   The Laocoön image as metaphor. Clockwise from top left: (a) Nicholas Garland, *Daily Telegraph*, March 27, 1981, © Telegraph Media Group Limited, image source British Cartoon Archive, University of Kent, www.cartoons.ac.uk. (b) Nicholas Garland, *Daily Telegraph*, November 19, 1999, © Telegraph Media Group Limited. (c) Steve Bell, *Guardian*, August 12, 1999, © Steve Bell. Used by permission of the artist. (d) Steve Bell, *Guardian*, January 28, 2011, © Steve Bell. Used by permission of the artist.

FIGURE 10.2 Continued

while Rome burns shows a leader willfully impotent in the face of some disaster; Sisyphus rolling his rock uphill shows a leader with a big recurring problem that won't go away.[6]

These are the visual equivalents of the "stock images and quotations from foreign languages" that form one of Partridge's (1978, xi) categories of clichés. He defines a cliché as
an "outworn commonplace; a phrase, or short sentence, that has become so hackneyed that
careful speakers and scrupulous writers shrink from it because they feel that its use is an
insult to the intelligence of their audience or public."[7] Yet the advantage of a cliché's inherent
familiarity is that it provides a rapid stimulus to a further idea: cartoonists' frequent repetition of the same base image populated by different characters appears to make them guilty of
Zijderfeld's (1979, 13) criticism that it is only by constant iteration that a cliché can "achieve
the thoughtless, mechanical response it set out to elicit." For the cartoonist, however, such a
stimulus is helpful not because it creates a thoughtless response but rather because the easy
apprehension of the underlying metaphor can rapidly provoke a thoughtful response to a
political situation. As Ricks (1980, 58) responds to Zijderfeld, "Clichés invite you not to
think—but you may always decline the invitation, and what could better invite a thinking
man to think?"

To demonstrate how the political cartoonist's toolbox of convenient classical clichés
stimulates thought and what relevance the classical prototype has for its modern political cartoons, consider a prolific example that can be easily traced back to a single classical source.
The statue of the death of Laocoön, attributed to Asegander, Polydorus, and Athenodorus
of Rhodes (Plin., *HN* 36.11), now housed in the Vatican Museums, depicts the Trojan priest
Laocoön and his two sons writhing in the grasp of a sea snake, their deaths portending the
destruction of Troy. The image has been used as a metaphor for groups of people being entangled in insurmountable problems. Among recent examples, we find Thatcher, Labour leader
Michael Foot, and Liberal leader David Steel being ensnared by the Roy Jenkins–headed snake
of the new British Social Democratic Party in 1981; Thatcher's legacy ensnaring Tory leaders
John Major and William Hague in 1999; Prime Minister Tony Blair, his spin doctor Alastair
Campbell, and Frank Dobson, the Labour party candidate for London mayor, being tied up by
the snake of rogue independent Ken Livingstone in 1999; and Rupert Murdoch running rings
around Prime Minister David Cameron and the police force in 2011 (figure 10.2). The image
is such a staple of the cartoonist's repertoire that Vicky (pen name of Victor Weisz) used it five
times between 1955 and 1965; Nicholas Garland used it eight times between 1966 and 2008;
between 2005 and 2011, Bell has drawn three.[8]

---

6. E.g., John Tenniel, *Punch*, February 1870; E. H. Shepherd, *Punch*, June 29, 1938 Nicholas Garland, *Daily
Telegraph*, March 2, 2001 (Hercules and the Hydra); David Low, *Star*, January 21, 1926; Low, *Evening Standard*,
March 18, 1940; Abu Abraham, *Observer*, January 5, 1964; Michael Cummings, *Daily Express*, September 20,
1985 (Ulysses and the Sirens); Low, *Evening Standard*, November 14, 1940, Emmwood, *Daily Mail*, July 14, 1960;
Garland, *Daily Telegraph*, October 28, 2003 (Nero); Vicky, *Daily Mirror*, April 16, 1956; Stanley Franklin, *Daily
Mirror*, December 14, 1964; Peter Schrank, *Independent*, July 15, 1996 (Sisyphus). Cf. Mitchell (2013).

7. The other categories are idioms that have become clichés, other hackneyed phrases, and quotations from
English literature (Partridge 1978, xii).

8. Mitchell (2013, 338–349) considers other Laocoön cartoons and explores their meaning in broader contexts,
including Canadian and American examples. Mitchell also considers examples that depict the Labors of Heracles
and Nero.

FIGURE 10.3 Caricature of the Laocoön group as apes. attributed to Nicolo Boldrini after Titian.

Its use in modern cartoons would seem to be more a result of its existence as an artistic trope than a contemporary reflection on classical art. The statue is itself iconic, described by Pliny the Elder (*HN* 236.11) as *opus omnibus et picturae et staturiae artis praeferendum* ("a work to be held in higher regard than every other work of art, both pictorial and statuary"). It was much copied in the Italian Renaissance; a competition for its restoration was judged by Raphael. Its vaunted perfection led to its being caricatured in a woodcut, sometimes attributed to Titian, dated to circa 1566, which shows apes, rather than men, ensnared in the snake's grasp (see figure 10.3).

Various explanations for what it is satirizing have been proposed, but perhaps the most convincing is that it was a comment on the dispute between the Galenist and Vesalian schools of medical thought in the late sixteenth century over the anatomical similarities between men and apes. In this interpretation, the epitome of representation of the human form in classical art is transformed into a reductio ad absurdum of the Galenist hypothesis that apes are enough like humans that they can be used as our anatomical analogues (Janson 1946). In other words, classical art is satirized in order to satirize classical ideas. William Blake similarly caricatured the statue in a print of circa 1820, which satirized the idea that classical art was primary to Judeo-Christian art and that modern imperialism following ancient precedents was good and correct. Blake titled the work "Jehovah & his two Sons Satan & Adam as they were copied from the Cherubim Of Solomon's Temple by three Rhodians & applied to Natural Fact or History of Ilium." Again, classical art is caricatured to caricature ideas about the classics.[9]

9. See Paley (2002) for a thorough exposition.

This is emphatically not the case in modern editorial cartoons that use the image. The heterogeneous political situations and characters to which the image is applied are united not by their having something scabrous to say about the nature of classical art but in their using this particular artwork as a skeleton from which to hang a comment on people being entangled in a deleterious situation. As such, the classical origins of the work are irrelevant to the modern cartoons' ability to make a political statement. In one telling instance, Vicky inserts an audience discussing the statue into the cartoon, which features Chancellor Rab Butler, Prime Minister Anthony Eden, and Labour Minister Walter Monckton entangled by an unlabeled snake. It is captioned "He's either wrestling with the snake of inflation, with the opposition, or with his conscience, dear . . ."[10] It is the image alone, divorced from its context, that has power; its prolificacy is predicated on its malleability to any number of perennial political situations, owing to the variety of possible opponents with which the protagonists can wrestle. Moreover, it is difficult to say whether modern cartoonists came to the image through the original statue and its place in the history of art and caricature,[11] from ancestral cartoonists, or, as is most likely, an indiscernible blend of the three.

The extent to which its classical origins are irrelevant is best shown by a hyperclassicizing example by Bell, who frequently deploys the statue in his work and used the image in the *Guardian* on August 12, 1999 (figure 10.2c) to show former Prime Minister Major, incumbent Tory leader Hague, and, oddly, Prince Philip being entangled by Thatcher's legacy. While Philip's presence is a separate joke,[12] the classical origins of the statue are used as an excuse to include several unrelated classical witticisms mediated through any desired later interpretation: the Thatcher snake says, "Hello Oedipus!" to Hague, who duly replies "Hello Mum!"— perhaps more in reference to Freud than to Sophocles. Major cries, "It's a Greek Tragedy I tell you!"—unlikely to be a reference to Sophocles' lost *Laocoön*. A classical canvas is a mere excuse to use classics en masse as a device to alienate readers from their current environment and thus make them reconsider the present political situation.[13]

Our engagement with the classical archetype in the Laocoön cartoons is diluted by the image's canonical status among cartoonists.[14] Other canonical classical images are watered down by more extreme means. The punishment of Prometheus, chained to a rock and about to have

10. Vicky, *Daily Mirror*, November 1, 1955.

11. A position cemented by Gottholm Lessing's 1766 book on the statue, *Laokoon oder Über die Grenzen der Malerei und Poesie*, which marked the first systematic assessment of aesthetics in the Enlightenment in its attempt to delineate the difference between the production of poetry and painting.

12. Philip is depicted drilling into his own forehead while shouting, "No no! It's an Indian fusebox!!"—a reference to his remarking, while touring a factory in Edinburgh in 1999, that a fusebox "looked like it had been put in by an Indian."

13. Similarly, a Martin Rowson cartoon in the *Guardian* on October 3, 2009, predominantly based on the "Nero fiddling while Rome burns" cliché and showing a defeated-looking Prime Minister Gordon Brown having fiddled the strings on his violin to the point of snapping, also shows Blair in the background offering daggers with which to stab him, simultaneously showing Brown as the megalomaniac Nero and Nero's arrogant ancestor Julius Caesar. Such is the generalizing power of the cartoon toga.

14. Lest one doubt the potential for a cartoon to become iconic, consider the manner in which the phrase *a curate's egg* has become a frequent metaphor for absurdly trying to find something good in a terrible situation since the publication of George du Maurier's cartoon "True Humility" in *Punch* (November 9, 1895).

his liver assailed by an eagle or vulture, is a common image in the toolbox of cartoon clichés; the eagle invariably wears some statement of the problem assailing the Prometheus figure.[15] In an early example by Tenniel, "King Cotton" is attacked by an eagle with the Union flag on its left wing and the Confederate flag on its right, representing the cessation of cotton exports to Europe in the American Civil War in 1861; in a more recent example by Garland from 2006, Charles Clarke, then Home Secretary, is assailed by the hepatophagic bird of "scandal latest."[16] In none of the cartoons is there any suggestion that the Prometheus character is being unjustly or tragically punished by a jealous higher force for bringing some power-redistributing benefit to mankind; rather, it is only important that the victim is helplessly under constant assault. The moral analysis of the victim is rarely positive. The emphasis of the punishment in the cartoon differs drastically, therefore, from that in the classical archetype in its simplification and stripping out of backstory.

The alienation of the cartoon from the source can, however, go further. In the Clarke example, as in some others by Garland, the cartoon comes with a caption: "He groaned slightly and winced, like Prometheus watching his vulture dropping in for lunch." The quotation, when used, is attributed to P. G. Wodehouse. Its specific provenance, the 1930 novel *Big Money*, is irrelevant. It is rather the fact that the scene is likened to something from a Wodehouse novel—where the ruling classes are portrayed as blithering idiots—that lends the image an additional bathos: Clarke is not the hero of classical myth, punished for bringing enlightenment to humanity, but a fool whose pomposity is deservedly being pricked. The classical source is thus open to abusive reinterpretation and transformation for the sake of a more devastating comment on political elites. Arguably, this more modern filter on the myth will, in time, become irrelevant as Wodehouse is read less, and reinterpretations of the scene will have to evolve further.

Cartoonists thus appear to rely on a small number of simplified snapshots of a classical image in order to make their points. This would suggest, however, that the toolbox of clichés is not dynamic. This is not the case for two reasons: first, the toolbox was not always fixed in its current form; and second, there are still exceptions to this toolbox that make detailed allusions to original classical material.

The toolbox has, over time, become more streamlined, with the fittest cliché supplanting others whose waning popular familiarity has made them moribund. Cartoons of Icarus flying too close to the sun, a symbol of overweening political ambition, occupy such a clichéd place in the cartoonist's arsenal that they are themselves the victim of Chris Morris's 1994 television news satire *The Day Today*. The repetitive and fossilized use of facile analogies in editorial cartooning is lampooned by the character of "Brant, the physical cartoonist from the *Daily Telegraph*," who enacts Bill Clinton as Icarus, flying too close to the sun of "political heat" over some "choppy waters" (Morris et al. [w.] and Gillman [dir.] 1994.)

Alongside the Icarus image in the nineteenth century are found several cartoons based on the similar story of Phaethon, another youth whose overambition ended in disaster. Phaethon was too weak to be able to heed his father the sun god's instructions on how to drive the

---

15. For the story of Prometheus' punishment by Zeus and rescue by Hercules, see Hesiod, *Theog.* 510–525.

16. *Punch*, November 1861; Tenniel (1868, pl. 74). Garland, *Daily Telegraph*, May 4, 2006.

FIGURE 10.4 **George W. Bush and the Hydra. Nicholas Garland,** *Daily Telegraph***, September 14, 2007,** ©
Telegraph Media Group Limited.

chariot of the sun and, in his youthful zeal, set fire to the Earth, the heavens, and himself (Ov.,
Met. 1.750–2.332). James Gillray used Phaethon in 1808 to show Foreign Secretary George
Canning's dangerous ambition of taking on Napoleon; Tenniel used it in 1877 to satirize the
Earl of Beaconsfield's doomed elevation of Sir Stafford Northcote to the leadership of the
House of Commons.[17] And yet we can find none from the twentieth century.

We can make a similar case for the slaughter of many-headed monsters. Tenniel in *Punch*
uses the image of Hercules killing the three-headed Cacus in February 1881 to show William
Gladstone's struggle with the terrorist Land League;[18] in September 1886, he used the image
of Lord Randolph Churchill killing the triple-headed Chimera to show his confronting the
military, naval, and civil services with a judicial inquiry; in December 1872, he portrayed the
president of the Third Republic, Adolphe Thiers, throwing a drugged cake to the three-headed
Cerberus, whose heads represent rival opposition Legitimist, Imperialist, and Orléanist fac-
tions. And yet the only image that survives into the twentieth century is that of Hercules
killing the Hydra, used by Tenniel to show the enormous number of problems that Gladstone
had to tackle, from Fenianism to sanitary reform, in the Parliament of February 1870. These
are different metaphors; the constant replication of the Hydra's severed heads to create an
ever larger enemy is used to great effect by Garland, for instance, to show George W. Bush's
futile attempt to kill a Hydra of Osama bin Laden–headed snakes in 2007 (figure 10.4). In

17. *Punch*, February 1877; Tenniel (1895, pl. 83).

18. Interestingly, Cacus does not have three heads in antiquity. Tenniel may have confused him with Geryon,
whose cattle Hercules was escorting at the time. We are grateful to an anonymous reviewer for this point.

FIGURE 10.5 "The Health Care Hydra." Karl Wimer, *Denver Business Journal*, May 2, 2008, © Karl Wimer. Used by permission of the artist.

contrast, the other monsters represent wars on several fronts, without the threat of the enemy multiplying. Nonetheless, it is evidence of a cultural loss that images are forced to drop out of the canon.

One consequence of this cultural loss is that cartoonists have come to use the Hydra image in a generic way to depict all multileveled political imbroglios, even those that are not likely to multiply in complexity as one component or another is addressed. An example of this is a 2008 cartoon by Karl Wimer entitled "The Health Care Hydra: (figure 10.5).[19] In the cartoon, the Colorado Legislature is collectively embodied in the person of Hercules, who is raising his sword against the beast while dressed in the armor of a knight from a much later period. The Hydra depicts the healthcare issue with its many stakeholder interests: the insurance industry, pharmaceuticals, patients, lawyers, hospitals, and doctors. There is no indication or reason to suppose that if one head were chopped off, two more would grow in its place. On the contrary, there are in this situation multiple interests of a fixed and identifiable number. This situation might have been more accurately depicted with a reference to some other multiheaded monster. Furthermore, in this cartoon, as with most other examples

19. This cartoon is, evidently, not British. It is, however, the best example we could find of this phenomenon contemporary with Garland's purer interpretation of the classical myth. It is not intended as any comment on the superiority or otherwise of British cartoonists over American ones.

of the Hydra cliché, the underlying message appears to be one of futility in the face of impossible odds. A fuller understanding of the myth, however, would convey the opposite: the Herculean politician will find a way to cauterize the stumps and kill the monster. This bit of optimism is rarely intended where the Hydra-headed cliché is used or misused in political cartooning.

The loss of a classical analogy from the canon can happen for various reasons. In some specific instances, we can point to a flash of popular relevance that quickly fades. David Low, for example, twice uses the same image from what would now generally be considered an extremely obscure play, the *Alcestis* of Euripides, in 1927 and 1931, each portraying two figures squaring off, as Hercules and Hades, fighting for the soul of Alcestis, who is lying, apparently dead, in a bed.[20] In the 1927 example, for instance, the caption reads, "Hercules about to wrestle with Ramsay MacDeath [Macdonald] for the soul of the Liberal Party [Alcestis]." After 1931, it is never seen again, a failure to stay in the toolbox. Gilbert Murray's translation of the *Alcestis* was published in 1915 and presented on BBC Radio in December 1928 alongside a number of other performances, mostly in schools; but it has since had a very low public profile.[21] It is likely that these cartoons appeared and disappeared on the same wave that briefly popularized the play. Similarly, the demise of the horse-drawn "phaeton" as a mode of carriage may have led to the diminution of knowledge of the etiology of the cart's name. To maintain relevance, then, cartoons appear to need some grounding in touchstones of popular culture, but that grounding does not need to be strongly tied to the classical sources.

In other instances, though, we can only point to a general attrition of the corpus of potentially relevant and identifiable images. Garland told us in an interview that he had a regular game with some fellow cartoonists in which they would construct a list of images they no longer felt able to use.[22] This perception of cultural ignorance among the wider public was not confined to classics (he recalled an editor of the *Daily Telegraph* failing to recognize Hamlet), but on the list of self-censored classical images, he included Perseus and the stand of Horatius Cocles against Lars Porsenna on the Pons Sublicius in the sixth century BCE (Livy 2.10). The fact that he came to this image from Thomas Babington Macaulay's 1842 poem *Horatius* and not from Livy (and possibly from earlier cartoonists; see Sidney Strube's cartoon "Holding the Bridge" in the *Daily Express* of March 17, 1947) implies a more widespread cultural loss that stretches to jingoistic Victorian reception of classics and the originals.

The attrition of the toolbox manifests itself not only in the absolute loss of images but also in the descriptions applied to them. For example, in the 1970s, Garland regularly uses images of Odysseus being tempted by the Sirens without a caption. If he does caption the cartoon, it is with reference to the *Odyssey*; for example, "But Ulysses escaped the sirens' blandishments by filling his companions' ears with wax and lashing himself to the mast." By the time he has reached the 2000s, however, he is captioning the cartoon with a dictionary definition of

20. *Evening Standard*, October 27, 1927; *Evening Standard*, March 20, 1931.

21. Archive of Performances of Greek and Roman Drama, Oxford University.

22. Telephone interview, July 1, 2011.

FIGURE 10.6 Gordon Brown as Achilles. Nicholas Garland, *Daily Telegraph*, January 6, 1999, © Telegraph Media Group Limited, image source British Cartoon Archive, University of Kent, www.cartoons.ac.uk.

what Sirens are: "Sirens: mythical monsters that called sailors to their destruction by the sweetness of their song."[23]

While there is no obligation to make a cartoon understandable to everyone, political incisiveness (and much of the humor) is lost when the image's point is delivered in so cumbersome a fashion. For a literary or historical allegorical cartoon to work well, it is usually sufficient to have a vague idea of what is going on through some received, unspecific cultural osmosis. There are rare occasions, however, when not only is knowledge of an image's classical background essential but readers are also required to form their own opinion about the cartoonist's interpretive nuances. The best individual example of this concerns not a single cliché but a character narrative. On January 5, 1999, Chancellor Brown's press adviser, Charlie Whelan, was forced to resign over revelations, attributed (incorrectly) to him, that Brown's cabinet colleague Peter Mandelson had received an undisclosed home loan from Paymaster-General Geoffrey Robinson. Brown was widely criticized for remaining silent over the issue, neither defending his spokesman nor passing comment on the loan scandal, which was seen as worsening the impression of a cabinet divided. Garland in the *Daily Telegraph* chose to depict this situation on January 6 with reference to Achilles (figure 10.6). When Garland refers to Achilles, he usually

23. *Daily Telegraph*, May 9, 1969; *Daily Telegraph*, May 31, 2001. In 2001, Garland appended a description similarly patronizing to a classicist to a cartoon of the Hydra representing the foot-and-mouth disease crisis: "Hercules and the Hydra: as soon as one of its heads was struck off two more grew in its place." But he did not do so later, in 2007, with Bush and bin Laden. Hence we must be aware of the cartoonist's (or editor's) caprice in these matters.

does so with a warrior fighting off a barrage of problems with his shield, only to be struck on the notoriously weak heel by a rogue single arrow—a cliché.[24]

In the Brown case, however, he goes for a much more obscure scenario. Brown is depicted as Achilles sitting glumly in his tent, chin in his hand, his weapons discarded to one side. John Prescott, the deputy prime minister, cast as an unlikely Patroclus, peers in with an anxious look. The first two lines of Alexander Pope's translation of the *Iliad* are quoted: "The wrath of Peleus' son, the direful spring/Of all the Grecian woes, O goddess sing!" The implications of this cartoon are beyond the unacquainted reader. It requires the reader to know that the plot of the *Iliad* revolves around Achilles' withdrawal from the Greek army over a quarrel with Agamemnon, which leads to the wholesale slaughter of the Greeks by the Trojans until he rejoins. This knowledge allows the reader to understand the political situation thus: Brown is an essential part of the Labour government, and without his strength at this time, it will be destroyed by the Conservative opposition until he chooses to return to the front rank.

To understand this perception of Brown, however, requires an interpretive level of analysis of the *Iliad*. There are at least two potential scenarios. In the first, Achilles is justified in leaving the army in response to Agamemnon's theft of his concubine; it requires the tragic death of his beloved Patroclus to spur him on to return. In this scenario, the cartoon suggests that Prescott would also have to fall before Brown would show his hand and that for the meantime, Brown is correct to withdraw over the unfair "theft" of his press officer to save the government's face over the Mandleson-Robinson debacle. On the other hand, the cartoon could be ridiculing Brown's withdrawal by relying on an interpretation of the *Iliad* whereby Achilles is portrayed as a petulant and petty character who would rather allow a vast number of his colleagues to be killed over a fuss about a slave woman than lose a shred of his own pride. A sound knowledge of current affairs would probably be enough to steer one away from the first interpretation; Prescott was vocal at the time in calling for unity.[25] The fact that this appears in the *Daily Telegraph*, a right-leaning paper, would also guide the reader against viewing Brown in a positive light. However, this is probably not enough to suggest that Brown should be viewed as petty; the ancient armor and his being named as the hero Achilles could even suggest that he be viewed positively as a strong if currently inactive Labour foot soldier.

We would contend that the "petty murderer by proxy" interpretation is at its most clear when considered within the history of caricature. In 1827, the Duke of Wellington resigned his position as commander-in-chief of the armed forces over the appointment of his political rival Canning as prime minister. The caricaturist T. Jones represented this on May 6, 1827, with the cartoon "Achilles in the Sulks after his Retreat, or, The Great Captain on the Stool of Repentance!!" (figure 10.7). The cartoon shows Wellington, his back to the fighting going on outside his window, his weapons cast aside, sitting and pouting under an absurdly large hat, wearing his absurdly large trademark boots. His commander-in-chief's baton is broken on the ground. Jones also quotes four lines from Book 18 of Pope's translation of the *Iliad* that more explicitly criticize the selfishness of Wellington's withdrawal from the forces: "Here, for brutal

---

24. E.g., in a *Daily Telegraph* cartoon of June 6, 1983, Thatcher successfully fends off the Franks Report, the Unions, the Sterling Crisis, and Inflation but is struck on the heel by Unemployment. In a *Daily Telegraph* cartoon of March 12, 2007, Blair fends off Iraq, Afghanistan, and Bosnia but is hit by the Cash for Honours Scandal.

25. www.guardian.co.uk/politics/1999/jan/02/uk.politicalnews?INTCMP=ILCNETTXT3487.

FIGURE 10.7 The Duke of Wellington as Achilles. T. Jones, May 6, 1827 © The Tabley House Collection, image source British Cartoon Archive, University of Kent, www.cartoons.ac.uk.

courage far renown'd,/I live an idle burden to the ground,/(Others in council fam'd for nobler skill,/More useful to preserve than I to kill)" (*Il.* 18.104–106). In quoting the opening lines of the *Iliad*, perhaps in an attempt to flag the cartoon's inspiration, rather than a more helpful interpretative passage, Garland's reliance on the same interpretation of events is rendered more ambiguous and does less to help a less knowledgeable reader into the message of the cartoon.

It is, however, extremely rare to find classical cartoons that rely on interpretation of the original source rather than merely extra knowledge. Added depth is lent to the Prometheus cliché by Peter Schrank, for example, in a cartoon that shows Major's Prometheus being assailed by a Thatcher eagle, while Hercules, in the form of new Tory leader Hague, runs away from Prometheus rather than rescuing him.[26] The visual metaphor is lent more force by this reworking, but it is an alteration, not an interpretation. Even among nineteenth-century cartoonists, the expectation is of factual knowledge, not interpretation. Among Tenniel's classically sourced cartoons, there is perhaps only one exception to this, a cartoon depicting Lord Selbourne as Medea throwing the children of Law and Equity into the cauldron, while John Bull as Jason looks on, saying, "Goodness gracious!—(Aside)—I hope it's all right—but there'll be an awful row!"[27] This is a subversive interpretation of the *Medea*: Selbourne appears not to be taking revenge on the nation but rather to be trying, and succeeding, to convince it that his Judicature Bill will combine the two qualities into a superior united force. Knowledge of the play reveals the cartoonist's scabrous criticism of Selbourne's murderous deception and the country's bathetic response; it does not rely on an interpretation of the play as having a sympathetic Medea and a feckless Jason.

The canon of cartoon clichés relies, then, on stock images based on basic knowledge that may, in fact, be flawed and increasingly not understood. We have shown how cartoonists are aware of this decline in the knowledge base through the self-censored trimming of the canon and selective increases in information given. They also display their awareness of the inaccessibility of classics. Low is perhaps the first to draw explicitly on the irrelevance of classics to the general public. In 1959, he satirizes the low-brow expectations of television by exploiting a letter from a reader saying, "If the money spent on TV had been applied to the encouragement of public enlightenment, we might have made a new Athens in Great Britain." He depicts a glum TV panel of Demosthenes, Aristotle, Socrates, and Plato being told to be "Louder and funnier."[28] Classics and modern mass media are depicted as mutually exclusive. And yet classical clichés have survived in both pictorial and written journalistic forms. The front cover of the *Economist* on May 21, 2011, depicted several nuclear workers pushing the red sun of the Japanese flag uphill, Sisyphus-like, following the earthquake; and yet inside, the newspaper asked, "Can fragile Japan endure this hydra-headed disaster?"

Perhaps the most frequently used classical word to describe any modern event is that it is a *tragedy*. Cartoonists, despite being key proponents of it, are acutely aware of this abuse of language. In 1999, Martin Rowson responded to the death of John F. Kennedy, Jr., with a cartoon depicting a newspaper seller shouting in the foreground, "Kennedy Shocker: Rich Yank We've Just About Heard of in New Terrifying Echo of Orestes Myth Thing!"[29] The phrase *Orestes*

26. *Independent*, August 15, 1999.

27. *Punch*, May 1873; Tenniel (1895, pl. 42).

28. *Guardian*, February 27, 1959.

29. *Guardian*, July 19, 1999.

FIGURE 10.8 Gordon Brown and the money plant. Andy Davey, *Sun*, April 12, 2011, © Andy Davey. Used by permission of the artist.

myth thing is highly telling; it suggests that the media does not appreciate the nuances involved when it refers to contemporary events or fictive family curses as tragedies; it also implies that the average newspaper reader does not know who Orestes is and hence that the power of so specific an analogy has been undermined by a lack of general knowledge of the classics. The accuracy or aptness of the classical analogies used in the past, it suggests, are being eroded; by losing our grip on knowledge, let alone interpretation, of the classics implies that we are losing touch with a set of images, stories, and concepts that are valuable in helping us understand and describe our political world.

Yet these references, however debased and however unfamiliar, have not been bested, made irrelevant, or replaced by modern narratives, references, or images. Classical sources speak to current political situations as much as they ever did, giving cartoonists ready access to apt images to depict perennial political situations. When compared with images or references of a more recent vintage, any of which might also be apt and provocative, classical references have at least one added advantage: they link current affairs to the ancient past and thereby emphasize the extent to which political situations are not only the products of our own immediate decisions but also outcomes entangled in persistent features of the human condition. The details of each situation and the casts of characters change, but the same images remain relevant through the ages. References to popular culture cannot fulfill this function in the same way.

Take, for example, a cartoon by Andy Davey from April 2011, in which former Prime Minister Brown is entangled in a money plant (labeled, in a nod to *Road Runner*, "Common Name: Big Banks; Latin Name: Globalis Banksii"), the label of which reads: "Vigorous succulent—will grow in any climate" (figure 10.8). Brown, who is depicted as Paw Broon from

the Scottish comic strip *The Broons*, is completely entangled by the plant, while the outreach-
ing fronds are pulling at the leg of an overtired, red-eyed Labour Party shadow chancellor Ed
Balls. Brown, in admitting that his government made mistakes in the way it regulated (or failed
to regulate) the banking sector, says: "Jings! I hadn't realised how tangled this thing could get."
This cartoon is an apt parody of the situation, but the oblique reference to *The Broons* does not
evoke quite the same timelessness that a reference to the Laocoön statue group might have done
if used to parody the same situation. Historical references in political cartoons, and especially
those of a classical vintage, concisely convey a sense of perennial inevitability; these are political
entrapments of a sort that we have found ourselves in before and are likely to find ourselves in
again in the not-too-distant future.

  This suggests that as the number and variety of familiar classical references are dimin-
ished, it will become increasingly difficult to parody the timeless features of our political world
effectively. There are, as we have seen, many serviceable classical references going to waste in
favor of an increasingly restricted toolbox of classical clichés. For example, a cartoon of the
judgment of Paris might be a welcome and more stable alternative to the similar, currently
much used, but ultimately ephemeral image of *X Factor* judges choosing among contestants in
a talent contest.

  More worrying still is the possibility that the very people who are charged with making
political decisions are themselves lacking any knowledge of the classics that might help them
navigate their own political obstacles. In a cartoon from 2009, Garland depicts Chancellor
Alastair Darling and Prime Minister Brown as big-game hunters about to be trampled by the
elephant of "Economic Downturn."[30] Darling helplessly asks, "Isn't this where we take a thorn
out of its foot or something?" This is a reference to the story of Androcles and the lion, where
the slave who soothes the lion's injured foot is subsequently not eaten by him in a later encounter.[31] It is obviously hopelessly late, and hopelessly the wrong animal, for the classical scenario
to recur. Once again, this cartoon must be set in the historical context of other cartoons, as it
is a politicization of a nonpolitical cartoon of the same image by John G. Walter, printed in
Punch in 1946. By politicizing a reference to ignorance of classics, Garland makes a wider statement about political failings: classics acts as a touchstone for general ignorance, without which
political situations are open to misinterpretation and ineptitude. Ironically, classical cartoons
assume a level of public ignorance that delimits the contents of their toolbox of analogies, and
they also rely on, at most, superficial knowledge of the classical background to fill out the innate
visual power of their images.

---

30. *Daily Telegraph*, January 14, 2009, www.telegraph.co.uk/comment/cartoon/?cartoon=4230500
&cc=4045421.

31. See, e.g., Gell., *NA* 5.14.

11

Eliot with an Epic, Rowson with a Comic

Recycling Foundational Narratives

FREDERICK WILLIAMS AND EDWARD BRUNNER

When is a parody more than a parody? In Petronius' *Satyricon*, Encolpius is dogged by the wrath of the small-time (but ultraphallic) deity Priapus, in a parody of Poseidon's stalking of Odysseus, but the resulting narrative, a taxonomy of social blundering, becomes a candidate for the earliest novel (Sullivan 1965, 17, 19). Ravel's *La Valse* (1919) takes up, as if in homage, the waltzes of Strauss but subjects them to unexpected instrumentation, dissonant modulations, and obsessive rhythms in a modernist *poème choréographique* that blocks return to the simplicity of prewar Vienna (Mawer 2006, 94–96). And Martin Rowson's remarkable distillation of T. S. Eliot's *The Waste Land* as a graphic novel in 1990 draws on the opportunism of *Classics Illustrated* and the subversions of *Mad* and *Humbug* in addition to critiques by Raymond Williams and Linda Hutcheon (1985, 98–99), an audacious project that recasts the events of Eliot's poem, including its esoteric allusions to works both ancient and modern, as a hard-boiled crime tale, adaptable to the crime-tale formulas of Raymond Chandler and Dashiell Hammett.

Written in 1922, Eliot's *The Waste Land* quickly became one of the pillars of high modernism. Eliot's protagonist, brooding in a London devastated by the Great War, pondered friends lost and lovers gone as he wandered through city streets that evoked the imagery of the desert, always recalling the great literature of the past in an effort to orient himself, even if that meant admitting that his civilization was wholly adrift. Written as a collage of ever-shifting fragments, many in languages other than English, the poem ultimately revealed a quest of sorts emerging from the tag lines and patches haunting its protagonist, whose initial confusion came to resemble a submission to suffering that could transmute pain into art. No text, at first, seems less likely to be adapted into a graphic novel, and Rowson's project, in one sense, rides on that incongruity. Yet the role of the private detective, as reconceived by Chandler and Hammett and as developed for the screen in film noir, is not just to solve a mystery but to portray a civilization whose social system tests rather than protects its citizens. The atmosphere of film noir is a visual rendering of the confusion and ambivalence central to the modernist works that Eliot helped inaugurate.

Modifications to Rowson's British Edition

As a deliberately unsettled mixture of parody, homage, and travesty, Rowson's *The Waste Land* has not gone unrecognized. (After all, Rowson is well known to readers of British newspapers such as *The Guardian* as a fiercely satirical editorial cartoonist whose caricatures of the powerful are designed for controversy.) Dettmar and Wicke (2006, 2533) selected its opening pages for the 2006 edition of the *Longmans Anthology of British Literature*, calling it a "loving parody of Eliot's poem, underscoring its air of mystery and menace"; though it makes "light of the gravitas of Eliot's poem . . . [it] also manages to retain Eliot's sense of real anguish." McHale (2000, 252) recognized Rowson's "comic-books version" as addressing readers as "detectives who piece together more or less plausible scenarios from fragmentary choices" while simultaneously turning the crime tale into an Eliotic "epistemological quest." Tabachnick (2001, 79–80) admired Rowson's ability to coax the reader into a sympathetic alliance with his frustrated detective (whose name, Christopher Marlowe, recalls Eliot's admiration for Elizabethan poetry while providing Chandler's Philip with an ancestor). As Tabachnick notes, in standard noir fashion, the clues add up to more meaning than the narrative requires, much as Eliot's numerous allusions expansively shape-shift as they reach across centuries. Bringing new details to this discussion, we contend that Rowson's work with the graphic novel extravagantly develops the opportunities available to the comics-art medium, demonstrating its capacity for generating meanings that use both the verbal and the visual to expand well beyond anyone's reasonable expectations. Rowson has indeed furthered this expansion of the visual-textual with an adaptation of *Tristram Shandy* (1996) that uses the possibilities of the illustrated page to be remarkably faithful to Sterne's experimentation, and also with an updated version of *Gulliver's Travels* (2012) in which a twenty-first-century descendent of Gulliver finds the cultures his forefather had earlier intruded on have now become all-too-recognizable sites of barbaric conflict. These ambitious works are fully anticipated in Rowson's 1990 text, in which every panel not only negotiates a place for itself in Eliot's original poem but also finds an equivalent in the noir formulaic, while also introducing new information that comments on the whole enterprise—an achievement on display most commandingly in the British edition (published by Penguin), a "second edition" that required Rowson to make numerous adjustments to a text whose more straightforward first edition was already in print in America (published by Harper & Row).

The sixty-plus highly detailed pages that Rowson spent, by his own calculation, eighteen months assembling reveal a remarkable immersion into the smallest corners of Eliot's text, a project whose lavish attention to detail was abruptly threatened when the Eliot estate filed legal objections to the numerous direct quotations from the poem that Rowson had assumed were available under the fair-use provisions of copyright law (Jackson 1994). Tolerant American copyright laws permitted an American edition by Harper & Row to reproduce numerous passages verbatim and to use the names of such characters as Stetson, who had been "in the ships at Mylae"; Mr. Eugenides, "the Smyrna merchant"; and Phlebas, "the Phoenician." But the more restrictive rule of British copyright law interrupted plans for a British edition by Penguin and subjected Rowson, as he recalled, to the wrath of the "zealous Widow Eliot" (Rowson 1995, 63). Although Rowson's illustrations would remain virtually unchanged, the British edition could proceed only after stripping out anything resembling a quotation that directly linked Rowson's text to Eliot's *The Waste Land*. Consequently, dialogue in word balloons was altered, as were segments in voice-over; characters were renamed (Stetson became Idaho Ez, Mr. Eugenides became Mr. Eumenides, and Phlebas the Phoenician became Mike the Minoan); and even passages in languages other than English—including the words of Virgil, Ovid, Dante, Baudelaire, and others—were replaced with new citations that, like those they supplanted, appeared in their original Greek and Latin, Italian and French.

In one sense, these revisions for the British edition further complicate an already dense product (with its multiple layers of parody) by folding in a level of referential material beyond even Eliot's extensive allusions. In another sense, though, these substitutions edify and even clarify, constituting an expanded layer of meaning. Rowson's response to a legal challenge was not to retreat but to open another front in his running engagement with Eliot's epic. (Indeed, England would be visited in 1994 by a Covent Garden festival operetta with a libretto by Andy Rashleigh and a score by Stephen McNeff based on Rowson's version, and in 2011, the graphic novel's pages became available, with their own running commentary, as an app for downloading to an iPad or iPhone.)[1] Eliot's lawyers may have been pleased to learn how many of Rowson's replacement quotations were in Latin, perhaps concluding that words in a dead language would further limit circulation of this travesty. Yet no such conclusion would be warranted by anyone familiar with the audience for graphic novels or, for that matter, *The Waste Land*. Rowson's pages were already peppered with so many arcane allusions and esoteric meanings to be discovered by the aficionado and the cognoscenti—in his visual imagery no less than in his verbal text—that material in Latin and Greek or Italian and French would only further intrigue readers. An interest in comics art and graphic novels, as Gardner (2006) has proposed, is often matched with an interest in things archival, a commitment to accuracy even down to small details, and a willingness to possess a text in its entirety. Indeed, Rowson's new quotations from "dead" languages—witty, elegant, learned juxtapositions that veer against Eliot's originals—might well have impressed Eliot himself, just as Rowson's whole concept might have delighted that side of Eliot's personality that authored an ode to "Macavity: The Mystery Cat"

---

1. McNeff's *Wasteland Wind Music*, a four-part suite for winds based on Rowson's version of the poem, not the poem itself, is collected on *Images in Stone*, in a performance by the Royal Northern College of Music, conducted by Mark Heron. While no print editions of Rowson's *The Waste Land* are currently available, a software application can be retrieved from Throwaway Horse (http://throwawayhorse.com/home/). The app has two merits: it accurately reproduces the fine lines of Rowson's drawing in a way no printed version can (the British edition, on inexpensive paper, has images with considerably less resolution of detail than the American edition), and it is accompanied by a "Reader's Guide" by Michael Barsanti which includes portions of Rowson's correspondence with Barsanti. The guide usefully emphasizes numerous connecting points between Eliot's poem, the formulaic devices of film noir, and Rowson's points of interplay between both. Rowson's alertness to visual culture is evident in his remarks on the numerous paintings placed in the background or used as the setting for a scene (artworks by Francisco Goya and Henry Wallis, for example, intermingle with scenes borrowed from *The Maltese Falcon* on Rowson's opening page). Although the app takes its text from the British edition, the "Reader's Guide" stops short of handling Rowson's footnotes and is content to translate most (though not all) of the quotations from foreign languages without adding background. Barsanti's running commentary usefully makes Rowson's text a helpful introduction to Eliot; Rowson's text "does more to help a reader learn how to read Eliot's poem than a hundred critical introductions could do," Barsanti notes in his foreword. (Barsanti's firm is dedicated to reproducing modernist texts in comics form, and an ongoing project involves panel illustrations for James Joyce's *Ulysses*). The guide, in short, makes Rowson's version a passageway via pop forms into a dauntingly complex modernist poem that lacks a clear plot; by contrast, we see Rowson's text as a tauntingly diverse, playful, and pleasure-driven postmodern counterpoint to a high modernity exemplified by Eliot that aligned art primarily with suffering, loss, and alienation.

and other light verse in intricate verse forms, that wrote an appreciative essay on Marie Lloyd and the British music-hall tradition, that exchanged correspondence with Groucho Marx, and that laced footnotes with traces of what he himself called "bogus scholarship" (Eliot 1939, 32–34; Eliot 1950, 405-408; Eliot 1957, 121; Ardis 2009, 312, 320).

We find every reason to support the idea that modifications at the micro-level for the "legitimate" British edition dramatically and meaningfully expand Rowson's province. Just as Eliot's own citations (in English as in non-English) acknowledged key texts in the Western literary tradition that represented both the values he saw in jeopardy in the ruins of postwar Europe and a source for imagining a resurgence of those values, so Rowson interpellates an alternative set of references that represent the values he would bring forward from the cultural history of his own time. Where Eliot's original epic privileges moments of individual courage, of prophetic greatness, of transformative beauty that emerge from suffering, Rowson privileges moments in which artists collaborated, in which the bonds of friendship outweighed the burden of history, and in which diversity and variety were seen not as fearful excess but as admirable traits. Where Eliot lingers over Ovid's *Metamorphoses* and recalls Sophocles and Homer while placing Petronius at the edge of his work in an epigraph, Rowson centers attention on Virgil's *Eclogues* (notably 6) and brings in the "confessional" Ovid of *Tristia* and the *Amores*, in addition to allowing Petronius the poet into the center of the noir *Waste Land*. This battle of the intertextual reference, this warfare of the footnote, fights major skirmishes in the critical territory held by Latin and Greek classics, but guerrilla activity in less developed regions occurs in substitutions in which the Shakespeare of *The Tempest* and the Dante of Purgatorial suffering whom Eliot favors are contested with examples from the Shakespeare who served as script doctor for Thomas Kyd's *The Spanish Tragedy* and the Dante who found words for Ulysses that anticipated, in the darkness of the late medieval era, the humanism of the Renaissance. Moreover, a fresh skirmish breaks out in mop-up operations as Rowson launches a campaign against the lawyers who assert Eliot's privileges; he stockpiles powerful evidence that demonstrates the fluidity of textual boundaries in writings whose authorship is uncertain or that were produced collaboratively or that echo the words of others. These are the very qualities, Rowson wants us to know, that (even as Eliot's estate cravenly mounts a counterargument to deny them) pertain to the making of *The Waste Land*, a poem with a line proposed by Vivienne Eliot, heavily edited by Ezra Pound, and a veritable echo chamber of ancestral voices.

Appropriating Eliot's Poetics

The Waste Land is an esoteric text; Rowson's can be no less so. His revised British edition trumpets his ability to use Eliot's means but go through them to a different end. Eliot's epic draws on poets at the dawn of literature, and Eliot's protagonist always pauses to hear the overtones in his situations, to speak words inhabited by the echoes of other speakers, echoes that stymie his ability to act even as they hold out the need for action. He is drawn toward themes whose recurrence crosses centuries and binds cultures—the prophet (Tiresias) whose words to Oedipus are difficult to hear because they identify an enemy within, the victim (Philomela) who finds alternative ways to express suffering, and the wise one (the Sibyl) who discovers that regret is often the beginning of understanding. By contrast, Rowson's graphic novel is voluble, expansive, unrestrained. He distributes the sequence of panels on a page in an arrangement whose visual structure changes according to the narrative. Sometimes it is driven by a sense of pace that dramatizes a harried, uncertain string of events; sometimes it serves as a visual counterpart to themes in Eliot and in Chandler and Hammett (figure 11.1; see the appendix to this chapter for further discussion of these images). Its ever-shifting and freewheeling arrangement recalls the sensational layouts that the production designers for *Classics Illustrated* favored to compete for the attention of adolescents in the American comic-book market in the 1940s and 1950s (figure 11.2). And every panel is packed with an overload of indirectly relevant and always irreverent data that recall the excessive detail of Will Elder or Jack Davis in the pages of *Mad* and *Humbug* (figure 11.3). That level of detail indicates that nothing is incidental in Rowson's production, that every object carries significance, and not even the smallest item is disposable—there is no waste in his land.

Such attention is in keeping with Rowson's (1995, 64) remark that he intended to create "what we might term some kind of postmodern dialectic, connecting the unconnectable by bringing Eliot and Chandler together to create a new, if mischievous, synthesis." As "postmodern dialectic," his parody acknowledges Williams's (1989, 34) concern that once-powerful modernist techniques have now been assimilated into entertainment: "The isolated, estranged images of alienation and loss" have become "easy iconography" as "the lonely, bitter, sardonic and skeptical hero takes his ready-made place as star of the thriller." Instead of contesting that trend, Rowson's "dialectic" embraces it, producing what Hutcheon calls an "ironic reprise" of parody, working a "self-reflexive technique that points to art as art" (Hutcheon 1989, 101); it locates a text "within an ever-expanding intertextual network that mock[s] any notion of either single origin or simple causality" (Hutcheon 1988, 129). The new citations from ancient (and sometimes modern) writers in the British edition promote an alternative classicism that makes it impossible to take Eliot's citations of predecessors as a noncontroversial identification of predominant works in a mainstream European literature; the "mainstream" traced in Eliot's citations and notes appears now as a specialized discursive system assembled to suit his needs.

Even before coming under fire from Eliot's estate, Rowson had already played around with Eliot's example by writing footnotes that identified certain references in his own parody. The four pages in which Rowson with mock pedantry acknowledges his forerunners and points out selected highlights of his text mimic Eliot's fussy donnishness by skipping around arbitrarily and offering explanations more fragmentary than complete. Where Eliot acknowledged a debt to James George Frazer's *Golden Bough* and Jessie Weston's study of the grail legend, Rowson acknowledges *his* forebears (on p. 72 of the 1990 Penguin edition): "To two cinematic works I am indebted in general, both of which have influenced our generation considerably; I mean *The Big Sleep* and *The Maltese Falcon*." Other Rowson annotations reveal an archive of the carnivalesque, a mélange of B-movie comedies, scraps of doggerel, off-color palindromes, hideous puns, and such dithery mutterings as "Carthage, California. Not to be confused with Carthage, Montana, or Carthage, Texas" (p. 74). Jutting out from such an errant mix is one footnote with a couplet in Latin identified as from Petronius (*Anth. Lat.* 700): *Foeda est in coitu et breuis voluptas/Et taedat Veneris statim peractae.* It is striking, of course, because it goes untranslated (as did several of Eliot's own footnotes). But the sudden opacity of foreign words recalls an older culture's readiness to shift a passage on a printed page from English to Latin

FIGURE 11.1 Eliot's Section II, "A Game of Chess." Script and art by Martin Rowson.

FIGURE 11.2 William Wilkins Collins, *The Moonstone, Classics Illustrated* 30 (September 1946). Art by Don Francisco Rico.

FIGURE 11.3 "Frankenstien [sic] and His Monster." *Humbug* 1.7 (February 1958): 6. Art by Will Elder. Used by permission of Fantagraphics Books.

when squeamish subject matter had to be discussed. Here was material, as Latin once signaled, that was "dangerous" and thus not surprisingly associated with Petronius, an author whose *Satyricon* was actively marketed in the 1920s as a scurrilous narrative.

This explosion into Latin, with shadowy words dimly lighted for the English-only reader (is that "voluptuous" in *voluptas*? is *coitu* what it seems to be?), stands at the outset of the longest of Rowson's annotations to his own book, which in turn parallels Eliot's longest footnote to his book, earmarking Tiresias as "the most important personage in the poem, uniting all the rest," although he was "a mere spectator" (Eliot 2005, footnote, line 218). Eliot's note was provocative, a remarkable moment in which a central "personage" was revealed, and it was followed, somewhat perversely, by a long quotation in Latin from Ovid's *Metamorphoses*. Ovid's words provided a backstory for Tiresias by explaining the quarrel between Juno and Jupiter about the relative pleasure during sex felt by men and women. Tiresias, whose ill-timed experiences with magic creatures led him to experience sex now as a man, now as a woman, was called upon to adjudicate the rift. When Juno disagreed with Tiresias' claim that sex was more enjoyable as a woman, she blinded him, and in compensation, Jupiter gifted him with the ability to prophesy. Eliot's note exists to set up a passage in "The Fire Sermon": when a Tiresias-like figure observes casual coupling between a male clerk and a female typist, he cannot associate their act with Juno and Jupiter; neither typist nor clerk finds pleasure. Their exchange is tainted with the mechanical and the routine that govern their lives, like laying out food in tins (the typist) or pausing cautiously to negotiate a dark stairway (the clerk).

Rowson goes about recording his unwillingness to share Eliot's mordant view, and he begins by dispossessing Tiresias of his stature as a sympathetic figure. Rowson's version of Tiresias is a cross-dressing sex worker whose age has reduced him to abject propositions. Rowson finds neither the typist nor the clerk as dismaying as Tiresias in his role as voyeur, a role that Rowson detaches from Eliot's poem the better to associate it with Eliot himself. The couplet indeed serves Eliot's cautionary view of sex as meaningless, fleeting, exhausting. As rendered with spectacular intensity by Ben Jonson: "Doing, a filthy pleasure is, and short;/ And done, we straight repent us of the sport." And yet Rowson's decision to reproduce only the opening two lines of a twelve-line poem is complicating. Investigating the whole poem reveals how poorly the first two lines represent the whole. The poem's later lines turn away from Eliotic disgust and counter the opening couplet's moment of grumpy *tristesse:* it is wrong (to continue with words from Jonson's translation) to "rush blindly" into lovemaking, "Like lustful beasts," for when two "together closely lie and kiss/There is no labour, nor no shame in this"—indeed, it is a delight that "never can decay, but is beginning ever." (American poet Robert Pinsky chose Jonson's version for his column's Valentine's Day selection of verse for *Slate* in February 2006, confirming that the poem still lives and lives well beyond its opening gambit; see Pinsky 2006.) Petronius isn't treating lovemaking as a contest with a specific economy of pleasure but as an event that is about renewal and that can be ever-renewed. To pursue the reference, then, is to contest the pessimism and perhaps even misogyny that many see in Eliot's poem, to expose his view as partial, with the added lesson that pertains to Eliot's observation and also to us: don't be just a spectator, taking only what is given; instead, engage, investigate, and change.

Illustrating Eliot's Notes

Always pursue the reference—following that advice opens a whole new dimension of Rowson's already complex work. And to follow it into truly shadowy corridors, we need to leave behind the relatively well-lit footnotes that Rowson supplied in the closing pages of his parody of Eliot and enter a territory that is deeply tangled: Rowson's parodic illustrations of and his substitutions for the footnotes that Eliot supplied for the final pages of *The Waste Land.* These footnotes by Eliot have always attracted attention. Kenner (1959, revised 1969) warned readers away from them as unnecessary distractions, but a half-century later, Kaufman (1995, 73-86) could draw on essays and chapters by an array of scholars who debated the notes' value. When Rowson set out to rectify his illegal transgressions for the British edition, he may have had his attention turned to Eliot's notes as one portion of the poem (though somewhat outside it) that the estate's lawyers could insist were covered by copyright. While Eliot's right to assert ownership of many of the lines of *The Waste Land* would have been in dispute (since so many were paraphrases and often straightforward reproductions of words that were not only by other authors but by long-dead authors whose words had never been in copyright), the footnotes that Eliot had dashed off quickly, to meet publisher Horace Liveright's request for a plumper volume, were indisputably his own words.

When Rowson came to illustrate the numerous footnotes that Eliot had placed at the end of his poem, he collapsed the whole enterprise into a one-page illustration. There, an indignant Marlowe forced his way into a strange backstage space to give Eliot a third-degree grilling that brought Pound out of the shadows to add his own remarks (figure 11.4; the images of both men in every panel were drawn from photographs or portraits of each). Tabachnick (2001) proposes that Marlowe's stance here, barraging the originators of the poem with assertive questions, appeals to the bruised and battered reader, exhausted and irritated after searching out one allusion after another. Tabachnick deftly characterizes Marlowe's stance: he is impatient, needs answers, wants to tie up loose ends.

FIGURE 11.4 "The Notes": Marlowe, Eliot, and Pound. Script and art by Martin Rowson.

Of course, noir itself usually fails to deliver such tidy closure. In this sense, Eliot's own poem is definitely noirish, and Eliot notably eludes any captor in the very section of his poem where he might be pinned down. The tolerant copyright provisions in America allowed the direct reprinting from the original, revealing Eliot's evasiveness in his own words. By contrast, when Rowson substituted words in the British edition, he had a chance not only to show Eliot speaking outside English to evade Marlowe's interrogation but also to choose quotations that critiqued, if not undermined, Eliot's project. In an early passage, Rowson's Eliot dodges Marlowe's inquiry by ducking behind lines from Ovid's *Metamorphoses* that he invokes to insist that his work is fixed on the page; neither fire nor sword nor the gnawing tooth of time can undo his words. Of course, what we are seeing is words becoming undone as their context is shifted about; no author is powerful enough to withstand questioning. A few panels later, Rowson's Eliot speaks lines from Charles Baudelaire's poem "The Albatross" to circumvent another question by Marlowe: he uses words from Baudelaire (whose poems were woven into the original of *The Waste Land*), who hailed the albatross as a "prince of the clouds," who scorned the archer below (a pun of sorts, incorporating Miles Archer, Spade's partner in *The Maltese Falcon*?). When asked by Marlowe whether "dames" are "the key" to the poem's riddles, Rowson's Eliot answers with phrases from Ovid's *Amores* that warn those who are easily scandalized to "keep away, keep far away." And rebuffing Marlowe's interrogation one last time, Rowson's Eliot replies with lines from Virgil's *Eclogues* 9, in which Lycidas defers to the superior skills of his fellow poets Varius and Cinna:

> *et me fecere poetam*
> *Pierides, sunt et mihi carmina, me quoque dicunt*
> *vatem pastores; sed non ego credulus illis.*
> *nam neque adhuc Vario videor nec dicere Cinna*
> *digna, sed argutos inter strepere anser olores.*

> Even me the muses made a poet, even I have songs, and shepherds also call me bard; but they don't fool me. So far, I seem to say nothing worthy of Varius or Cinna, but to honk like a goose amid melodious swans. (*Ecl.* 9.32–36)

What mischief lies behind Rowson's decision to choose these words from Virgil's *Eclogues* as a substitute for Eliot's originals? The words Rowson has Eliot speak are confessing to a dependency on others; the solution, that is, that Rowson crafts to meet the challenges of the estate features Eliot confessing, courtesy of Virgil's Latin, that he had borrowed the best parts of his own poem. This is not entirely a malicious joke on Rowson's part. Creativity is, for Rowson, not the product of a single mind working alone but a series of collaborations, which is exactly what Eliot's own work dramatically testifies to. Perhaps, then, the most powerful message that Rowson sends on this page is not in its words but in its images, for this page offers a panel in which Eliot and Pound together appear, though in silhouette, as themselves. Earlier, they had been unidentified presences in the backgrounds of panels. Indeed, Pound had been physically present on most pages of Rowson's parody, sometimes lurking in a corner, sometimes at the center of attention, sometimes as a figure being pursued (as Idaho Ez), as befits one whose editing altered significantly a late draft of Eliot's poem through numerous small adjustments and by eliminating such extensive portions as a page-long prologue, an extended introduction to "The Game of Chess," and a lengthy sea voyage in "Death by Water." One scholar goes so far as to say that Eliot's poem in draft form "reads like the premonition of Pound's arrival." What the draft needed, Koestenbaum (1989, 138) has argued, was someone who could take Eliot's fragments and "redefine disjunction," to convert Eliot's confusion bordering on hysteria "back into a powerful discourse." To produce *The Waste Land*, then, Eliot needed not just the suffering that he appeared to be asserting as a prelude to transformative creativity but also the collaboration of an understanding companion—the very understanding of creativity that Rowson celebrates and whose traces he finds in his group of ancients and moderns.

Eliot's Ending, Rowson's Beginning

Even multilingual readers of Eliot's original poem may not have been able to resist a look into Eliot's notes after reading the curious and disarming close to his poem, where words cascade around us in multiple languages:

> London bridge is falling down falling down falling down
> *Poi s'ascose nel foco che gli affina*
> *Quando fiam ceu chelidon*—O swallow swallow
> *Le Prince d'Aquitaine à la tour abolie*
> These fragments I have shored against my ruins
> *Why then Ile fit you. Hieronymo's mad againe.* (426–431)

Although the words are borrowed from other writers, they are so strikingly arranged and so indelibly a part of the original poem that lawyers could make a case for them as being so distinctive that they surely are copyright-protected. Whatever the reason prompting Rowson, he found substitutes for each one of the quotations in the lines above, some of them decidedly unflattering to Eliot. A new children's rhyme—"Tom Tom the Piper's son stole a pig and away he run"—replaces "London bridge is falling down," explicitly naming Eliot as a thief.

Cover-ups and covert actions remain as a subtext in lines that Rowson inserts in place of fragments ("Why then I'll fit you" and "Hieronymo's mad again") that Eliot drew from Thomas Kyd's *Spanish Tragedy* (1587), a revenge tragedy of remarkable violence whose many overstated passages invited numerous parodies from Elizabethan playwrights, including Jonson. Rowson replaces the first of the two quotations with an observation that encourages drink—"there is no drinking after death"—instead of Kyd's invitation to battle ("fit you" translates as "fight you" in Kyd). Here it helps to know how Rowson brings a noirish twist to his illustration of Eliot's disheveled ending. In Rowson, the chalice that all had been greedily fighting over ends up in Marlowe's possession, and, having no use for it, he hands it over to the corpulent expatriate Marie, whose inquiry at his office had first launched Marlowe on his frustrating quest. A besotted Marie says: "There ish [*sic*] no drinking after death" as she converts chalice into drinking goblet, filling it with "Old Possum's Bourbon" ("Possum" was Pound's nickname for Eliot). Marie's words originate, according to Rowson's brief footnote, with "the drinking song from Fletcher and Jonson's *The Bloody Brother*"—a play that, while often attributed to John Fletcher and Ben Jonson, in fact lacks a clear provenance. "It is clear," concludes one scholar after extensive research, "that the play is the work of [John] Fletcher and [Philip] Massinger, assisted by one, two, or three collaborators, most likely [Michael] Field for one, possibly Field or [John] Chapman, or Field and Chapman for another, and improbably [Ben] Jonson for a third" (Williams 1989, 159).

The impossibility of untangling authorship and confirming ownership is handled no less dramatically when Rowson replaces Eliot's second quotation from Kyd, "Hieronymo's mad again," with a new quotation, "wicked wicked plant," a truly odd substitution, as the only sign of vegetation in Marie's domicile is Marie herself. Rowson clues us to look elsewhere, in his note linking the passage to *The Spanish Tragedy*'s "additions." When Kyd's play was republished in 1602, new scenes were commissioned for an edition whose frontispiece trumpeted a volume "newly corrected, amended, and enlarged with additions" (Thompson 2011, 4). Just as in Rowson's corrected and amended British edition, these "additions" to Kyd's text were more than touch-ups. The five additional segments—one several hundred lines in length—have been attributed, moreover, to no less a script doctor than William Shakespeare, at the time fortuitously writing *Hamlet*, a play that not coincidentally happens to recast important aspects of the revenge drama (Cannon 1962; Stevenson 1968; Thompson 2011, 70–71). To answer the charge against him by Eliot's estate, that is, Rowson replaces words that Eliot ascribed to Kyd with words ascribed to Kyd but possibly added by Shakespeare. Texts can be the product of many hands, with sources freely taken; copyright rules inhibit creativity. Rowson's referral to the "additions" to Kyd can lead us to information reminding us that Shakespeare toiled at reworking, enhancing, and even lifting work by others. The "plant" in the quotation, then, that is "wicked wicked" is this very substitution that has been planted to expose collaborative activity at the very highest level of the literary canon.

Numerous examples might have been chosen to demonstrate authors taking up and adding to the work of others, but Rowson's examples continually promote a point of view that challenges Eliot's estate and sometimes Eliot himself. Consider, for example, that the figure of Odysseus lacks even a passing acknowledgment in *The Waste Land*; he exists in Eliot's text, if *exist* is the word, deep in the background, as the personage who we might know is responsible for summoning Tiresias, who, in Eliot's quotation, "walked among the lowest of the dead" (Eliot 2005, line 246). Strikingly different, though, is the Odysseus whose words Rowson reproduces: Odysseus as Ulysses the adventurer eager to break boundaries. In the pile of quotations that Eliot heaped together at the end, one phrase from Dante stands out, a moment in the *Purgatorio* when Arnaut Daniel (inspiration for Dante when young) fades into the *foco che gli affina*, the refining fire into which Dante will soon plunge; he will realize on emerging that he can now speak to Beatrice, but he has forever left behind Virgil (Canto 26, line 148). Eliot's choice helps establish, once again, an art that has a basis in suffering (and this powerful moment meant a good deal to Eliot, who employed the passage as an epigraph to "The Love Song of J. Alfred Prufrock" and gave it prominence in his 1929 essay on Dante). Rowson, though, supplants this "refining fire" passage from Dante with a far different quotation from an earlier point in Dante's journey, when he finds Odysseus (as Ulysses) rising interactively within a flame in the *Inferno*. Ulysses endures the fire, not expecting a transformation; his "sin" lay in his curiosity, in his desire to explore, which led him too close to the sacred mount of Purgatory, so he and his crew were wrecked as punishment. Answering questions from Dante, he recalls the words he had once used to summon his crew to a post-Ithacan adventure, a renewal of companionship powerfully unlike Eliot's vision of loss and abandonment. These are the words that Rowson takes from an *Inferno*-based Dante to overwrite Eliot's *Purgatorio*-based Dante; they are spoken by Ulysses (they are the basis for Tennyson's "Ulysses"), and they have a grandeur quite unlike anyone else's in the *Inferno: Considerate la vostra semenza:/fatti non foste a viver come bruti*" (*Inferno* 26, 118–119). As translated by Merwin (1993, 121): "Consider what you rose from: you were not/made to live like animals" but (in the sentence's conclusion not reproduced by Rowson) "for the pursuit of virtue and knowledge" (*virtute et conoscenza*). Ulysses' words to his shipmates offer a gleam, deep within the darkness of a late-medieval poem, of what will become Renaissance humanism with its emphasis on the pursuit of knowledge, wherever it will lead, not the caution of tradition.

Of all these citations that Rowson offers in place of these last quotations by Eliot, the subtlest but most disruptive may be his substitution of a line quoted from "The Vigil of Venus": *Quand fiam ceu chelidon* [when shall I become like the swallow]—O swallow swallow" (1.428). To displace this quotation is to intrude upon the last in an unusually long string of allusions that Eliot had carefully threaded through *The Waste Land* that evoke the Philomela and Procne legend. It is a legend Eliot finds deeply moving, with its narrative of intense suffering transformed, with women becoming nightingale (Philomela) or swallow (Procne), their pain now transvalued as song. This was one set of references, judging from their recurrence in the notes, that Eliot did not want missed. Though glimpsed only in fragments, the Philomela tale served as a point of orientation in a sea of confusion, mentioned obliquely in sections II, III, and V but specifically identified in three of Eliot's footnotes, beginning with line 99's attribution to a version of the tale in Ovid, then further specified in a note to line 100 that points ahead to line 204, and finally recapitulated in a note to line 428 that points back to sections II and III. Eliot is seldom so explicit in making connections emerge within a poem otherwise notable for its disconnection, nor is Rowson always so eager to disrupt Eliot's plan.

Rowson takes equal pains not only to overwrite the Philomela legend but also to modify it. Rowson's Eliot cites Ovid, the poet Eliot draws on for the backstory of Philomela, but Rowson supplants the anthologizing poet of *Metamorphoses* with the autobiographical poet of *Tristia*. There, Ovid recalls the ease with which he once wrote verse: *Quod temptabam scribere versus erat* ("whatever I attempted to write became verse"). (Rowson replaces *scribere* with *dicere*, a manuscript variant, because the panel shows someone talking.) The passage is from *Tristia* 4.10.26, and Ovid's words affirm a sure-footed confidence that differs from Eliot's broken phrasings. But if this passage displays a confidence that Rowson is himself wont to display, he is not always so sure-footed. His own footnote for this panel directs us to *Tristia* 3.12.47, an irrelevant connection. Clearly, he meant to cite lines that begin at *Tristia* 3.12.7, a passage that specifically uncouples the swallow from the narrative of suffering in the *Metamorphoses*: "and the meadows begin to flourish with the splendor of manifold colors,/and the chattering bird resounds with her untaught throat;/and to lay aside the crime of her wicked mother [i.e., Procne], the swallow/builds her nest and little roof under the timbers." Throughout the British edition, Rowson's replacements for Eliot's citations reveal an alternative archive of classical and European writings that contest Eliot's selections of a "mainstream" literature. Rowson is particularly drawn, it seems, to undermining the Philomela tale—he organizes one entire page around a dislocation of its centrality—but in this example, if Rowson indeed had in mind such an allusion, he is both vindictive and recuperative (figure 11.5). He finds within one of Eliot's most esteemed classical poets an alternative version of Eliot's most esteemed myths, and, not surprisingly, it highlights a variant that emphasizes splendor, pleasure, and delight; crime has been laid aside, and suffering is forgotten.

Rewriting Eliot's Epigraph and Rowson's "Bogus Scholarship"

If Ovid's *Metamorphoses* is the classical text that Eliot often stands on—its influence further deepened in Eliot's many references to that most sea-change-like of all Shakespearean plays, *The Tempest*—Virgil's *Eclogues* stand as the classical text most akin to Rowson's parody, a sequence with recurring characters that outrageously mixes styles, wearing its politics lightly but insistently. Ostensibly, the *Eclogues* are simply pastoral poems, dialogues among shepherds who pass the time on their hands as lightly as they can. But in Virgil's hands, the ten poems actually function as a complex production that registers a republic in disorder. In one sense, the *Eclogues* are a forerunner text to *The Waste Land* in the same odd, indirect, and provocative way that *The Waste Land* is proleptic to *The Big Sleep*. In another sense, the *Eclogues* align more directly with Rowson's burlesquing. After all, Virgil's poem openly embraces Thalia, the muse of comedy, as its central figure, Tityrus, notes when he sheepishly explains to Varus (in absurdly tangled convolutions) why the sixth *Eclogue* fails to celebrate military might. This very portion of the Virgilian oeuvre was conspicuously neglected by Eliot himself, whose "acquaintance with Virgil's work appears to be quite circumscribed," according to Ziolkowski (1993, 120), limited to "what he remembered from his schooldays"—that is, the first six books of the *Aeneid* and, more precisely, two episodes therefrom, Dido and the visit to the Underworld. The *Eclogues* go unmentioned in Eliot's poems and essays except in a 1951 radio talk that approves of the fourth as "peculiarly sympathetic to the Christian mind" and admires the *Georgics* for having "affirmed the dignity of manual labor" (Eliot 1957, 135, 141).

Virgil's shepherds aren't contenders for Eliot's admiration. They aren't interested in dignity, and they'll do everything and anything—sing, argue, drink, reminisce, seduce, lament—*except* labor. Commentary about them, Rieu (1949, 165) warns, leads down "labyrinthine ways of hypothesis, allegory, and reconstruction"—a warning that we might have posted at the opening of this essay. The sixth especially floats on an airy skein of references, an "intertextual fabric" so "dazzlingly elaborate and densely woven . . . that it is still only partly understood" (Farrell 1997, 230). Silenus' songs of creation in the sixth are a fractured catalogue, a compote of predecessors and contemporaries, echoing Lucretius and Gallus, a "mini-epyllion, a miniaturization of the miniature epic" (Martindale 1997, 112) associated with Callimachus, who found "the sub-heroic side of the heroic age, the sensational tales of love and fantasy" his main interest (Coleman 1977, 204). These elements of the sixth *Eclogue* are homologous with Rowson's overstuffed panels, his inveterate clashing of high art and mass culture in numerous visual reproductions drawn from the British art tradition, and his identification with predecessors whose disorderly practices obliterate any chance of pretension.

FIGURE 11.5 Philomela in Rowson's "The Waste Land," 203–206. Script and art by Martin Rowson.

Scholars reading the *Eclogues* have long sensed the presence of other styles, distinctive voices, celebratory echoes lying within but beyond Virgil's words that can only be guessed at. "If we had the poems of Gallus and Virgil's other friends in our hands," Rieu (1949, 13) wistfully writes, "we would find a wealth of subtle allusions, even of parody." In a similar way, numerous facets of Rowson's text are always slipping over and beyond a horizon of meaning, often gesturing happily to us as they go off into clouds of obscurity. At no moment is this more vivid than in the first words spoken in Rowson's parody. Eliot's original begins with an epigraph from Petronius' *Satyricon* that cites Trimalchio's gassy reminiscence of the Cumean Sibyl trapped in a glass; having asked for longevity but not eternal youth, she is reduced to a husk, answering the question "what do you want?" (in her Greek, *apothanein thelo*) with "I want to die." Rowson proffers an alternative text that has words in Greek within a Latin discourse and even includes talk about death (in a passage that appears as prose but lends itself to scansion as rough hexameter; p. 11 of the UK edition):

> *Dictur de pharetra Herculis cecidesse* [sic] *sagitta*
> *veneno Hydrae oblita in pedem Cheirontis: Magna*
> *voce clamabat: succurrit Theseus . . . At ille:*
> Τίπτε, διδασκαλε, κραυγη? Μη αθανατος θελω ειναι!!!

> They say that an arrow smeared with the poison of the Hydra fell from the quiver of Hercules onto the foot of Chiron. He began to cry out in a loud voice. Theseus ran to help. "Why on earth, my teacher, (such a) cry?" And he: "I don't want to be immortal!"

In Rowson's version, these words are spoken by Marlowe's partner just as he is about to be brutally shot in a back alley. In this one-page prologue that offers a backstory to the events that the private detective will investigate—the noir version of an epitaph?—the partner's words only loosely illustrate the actions in the panels (the response to the partner's plea will be a volley of deadly gunshots that in effect answers his cry). The Greek words are a shout from the centaur Chiron, who is telling Theseus that his immortality has become a handicap now that one of Hercules' ultratoxic arrowheads has accidentally injected poison into his system. Rowson's footnote to this quotation, however, is remarkably unhelpful; it directs us to Virgil's sixth *Eclogue*, to the middle of a long speech in which Silenus the satyr, attempting to entertain those who have captured him and still woozy from too much drink, offers an episodic history of humankind's achievement. Specifically, the passage that Rowson singles out describes, among other things "natural and ancient," the torture of Prometheus by Zeus' eagle:

> *hinc lapides Pyrrhae iactos, Saturnia regna,*
> *Caucasiasque refert volucres furtumque Promethei.*

> From this point he tells of Pyrrha's hurled stones, the Saturnian realms, and the Caucasian birds and the theft of Prometheus. (*Eclogues* 6.41–42)

That line, of course, is not implausible as a link to the figure of Chiron the centaur. In one telling, Chiron replaced Prometheus, an arrangement whereby one immortal substituted for another, as Zeus had stipulated as a condition if Prometheus were ever to be freed, an exchange involving a healer of great renown for the figure who stole fire from the gods for mankind. Negotiations, compromises, and arrangements sometimes foster unlikely relationships, as Rowson surely feels after tangling with the Eliot estate.

Yet the strangest aspect of this already-tangled footnote by Rowson is that it further directs us to consider, in Rowson's words, "Varus quoted by Servius in his note to Virgil, *Eclogues* 4.42" (UK edition, 72)—a baffling annotation, given the absence of Varus from any point in Servius' commentary to line 42, although Servius' commentary famously complicates the identification of Varus by now calling him Publius Alfenus Varus, who oversaw allotment of lands to Octavian's soldiers, including Virgil's farmland, and then aligning him with Publius Quinctilius Varus, who lived fifty years after the *Eclogue* was composed (Servius 1881, 70–74; Rieu 1949, 149). Commentators, of course, make the occasional error. Is this, then, Rowson's occasional error? And has it been placed here in a premier position with the assumption that the Eliot legal team would check every substitution and unimaginatively begin at the beginning? Searching, searching, searching. And where, above all, is the original source of the exchange between Chiron and Theseus? Though copied by Rowson as prose, the hexameter lines imply an epic narrative. Here at the opening of Rowson's British edition, then, exists a tangle of references, perhaps a flawed transcription, as if accident could not be avoided. Eliot's opening features a prophet trapped for display, but Rowson's opening features an accidental juxtaposition (the falling poison arrow) with further ramifications, even further accidents (Servius on Varus). This is a dynamic, uncertain, explosive world, with one allusion spilling into another, not the endlessly narrowing world in which the Sibyl, kept under glass, is ever shrinking as time passes.[2]

The classical world as imagined by Pound was explosively close to the everyday world of the early twentieth century, as his Propertius translations with their references to flats and Frigidaire attest (these caused apoplectic reactions from classical scholars when they were first printed in *Poetry*; Hale 1919). Rowson is closer to Pound in this regard. When Eliot considered classical theater, it was in the context of restoring ritual to a world that had drifted away from it, as in the chorus he employed in *Murder in the Cathedral*. But Rowson's agenda also includes a defense of the very vehicle he is operating, affirming the excess and collaborative energy of comics art, of robust caricatures that exceed all bounds, of material that celebrates and delights rather than controlling and placing, that challenges taboos with disarming brio. Competing with the high culture of Eliot's epic even at the level of the footnote, he sets new standards for what may be accomplished when visual representation is set in productive tension with verbal registration. Rowson's translation expands the boundaries of the graphic novel to incorporate a cornerstone work of experimental poetry, a countertradition of classical verse, and the modern epic tradition.

---

2. We have left these speculations intact, although Martin Rowson has clarified this point in answer to our query. He identifies the Greek and Latin quotation as a "cod quotation made up for me by an old school teacher of mine (alas now dead) who taught Classics, though not to me" (personal correspondence, November 15, 2011). The Servius and Varus link can thus be described as a cod citation. (In British slang, to *cod* is to hoax or joke.)

Appendix: Further Notes on the Images
Figure 11.1

Eliot's Section II, "A Game of Chess," depicts the faltering relations between men and women as a trait common to all social classes. Rowson transfers Eliot's tense conversation between an upper-class couple, surrounded by signs of wealth and culturally sanctioned acquisitions, to the moment in film noir where a tense exchange between people who should be close (here Marlowe and his partner's wife, named Sibyl) discloses a lack of trust. The squares of chess serve as panels, occupied by only one player at a time, as in a game where moves are blocked. Marlowe fills his panels, while in her panels, Sibyl fragments into distracting details, fetishized bodily parts that never add up. As one in hiding, she is associated with Madame Sesostris, removing a mask in an earlier panel without showing her face (just who is under that mask Rowson never bothers to reveal, meaning that we must already know). Background decor includes a sculpture of the "dingus" that provides a title to *The Maltese Falcon* (panel 5), along with items taken from Eliot's descriptions (a carved dolphin in panel 3, a nightingale in panel 7). In Eliot's poem, the protagonist fails to answer the jabbing questions a woman asks, while his thoughts turn to "rats' alleys/Where the dead men lost their bones" (lines 115–116), an allusion to the network of trenches at the front of the Great War. Rowson's detective sees rats looking up at him from the "mean streets" that Chandler said his private eye must walk down.

Figure 11.2

Between 1945 and 1953, the Gilberton company operating *Classics Illustrated* outsourced production to Samuel "Jerry" Iger, an impresario of the earliest days of comic-book publishing, who oversaw a shop of artists and writers to develop titles and stories for various publishers. The "Iger shop" specialized in "Good Girl art," accurately characterized by Jones (2002, 37) as "drawings of pouting-lipped, ample-bosomed, minimally-clothed heroines." Iger's page also had a distinctive look; its panels departed from the orderly parade of same-size squares that were required for the standardized spaces in newspapers and offered instead jangling arrangements, panels at off angles to one another, circles and ovals suddenly appearing. The underdressed heroine on an Iger page, then, emerged from an already unsettled environment, and she was often drawn as stepping or reaching beyond a panel, arms and legs extended past the frame, for a 3-D effect. Iger brought that intensifying technique to adaptations of classics, although in this example, it is only the moonstone on display, and the hand of Mr. X remains behind the circular frame. When Rowson disrupts the orderly look of the comics page, he is also working in a visual tradition that used sensational visual effects to amplify the work of delivering a narrative.

Figure 11.3

This version of the Frankenstein story follows not the Mary Shelley novel but the 1932 movie in which the monster is trapped in a windmill by an angry mob. Emphasizing the fate of the classic that has become a movie franchise, these concluding panels reveal the overlay of other popular genres, as when *Gunsmoke*'s Marshal Dillon shows up too late to restore order. Elder, like Rowson, builds levels of detail into every panel, rewarding readers who look deeper and deeper, even changing font sizes at the close, in a process that recalls the footnote tradition which embeds multiple levels of importance into a text. The persistence of the good doctor and his assistant can be glimpsed as silhouettes through a window as they retrieve another body for their experiment.

Figure 11.4

Traditionally, the notes that poets add to their works, whether by those such as Edmund Spenser (*The Shepherd's Calendar*) or Melvin B. Tolson (*Libretto for the Republic of Liberia*), don't resolve issues in the text; instead, they continue the text by other means. Eliot's notes centralize Tiresias as a major figure, indicate the repetition of the Philomela tale, and underscore recurring metamorphoses. Rowson stresses instead Eliot's readiness to escape into a public self, to defer explanation, and to prefer mystification. Not surprisingly, all images here are based on actual portraits of both Eliot and Pound. We are behind the scenes now, although Marlowe hears Eliot's snipping as he crosses London Bridge (which did not fall down). Pound emerges as a coconspirator but, unlike Eliot, talking as bluntly as Marlowe. The poster advertising Wyndham Lewis's journal *Blast* (adjacent to a gun to underscore the title's violence) echoes the extreme rhetoric of "Salutation the Third," a Pound poem in the journal's first issue (see Pound 1982 [1913]), but here its virulence is leveled not at the Jews but at Pound ("smart-arse émigré . . . fellow travellers of tough-guy Italian") and Eliot ("mean-minded metaphysics . . . cat-fancying prudery"). Cats abound, as Eliot works at cutting-and-pasting his material, beginning with the Owl and the Pussycat of Edward Lear but ending with two recognizable brands of rival studios, Warner Brothers' Sylvester and MGM's Tom (of Tom and Jerry), as if modern poetry had been colonized by Pound and by Eliot, figured as opposing brands that establish the perimeters of poetic discourse but are at base remarkably alike, covering the same territory and defining the product.

Figure 11.5

The panels on this page illustrate a compressed shorthand that brushes up against the Philomela legend touched on in earlier lines:

> Twit twit twit
> Jug jug jug jug jug jug
> So rudely forc'd
> Tereu (Eliot, *The Waste Land*, lines 203–206)

Reproducing the nightingale's song, its odd throat-clearing chortle before its delicate trill orthographically reproduced by Elizabethans as "jug jug," coincides in a sound aligned with the name of Philomela's rapist, Procne's husband, Tereus. In Eliot's poem, suffering and injustice are partially redeemed by transformative song, as if art must be steeped in sorrow. But Rowson handles this same passage with a brio unusual even for him, moving us through a dusty museum with sexually explicit but antiquated artifacts that Eliot, then Pound, then Lewis anxiously scan (three twits, one after the other) and following up with six vases, or jugs, in a display that moves increasingly away from erotic ancient figures toward abstract modern design. Marlowe is escorted with rude force outside the museum by the gunsel from *The Maltese Falcon*, and in the page's last panel, a songbird on a branch cries out "Tereu"—except in the British edition, it is an unexpected and inappropriate "Quack!" Signs of an anxious masculinity abound, against an identifiable backdrop, the British Museum (its columnar façade and distinctive three-pronged outdoor lamps evident in the middle and final panels). The voice-over declares, "I made for the exit," even as the detective edges toward a sign that says "Enter," a clear indication that things are awry.

12

Ozymandias the Dreamer

Watchmen and Alexander the Great

MATTHEW TAYLOR

If 1986 was truly "The Year That Changed Comics,"[1] it was thanks in no small part to Alan Moore (w.) and Dave Gibbons's (a.) highly acclaimed *Watchmen*. The twelve-issue series—which, in its collected edition, was instrumental in legitimizing the term *graphic novel*—is still considered a watershed for its innovations in formal technique and thematic content, pushing as it did what Moore calls the "underlanguage" of comics—the unique marriage of image and text that they present—to new extremes, in order to produce "a moral and political fable that used the icons of superhero adventure fiction to make its point."[2]

At the climax of their fable, Moore and Gibbons chose to supplement these icons with one from the classical tradition: Alexander the Great. This invocation of Alexander can be considered a thematic linchpin for *Watchmen*, since it serves a pivotal role in the characterization of the series' primary antagonist, Adrian Veidt, informing and expanding his role in the moral and political questions that lie at its very core. With a depth typical of *Watchmen*, the textual and iconic registers of the comic work in harmony to build a powerful resonance between the life of the Macedonian king and the action of the series' climax, such that both the details of Alexander's career and the way in which they are interpreted become key to the articulation of Veidt's motivation and how we are to understand it. Moreover, the use of the reception of Alexander in this fashion serves as a perfect demonstration of the plasticity of this historical figure, the manner in which he can be and has been shaped to fit the agendas of individual subjects, and why perhaps it is important that we interrogate all our encounters with him more carefully.

I would like to express my gratitude to the editors of this volume for their support and encouragement. I would also like to thank Lisl Walsh, Daniel Richter, and the anonymous readers for all their help and comments.

1. Such was the title of a lecture series held in 2006 at the Museum of Comic and Cartoon Art in New York (Carey 2006). The year 1986 also saw the publication of Frank Miller's *Batman: The Dark Knight Returns* and Art Spiegelman's *Maus*. For a thorough account of the impact of *Watchmen* and the critical response it has received, see especially Van Ness (2010, chap. 1); also Kovacs and Marshall (2011, x); Kovacs (2011, 14); Millidge (2011, 132–133).

2. For Moore on comics' "underlanguage," see Sharrett (1988, 13), reprinted in Berlatsky (2012, 44–60); and Wiater and Bissette (1993, 163). For *Watchmen* as "moral and political fable," see Sharrett (1988, 16–17).

No More Heroes

The central aim of Moore and Gibbons's fable was to problematize the dichotomy of heroes and villains, which they believed represented "the two most dangerous fallacies" plaguing both comic-book fiction and real-world politics.[3] This included establishing a moral imperative to question the people who would claim to protect us, an idea encapsulated by the quote from Juvenal from which the series draws its name: "Who watches the watchmen?"[4] The comic broaches this question by imagining a contemporary America in which costumed vigilantes have long been a reality. Public concern over their activity eventually led to these would-be heroes being outlawed in 1977, but the questions they raised about power and authority are still current in 1986 (thanks in no small part to the continuing existence of Dr. Manhattan as part of America's strategic defense platform), and Juvenal's aphorism still haunts the graffitied streets of the comic's New York City. Against this backdrop, *Watchmen* projects a continuing discourse on the question of authoritarianism as embodied by both vigilantes and governments, which elevates Juvenal's conceit to one of major civic and political importance and primes the reader to engage in his or her own evaluation of heroes, both within the text and outside it.

In service of this, *Watchmen* presents a systematic examination of two generations of costumed crime-fighters. Over the course of the series, we are given relatively detailed insights into their psychology and motivation, through flashback, exposition, and the secondary materials (biographical excerpts, news clippings, police reports) that are included as back matter to each of the twelve issues. Each character is explored in turn, with a particular focus on the reasons they have for dressing up and fighting crime, be it genuine altruism, psychological trauma, sexual fetishism, or some other cause (Millidge 2011, 125; Sharrett 1988, 11). In classic superhero fashion, all of them have adopted alternative identities in the course of becoming heroes and, as we learn, they generally made use of some model or archetype in the process. Dan Dreiberg models himself on his boyhood idol, the original Nite Owl, while Laurie Juspeczyk was forced to become her mother as the second Silk Spectre. Rorschach's persona (or psychosis) is to a certain degree based on his idealization of his absent father. Even the generally aloof Dr. Manhattan makes conscious choices in his self-representation, revealed by his rejection of the US military's branding efforts in favor of the symbol for a hydrogen atom and, more broadly, in his continuing decision to occupy a human form (and a very male one at that), even though he can now control and configure every atom in his body.[5]

The Veidt Method

The very last of the Watchmen to receive this treatment is Adrian Veidt, the "Smartest Man on Earth." Unlike many of his contemporaries, Veidt made his secret identity public in 1975 and not only acknowledges his alter ego, Ozymandias, but has even built a media and merchandising

3. Moore, quoted in Sharrett (1988, 7).

4. Juv. 6.347–348: *quis custodes ipsos custodiet?* As the backplate to the graphic novel notes, the same quote also graced the text of the 1987 Tower Commission report into the Iran-Contra affair, confirming the degree to which Moore and Gibbons had captured the zeitgeist of their political climate.

5. *Watchmen* 4, 12 (DC, December 1986).

empire on the back of this persona. Indeed, he seems to perceive no fundamental separation between the personas of Adrian Veidt and Ozymandias; the latter merely represents the culmination of Veidt's quest for personal development and fulfillment, and the origins of the Ozymandias identity are therefore tied directly to everything that Veidt himself has become (Van Ness 2010, 114–115, 161). Issue 11 explores how Veidt, resolving "to apply antiquity's teachings to today's world," selected his models for this persona from history: the first and most obvious was the Egyptian pharaoh Ramses II (1279–1213 BCE), from whose Greek name Veidt adopted the alias Ozymandias; the other, as he now reveals, was "Alexander of Macedonia."[6]

This new information arrives at a critical juncture in the series. By issue 11, it has become apparent that the sequence of seemingly coincidental events that form *Watchmen*'s narrative—beginning with the murder of the Comedian in issue one—are all part of a complicated scheme devised by Veidt, the goals of which are still unclear. As will soon emerge, he has taken it upon himself to save mankind from incipient self-annihilation by uniting them against a common enemy and so has faked an alien attack on New York City, killing millions of innocent people (besides those he has murdered in order to keep his plan a secret). The scale of the carnage he has wrought in the name of peace is brought home by a sequence of six splash pages that begin issue 12 (the only time this visual device is used in *Watchmen*), which, absent any captions or dialogue, illustrate in stark and lurid detail the devastation of New York and the deaths of most of the incidental characters we have encountered in the course of the series.[7] The position and impact of Veidt's exposition, paired as it is with the revelation of his scheme, are thus crucial to understanding both the narrative and thematic content of *Watchmen*, since, as becomes apparent, the reader is here given access to the motivation of what would conventionally be considered the series' villain and, at the same time, of what could actually be the most extreme articulation of heroism that it has to offer.

It should be emphasized that it is only here, for the first time, that we discover that Veidt considers Alexander to be the primary inspiration for both his career and his plan (*Watchmen* 11, 8.6).[8] Until this point, both the textual and iconic registers of *Watchmen* have reflected only the influence of Ozymandias's namesake, Ramses II, through Egyptian artifacts, architectural nods, and passing references to Egyptian philosophy or history.[9] Now, in the context of his killing of millions, Veidt finally confesses the influence of Alexander on his life (figure 12.1):

> My intellect set me apart. Faced with difficult choices, I knew nobody whose advice might prove useful. Nobody living. The only human being with whom I felt any kinship died three hundred years before the birth of Christ.

6. The primary narrative concerning the inspiration Veidt has taken from Alexander is accomplished in a monologue in *Watchmen* 11, 7–11 (DC, August 1987). Later, after the arrival of Rorschach and Nite Owl, Veidt resumes his monologue with only minor interruptions, focusing now on the details of his scheme (18–27).

7. *Watchmen* 12, 1–6 (DC, October 1987). Moore acknowledges that the use of splash pages prior to this moment was specifically avoided in order to add weight here (Sharrett 1988, 13). See Van Ness (2010, 54–60) on the layering of image and text in these pages.

8. There are clues to the influence of Alexander earlier in the series, e.g., in the references to the Gordian Knot Lock Company (*Watchmen* 3, 7.4 [DC, November 1986]) or the Nodus Gordii mountains on Mars (*Watchmen* 4, 28.5). Moore has denied that these were deliberate attempts to foreshadow issue 11 (Kavanagh 2000), and he makes no mention of Alexander in the original proposal for the series, appended to the *Absolute Watchmen* edition of the graphic novel (DC, 2005).

9. The astute reader might also detect a nod to Alexander in the diadem Veidt wears as part of his Ozymandias costume. On the significance of the diadem, see, e.g., Fredricksmeyer (1997); for its symbolic value among Alexander's

FIGURE 12.1 Adrian Veidt's backstory in *Watchmen* 11, 8.4–9 (DC, August 1987). Art by Dave Gibbons.

Alexander of Macedonia. I idolized him. A young army commander, he'd swept along the coasts of Turkey and Phoenicia, subduing Egypt before turning his armies towards Persia . . . He died, aged thirty-three, ruling most of the civilized world. Ruling without barbarism!

At Alexandria, he instituted the world's greatest seat of learning. True, people died . . . perhaps unnecessarily, though who can judge such things? Yet how nearly he approached his vision of a united world! (11, 8.5–7)

successors, see Waterfield (2011, 7, 20, 142, 205). I would, however, argue that this visual element alone is insufficient to summon the specter of Alexander prior to the revelations of issue 11 and that it is generally overpowered by the more overt Egyptian symbolism.

Here lie the seeds of Veidt's plan, modeled on the career of Alexander, whose "united world" he believes justified the deaths that brought it into being. Veidt reads Alexander's career as a "conquest not of men, but of the evils that beset them," and it is just such a project in which he sees himself engaged (11, 11.2).

Veidt does not just credit Alexander with giving him this vision of a united world but also with inspiring his means for achieving it. We learn that the young Veidt set out on a journey to follow in the footsteps of Alexander, and for him the most salient event was the episode of the Gordian knot:

> I followed the path of Alexander's war machine along the Black Sea coast, imagining his armies taking port after port; ancient blood on ancient bronze. Strangely, before subduing Phoenicia, he struck north towards Gordium . . .
>
> . . . perhaps because of the challenge it presented: the world's greatest puzzle was there, a knot that couldn't be untied. Alexander cut it in two with his sword. Lateral thinking, you see. Centuries ahead of his time. (11, 10.1–2)

For Veidt, cutting the knot embodied not only a genuine solution but also the kind of pragmatism that could inform action on a grander scale; as he puts it, "an intractable problem can only be resolved by stepping beyond conventional solutions" (11, 25.5). He confirms the analogy between the knot and his own actions in the course of his subsequent confrontation with Nite Owl and Rorschach, during which he refers to the impending nuclear war as "a knot to try even Alexander's ingenuity" (11, 21.4). Moore and Gibbons supplement these textual references with supporting imagery; a huge painting depicting the scene from Gordium can be seen hanging in Veidt's monitor room, and through the visual field it punctuates the action of issue 11, reactivating the specter of Alexander throughout this chapter's revelations. This recurring resonance between image and text reaches a striking climax when, at the end of his monologue, Veidt stands in front of the painting and calmly informs Nite Owl and Rorschach that they are too late to stop him and that he has already made good his plan to destroy New York (figure 12.2).[10] Over his shoulder hangs the knot, already cut in two.

The one reservation Veidt confesses about his hero is that he failed to realize his dream, that he'd "not united all the world, nor built a unity that would survive him" (11, 10.5). Indeed, his journey in the footsteps of Alexander apparently ended in disillusionment at this very realization. This, Veidt claims, is why he combined the dream of Alexander with the name of Ramses II, because he eventually came to the realization that "Alexander had merely resurrected an age of pharaohs." For Veidt, Egypt then came to represent the perfection of Alexander's vision, one that had enjoyed a meaningful longevity and was perhaps even the model for Alexander himself; as he says, "*Their* wisdom, *truly* immortal, now inspired *me*" (11, 10.7; emphasis in original). The relationship that he perceives between the pharaohs and Alexander is important for his conception of his own life; he characterizes his decision to move away from small-time

---

10. The painting, which can first be seen in *Watchmen* 10, 8.1 (DC, July 1987), appears throughout issue 11: first right before Veidt pushes the button to set his plan in motion at 4.5, then looming over Nite Owl and Rorschach as they arrive in his lair at 15.4, and finally when he reveals his plans are a fait accompli at 27.1. It is also visible in issue 12, esp. 19.7.

FIGURE 12.2 A painting of the Gordian knot stands behind Veidt/Ozymandias in *Watchmen* 11, 27.1 (DC, July 1987). Art by Dave Gibbons.

FIGURE 12.3 Veidt's collection in *Watchmen* 11, 22.4 (DC, August 1987). Art by Dave Gibbons.

crime-fighting—the contingent and ephemeral activity of his fellow Watchmen—and toward a project designed to save the entire world as the moment when he would "assume the aspect of kingly Ramses, leaving Alexander the adventurer and his trappings to gather dust." In another example of the careful layering of graphic and textual information, Veidt proclaims this while passing display cases that contain a war chariot and a set of ancient armor (including a breastplate that resembles that depicted on the Alexander mosaic; 11, 22.4; see figure 12.3).

Of course, if Veidt chose his namesake to symbolize the permanence of his united world, it was a bitterly ironic choice, since the name Ozymandias is perhaps most familiar to modern readers from the sonnet by Percy Bysshe Shelley, excerpted in the endnote to issue 11: "My name is Ozymandias, king of kings:/Look on my works, ye mighty, and despair!" The immediate reference would appear to be to Veidt's destruction of New York, but readers who are familiar with the rest of the sonnet will be aware that this legend is reported to appear on the ruins of a statue, the point being that the pharaoh was himself deluded regarding the longevity of his empire. Moore himself has acknowledged that there exists in this connection an implicit undermining of Veidt's project, which works in tandem with the device of *Tales of the Black Freighter* (the comic within the comic) to imply that Veidt's plan is delusional.[11] There is, therefore, a suggestion that Veidt's united world will not last any longer than Alexander's and that he is perhaps not quite the careful reader of history that he thinks himself to be.

In sum, then, Veidt claims he took three lessons from Alexander: the inherent beauty of a quest to unite mankind, the need to seek unconventional solutions to difficult problems, and the necessity to build a union that will outlast its maker. Because of the action he takes on the basis of these lessons, Wolf-Meyer (2003, 497–501) has identified Veidt as the only example of a true Nietzschean Übermensch in *Watchmen* (and, indeed, one of the few in comics in general), primarily because he is the only character invested in altering, rather than protecting, the status quo (likewise Keeping 2009, 57). As Hughes (2006, 551) has similarly observed, it was only Veidt who proved himself capable of taking up the challenge issued by the Comedian earlier in the series: to step outside the dominant paradigm and try to change it.[12] This is why his actions and character are so critical to the thematic payload of *Watchmen* and why his relationship with Alexander is so important to how we approach it. Veidt's picture of Alexander is rendered as the blueprint for more than just the last of *Watchmen*'s would-be heroes but possibly for its only true superhero (in the Nietzschean sense). As a corollary to this, it becomes the blueprint for all the events of the comic's narrative, including an act of mass murder committed in the name of pragmatism and world peace.

The final issue of *Watchmen* confronts us directly with the ramifications of Veidt's philosophy, as the other characters attempt to come to terms with what he has done, judge his actions, and decide whether to become accomplices after the fact by staying silent about his role in the staged attack. In dedicating so much space to the analysis of Veidt's actions, Moore and Gibbons invite serious deliberation on their moral implications, perhaps only intensified in the original publication by the prolonged wait readers experienced between issues 11 and 12.[13] The other heroes react with horror and disapprobation but have to admit, judging by the news filtering in on Veidt's monitor array, that he seems to have achieved his ultimate goal. With that in mind, Nite Owl, Silk Spectre, and the ever-rational Dr. Manhattan decide they have no choice but to protect Veidt and his secrets for the greater good (i.e., to protect the new status quo). Only Rorschach, with his black-and-white view of morality, refuses to compromise on this point, insisting that absolute truth and the punishment of evil are more important than Veidt's utopia.

---

11. Sharrett (1988, 8). The proposal included in *Absolute Watchmen* shows that he had always planned for the connection to Shelley's Ozymandias to exist. See also Fishbaugh (1998, 197); Thomson (2005, 15 n. 40); Loftis (2009, 70). For the *Black Freighter*, see Sharrett (1988, 6); Kavanagh (2000). As Parr (1957) discusses, by Shelley's time, the inscription he reports wasn't even visible on the remains of what is thought to be the statue in question. The text was best known from the account of Diod. Sic. 1.47.4; see also Tac. *Ann.* 2.60.3.

12. Discussing *Watchmen* 2, 10–11 (DC, October 1986).

13. I am grateful to the anonymous reader for this observation.

This clash in ideologies that Veidt and Rorschach demonstrate has been characterized by Loftis (2009) as a confrontation between "consequentialist" and "deontologist" worldviews.[14] Veidt, the consequentialist, believes that the end justifies the means, that achieving his vision of a united world rationalizes "his bizarre murderous scheme." Rorschach, the deontologist, believes that "we should act in ways that express essential moral values" and would rather scupper the peaceful world Veidt has created than be a party to what he can only comprehend as murder and madness (Loftis 2009, 64). Both men believe they are behaving as heroes. Together they present a moral and political quandary, since, while one cannot deny Rorschach's definition of Veidt's actions, it is perhaps all too easy to agree that it is in no one's interest now to expose them.[15] This, then, is the challenge of *Watchmen*: to examine and evaluate the actions and motivations of those who would make themselves "the guardians of society," proponents of what Loftis (2009, 65) calls "authoritarianism."[16] While the comic seems to assert that this is necessary, it does not promise that it will be easy.

Veidt's actions, and his ethically questionable rationale for these actions, form the crux of the comic's moral exploration, and issue 11 is therefore critical in that it proposes in some detail an argument for why a certain model of action is morally justifiable and, indeed, may even be heroic. Veidt's monologue traces a line from Alexander to his own actions, explains why what he has done was both necessary and defensible, and adduces Alexander as his primary model and justification (as both dreamer and lateral thinker). If we are to judge Veidt's actions responsibly, it would seem that we must first confront the way he uses Alexander.

"A Dream More Than Two Thousand Years Old"

For all this, the reception of Alexander in *Watchmen* has received comparatively little attention in critical studies on either the reception of Alexander or *Watchmen* itself. Scholars approaching the comic as the primary object of analysis generally contend that Veidt's fascination with Alexander is simply a manifestation of his "megalomania" and leave it at that.[17] Meanwhile, in the field of classics, none of the more recent monographs that address the reception of Alexander in the modern era even acknowledges the existence of *Watchmen*.[18] This critical

14. Keeping (2009, 57) similarly labels Veidt's actions as "utilitarianism." See also Wolf-Meyer (2003, 508–511), who argues that, if readers side with Rorschach, it is "the conservative ideology of [comic-book] readers that structures this discourse," because they prefer stories that maintain a status quo.

15. Loftis (2009, 68–72) points out several further complications, such as the fact that Rorschach himself has previously espoused consequentialist thinking to justify his violence toward criminals (e.g., at *Watchmen* 5, 6.4 [DC, 1986]). Thomson (2005) agrees there is no clear winner between consequentialism and deontology. Moore claims they wanted the questions to be as problematic as possible, pointing to the fact that "the perpetrator is a liberal humanitarian" (Sharrett 1988, 16). Van Ness (2010, 118–119) concurs that this confrontation is an interpretive crux.

16. As Loftis (2009, 75) observes, the Iran-Contra affair was a perfect example of authoritarian activity (see note 4 above).

17. See, e.g., Spanakos (2009, 36, 38–39); Keeping (2009, 58). Loftis (2009, 67) and White (2009, 79) also call Veidt a megalomaniac. Van Ness (2010, 112) holds that Alexander is symbolic of Veidt's belief in his own nobility, wealth, and power.

18. Spencer (2002); Cartledge (2004); Mossé (2004); Stoneman (2008).

blind spot may be the result of the fact that the allusion is made to seem so straightforward; indeed, since in his monologue Veidt provides the reader with a potted history of Alexander sufficient to make his significance clear even to the layman, it may seem as though the reference does not require much further scrutiny.

And yet this scene actually constitutes a remarkable analytical opportunity, precisely because what we are given here is only Veidt's reading of Alexander; it is not, in fact, a real history lesson but rather a lesson in how Veidt reads the legacy of Alexander and how he modeled his life on that legacy. Veidt's reception of Alexander is instrumental to his characterization and to our understanding of the particular moral and political position he embodies. We have already seen that the way Veidt understands Alexander reveals more about him than it does about Alexander himself; his reading of Alexander's conquest and his cutting of the knot perfectly explain the rationale for his plot and establish him immediately as a proponent of the consequentialist school of thought.

Veidt's reading of Alexander also tells us something significant about his bookshelf, because his Alexander is not just any Alexander but rather an iteration of the particular Alexander canonized by Sir William Woodthorpe Tarn, a version that has come to be known as "Alexander the Dreamer." This Alexander also dreamed of the "Unity of Mankind," or *homonoia*, and Tarn dedicated much of his career to fostering the reception of him as an ecumenicist conqueror.[19] In a startling parallel to Veidt's scheme, Tarn (1933, 124–126) argued that Alexander, motivated by genuine *philanthropia* and the desire to achieve "something better than constant war," sought to "utilize [the Greeks'] enmity to barbarians as a bond of union." Like Veidt, Tarn valued Alexander even more for what he "dreamt" than for what he was able to achieve, and in his devout focus on what he perceived as the ends of Alexander's conquests, Tarn (1948, vol. 1, 146–148; 1933, 148) seems likewise to have received him in a considerably consequentialist mode, proclaiming him "the pioneer of one of the supreme revolutions in the world's outlook."

In the years since his death, there have been significant and continuing attempts to demonstrate the problems with Tarn's version of Alexander and to negate the influence it has had on his reception. Badian (1958, 130) led what he hoped was a preemptive charge against "Alexander the Dreamer," seeking to expose the problems with Tarn's reading of the primary texts and to restore instead the "Alexander of history, who did not gain his Empire by well-meaning muddle-headedness." Yet Lane Fox (1973, 501) acknowledged that Tarn's monograph remained "the most influential work in English for both critics and admirers," despite being "persistently mistaken both in method and evidence."[20]

More recently, Stoneman (2008, 2, 228, n. 3) has cited Tarn's Alexander, the "visionary who aspired to unite the whole world in brotherhood," as an example of what he calls Alexander's "protean" nature: his persistent ability to conform or be shaped to fit the purposes

---

19. The classic text for Tarn's Alexander is the Raleigh Lecture on History, which he delivered to the British Academy (Tarn 1933), but the reading also colors his sections of the *Cambridge Ancient History*, Vols. 6 and 7 (1927, 1928), and is the central thesis underlying his two-volume monograph, *Alexander the Great* (Tarn 1948; esp. Vol. 2, 399–449). "Alexander the Dreamer" was coined by Badian (1958, 425). I am indebted to the recent discussion of Tarn's Alexander and its reception in Richter (2011, 13–16).

20. See also Green (1991, 483–486). Savill (1956, 142–143, 202–203) is indicative of Tarn's influence.

and tastes of individuals and societies (see also Spencer 2002, xiii). As Richter (2011, 13 n. 2, citing Adcock 1958) has noted, Tarn's obituary contains a wealth of information about his lifestyle as an English gentleman that could be said to have informed his particular vision of Alexander the Dreamer. Likewise, Green (1991, 484) has argued that Tarn's "personal political convictions strongly affected his subsequent treatment of his hero," producing a vision of imperialism tempered with humanism that Green calls "the League of Nations Alexander." Veidt's connection of the Gordian knot to lateral thinking, a popular element of 1980s corporate thinking and his own lifestyle, is an example of the same phenomenon.[21] The critical response to Tarn thus provides a model for how to unpack the self-interest at work in Veidt's own version of Alexander.

This version differs from Tarn's in one important respect: the Gordian knot. As we have seen, this episode is quite crucial in the history of Veidt's hero, and it appears that it was similarly critical to Tarn's conception of his, although he denied that the story was true. Tarn confronts the issue in the appendices to his monograph *Alexander the Great*, where, based on a series of decisive inferences about the primary sources, he claims to debunk the authority of the anecdote, before adding that cheating in this fashion "would have been utterly out of character" for Alexander (Tarn 1948, vol. 2, 262–265).[22] Even without exploring his rationale more fully, we can find Tarn's confidence and obvious investment in the question instructive, since they could be said to mirror Veidt's self-involvement in his own version of Alexander.

Despite this disagreement, the Alexander whom Veidt admires does appear strikingly similar to Alexander the Dreamer; given the influence of Tarn's reading, this is perhaps not surprising. Moore, unfortunately, does not cite his sources, either in the work itself or in subsequent interviews, and *Watchmen* lacks an appendix like the one in the collected edition of *From Hell* (Top Shelf, 2011).[23] A quite direct connection between Tarn and *Watchmen* does seem to be indicated at the very beginning of Veidt's monologue, when he claims that his plot "represents the culmination of a *dream* more than two thousand years old" (*Watchmen* 11, 7.3; my emphasis). At the very least, the similarities between these readings suggest that, however self-consciously, Moore (and thus Veidt) received some measure of his Alexander from the tradition established by Tarn; certainly, it should invite similar criticism. Whether or not Moore knowingly employed such a problematic reading, it constitutes a further invitation to question Veidt's justification for his actions and perhaps to start interrogating his philosophy on a grander scale. It also demonstrates the degree to which a similarly protean reading of Alexander

21. Tomasso (2014) has recently argued that there arose a general enthusiasm for Alexander in the 1980s, especially in popular culture, likely inspired by the traveling museum exhibition "In Search of Alexander" (see Yalouris et al. 1980) and deployed by an equally "corporate" villain in the movie *Die Hard* (20th Century Fox, 1988). Umurhan 2012 has likewise demonstrated that Tarn's reading of Alexander specifically informs Iron Maiden's song "Alexander the Great" from its album *Somewhere in Time* (EMI, 1986) and further adds Droysen (1856) into the mix of mediating influences.

22. *Contra* Lane Fox (1973, 150). Both concentrate in particular on Arrian's account (*Anab.* 2.3.7–8).

23. Moore admits in passing his lack of scholarly diligence in Sharrett (1988, 13). The inclusion of the knot could indicate a familiarity with Lane Fox.

could be exploited by both Veidt (as the justification for his plan) and Moore (for the characterization of Veidt); the departure from Tarn over the Gordian knot perhaps only illustrates this more keenly.

The Roman Alexander

If Alexander has always been such a protean figure, then it follows that we are always receiving a tradition of similarly interested readings. Indeed, Tarn was not the first to read Alexander the way he did: his Alexander the Dreamer was, in turn, a very Roman Alexander. For the Romans, Alexander was the quintessential benevolent conqueror, the poster child for *iustum imperium, pax Romana*, and the consequentialist rationalization of ambitious conquest through (supposedly) egalitarian government. Such is the ideology summarized in Book 6 of Virgil's *Aeneid*:

> *tu regere imperio populos, Romane, memento*
> *(hae tibi erunt artes), pacique imponere morem,*
> *parcere subiectis et debellare superbos.*

> Remember, Roman, to rule peoples through empire:
> These will be your arts: to impose the custom of peace,
> To spare those you have subjected, and to cast down the proud. (6.851–853)[24]

The reception of Alexander in Roman culture has exerted considerable influence on the Alexander who is available to modernity. As Spencer (2002, xiv–xvi) notes, "the early story of Alexander as we receive it today is essentially a Roman story," and our primary sources for him "are all inextricably texts of and about the Roman world that produced them."[25] Their engagement with Alexander has to some extent defined him for all time as committed to the same type of "cultural imperialism" as Rome, a project of forced enlightenment that we can see reflected in Veidt's plans for the world.

The Roman reception is informative for *Watchmen* because it can be schematized on two levels: Alexander's exploitation by individuals (such as Veidt) and by authors (such as Moore and Gibbons). In the former category, we could number the generals and emperors who did the most obvious work to connect him to both Rome's empire and their own ambitions; the primary example of this practice would perhaps be Augustus. In Egypt, he was said to have sought out and viewed the body of Alexander; famously, and in counterpoint to Veidt, he had no interest in the corpses of the pharaohs.[26] As emperor, he would go on to use Alexander's image on his signet ring to seal the documents of the early empire, one for which *concordia* (a

---

24. A further version of Rome as the ecumenicist conqueror is projected by Aelius Aristides' *To Rome*, on which see Richter (2011, 3–4).

25. The Romans were not the only ones who worshipped Alexander. See, e.g., Mayor (2010, 65–67) for his influence on Mithridates of Pontus.

26. Suet., *Aug.* 18.1; Cass. Dio 51.16.5.

Latin cognate for *homonoia*) was a central tenet.[27] Similarly, Zanker (1990, 10) has shown how imperial portraiture came to be modeled on that of Alexander, based on a practice established by Pompey the Great (whose own epithet was, of course, no coincidence).[28] Tarn himself actually saw the similarity between his vision of Alexander and the Augustan reception of him, and, as if he had anticipated Spencer's monograph, he took pains to argue that the Alexander he had recovered was not merely a byproduct of the ideology of imperial Rome.[29] In another parallel to Veidt, by dismissing his Alexander's likely roots in Roman imperialism, Tarn was effectively refusing to confront the complex historical and moral ambiguities at play in his reading.

The second category of reception is best illustrated by a famous anecdote concerning Julius Caesar. At the age of thirty-three, he supposedly encountered a statue of Alexander and was stricken with grief, because by that age the Macedonian had already conquered the known world, while he had done so little. In one version of the story, it was simply reading a history of Alexander's conquests that had this effect on him.[30] Moore has admitted to being aware of this story and the obvious parallel with Veidt, characterizing both men's careers as efforts to compete with Alexander, with similarly catastrophic results (Sharrett 1988, 11–12). The reception here operates on multiple levels. The anecdote tells us more about Caesar's reading of Alexander than it does about Alexander himself but also about how the authors understood Caesar, since they have all chosen to make this act of reception part of his myth. In Plutarch, this textual effect is compounded by the pairing of Caesar's *Life* with that of Alexander. This is itself an act of reception, one that is intended to tell us something about both of its subjects but arguably has as much effect on Alexander's tradition as it does on Caesar's (Buszard 2008). Like the representative projects of Roman leaders themselves, the intermingling of Alexander's legacy in their reception by Roman authors changes the way he can and will be read.

Alexander was certainly not immune to this same practice. It is a famous feature of his story that he admired Hercules, Dionysus, and Achilles and slept with a copy of the *Iliad* under his pillow; indeed, according to one reading, it was his overwhelming desire to follow in his heroes' footsteps and to surpass their achievements that pushed him to such great conquests—much like Veidt.[31] As with Spencer's Romans, it is perhaps impossible to separate completely the influence these figures have had on each other's reception, but it must be emphasized that these are as much the heroes of the textualized Alexander as they are of the historical one, factoring into the way we read Alexander and understand what he did in his lifetime.

These two categories of reception share a more complicated relationship than I can examine here, but they are inextricably linked in the effect they have had on Alexander's tradition,

---

27. Suet., *Aug.* 50; Plin., *HN* 37.4.

28. Pompey's own enthusiasm for Alexander was apparently so great and well known that it was openly lampooned by his peers (Plut., *Pomp.* 2.1–2).

29. Tarn (1938, 132–138), which recognizes that *homonoia*, as *concordia*, was a component of Augustan ideology. When Spencer (2002, 180) labels Andrew Anderson's assertion that the "Roman empire was in essence the realization of the ideal of Alexander" as "a vast over-simplification," she is in essence disagreeing with Tarn's position.

30. Statue: Suet., *Jul.* 7.1; Cass. Dio 37.52.2. History: Plut. *Caes.* 11.3.

31. Plut. *Alex.* 8.2; Stoneman (2008, 2, 68, 76).

exerting considerable influence on the circumstances of his reception by even the earliest of our primary sources. Spencer (2002, 15–38) analyzes this phenomenon in more intricate detail and, moreover, argues that the role Alexander came to enjoy in Roman cultural and historical discourse also influenced Rome's reception of its own history. She contends that the impression we gain of the first century BCE as being "dominated by a series of powerful and power hungry dynasts," a type of mythology in and of itself, was in part the product of a "post-Julio-Claudian narratology" that had come under the influence of Greek Alexander mythology, fostering a tendency to attribute the revolutions of history to individual agents (which suited both Alexander and the Principate).[32] This affected the way Roman history was read by Imperial authors and, in turn, our reception of it. As she concludes, "There is a mutuality, indeed an almost parasitic relationship between Alexander and the development of a Roman discourse of empire, which involves us in thinking about how these Roman super-heroes are bound together by their connexion to Alexander" (165–166).[33]

If we follow Spencer, Roman hero worship of Alexander could be said to have made possible the very idea of the superhero: that one man could affect the course of history and change the world for the better. To call this simply megalomania is to deny its singular relevance to comic-book fiction. Perhaps, then, this was the true "revolution in the world's outlook" of which Alexander was the pioneer; if so, it only makes him more relevant as the archetype for Veidt's character and to the thematic and generic concerns of *Watchmen* as a whole.

Conclusion

Watchmen participates in an ongoing tradition of reception that exploits what Spencer (2002, xiii) calls "the flexibility of the Alexander myth as a significatory paradigm." It does so on two levels: the character Adrian Veidt exploits the protean myth of Alexander to explain and justify his radical scheme to save the world, and the creators Moore and Gibbons exploit Veidt's self-interest in the presentation of that myth in order to undermine his rationalizations. Besides the lessons to be learned about authoritarianism and consequentialism, there is also in *Watchmen* an abject lesson about the interrogation and exploitation of history, for which Alexander is the perfect example. A close reading of the way Veidt receives Alexander exposes both his rationale and his credibility to deeper criticism, since he seems to adopt unproblematically a version of Alexander the Dreamer that supports his consequentialist philosophy and, yes, his megalomania. Veidt is either unaware or, like Tarn, unwilling to accept that his Alexander represents an accretion of similarly imperialist traditions from Western history, all of which have condoned instrumental violence and all of which have proved transitory.

Watchmen also has something to offer the study of Alexander's reception: as speculative fiction, it can dramatize and explore the results of an individual—a modern-day Julius Caesar—following the example of this idealized Alexander to its logical ends. The peculiar

---

32. The Roman reception of Alexander was, of course, likely mediated through the Hellenistic kings who followed in his wake. For a representative account of the influence of Alexander's life on—and the manipulation of his image by—his successors, see Waterfield (2011).

33. The preface to Lane Fox (1973) evinces a similar belief in individual agency.

FIGURE 12.4 Veidt/Ozymandias celebrates in *Watchmen* 12, 19.7 (August 1987). Art by Dave Gibbons.

"underlanguage" of comics lets it do so through a mixture of image and text that permits imaginative juxtaposition between this construction of Alexander and the actions of Veidt. Finally,
in the elaboration of its particular moral preoccupations, *Watchmen* deploys this Alexander
in confrontation with competing models and worldviews, implicating him, and his reception,
within its central moral and philosophical debate, one that reaches beyond the panels of the
comic itself to both the generic and political context of its production. This effectively politi-
cizes one's response to Alexander the Dreamer in a way that dispassionate academic study generally does not. If the problems with Veidt's reading are meant to hint at how questionable his
position is, then perhaps, by extension, *Watchmen* shows us how questionable it is to invoke
Alexander in support of anything (figure 12.4).

13

And They Call That Poison Food

Desire and Traumatic Spectatorship
in the *Lucifer* Retelling of Genesis

KATE POLAK

Recontextualizations of biblical stories tend to open up other possibilities of interpretation by redefining the parameters of the initial narrative. Creation stories change the way in which the individual orients himself or herself in the world. In light of the ambivalence of the Creation accounts in Genesis—the first of which relates a concurrent creation of the sexes (Genesis 1:1–2:2), the second of which stresses Eve's origin in Adam (Genesis 2:3–3:24)—Jewish, Christian, and Muslim interpreters have handled the story of the Fall of Adam and Eve differently. These different approaches offer us one way of understanding retellings not as counter to but rather as commentary on biblical narrative:

> in [Jewish] midrashic treatments of scripture, the reader is free (even encouraged) to ask questions of the text. . . . While Christian doctrine developed concepts of "sin" and "fall" based on Eve's disobedience, the corresponding rabbinical tradition of Israel's "pollution" after Eden was never, to any degree, central to Jewish thought. . . . Christians have typically concluded that God created woman after man to be his subordinate. That woman was first to disobey God was proof of her derivative status. . .] [T]he Qur'an offers several accounts of the first act of disobedience. Q. 7:19–24 presents Adam and his mate as equally responsible for straying from God's command, while Q. 20:120–21 underscores Adam's culpability. (Kvam, Schearing, and Zeigler 1999, 3–5)

When we approach modern retellings of the Creation story, some of these impulses to develop and change narrative reinscribe the dominant paradigms present in the original text, including simplistic interpretations such as "the woman is the source of sin." Others depart from these popular readings to offer a space of resistance for contexts that relate to the primary thrust of the narrative, including repositioning humans in relation to God. The Creation accounts in Genesis have provided a framework for thousands of retellings beyond those specific to a theological interpretive framework, including John Milton's *Paradise Lost*. These retellings also include hundreds of paintings depicting the Garden of Eden, Adam and Eve's transgression, and thousands of tangential references to the Fall. The visual work of Michelangelo, Rubens, and others shows us the basic elements present in the Genesis account: man, woman, tree, snake, fruit. Conspicuously absent from most of these depictions is God and his entry into the garden after the first two humans eat of the Tree of Good and Evil.

Alexandre Cabanel's *The Expulsion of Adam and Eve from the Garden of Paradise* (figure 13.1) is notable in its divergence from the dominant depictions, actually rendering God and his attendant angels within the garden, an artistic choice that at first seems to resist the ban on graven images (Exodus 20:3–6), but it also gives the viewer a wholly human tempter.[1] One should note the orientations of the gaze within the painting; God's gaze is directed out of the painting—one can assume at the exit to Eden—with his hand raised in a gesture that mimics the bearing of the gaze. The angels to either side of God gaze at him, but the angel beneath takes a sidelong glance at the doomed couple. The tempter regards, oddly enough, in the same direction as God, and from his malevolent and gleeful expression, one can only assume that the path gestured to by God is less of a punishment than a manifestation of his will. Eve's face is directed upward, her eyes closed in despair, and Adam looks directly at the viewer. In Adam's face lies a challenge, as the viewer appreciates the desire or need to accompany the sinner in his expulsion from Paradise. This is at its surface an easy thing to appreciate—none of us wants to drink alone, after all. More important, a challenge lies in the gaze, as Adam views us with suspicion equal to our own. Adam is partially covered by the apron of leaves he and Eve wove upon gaining the knowledge of good and evil; our viewpoint as spectator is no longer divine, with one being wholly the observer and the other wholly the observed. Instead, both are locations of the gaze, but neither is wholly revealed. This painting is important to consider alongside textual retellings, such as Milton's *Paradise Lost*, as they distinguish between two types of readership: the textual and the visual. While these retellings offer alternative windows into the story, graphic narratives offer both simultaneously. The comics series *Lucifer* offers another take on how our eyes should come to rest on the garden. In *Lucifer*, Mike Carey presents an alternative retelling of Genesis, in which the reader is placed as a witness to the trauma of the Creation.

Mike Carey's *Lucifer* comics series[2] is a mythic retelling partially based on Judeo-Christian theology that also incorporates multiple other mythological and theological frameworks. Lucifer[3] is the main character in the series, but the series draws on multiple religious frameworks while still maintaining the primacy of YHWH. This primacy is what Lucifer seeks to escape, and his goal is to locate a way in which he can exit YHWH's creation. He seeks to exit created space both as a method of circumventing the divine plan so as to define his own providence and as an attempt to be himself a creator, although this project is later abandoned when

1. Most of the scholarship on Cabanel focuses on *The Birth of Venus*. *The Expulsion of Adam and Eve* is housed in a private collection and is rarely mentioned in the literature.

2. *Lucifer* was a spin-off from *The Sandman*. The character's first appearance came in Neil Gaiman (w.) and Sam Keith (a.), "A Hope in Hell," *The Sandman* 4 (Vertigo, April 1989).

3. In *The Oxford Companion to the Bible*, "Lucifer" is included under the heading of "Satan," from the Hebrew root *śṭn*, which is variously glossed as "to be remote" and "to obstruct" (Avallos 1993). Lucifer as he is depicted in Milton's *Paradise Lost* is at his core related to the figure we see in the comic—compelling, seductive, beautiful—but the Miltonic Lucifer differs in one core respect. In spite of the interpretation offered by Fish (1967) that Milton intended to create an attractive devil so as to seduce the reader, the Miltonic Lucifer ultimately begins to decay, and over Books 11 and 12 turns into an almost bestial figure.

FIGURE 13.1 *The Expulsion of Adam and Eve from the Garden of Paradise.* Alexandre Cabanel (1823–1889), private collection.

he realizes that it runs counter to his own philosophies. In *Lucifer*, YHWH has effectively departed creation so as to allow for some freedom of movement for his creatures in his plan. However, in Carey's retelling, YHWH's name is what ostensibly holds the particles of creation together, so that all of the inhabitants of creation may be annihilated as the name fades at the atomic level, an event referred to in the comic as the Great Fading. During this period, ennui overtakes the world, and the inhabitants slowly lose their interest in life. The series concerns multiple characters attempting either to halt or to hasten this destruction, and this leads to the creation of two universes alongside YHWH's, one of which belongs to Lucifer. Although he uses YHWH's creation as a template, it is a repetition with difference that develops an argument against worship.

The retelling of the Creation story is presented in a single issue, *Lucifer* 16.[4] "The Ancestral Deed" is the third of three single-issue stories (collectively labeled as "Triptych") between larger story arcs. In Lucifer's newly created garden, the trope of sin is presented as worship rather than knowledge, and the man (rather than the woman) violates this law when he chooses to worship his maker. Lucifer, after annihilating the man as he promised (in contrast to YHWH's unfulfilled threat of death in Genesis), tells the woman that he will make her a new companion. She instead chooses her death, which Lucifer appreciates because it indicates, as he says, "You have your own agenda. I like that" (*Lucifer* 16, 65.5). In Lucifer's universe, agency is situated as the primary productive agent, and he demands an agency in his own creations that denies their subordination to him, in spite of that fact that he is both "the giver of life and of death" (53.3). In this conceptualization of agency, the primary mover is effaced as the sole locus of power, and the man and the woman are told to "enjoy the garden. It's almost unique" (53.6) This ironic reference to YHWH's garden accompanies the introduction of a snake, who in Carey's retelling is a disguised angel manipulating the man in order to tempt him to worship.

The Fall of Mankind can serve as a paradigmatic event of trauma, and its analysis requires theoretical models that recognize this. As Foster (1996, 107) discusses, the understanding of "the real" has shifted "from the real understood as an effect of representation to the real understood as an event of trauma." For Foster, reality is located primarily within the act of traumatic witness and becomes chiefly defined by its ability to induce a traumatic reaction in the witness. When we approach a text such as *Lucifer* 16, we see panels that mimic various traumatic reactions, as they incorporate both textual and visual allusions to the historical treatments of the Fall of Adam and Eve and provide a new context for understanding the transgressed command, the access to (or denial of) alternative modes of knowledge of the world, and the problematic intervention of the man-made between the creator and the body of the created.

The biblical account of the Fall in Genesis 3:1–24 orients Adam and Eve in relation to their creator and other creations. It focuses on aspects of communication and the connections between individual elements of the Creation wherein the serpent

> said to the woman, "Did God say, 'You shall not eat from any tree in the garden?'" The woman said to the serpent, "We may eat of the fruit of the trees in the garden; but God said, 'You shall not eat of the fruit of the tree that is in the middle of the garden, nor shall you touch it, or you shall die.'" But the serpent said to the woman, "You will not die; for God knows that when you eat of it your eyes will be opened, and you will be like God, knowing good and evil." (Genesis 3.1–5).[5]

---

4. M. Carey (w.), P. Gross (a.), and R. Kelly (a.), *Lucifer* 16 (Vertigo, September 2001). Collected in *Lucifer: A Dalliance with the Damned*, Vol. 3, 51–68 (DC Vertigo, 2002). Page numbers refer to the collected edition.

5. All translations are from the New Revised Standard Version, unless stated otherwise.

Here God attempts to limit knowledge acquisition, not because knowledge is itself a sin but rather because "the maturing of humans into civilized life involved damage of connections established in 2.4–2.5 between the LORD God, man, woman, and earth" (Coogan 2010, 14). By this reading, the "connections" are those established between the deity, humans, and the land. This formulates a social matrix, and the connection between God and the humans is damaged by their disobedience, while God damages the connections between the humans and the Earth. The prohibition of violation of connections is at the core of sin in the biblical account of the Creation, and YHWH's punishments of each individual character reflect this by inscribing antagonism and power into all of the existing relationships: by putting "enmity between [the snake] and the woman" (Genesis 3.15); by creating a hierarchy between the man and the woman by decreeing that "your desire shall be for your husband, and he shall rule over you" (Genesis 3.16); and by telling the man that "By the sweat of your face you shall eat bread until you return to the ground" (Genesis 3.19). All of these punishments exaggerate the already violated connection between the elements of creation. For Lucifer, it also means that the original promise of death in the case of non-compliance is unfulfilled.

Control and trauma, both aspects of the violation of connections between individuals, help to define creation within these texts. We can therefore ask to what extent Lucifer's replication of YHWH's originary structures may be read as a site of resistance to divine power and how his ultimate departure from created space (and the divine plan) complicates any reading of resistance. To what extent can trauma be productive of spiritual growth and/or resistance? The Fall is the primary traumatic event in human history, and this defines the possibilities either offered or withheld in Lucifer's universe. Runions's (2003) work on the destabilization of gender and the gaze would appear to be particularly relevant here, as Lucifer's attempt to mimic the creation of YHWH changes creation, while embracing an alternative prohibition (a ban on all worship, rather than merely graven images, as opposed to a forbidden fruit). In addition, while the serpent in YHWH's garden was not initially seen as equivalent to Satan, this interpretation became established in postbiblical scholarship (Kvam, Schearing, and Zeigler 1999, 32–33). Carey's Creation account shows the extent to which power is inherent in the act of "creation" and can be undercut by the creative reenvisioning of that space. All of the ways out lead only into another similarly structured space, but both the existence of an internal space and the way in which one performs as a spatial inhabitant offer the possibility of sites of resistance. While there seems to be no true escape from the YHWH-Lucifer dialectic, another space is opened by Lucifer's Adam and Eve equivalents, who demonstrate their resistance to preordination in the choice to worship and the choice of death. This opposition reveals the extent to which Lucifer offers a radical reinterpretation of the creation of life, in spite of the mimicry inherent in the creation of another garden.

Both classical and contemporary conceptualizations of trauma can inform our understanding of retellings of the biblical account of Creation, and Sigmund Freud's work on hysteria and traumatic neurosis provides a vocabulary for considering this process. Whenever the Fall has been replicated in visual art and literature, Freud would identify traumatic memories being repressed and the consequences of that repression: the patient, after suffering a shock or fright of some kind, is no longer able to fully access the memory and "is obliged to *repeat* the repressed material as a contemporary experience instead of, as the physician would prefer to see, *remembering* it as something belonging to the past" (Freud 1961, 9). *Remembering* denotes the incorporation of a traumatic event into the consciousness; events return when they are instead residing in the unconscious, where they inform behavior but cannot be consciously accessed. Without access to a traumatic memory, Freud contends, the individual is nonetheless negatively influenced by it. The Fall may be seen as a traumatic moment, in that, as Herman (1992, 51) argues, "traumatic events call into question basic human relationships . . . violat[ing] the victim's faith in a natural or divine order." In a world informed by an early traumatic event in which the social relationships between individuals have been damaged, the reintegration of the nature of the Fall into the consciousness becomes a form of salvation. But this salvation is elusive, given how the story of the Fall is endlessly replicated, rather than explicitly *remembered*. *Lucifer* offers a rereading of the source of trauma in the Creation: to repress any particular behavior encourages its rebellious return. Furthermore, in *Lucifer*, trauma occurs at the point at which decontextualized violence is introduced. The act of retelling the Genesis story reframes the readers' positions regarding human suffering.

Reframing our relationship to this originary account of trauma can only be done through remembering, rather than reenacting. Runions's work focuses on how readings (and misreadings) of films with biblical allusions influence ideological positions of the audience members, a key aspect of the integration of a traumatic event into the everyday.[6] She argues that viewer identification with images plays a powerful role in the consumption of retellings and popular works that draw on biblical sources and that examining what types of identifications are encouraged can promote a better understanding of how the Bible is presently positioned in culture. Furthermore, she argues that resistance to these encouraged identifications is politically productive, noting, "In psychoanalytic terms, hysteria is considered failed identification with the dominant, patriarchal (symbolic) order" (Runions 2003, 8). Hysteria as defined by Freud was the repression of a traumatic memory and its replication, which, in Runions's terms, becomes the inability to integrate oneself appropriately into the (gendered) social order. Runions's work with film informs my own work with comics because, while the genres differ in terms of formal properties, comics and film still provide similar cultural surfaces that combine image and text. Further, both media encourage broad cultural consumption, a collective response and an individual one. Runions (2003, 85) notes, "Hysterics, in Freud's terms, 'express in their symptoms not only their own experience but those of a large number of other people; it enables them, as it were to suffer on behalf of a whole crowd of people.'" Here the connection is not only to the single reader but also to the text as it represents the collective cultural consciousness. Earlier in his work, Freud (1961 [1896], 96) articulated the onset of hysteria as "the *manifestation of fright* accompanied by a *gap* in the psyche.". The gap is an aporia that plagues the victim in terms of both memory and sociality, but it is also something that is shared to some extent by the entire reading community.

While the diagnosis of hysteria has been replaced in modern medical contexts by post-traumatic stress disorder (PTSD), when dealing with *Lucifer*, I prefer to retain the earlier terminology because of its pejorative connotations. *Hysteria*, in addition to being a term classifying a type of mental illness, has also been used to denote "excessive" displays of emotion and to

---

6. For example, she considers films such as *Boys Don't Cry* (1999, directed by Kimberley Peirce) for the ways in which they offer readings that either adhere to or resist normative biblical readings.

dismiss reactions perceived as out of proportion to a transgression. It is also a term that has historically been gendered female, owing in part to its etymology. From the Greek ὑστερικός and the Latin *hystericus*, meaning "belonging in the womb," and so termed because a disruption of the normal functioning of the uterus was thought to cause the emotional upheaval treated as a symptom of the disorder. The historical gendering of this term caused an inability among clinicians to see the connections between women's "hysteria" and men's "shell shock" until late in the twentieth century. While using *PTSD* would perhaps be a more accurate way to align my analysis with contemporary usage, reintegrating the notion of *hysteria* preserves both the term's pejorative qualities and its historical capacity for the erasure of marginalized experiences. This is essential, because it speaks to the ways in which *Lucifer* regards whose emotions matter.

Retellings of the Genesis narrative often focus on Adam and Eve's transgression, and in some sense, this undermines the importance of God's reaction to that act of resistance. God's reaction can be read as hysterical to the extent that it seems a disproportionate response to the nominal transgression. It is also not the promised response; rather than inflicting the promised death, they are instead further divided from other elements of creation and are cast out. This is reconfigured through a number of retellings of the biblical narrative,[7] all of which demonstrate a different understanding of the extent to which Adam and Eve have in fact transgressed but most of which fail to question God's reaction to the act of eating.[8] Each of these retellings either inadvertently or purposefully presents some sort of limit on God's power in failing to question his reaction ("a gap in the psyche"). In *Lucifer,* the act of creation is retold in such a way as to offer a nonhysterical response to the act of transgression. This moment opens a space for a radical departure from the way in which power may open a space for agency, opening possibilities for acts of resistance: "Resistance is not the most obvious or usual response to the oppressions established through identification with dominant norms" (Runions 2003, 8). For these purposes, Runions uses Homi Bhabha's idea of "liminal identification" to gesture toward a point between the poles of identification with and resistance to paradigms of power. *Hysteria* becomes a term that "represents a different kind of identification, an identification with difference" (Runions 2003, 9), and the term incorporates into itself the extent to which the subject rejects the social structure through alternative subject formation. Rather than reading hysteria as pathological, Runions emphasizes how it can provide alternative methods of identity performance. In arguing for a productive view of hysteria, she argues that "the hysterical symptom is the excessive remainder of a lost or forgotten trauma; like the sublime, it represents the unrepresentable; like apocalypse, it cryptically makes known things hidden" (Runions 2003, 9). This "excessive remainder" is the tendency for disruption, the return of the repressed. In *Lucifer*, Lucifer willfully reenacts Creation and the Fall to discover whether there is a space outside of divine will. If the Fall is read as a moment of traumatic rupture, dividing human beings from YHWH, Lucifer's repetition of the Genesis narrative can be interpreted as an attempt to reintegrate this traumatic memory into the consciousness. He does so, however, by both mimicking and undermining the structure of the narrative determined by YHWH.

7. A number of examples immediately suggest themselves, although perhaps the most pertinent are Steinbeck (1952) and Crumb (2009).

8. Eating is normally an act of incorporation; here it causes separation.

The reader's recognition of the Genesis story in *Lucifer* 16 is intimately related to many of our modern Western ideas about sin and gender/sex difference, and because of the cultural primacy of the Christian interpretation of the Genesis narrative, we often read sin onto female characters who have been identified with Eve. The question is whether the *Lucifer* retelling subverts the original story in potentially productive, resistant ways that offer a new, more positive reading of the woman (and, implicitly, of women in general). To what extent is the reaction of God to the first resistant act subverted? Lucifer creates his first humans concurrently, raising them from the ground at the same time. This essentially follows the account as it is related in Genesis 1:27 ("God created man in his own image, in the image of God created he him; male and female created he them"), rather than the sequential creation in Genesis 2. This implicit privileging of the summative account of human creation is interesting partly in light of the fact that Lucifer tells them that they are "the man and the woman" (*Lucifer* 16, 53.2). In Genesis, the man is only referred to as Adam after God has both commanded him not to eat of the tree (Genesis 2:16) and brought him animals to name (2:19). Lucifer forgoes naming entirely, even denying his own name when Adam questions him. He instead calls himself "the Maker—of all this, and of you yourselves" (*Lucifer* 16, 53.3). Lucifer positions himself as one agent within creation, rather than attempting to denote any core quality through names (figure 13.2).

This denial of names and naming can be seen to relate to the fear of many ancient peoples about the meaning and power that names possess. Nowhere is this seen more clearly than in the Tetragrammaton *YHWH*, where the four consonants in God's proper name remain ineffable.[9] In Genesis 2:23, Eve is named "Woman": "This is now bone of my bones, and flesh of my flesh: she shall be called Woman, because she was taken out of Man." Kvam, Schearling, and Zeigler (1999, 30) approach this phrase first by identifying the two potential positions one can take on this naming: (a) that there is no naming formula since the Hebrew roots are not etymologically related, or (b) that naming does take place, whether or not it follows a specific linguistic pattern:

> Naming, it is argued, implies domination in the ancient world. If a woman's naming takes place on verse 23b, then it might suggest that a hierarchical relationship existed between man and woman as part of the created order (not the result of disobedience). If woman's naming by man does not take place until 3:20 ("The man named his wife Eve") then hierarchy can be seen as a perversion of creation's original order.

In light of these alternatives, Lucifer's denial of names is not particularly surprising. In Genesis 2:7, Adam has already been named, at least in some sense: "in the Hebrew there is a word play (paronomasia) between the terms 'adam ('man') and 'adamah ('ground'). Scholars disagree, however, on how 'adam should be translated and whether or not this word play is significant enough to be retained in translations" (Kvam, Schearing, and Zeigler 1999, 27). Eve's eventual naming in 3:20 can be contrasted with this, as she is given a name that does not denote either her specific embodied character (sex, etc.) or the stuff from which she was made but rather her function:

---

9. To avoid "taking the name of the Lord in vain" (Exodus 20:6), many Jews today will not even say or write the *substitute* for the Tetragrammaton (let alone write the Tetragrammaton itself).

FIGURE 13.2 The Maker introduces himself. *Lucifer* 16, 53 (DC, September 2001). Art by Peter Gross.

In token of her role as human genetrix, the man gave to the woman a new name: she was thenceforth called Eve—"for she was the mother of all life" (*Gn.* 2:19). This new name, *Eve* (Heb., *Ḥavvah*), is in fact a pun on the noun for "life" (Heb., *ḥay*), since both *ḥavvah* and *ḥay* allude to old Semitic words (in Aramaic, Phoenician, and Arabic) for "serpent," as the ancient rabbis noted. (Fishbane 2005, 2896)

In the retelling, the first man and woman retain their general referents ("man" and "woman") but are never specified. By declining to specify a given name, Lucifer rejects one aspect of the power dynamic at work in the biblical Creation story, although the rejection is in one sense incomplete. He still identifies them in terms of gender and in this fails to restage the power inherent in the terms *man* and *woman*. *Woman* remains a derivative term etymologically, even though the genesis of the woman in the *Lucifer* retelling is concurrent with that of the man.

Lucifer's commandment to the man and the woman bears a striking relationship to his retention of the terminology of gender. He tells them, "I will withhold death from you as long as you obey my one command. Bow down to no one. Worship no one. Not even me. Do you understand?" (*Lucifer* 16, 53.5). Like YHWH, Lucifer defines only one prohibited action, but this is a repetition with difference. The command not to worship does not, of course, have its counterpoint in the Bible. YHWH's command to the first man and woman is not to eat of the tree. By telling them not to worship, Lucifer is asserting no primacy beyond a command that essentially denies hierarchy. This command is, of course, counterintuitive for those who have actually "met their maker"; while we do not worship our parents, we do tend to venerate them for giving us life. When the man is confronted with the paradoxes of the snake, however, he encounters increasing difficulty in upholding the commandment, as his interiority is pulled toward the one activity explicitly prohibited in the social order.

The snake first appears while the man and the woman are making love, and Adam asks, "Why do you watch us, creature without limbs?" The snake responds, asking, "Why should I not watch? Are you ashamed of what you do?" (*Lucifer* 16, 54.5). This is interesting in several respects. First, the man is the first to notice the presence of the snake and engage with it. Second, the snake already appears as a snake, whereas the curse to "creep upon the ground" follows the Fall in the Bible. Third, the man seems to have none of his predecessor's desire to name; this absence of naming is conspicuous throughout, most important in the context of the man and the woman themselves, but the absence in reference to the snake also points toward a lack of desire to reformulate creation according to language (naming is part of Adam's duties in the garden; Genesis 2:19). Fourth, the relationship between the reader and the scene changes over the course of the page. The first several panels are at ground level, the first and third being directly from the position of the snake as the voyeur to the lovemaking scene, while the penultimate panel suddenly removes the perspective to a tree filled with fruit (figure 13.3). This panel, an aerial view, enhances the sensation of voyeurism and also positions the reader at the common vantage point of the snake, which is usually depicted in the Tree of Knowledge, rather than on the ground. The panel, in which the reader is positioned in the vantage point normally reserved for the snake, underscores the extent to which the reader is typically occupying a position of divinity in the scenes. The account in Genesis 2–3 has four primary actors: the man, the woman, the snake, and God. While the *Lucifer* retelling depicts Lucifer himself as a creator, readers of

FIGURE 13.3 Perspectival alterations. *Lucifer* 16, 54 (DC, September 2001). Art by Peter Gross.

the series are already aware of a divinity that exists outside of Lucifer. Positioning the reader in this fashion invites identification with the observing divinity, particularly because Lucifer soon reappears in his garden. At this point, the identification of the snake within Lucifer's garden (an unexpected addition to the created world) has not been clarified.

This identification with an outside observer creates a gap in the consciousness of the reader. Identification with particular characters in graphic narratives often involves framing characters' perspectives so that the reader occupies a vantage point that gives insight into the way that character views the world of the narrative. In the case of the Genesis retelling in *Lucifer*, the reader is never invited into the position of the actors but instead occupies a space at a distance. This reinscribes the possibility of resistance to commandments: the space between the reader and Lucifer gestures toward a space outside of the matrix of Lucifer's creation. This is further developed by the man's encounters with the snake. When the man goes to find the snake after intercourse with the woman, the snake asserts, "The path that leads to wisdom is hard. Tell me: when you lie with the Woman, do you enjoy it?" (*Lucifer* 16, 55.2). The man responds, "Of course I do. We both do," to which the snake queries, "But if it gave her pain rather than pleasure, would you not still desire it? . . . Then there is your first lesson . . . You can't always trust your desires" (55.3–5). This paradox opens the door through which the potential for resistance to Lucifer's command may enter. This lesson in not trusting your desires at first appears to run counter to the Genesis fable, in which the command is framed partly as a resistance of desire (as for whether that desire would have existed had the command not been uttered is a matter of ambivalence).

In addition to the difference in the content of the command, the reader's reception of that command also differs. In Genesis, the command is framed by Eve (Genesis 3:3). We do not in fact have even textual access to the narration of the original edict; there is no scene in Genesis that depicts YHWH telling Eve of the command. It comes to her only through the mediation of Adam, who originally receives the instruction in Genesis 2:16–17. This original command is both textually and visually depicted in *Lucifer*, and this reinforces the general tenor of Lucifer's desire for a greater visibility as creator and, furthermore, demonstrates his egalitarian leanings in regard to gender. The rhetorical framing of the decrees also suggests a disruption of the hierarchical model. While Lucifer begins with the threat of death, he ends on the question "Do you understand?"—effectively inverting Genesis 2:16–17. As I have shown above, this is only one of many inversions in this retelling, but these inversions share a core tenet: the desire for an identity outside of the recognized social order, in which YHWH is not the source from which sociality devolves.

The question of desire is the major turning point in the *Lucifer* retelling of Genesis. Desire is the acknowledgment of a missing element and a drive to acquire that missing element. This aporia signifies the man's failed identification with his creator. In the man's continued conversation with the snake, he asks, "But is it not that desires come from the Maker, as all things do? . . . and are they not therefore good?" (*Lucifer* 16, 57.1). The questioning of the interloper does not appear in the original Genesis account, which is interesting in respect to the snake's response, asking the man to "suppose the Maker himself is only a part of something greater. Suppose good and evil are things that exist above him—eternal principles that he cannot manipulate" (57.2). This supposition is meant to point to that space outside of Lucifer's creation, a space that is unknown to the man. The snake expounds on this point, saying that "good and evil are the twin poles on which all things are built. They are what is left when illusion is winnowed away" (57.3). The idea of twin poles has particular importance in the *Lucifer* comics series, as evil is defined not as a moral valence but rather as the location of the individual will—the extent to which the will may work on the world and the points at which the will is subsumed in the larger power structure.

The man's confusion over desire and the abstract concepts of good and evil again resonates with the biblical account. Commandments are given but not explained. The power to command is not accompanied by an explanation imparting knowledge. The man says, "I would not wish to disappoint the Maker. I would like to be good. But it is too confusing. There is no way to tell acts that are good from those that are evil," to which the snake replies, "Acts, in themselves, cannot be either. What matters is intent. Anything done out of selfish desire is tainted. Anything done out of love for the Maker is sanctified" (57.5). This assertion of sanctification in intent is important to how sin is reconfigured here. Sin becomes a matter not of action but rather of premeditation. While an action itself may be beneficial, if the intent is not within the bounds of selflessness, it is positioned as evil. This runs counter to Eve's discussion with the serpent in Genesis, in which she initially relates the commandments that she and Adam received from YHWH regarding the tree. This scene is important in its narrative framing, as it does not directly show YHWH commanding the pair but rather refers to a conversation that took place elsewhere. As Eve describes it, the serpent claimed that "you will not die; for God knows that when you eat of it your eyes will be opened, and you will be like God, knowing good and evil" (Genesis 3:4–5). The serpent's "outside knowledge" is remarkable in both stories but seems to go uncommented on by the recipients of this knowledge.

In the comic, Lucifer intervenes to address the man's concerns personally, and this inadvertently ensures his disobedience. After speaking with the snake, the man goes out into the garden to think over his debate with the snake. Lucifer approaches him and offers to show him "something that may be relevant to your deliberations" (*Lucifer* 16, 59.5). In these frames, panels rise out of the forest of the garden, and as the panels float before the man's eyes, we are given a view of various scenes of torture (figure 13.4) drawn from outside of Lucifer's peculiar world, from the larger creation, the "something greater" that the snake had intimated as existing. These panels within the larger panel are red and transparent—Lucifer and the man appear through the frames as they float past, furthering the visual effect common in graphic narratives that position panels as "windows" into the action. This transparency also serves to show how pain can be mapped onto more bodies than just the one that has been tortured. As the man witnesses these scenes, his face is contorted in shock and horror. The man exclaims, "Maker! What am I seeing?" Lucifer responds, "A place made by a colleague of mine. Don't look away. The path that leads to wisdom is hard . . . These people have will and desire too. But in this world a hundred codes and schools tell them not to exercise it—to restrain desire, until desire turns to poison. And then to tell their children that poison is wholesome food" (60.1–2). The scenes appear almost as comic panels floating into the sky, and given the multiple changes in perspective in this story, this creates a metacommentary on position, in which "formal codes produce certain positions for the spectator" (Harries 2007, 8), which refigures the way we view disasters that befall others as specifically traumatic for the witness.

FIGURE 13.4 Scenes of torture. *Lucifer* 16, 60 (DC, September 2001). Art by Peter Gross.

This position as spectator of another universe that the man briefly occupies clearly traumatizes him, even as it makes him, like us, readers of scenes from another's imagination. His reaction is hysterical in precisely the sense that it renders the social structure in which he exists illegible to him.[10] The scenes of torture relate to Lucifer's points about the problem with overweening restraint of desire, but the man interprets this to mean that "desire without restraint is an abomination" (*Lucifer* 16, 63.3). The depiction of the man's viewing of the torture clearly relates the shock he feels. The way he is framed by the various panels depicting the abuses endured by people in YHWH's creation surround and overlap him, creating a scene that foreshadows his future disobedience, as he is overlaid by the wounds of multiple people. In a quasi-penitential act in response to seeing these horrors, the man wraps himself in thorns that visually resemble barbed wire. The man implicates himself and feels guilt for his participation in the events, even if it was only as an observer. The man's decision to repeat what he has seen, to inflict pain on himself, demonstrates Freud's notion that the traumatized individual is compelled to replicate the originary traumatic moment, even though the victim may not have access to the full memory. The man does not have context for the images he has seen but has nevertheless decided to reproduce the experiences he perceives on his own body as a way to avoid reproducing them on the body of another. The man's interpretation of this traumatic spectatorship shows the extent to which he attempts to empathize with these destroyed people of another creation. He has not experienced their physical trauma, but in the act of witnessing, he connects his own desires to the suffering they have undergone. He formulates his worldview around it, which stands in direct contrast with the world the Maker/Lucifer articulated for him.

Recalling Freud's definition of hysterics, the scenes of torture become "a representation of the body turned inside out . . . this is also the condition of the outside turned in, of the invasion of the subject-as-picture by the object-gaze" (Foster 1996, 112). The man internalizes these images and then chooses to mimic them, so that he may suffer along with those who undergo the trauma. He reinscribes the horrors he witnessed onto his own flesh, and this creates a boundary for desire. It is significant that in the scene depicting his self-mortification with thorns, the man's eyes are tightly shut against the garden, Lucifer, and himself (figure 13.5). In the Genesis account, Adam and Eve are not exposed to the experiences of anyone outside of their world (as, ostensibly, there *is* no one outside of their world other than their creator); in the *Lucifer* account, the exposure to other experiences provokes an immediate traumatic reaction, and this identification invokes the man's first (and last) act of worship. The man's hysteria is the rejection of the social order established by Lucifer, but Lucifer, in spite of his calm demeanor, can also be read as "hysterical."

Lucifer's Creation and Genesis retelling is not, at its core, an entire subversion of YHWH's Garden of Eden or the events of Genesis 2–3. In spite of the fact that Lucifer provides a different commandment to those inhabiting his garden and that he keeps his promise for their deaths, the man's act of resistance is still met with a "hysterical" reaction, the discorporation of his body only recently formulated. This is problematic within the narrative in several respects.

---

10. This scene echoes Siddhartha Gautama's "discovery" of the suffering surrounding him in the world, which eventually led to his departure from his aristocratic life to seek transcendence through various means (including ritual self-mortification), until he eventually settled on meditation as the appropriate path to enlightenment.

FIGURE 13.5 Self-mortification. *Lucifer* 16, 64.4 (DC, September 2001). Art by Peter Gross.

First, Lucifer sets out to radically alter the paradigm of power as it is structured in YHWH's universe; he creates so as to provide an alternative method of the deployment of power within the context of maker/creator. Second, he fails to provide alternatives for resistance within his paradigm. Finally, the woman chooses her own death (rather than another partner) after witnessing the man's choice. When Lucifer notices that she has seen the man's disambiguation, he tells her, "Don't be afraid. You've done very well, all things considered. I'll make you a new companion" (*Lucifer* 16, 65.3–4). Her preference for death rejects his offer and thereby rejects his commandment, too. Lucifer fundamentally misrecognizes the woman, thinking of her as simply obeying his injunction, but her choice of death demonstrates her resistance to the same structure that Lucifer himself once rebelled against. The final scene in the issue reveals that the tempter was Amenadiel, an angel who remains loyal to God. The irony of this is not unremarked on by Lucifer, who thanks the angel for his temptation of the humans, observing that "any prototype that can't resist the old celestial party line isn't worth the effort of mass production" (67.6).

Lucifer offers an alternative to the Genesis Creation accounts in underscoring the extent to which individual elements of the Genesis story, slightly reinterpreted, can offer a different vision of our social structure. When the commandment is to deny reverence rather than to deny knowledge, how does this change the readers' understanding of their own resistant acts? When the resistant act is to worship and venerate rather than to gain knowledge, what does that mean for our culture? When we experience shock at what we see, what is the appropriate response? *Lucifer* raises these questions to illuminate the extent to which the Fall in Genesis has articulated a particular vision of what can constitute large, existential questions. As one of the archetypal narratives of our culture, it is deeply ingrained in our consciousness, so much so that its meaning becomes less accessible than a newer narrative might. *Lucifer* questions the ways Genesis influences the reader unconsciously and attempts to articulate a path for future resistant readings that acknowledge the core of both God's original commandment and Lucifer's reworking. We would all like to be good, but how do we know what that is?

Bibliography

Adcock, F. E. 1958. "Sir William Woodthorpe Tarn." *Proceedings of the British Academy* 44: 253–262.

Almagor, Eran. 2005. "Who Is a Barbarian? The Barbarians in the Ethnological and Cultural Taxonomies of Strabo." In *Strabo's Cultural Geography: The Making of a Kolossourgia,* edited by D. Dueck, H. Lindsay, and S. Pothecary, 42–55. Cambridge: Cambridge University Press.

Almagor, Eran, and Joseph Skinner, eds. 2013. *Ancient Ethnography: New Approaches.* London: Bloomsbury.

Arakawa Hiromu. 2006. *Fullmetal Alchemist Profiles.* Translated by Akira Watanabe. San Francisco: Viz Media.

Ardis, Ann. 2009. "T. S. Eliot and Something Called Modernism." In *A Companion to T. S. Eliot,* edited by David E. Chinitz, 311–322. Oxford: Wiley-Blackwell.

Aretz, S. 1999. *Die Opferung der Iphigeneia in Aulis: Die Rezeption des Mythos in antiken und modernen Dramen.* Stuttgart and Leipzig: Teubner.

Ashby, Madeline. 2009. *Transformative Bodies: Anime, Fandom, and Cyborg Sub-Cultures.* MA Dissertation. York University, Toronto.

Avallos, Hector. 1993. "Satan." In *The Oxford Companion to the Bible,* edited by M. Coogan and B. Metzger, 678–679. Oxford: Oxford University Press.

Badian, Ernst. 1958. "Alexander the Great and the Unity of Mankind." *Historia* 7, no. 4: 425–444.

Balsdon, J. P. V. D. 1979. *Romans and Aliens.* London: Duckworth.

Barber, Benjamin. 1996. *Jihad vs. McWorld.* New York: Ballantine.

Barrett, Amy. 1999. "After His Success against Caesar, Asterix Gets a Modern Assignment." *Wall Street Journal,* February 4, 1999.

Barthes, R. 1972. *Mythologies.* Translated by Annette Lavers. New York: Hill and Wang.

Baur, U. 2004. "Superman—Asterix. Mythisierte Körperbilder im seriellen Comic." *Zagreber Germanistische Beiträge* 13: 149–158.

Bell, Anthea. 2004. "Translation as Illusion." *EnterText* 4.3. http://www.brunel.ac.uk/__data/assets/pdf_file/0005/110696/Anthea-Bell-pdf,-Translation-as-Illusion.pdf.

Berlatsky, Eric. 2012. *Alan Moore: Conversations.* Jackson: University Press of Mississippi.

Berlatsky, Noah. 2010. "Hooded Polyp—Stupid Spaces." *Hooded Utilitarian.* http://hoodedutilitarian.com/2010/05/hooded-polyp-—-stupid-spaces.

Bostock, J. and Riley, H. T., trans. 1855. *Pliny the Elder: The Natural History.* London: Taylor and Francis.

Brenne, Stefan. 1999. "Asterix und die Antike." In *"Antico-mix": Antike in Comics,* edited by T. Lochman, 106–119. Basel: Skulpturhalle.

Bridgeman, T. 2005. "Figuration and Configuration: Mapping Imaginary Worlds in BD." In *The Francophone Bande Dessinée,* edited by C. Forsdick, L. Grove, and L. McQuillan, 115–136. New York: Rodopi.

Brodersen, Kai, ed. 2001. *Asterix und seine Zeit: Die grosse Welt des kleinen Galliers.* Munich: Beck.

Broeniman, Clifford. 1996. "Demodocus, Odysseus, and the Trojan War in *Odyssey* 8." *Classical World* 90: 3–13.

Brunetti, Ivan, ed. 2008. *An Anthology of Graphic Fiction, Cartoons and True Stories,* Vol. 2. New Haven, CT: Yale University Press.

Buszard, Bradley. 2008. "Caesar's Ambition: A Combined Reading of Plutarch's Alexander-Caesar and Pyrrhus-Marius." *Transactions of the American Philological Association* 138: 185–215.

Cairns, D. 1994. "Review of Fisher, Hybris: A Study of Values of Honour and Shame in Ancient Greece." *Classical Review* 44: 76–79.

Cairns, D. 2005. "Values." In *A Companion to Greek Tragedy*, edited by Justina Gregory, 305–320. Malden, MA: Blackwell.

Campbell, Joseph (with Bill Moyers). 1988. *The Power of Myth*. New York: Doubleday.

Cannon, Charles K. 1962. "The Relation of the Additions of *The Spanish Tragedy* to the Original Play." *Studies in English Literature, 1500–1900* 2: 229–239.

Carey, Edward. 2006. "MoCCa Presents: '1986: The Year That Changed Comics.'" Comic Book Resources. http://www.comicbookresources.com/?page=article&old=1&id=8916.

Carlà, Filippo. 2014. *Caesar, Attila und Co. Comics und die Antike*. Darmstadt, Germany: Philipp von Zabern.

Carrier, David. 2000. *The Aesthetics of Comics*. University Park: Pennsylvania State University Press.

Cartledge, Paul. 2004. *Alexander the Great: The Hunt for a New Past*. Woodstock, NY: Overlook Press.

Cavallaro, Dani. 2006. *The Anime Art of Hayao Miyazaki*. Jefferson, NC: McFarland.

Celotti, Nadine. 2008. "The Translator of Comics as Semiotic Investigator." In *Comics in Translation*, edited by Federico Zanettin, 33–49. Manchester, UK: St. Jerome.

Chandler, Benjamin. 2010. "Alchemic Heroes." In *Anime and Philosophy*, edited by J. Steiff and T. D. Tamplin, 171–180. Chicago: Open Court.

Chante, A. 1982. "Les Gaulois dans l'Hebdomadaire Tintin." In *Nos ancêtres les Gaulois: Actes du Colloque International de Clermont-Ferrand II, les Gaulois aujourd'hui*, edited by P. Viallaneix and J. Ehrard, 421–426. Clermont-Ferrand, France: Institut d'études du Massif central.

Chapman, Malcolm. 1992. *The Celts: The Construction of a Myth*. Basingstoke, UK: Macmillan.

Clark, Andrew. 2004. "Imperialism in *Asterix*." *Belphégor* 14, no. 1. http://etc.dal.ca/belphegor/vol4_no1/articles/04_01_Clark_Asterx_fr.html.

Clark, Matthew. 1998. "Chryses' Supplication: Speech Act and Mythological Allusion." *Classical Antiquity* 17: 5–24.

Coffin, Bill. 2011. "Tragic Tale." *National Underwriter Life and Health Magazine* 7 (November 2011). http://www.lifehealthpro.com/2011/11/07/tragic-tale.

Cohn, Neil. 2010. "Japanese Visual Language: The Structure of Manga." In *Manga: An Anthology of Global and Cultural Perspectives*, edited by Toni Johnson-Woods, 187–203. New York: Continuum Press.

Coleman, Robert. 1977. *Vergil: Eclogues*. Cambridge: Cambridge University Press.

Collis, John. 2003. *The Celts: Origins, Myths and Inventions*. Stroud, UK: Tempus.

Coogan, Michael, ed. 2010. *The New Oxford Annotated Bible: With the Apocrypha*. New York: Oxford University Press.

Cook, Erwin. 1992. "Ferrymen of Elysium and the Homeric Phaeacians." *Journal of Indo-European Studies* 20: 239–264.

Creed, Barbara. 1986. "Horror and the Monstrous-Feminine: An Imaginary Abjection." *Screen* 27: 44–71.

Crumb, R. 2009. *The Book of Genesis Illustrated*. New York: Norton.

Dandridge, Eliza Bourque. 2008. *Producing Popularity: The Success in France of the Comics Series "Astérix le Gaulois."* Master's thesis. Virginia Polytechnic Institute and State University, Blacksburg. http://scholar.lib.vt.edu/theses/available/etd-05142008-162029/unrestricted/thesis_final_060308.pdf.

Dauge, Yves-Albert. 1981. *Le barbare: Recherches sur la conception romaine de la barbarie et de la civilisation*. Brussels: Latomus.

Davenport, Guy. 1978. "Ozymandias." *New York Times* (May 28): 15.

Delesse, Catherine. 2004. "Accents étrangers et régionaux: Le cas des séries Astérix et Tintin et leurs traductions anglaises." *Ateliers* 31: 113–126.

Delesse, Catherine. 2008. "Proper Names, Onomastic Puns and Spoonerisms: Some Aspects of the Translation of the Astérix and Tintin Comic Series, with Special Reference to English." In *Comics in Translation*, edited by Federico Zanettin, 251. Manchester, UK: St. Jerome.

Detienne, Marcel. 2003. *Comment être autochtone? Du pur Athénien au Français raciné*. Paris: Seuil.

Dettmar, Kevin, and Jennifer Wicke. 2006. "Martin Rowson: From *The Waste Land*." In *The Longman Anthology of British Literature*, Vol. 2C, *The Twentieth Century*, 3rd ed., edited by Kevin Dettmar and Jennifer Wicke, 2533–2538. New York: Longman.

Dev, K. 2012. *A Discussion of the Reception of Homer's* Odyssey *in the Graphic Novel of Gareth Hinds'* The Odyssey. MA thesis, University College, London.

Dietler, Michael. 1994. "Our Ancestors the Gauls: Archaeology, Ethnic Nationalism, and the Manipulation of Celtic Identity in Modern Europe." *American Anthropologist* 96: 584–605.

Dinter, Martin. 2011. "Francophone Romes: Antiquity in *Les Bandes Dessinées*." In *Classics and Comics*, edited by George Kovacs and C. W. Marshall, 183-192. New York: Oxford University Press.

Dowden, Ken. 1989. *Death and the Maiden: Girls' Initiation Rites in Greek Mythology*. London and New York: Routledge.

Droysen, J. G. 1856. *Geschichte des Hellenismus*. Hamburg: Friedrich Perthes.

Du Chatenet, Aymar, et al., eds. 2003. *Le dictionnaire Goscinny*. Paris: Editions Jean-Claude Lattès.

Du Chatenet, Aymar, and Christian Marmonnier. 2005. *René Goscinny: La première vie d'un scénariste de genie*. Paris: Editions de la Martinière.

Duhamel, Alain. 1985. *Le complexe d'Astérix: Essai sur le caractere politique des Francais*. Paris: Gallimard.

Duval, Paul-Marie. 1952. *La vie quotidienne en Gaule*. Paris: Hachette.

Eaton, Anne. 2003. "Where Ethics and Aesthetics Meet: Titian's Rape of Europa." *Hypatia* 18: 159–188.

Economist. 1999. "Worrying Statistix." http://www.economist.com/node/185310.

Economist. 2002. "National Champions." http://www.economist.com/node/1416278.

Ehrhart, Hans-Georg. 2000. "France and NATO: Change by Rapprochement? Asterix' Quarrel with the Roman Empire." *Hamburger Beiträge zur Friedensforschung und Sicherheitspolitik* 121: 1–32.

Eisner, Will. 1985. *Comics and Sequential Art: Principles and Practice of the World's Most Popular Art Form*. Tamarac, FL: Poorhouse Press.

Eliot, T. S. 1939. *Old Possum's Book of Practical Cats*. New York: Harcourt, Brace.

Eliot, T. S. 1950. "Marie Lloyd." In *Selected Essays*, 405–408 New York: Harcourt, Brace.

Eliot, T. S. 1957. "Vergil and the Christian World." In *On Poetry and Poets*, 135–148. New York: Farrar, Straus and Cudahy.

Eliot, T. S. 2005. *The Annotated Waste Land with Eliot's Contemporary Prose*, edited by Lawrence Rainey. New Haven, CT: Yale University Press.

Embleton, Sheila. 1991. "Names and Their Substitutes: Onomastic Observations on *Astérix* and Its Translations." *Target* 3: 175–206.

Emmer, Michele. 1982. "Art and Mathematics: The Platonic Solids." *Leonardo* 15: 277–282.

Espino Martín, Javier. 2002. "La reinterpretación del mito clásico en el comic book USA. Un análisis del mito en el Sandman de Neil Gaiman y el Epicurus el sabio de Messner-Loebs." In *El mito, los mitos*, edited by Carlos Alvar, 45–54. Madrid: Sociedad Española de Literatura General y Comparanda.

Evslin, Bernard. 1975. *Gods, Demigods, and Demons: An Encyclopedia of Greek Mythology*. New York: Scholastic Books.

Fagles, Robert, trans. 1997. *Homer: The Odyssey*. New York: Penguin Books.

Farrell, John. 1997. "The Virgilian Intertext." In *The Cambridge Companion to Virgil*, edited by Charles Martindale, 222–238. Cambridge: Cambridge University Press.

Feuerhahn, Nelly. 1996. "Astérix dans la B.D." In *Ils sont fous . . . d'Astérix!: Un mythe contemporain*, edited by Michel Colardell et al., 77–88. Paris: Éditions Albert René.

Fibonacci. 2002. *Fibonacci's* Liber Abaci: *A Translation into Modern English of Leonardo Pisano's Book of Calculation*. Translated by L. E. Sigler. New York: Springer.

Finkelberg, Margalit. 1991. "Royal Succession in Heroic Greece." *Classical Quarterly* 41: 303–316.

Finkelberg, Margalit. 1995. "Odysseus and the Genus 'Hero.'" *Greece and Rome* 42: 1–14.

Finkelberg, Margalit. 2005. *Greeks and Pre-Greeks: Aegean Prehistory and the Greek Heroic Tradition*. Oxford: Oxford University Press.

Fish, Stanley. 1967 [1997[2]]. *Surprised by Sin: The Reader in "Paradise Lost"*. New York: St. Martin's Press [[2]Cambridge: Harvard University Press].

Fishbane, Michael. 2005. "Eve." In *The Encyclopedia of Religion*, 2nd ed., Vol. 5, edited by Lindsay Jones, 2896–2897. Detroit: Macmillan Reference USA.

Fishbaugh, Brent. 1998. "Moore and Gibbon's *Watchmen*: Exact Personifications of Science." *Extrapolation* 39, no. 3: 189–198.

Foley, Helena. 1985. *Ritual Irony: Poetry and Sacrifice in Euripides*. Ithaca, NY: Cornell University Press.

Forsdick, C., L. Grove, and L. McQuillan, eds. 2005. *The Francophone Bande Dessinée*. New York: Rodopi.

Foster, Hal. 1996. "Obscene, Abject, Traumatic." *October* 78: 106–124.

Fotheringham, L. S. 2012. "The Positive Portrayal of Sparta in Late-Twentieth-Century Fiction." In *Sparta and Modern Thought*, edited by Stephen Hodkinson and Ian Macgregor Morris, 393–428. Swansea: Classical Press of Wales.

Fotheringham, L. S., and Matt Brooker. 2013. "Storyboarding and Epic." In *Epic Visions: Visuality in Greek and Latin Epic and Its Reception*, edited by Helen Lovatt and Caroline Vout, 168–190. Cambridge: Cambridge University Press.

Fredricksmeyer, E. A. 1997. "The Origin of Alexander's Royal Insignia." *Transactions of the American Philological Association* 127: 97–109.

Fresnault-Deruelle, Pierre. 1972. *La bande dessinée: Essai d'analyse sémiotique*. Paris: Hachette.

Freud, Sigmund. 1961. *Beyond the Pleasure Principle*. New York: Norton.

Friedrich, Rainer. 1991. "The Hybris of Odysseus." *Journal of Hellenic Studies* 111: 16–28.

Frings, U. 1978. "Comics im Lateinunterricht?" *Gymnasium* 85: 47–54.

Fuhrmann, M. 1976. "Asterix der Gallier und die 'römischen Welt.'" In *Alte Sprachen in der Krise? Analysen und Programme*, edited by M. Fuhrmann, 105–127. Stuttgart: Klett.

Gallacher, Lesley-Anne. 2011. "(Fullmetal) Alchemy: The Monstrosity of Reading Words and Pictures in Shonen Manga." *Cultural Geographies* 18: 457–473.

Gantz, Timothy. 1993. *Early Greek Myth: A Guide to Literary and Artistic Sources*. Baltimore and London: Johns Hopkins University Press.

Gardner, Jared. 2006. "Archives, Collectors, and the New Media Work of Comics. *Modern Fiction Studies* 52: 787–806.

Gaumer, Patrick, and C. Moliterni, eds. 1994. *Dictionnaire mondial de la bande dessinée*. Paris: Larousse.

Gay, Karine. 2001. *Astérix: An Analysis of the Strategies Used to Translate Culturally Bound Elements in the Comic Book Series*. Master's thesis. University of the Witwatersrand, Johannesburg.

Gentry, F. G. 2004. "Asterix and Obelix: The Genesis of the Vernacular Heroic Tradition." In *Paare und Paarungen: Festschrift für Werner Wunderlich*, edited by U. Müller and M. Springeth, 373–386. Stuttgart: Heinz.

Geschiere, Peter. 2009. *Perils of Belonging: Autochthony and Citizenship in Africa and Europe*. Chicago: University of Chicago Press.

Geus, Klaus, and Birgit Eickhoff. 2006. "Comics." In *Brill's New Pauly, Classical Tradition*, Vol. 1, edited by Hubert Cancik et al., 985–999. Leiden: Brill.

Gindhart, Andreas, and Marion Gietzen. 2015. "Project(ion) Wonder Woman—Metamorphoses of a Superheroine." In *Ancient Magic and the Supernatural in the Modern Visual and Performing Arts*, edited by Filippo Carlà and Irene Berti, 135–150. London: Bloomsbury Academic.

González Delgado, R. 2010. "Orfeo y Eurídice en el comic." *Cuadernos de Filología Clásica, Estudios Latinos* 30: 193–216.

Graf von Rothenburg, K.-H. 1989. "Comics im Lateinunterricht." *Latein und Griechisch in Berlin* 33: 2–10.

Graves, Robert. 1960. *The Greek Myths*. Revised Edition, Vols. 1–2. Harmondsworth: Penguin.

Green, Peter. 1991. *Alexander of Macedon, 356–323 B.C.: A Historical Biography*. Berkeley: University of California Press.

Greene, E. 1998. *Planet of the Apes as American Myth: Race, Politics, and Popular Culture*. Middletown, CT: Wesleyan University Press.

Griffiths, J. Gwyn. 1948. "Shelley's 'Ozymandias' and Diodorus Siculus." *Modern Language Review* 43: 80–84.

Grove, Lawrence. 2010. *Comics in French: The European* Bande Dessinée *in Context*. New York: Berghahn Books.

Guillaume, Marie-Ange. 1987. *Goscinny. Les Auteurs par la band*, Vol. 72. Paris: Seghers.

Gurgand, Jean-Noel 1966. "Le phénomène Astérix, la nouvelle coqueluche des Français." *L'Express* 795: 24-26.

Guthrie, William Keith Chambers. 1966. *Orpheus and Greek Religion: A Study of the Orphic Movement*. New York: Norton.

Hale, W. G. 1919. "Pegasus Impounded." *Poetry* 14: 52–55.

Hall, Edith. 2005a. "Iphigenia and the Glorious Revolution." In *Greek Tragedy and the British Theatre 1660–1914*, edited by Edith Hall and Fiona Macintosh, 30–63. Oxford: Oxford University Press.

Hall, Edth. 2005b. "Iphigenia and Her Mother at Aulis: A Study in the Revival of a Euripidean Classic." In *Rebel Women: Staging Ancient Greek Drama Today*, edited by J. Dillon and S. E. Wilmer, 3–41. London: Methuen.

Hall, Edith. 2010. *Greek Tragedy: Suffering under the Sun*. Oxford: Oxford University Press.

Hall, Edith. 2013. *Adventures with Iphigenia in Tauris: A Cultural History of Euripides' Black Sea Tragedy*. Oxford: Oxford University Press.

Hammersley, Martyn, and Paul Atkinson. 1983. *Ethnography: Principles in Practice*. London and New York: Routledge.

Hampton, Timothy. 2001. *Literature and Nation in the Sixteenth Century: Inventing Renaissance France*. Ithaca, NY: Cornell University Press.

Hardie, Philip R. 1993. *The Epic Successors of Virgil: A Study in the Dynamics of a Tradition*. Cambridge: Cambridge University Press.

Harries, Martin. 2007. *Forgetting Lot's Wife: On Destructive Spectatorship*. New York: Fordham University Press.

Harvey, Keith. 1995. "A Descriptive Framework for Compensation." *Translator* 1: 65–86.

Hatfield, Charles. 2010. "*Asterios Polyp* Reviewed by Charles Hatfield." *Comics Journal* 300. http://classic.tcj.com/ tcj-300/tcj-300-asterios-polyp-reviewed-by-charles-hatfield.

Hayward, Susan. 2005. *French National Cinema*. London: Routledge.

Henderson, Mary. 1997. *Star Wars: The Magic of Myth*. New York: Bantam.

Henrichs, Albert. 2000. "Drama and Dromena: Bloodshed, Violence, and Sacrificial Metaphor in Euripides." *Harvard Studies in Classical Philology* 100: 173–88.

Herman, Judith. 1992. *Trauma and Recovery: The Aftermath of Violence—From Domestic Abuse to Political Terror*. New York: Basic Books.

Hernández Reyes, A. 2008. "La Antigüedad en las artes visuales: cómic y publicidad. Los mitos griegos en el manga japonés." In *Congreso Internacional "Imagines": La Antigüedad en las Artes escénicas y visuales*, edited by M. J. Castillo Pascual, 633–644. Logroño: Universidad de La Rioja.

Herreros Tabernero, Elena. 2002. "Mitología clásica y comic." In *Actas del X Congreso Español de Estudios Clásicos*, edited by J. F. González Castro and J. L. Vidal, 619–626. Madrid: SEEC.

Hobden, Fiona. 2009. "History Meets Fiction in *Doctor Who*, 'The Fires of Pompeii': A BBC Reception of Ancient Rome Onscreen and Online." *Greece and Rome* 56: 147–163.

Hughes, Jamie A. 2006. "'Who Watches the Watchmen?': Ideology and 'Real World' Superheroes." *Journal of Popular Culture* 39, no. 4: 546–557.

Hutcheon, Linda. 1985. *A Theory of Parody: The Teachings of Twentieth-Century Art Forms*. New York: Methuen.

Hutcheon, Linda. 1988. *A Poetics of Postmodernism: History, Theory, Fiction*. New York: Routledge.

Hutcheon, Linda. 1989. *The Politics of Postmodernism*. London: Routledge.

Ils sont fous . . . d'Astérix!: Un mythe contemporain. 1996. Catalogue de l'Exposition, Musée National des Arts et Traditions Populaires. Paris: Éditions Albert René.

Inaba, Shin'ichirō. 1996. *Naushika kaidoku: Yūtopia no rinkai* [*Reading Naushika: The Crisis of Utopia*]. Tokyo: Madosha.

Isaac, Benjamin. 2004. *The Invention of Racism in Classical Antiquity*. Princeton, NJ: Princeton University Press.

Jackson, Kenneth. 1964. *The Oldest Irish Tradition: A Window on the Iron Age*. Cambridge: Cambridge University Press.

Jackson, Kevin. 1994. "T. S. Eliot: The Sequel." *Independent*, May 4. http://www.independent.co.uk/ arts-entertainment/t-s-eliot-the-sequel-first-that-film-now-this-waste-land-opera-based-on-a-comic-no- wonder-lawyers-acting-for-the-eliot-estate-are-so-busy-1433576.html.

Janson, H. W. 1946. "Titian's Laocoön Caricature and the Vesalian-Galenist Controversy." *Art Bulletin* 28, no. 1: 49–53.

Jenkins, Thomas. 2011. "Heavy Metal Homer: Countercultural Appropriations of the *Odyssey* in Graphic Novels." In *Classics and Comics*, edited by George Kovacs and C. W. Marshall, 221–235. New York: Oxford University Press.

Johnson-Woods, Toni, ed. 2010. *Manga: An Anthology of Global and Cultural Perspectives*. New York: Continuum Press.

Jones, William B., Jr. 2002. *Classics Illustrated: A Cultural History, with Illustrations*. Jefferson, NC: McFarland.

Kaelin, Oskar. 1999. "Gespräche über Atlantis." In *"Antico-mix": Antike in Comics*, edited by T. Lochman, 88–91. Basel: Skulpturhalle.

Kahn, Didier. 2008. "Alan Pritchard. Alchemy: A Bibliography of English Language Writings (Review)." *Isis* 99: 829–830.

Kamp, Marcel Alexander, Phillip Slotty, Sevgi Sarikaya-Seiwert, Hans-Jakob Steiger, and Daniel Hänggi. 2011a. "Reply to the comment re: 'Traumatic Brain Injuries in Illustrated Literature: Experience from a Series of over 700 Head Injuries in the *Asterix* Comic Books' by Nikolas Lloyd." *Acta Neurochirurgica* 153: 2501.

Kamp, Marcel Alexander, Phillip Slotty, Sevgi Sarikaya-Seiwert, Hans-Jakob Steiger, and Daniel Hänggi. 2011b. "Traumatic Brain Injuries in Illustrated Literature: Experience from a Series of over 700 Head Injuries in the *Asterix* Comic Books." *Acta Neurochirurgica* 153: 1351–1355.

Kannenberg, Gene, Jr. 2001. "Graphic Text, Graphic Context: Interpreting Custom Fonts and Hands in Contemporary Comics." In *Illuminating Letters: Typography and Literary Interpretation*, edited by Paul Gutjahr and Megan Benton, 163–192. Amherst: University of Massachusetts Press.

Kaufman, Michael Edward. 1995. "T. S. Eliot's New Critical Footnotes to Modernism." In *Rereading the New: A Backward Glance at Modernism*, edited by Kevin J. H. Dettmar, 73–86. Ann Arbor: University of Michigan Press.

Kavanagh, Barry. 2000. "The Alan Moore Interview." http://www.blather.net/articles/amoore/alanmoore.txt.

Keen, Anthony. 2006. "The 'T' Stands for Tiberius: Models and Methodologies of Classical Reception in Science Fiction." *Memorabilia Antonina*. http://tonykeen.blogspot.ca/2006/04/t-stands-for-tiberius-models-and.html.

Keeping, Joseph. 2009. "Superheroes and Supermen: Finding Nietzsche's Übermensch in *Watchmen*." In *Watchmen and Philosophy: A Rorschach Test*, edited by Mark D. White, 47–60. Hoboken, NJ: John Wiley.

Kenner, Hugh. 1969 [1959]. *The Invisible Poet: T.S. Eliot*. Revised. New York: McDowell.

Kenner, Hugh. 1980. *Ulysses*. London: George Allen & Unwin.

Kepler, Johannes. 1952. *The Harmonies of the World, Book Five*. In *Great Books of the Western World*, Vol. 16. Chicago: Encyclopaedia Britannica.

Keslassy, Elsa. 2010. "Fidelite Filmmakers Win Rights to 'Asterix' Franchise." *Variety*. http://www.variety.com/article/VR1118016970?refCatId=13.

Kessler, Peter. 1995. *The Complete Guide to Asterix*. London: Hodder.

Keun Kim, Joong. 2010. "The Korean Wave: Korea's Soft Power in Southeast Asia." In *Korea's Changing Roles in Southeast Asia*, edited by David I. Steinberg, 283–303. Singapore: Institute of Southeast Asian Studies.

Khordoc, Catherine. 2001. "The Comic Book's Soundtrack: Visual Sound Effects in *Asterix*." In *The Language of Comics: Word and Image*, edited by Robin Varnum and Christina Gibbons, 156–203. Jackson: University Press of Mississippi.

Khoury, George. 2007. *Image Comics: The Road to Independence*. Raleigh, NC: TwoMorrows.

Kidd, I. G. 1988. *Posidonius*, Vol. 2. Cambdridge: Cambridge University Press.

King, Anthony. 2001. "Vercingetorix, Asterix, and the Gauls: Gallic Symbols in French Politics and Culture." In *Images of Rome: Perceptions of Ancient Rome in Europe and the United States in the Modern Age* (Journal of Roman Archaeology Supplementary Series 44), edited by R. Hingley, 113–123. Portsmouth, RI.

Kirk, Gregory. 1981. "Some Methodological Pitfalls in the Study of Ancient Greek Sacrifice (in Particular)." In *Le sacrifice dans l'antiquité*, edited by O. Reverdin and J. Rudhardt, 1–90. Geneva: Fondation Hardt.

Koestenbaum, Wayne. 1989. *Double Talk: The Erotics of Male Literary Collaboration*. London: Routledge.

Kovacs, David. 2003. "Toward a Reconstruction of Iphigenia Aulidensis." *Journal of Hellenic Studies* 123: 77–103.

Kovacs, George. 2011. "Comics and Classics: Establishing a Critical Frame." In *Classics and Comics*, edited by George Kovacs and C. W. Marshall, 3–24. New York: Oxford University Press.

Kovacs, George. 2013. "Truth, Justice, and the Spartan Way: Affectations of Democracy in Frank Miller's *300*." In *Classics in the Modern World: A Democratic Turn?* edited by Stephen Harrison and Lorna Hardwick, 381–392. Oxford: Oxford Classical Press.

Kovacs, George. 2015. "Moral and Mortal in *Star Trek: The Original Series*." In *Classical Traditions in Science Fiction*, edited by Brett M. Rogers and Benjamin Stevens, 199–216. Oxford: Oxford University Press.

Kovacs, George, and C. W. Marshall. 2011. *Classics and Comics*. New York: Oxford University Press.

Kremer, Bernhard. 1994. *Das Bild der Kelten bis in augustische Zeit*. Stuttgart: Franz Steiner.

Kullmann, Wolfgang. 1960. *Die Quellen der Ilias*. *Hermes Einzelschriften* 14. Wiesbaden, Germany: F. Steiner.

Kumi, Kaoru. 2004. *Miyazaki Hayao no shigoto: 1979–2004 [The Works of Miyazaki Hayao: 1979–2004]*. Tokyo: Chōeisha.

Kvam, Kristen, Linda Schearing, and Valerie Zeigler. 1999. *Eve and Adam: Jewish, Christian, and Muslim Readings on Genesis and Gender*. Bloomington: Indiana University Press.

LaMarre, Thomas. 2009. *The Anime Machine: A Media Theory of Animation*. Minneapolis: University of Minnesota Press.

Lambert, Pierre-Yves. 1994. *La langue gauloise: Description linguistique, commentaire d'inscriptions choisies*. Paris: Editions Errance.

Lane Fox, Robin. 1973. *Alexander the Great*. London: Dial Press.

Le Corbusier, Charles-Édouard. 1954 (facsimile reprint 2000). *The Modulor: A Harmonious Measure to the Human Scale, Universally Applicable to Architecture and Mechanics*. Boston: Birkhäuser.

Lee, Wood-hung, and Yomei Shaw. 2006. "A Textual Comparison of Japanese and Chinese Editions of Manga: Translation as Cultural Hybridization." *International Journal of Comic Art* 8, no. 2: 34–55.

Leerssen, Joseph. 2006. *National Thought in Europe: A Cultural History*. Amsterdam: Amsterdam University Press.

Lentz, Serge. 1967. "La folie Astérix." *Le Nouveau Candide* 348: 4.

Lesky, A. 1966. "Decision and Responsibility in the Tragedy of Aeschylus." In *Oxford Readings in Greek Tragedy*, edited by Erich Segal, 78–86. Oxford: Oxford University Press.

Llewellyn-Jones, Lloyd. 2010. *Ctesias' "History of Persia": Tales of the Orient*. New York: Routledge.

Lloyd, N. 2011. "Comment re: 'Traumatic Brain Injuries in Illustrated Literature: Experience from a Series of over 700 Head Injuries in the *Asterix* Comic Books.'" *Acta Neurochirurgica* 153: 2499.

Lloyd-Jones, H. 1982. "The Guilt of Agamemnon." In *Oxford Readings in Greek Tragedy*, edited by Erich Segal, 57–72. Oxford: Oxford University Press.

Lloyd-Jones, H. 1983. "Artemis and Iphigeneia." *Journal of Hellenic Studies* 103: 87–102.

Lochman, Tomas. 1999. *"Antico-mix": Antike in Comics*. Basel: Skulpturhalle.

Loftis, J. Robert. 2009. "Means, Ends, and the Critique of Pure Superheroes." In *Watchmen and Philosophy: A Rorschach Test*, edited by Mark D. White, 63–77. Hoboken, NJ: John Wiley.

Loraux, Nicole. 1987. *Tragic Ways of Killing a Woman*. Translated by Anthony Forster. Cambridge, MA: Harvard University Press. Originally published as *Façons tragiques de tuer une femme*. Paris: Hachette, 1985.

Loraux, Nicole. 1994. *The Children of Athena: Athenian Ideas about Citizenship and the Division between the Sexes*. Translated by Caroline Levine. Princeton, NJ: Princeton University Press.

Loraux, Nicole. 2000. *Born of the Earth: Myth and Politics in Athens*. Translated by Selina Stewart. Ithaca, NY: Cornell University Press.

Lüthje, E. 1979. "Asterix als Motivationshelfer im lateinischen Grammatikunterricht." *Der altsprachliche Unterricht* 22: 34–47.

MacLeod, C. W. 1982. *Homer: Iliad XXIV*. Cambridge: Cambridge University Press.

Malitz, Jürgen. 1983. *Die Historien des Poseidonios*. Munich: Beck.

Manson, Anne. 1966. "Grâce à 'Astérix, le nouveau rival de Tintin.'" *L'Aurore*, March 22, 1966.

Marshall, C. W. 2001. "The Next Time Agamemnon Died." *Classical World* 95: 59–63.

Marshall, C. W. 2011a. "Ali, Aliens, and Athena." *OUPblog* (2011), http://blog.oup.com/2011/02/superman-ali/.

Marshall, C. W. 2011b. "The Furies, Wonder Woman, and Dream: Mythmaking in DC Comics." In *Classics and Comics*, edited by George Kovacs and C. W. Marshall, 89–102. New York: Oxford University Press.

Marshall, C. W. 2012. "Seeing Sound." In *Cerebus the Barbarian Messiah: Essays on the Epic Graphic Satire of Dave Sim and Gerhard*, edited by Eric Hoffman, 127–147. Jefferson, NC: McFarland.

Marshall, C. W. 2014. "Frank Miller's *300*, before and after 9/11." In *Muslims and American Popular Culture*, edited by A. Richards and I. Omidvar, Vol. 1, 349–357. Santa Barbara, CA: Praeger.

Marshall, C. W. 2015. "Jonathan Hickman's *Pax Romana* and the End of Antiquity." In *Classical Traditions in Science Fiction*, edited by Brett Rogers and Benjamin Stevens, 307–325. Oxford: Oxford Classical Press.

Marshall, C. W. Forthcoming. "Zeno, Childhood, and *The Three Paradoxes*." In *Representations of Childhood in Comics*, edited by Mark Heimermann and Brittany Tullis. Austin: University of Texas Press.

Marshall, C. W., and George Kovacs. 2011. "Introduction." In *Classics and Comics*, edited by George Kovacs and C. W. Marshall, vii–xiii. New York: Oxford University Press.

Martindale, Charles. 1997. "Green Politics: *The Eclogues*." In *The Cambridge Companion to Virgil*, edited by Charles Martindale, 107–124. Cambridge: Cambridge University Press.

Masson, Pierre. 1985. *Lire la bande dessinée*. Lyon: Presses Universitaires de Lyon.

Mawer, Deborah. 2006. "Balanchine's *La Valse*: Meanings and Implications for Ravel Studies." *Opera Quarterly* 22, no. 1: 90–116.

Mayor, Adrienne. 2010. *The Poison King: The Life and Legend of Mithridates, Rome's Deadliest Enemy*. Princeton, NJ: Princeton University Press.

McCarthy, Helen. 1999. *Hayao Miyazaki: Master of Japanese Animation*. Berkeley, CA: Stone Bridge Press.

McCloud, Scott. 1993. *Understanding Comics: The Invisible Art*. Northampton, MA: Kitchen Sink Press.

McHale, Brian. 2000. "Telling Stories Again: On the Replenishment of Narrative in the Postmodernist Long Poem." *Yearbook of English Studies* 30: 250–262.

McKinney, Mark, ed. 2008. *History and Politics in French-Language Comics and Graphic Novels*. Jackson: University Press of Mississippi.

Meineck, Peter. 2009. "'These Are Men Whose Minds the Dead Have Ravished': Theater of War/The Philoctetes Project." *Arion* 17: 173–191.

Merwin, W. S. 1993. "Canto XXVI." In *Dante's Inferno: Translations by Twenty Contemporary Poets*, edited by Daniel Halpern, 118–122. New York: Ecco.

Michallat, Wendy. 2005. "*Pilote*: Pedagogy, Puberty and Parents." In *The Francophone Bande Dessinée*, edited by C. Forsdick, L. Grove, and L. McQuillan, 83–95. New York: Rodopi.

Michaud, Nicolas. 2010. "Is Al Still Ed's Brother, or Is He Already Dead?" In *Manga and Philosophy*, edited by J. Steiff and A. Barkman, 141–148. Chicago: Open Court.

Michelakis, Pantelis. 2006a. *Euripides: Iphigenia at Aulis. Duckworth Companions to Greek Tragedy*. London: Duckworth.

Michelakis, Pantelis. 2006b. "Reception, Performance, and the Sacrifice of Iphigenia." In *Classics and the Uses of Reception*, edited by Charles Martindale and D. F. Thomas, 216–226. Malden, MA: Blackwell.

Miller, Ann. 2008. *Reading Bande Dessinée: Critical Approaches to French-Language Comic Strip*. Bristol, UK: Intellect.

Millidge, Gary Spencer. 2011. *Alan Moore: Storyteller*. New York: Universe.

Mitchell, Alexandre. 2013. "Democracy and Poular Media: Classical Receptions in Nineteenth, Twentieth, and Twenty-First Century Political Cartoons—Statesmen, Mythological Figures, and Celebrated Artworks." In *Classics in the Modern World: A Democratic Turn?* edited by Lorna Hardwick and Stephen Harrison, 319–349. Oxford: Oxford University Press.

Miyazaki Hayao. 1995. "I Understand Nausicaa a Bit More Now Than I Did a Little While Ago." Interview with Saitani Ryō. *Comic Box* (January 1995). http://www.comicbox.co.jp/e-nau/e-nau.html.

Mondi, Robert. 1983. "The Homeric Cyclopes: Folktale, Tradition, and Theme." *Transactions of the American Philological Association* 113: 17–38.

Morris, C., et al. (writers), and A. Gillman (director). 1994. *The Day Today*, episode 3. BBC television broadcast.

Mossé, Claude. 2001. *Alexander: Destiny and Myth*. Baltimore, MD: Johns Hopkins University Press.

Most, Glenn W. 1989. "The Structure and Function of Odysseus' Apologoi." *Transactions of the American Philological Association* 119: 15–30.

Moula, E. 2012. "Greek Classics through Comic Books: Negotiating Cultural Tradition under the Fidelity Pseudo-Dilemma." *Journal of Literature and Art Studies* 2: 587–605.

Nadel, Dan. 2010. *Art in Time: Unknown Comic Book Adventures, 1940–1980*. New York: Abrams Comics Arts.

Napier, Susan. 2001. *Anime from Akira to Howl's Moving Castle: Experiencing Contemporary Japanese Animation*. New York: Palgrave.

Napier, Susan. 2005. *Anime from Akira to Howl's Moving Castle: Experiencing Contemporary Japanese Animation*, rev. ed. New York: Palgrave Macmillan.

Napier, Susan. 2007. "When the Machines Stop: Fantasy, Reality and Terminal Identity in *Neon Genesis Evangelion* and *Serial Experiments: Lain*." In *Robot Ghosts and Wired Dreams*, edited by C. Bolton et al., 101–122. Minneapolis: University of Minnesota Press.

Nash, Daphne. 1976. "Reconstructing Poseidonus' Celtic Ethnography." *Britannia* 7: 111–126.

Nye, Russel. 1980. "Death of a Gaulois: René Goscinny and Astérix." *Journal of Popular Culture* 14: 181–195.

O'Connor-Visser, E. A. M. E. 1987. *Aspects of Human Sacrifice in the Tragedies of Euripides*. Amsterdam: B. R. Grüner.

Oda, Minoru. 1998. (小田稔). 理化学英和辞典 *(Rikagaku Ei-Wa Jiten; An English-Japanese Dictionary of the Physical Sciences)*. Tokyo: Kenkyusha.

Olivier, Laurent. 1997. "Bibracte ou l'invention des origins nationals." *Journal of European Archeology* 5: 173–188.

Ory, Pascal. 2007. *Goscinny (1926–1977): La liberté d'en rire*. Paris: Perrin.

Osmond, Andrew. 1998. "Nausicaä and the Fantasy of Hayao Miyazaki." *Foundation* 72: 57–81.

Ōtsuka, Eiji. 1998. *Manga no kōzō: Shōhin, tekisuto, genshō* [*The Structure of Manga: Goods, Text, Phenomenon*]. Tokyo: Yudachisha.

Padovan, Richard. 1999. *Porportion: Science, Philosophy, Architecture*. New York: Routledge.

Paik, Peter. 2010. *From Utopia to Apocalypse: Science Fiction and the Politics of Catastrophe*. Minneapolis: University of Minnesota Press.

Paley, M. D. 2002. "הו and His Two Sons Satan and Adam." *Studies in Romanticism* 41: 201–235.

Parr, Johnstone. 1957. "Shelley's 'Ozymandias.'" *Keats-Shelley Journal* 6: 31–35.

Partridge, Eric. 1978. *A Dictionary of Clichés*, 5th ed. London: Routledge.

Peeters, Benoit. 1991. *Case, planche, récit: Comment lire une bande dessinée*. Tournai, Belgium: Casterman.

Pellegrin, A. 2013. "'*Ils sont fous ces Gaulois!*': *Astérix, Lucky Luke*, Freedom Fries and the Love-Hate Relationship between France and the US." In *Comics as History, Comics as Literature: Roles of the Comic Book in Scholarship, Society, and Entertainment*, edited by A. A. Babic, 47–64. Teaneck, NJ: Fairleigh Dickinson University Press.

Pelling, Christopher, ed. and trans. 2012. *Plutarch: Caesar*. New York: Oxford University Press.

Penndorf, Gudrun. 2001. "Asterix Übersetzen: Oder das Wechselspeil in Bild und Sprache." In *Asterix und seine Zeit*, edited by Kai Brodersen, 212–230. Munich: Beck.

Peradotto, J. J. 1969. "The Omen of the Eagles and the ΗΘΟΣ of Agamemnon." *Phoenix* 23: 237–263.

Pernoud, Régine. 1957. *Les Gaulois*. Paris: Scuil.

Petersen, Robert. 2011. *Comics, Manga, and Graphic Novels: A History of Graphic Narratives*. Santa Barbara, CA: Praeger.

Petruso, Karl. 2006. "Review of *Age of Bronze*." *Bryn Mawr Classical Review* 2006.1.04.

Piggott, Stuart. 1968. *The Druids*. London: Praeger.

Pinet, Christopher. 1980. "Myths and Stereotypes in *Astérix le Gaulois*." *Canadian Modern Language Review* 34: 149–162.

Pinsky, Robert. 2006. "Love Isn't Always Pretty." *Slate*. http://www.slate.com/id/2135749/.

Pitcher, Luke. 2009. "Saying 'Shazam': The Magic of Antiquity in Superhero Comics." *New Voices in Classical Reception* 4: 27–43.

Polak MacDonald, Katharine. 2012. "'It Accreted around Me': Created Space and the Problem of the Name in *Lucifer.*" *Trespassing Journal* 1 (Spring 2012). http://trespassingjournal.com/?page_id=243.

Pomian, Krzysztof. 1996. "Franks and Gauls." In *Realms of Memory: Rethinking the French Past*, Vol. 1, *Conflicts and Divisions*, edited by Pierre Nora, 27–78. New York: Columbia University Press.

Pound, Ezra. 1982 [1913]. "Salutation the Third." *Blast* 1: 45. Edited by Bradford Morrow. Santa Rosa, CA.: Black Sparrow.

Pritchard, Alan. 1981. *Alchemy: A Bibliography of English-Language Writings*. New York: Viking Press.

Prot, Benedicte. 2009. "Positive 2008 Results." *Miracle Screenings*. http://www.worldcontentmarket.com/download/ex_cinema.pdf.

Rabinowitz, N. 1993. *Anxiety Veiled: Euripides and the Traffic of Women*. Ithaca, NY: Cornell University Press.

Rankin, H. D. 1987. *Celts and the Classical World*. London: Routledge.

Richter, Daniel S. 2011. *Cosmopolis: Imagining Community in Late Classical Athens and the Early Roman Empire*. Oxford: Oxford University Press.

Ricks, Christopher. 1980. "Clichés." In *The State of the Language*, edited by Leonard Michaels and Christopher Ricks, 54–63. Berkeley: University of California Press.

Riese, Alexander, ed. 1884. *Die Gedichte des Catullus*. Leipzig: Teubner.

Rieu, E. V., trans. 1949. *Virgil: The Pastoral Poems*. Harmondsworth, UK: Penguin.

Riggsby, Andrew. 2006. *Caesar in Gaul and Rome: War in Words*. Austin: University of Texas Press.

Rogers, Brett, and Benjamin Stevens. 2015. *Classical Traditions in Science Fiction*. Oxford: Oxford University Press.

Romm, James. 1992. *The Edges of the Earth in Ancient Thought: Geography, Exploration and Fiction*. Princeton, NJ: Princeton University Press.

Rosivach, V. J. 1987. "Autochthony and the Athenians." *Classical Quarterly* n.s. 37: 294–306.

Rouvière, Nicolas. 2006. *Astérix ou les lumières de la civilisation*. Paris: Presses Universitaires de France.

Rouvière, Nicolas. 2008. *Astérix, ou, la parodie des identités*. Paris: Flammarion.

Rowson, Martin. 1995. "Hyperboling Gravity's Ravelin: A Comic Book Version of Tristram Shandy." *Shandean* 7: 63–75.

Runions, Erin. 2003. *How Hysterical: Identification and Resistance in the Bible and Film*. New York: Palgrave Macmillan.

Ryan, Marie-Laure. 1992. *Possible Worlds, Artificial Intelligence and Narrative Theory*. Bloomington: Indiana University Press.

Sadoul, Jacques. 1976. *Panorama de la bande dessinée*. Paris: J'ai Lu.

Savill, Agnes. 1956. *Alexander the Great and His Time*. New York: Citadel Press.

Scarry, Elaine. 1985. *The Body in Pain: The Making and Unmaking of the World*. New York: Oxford University Press.

Schadee, Hester. 2008. "Caesar's Construction of Northern Europe: Inquiry, Contact and Corruption in *De Bello Gallico*." *Classical Quarterly* 58: 158–180.

Schein, Seth L. 1996. "Introduction." In *Reading the* Odyssey: *Selected Interpretive Essays*, edited by Seth L. Schein, 3–31. Princeton, NJ: Princeton University Press.

Schnitzler, Bernadette. 1999. "Gallisches in den französischen BD's." In *"Antico-mix": Antike in Comics*, edited by T. Lochman, 120–125. Basel: Skulpturhalle.

Schodt, Frederik L. 1996. *Dreamland Japan: Writings on Modern Manga*. Berkeley, CA: Stone Bridge Press.

Segal, Charles. 1994. *Singers, Heroes, and Gods in the Odyssey*. Ithaca, NY: Cornell University Press.

Servius. 1881. *Commentary on Vergil's Bucolics and Georgics*, edited by Georg Thilo. Leipzig: Teubner.

Shanower, Eric. 2011. "Twenty-First-Century Troy." In *Classics and Comics*, edited by George Kovacs and C. W. Marshall, 195–206. New York: Oxford University Press.

Sharrett, Christopher. 1988. "Alan Moore." *David Anthony Krafts Comics Interview* 65: 5–23.

Shay, Jonathan. 1994. *Achilles in Vietnam: Combat Trauma and the Undoing of Character*. New York: Scribner.

Shay, Jonathan. 2002. *Odysseus in America: Combat Trauma and the Trials of Homecoming*. New York: Scribner.

Sherwin-White, Adrian. 1967. *Racial Prejudice in Imperial Rome*. Cambridge: Cambridge University Press.

Shirbon, Estelle. 2009. "Asterix the Gaul Rises Sky High for 50th Birthday." Reuters. http://www.reuters.com/article/2009/10/08/idINIndia-43015020091008.

Silk, Michael. 1985. "Heracles and Greek Tragedy." *Greece and Rome* 32: 1–22.

Simms, R. Clinton. 2011. "The Burden of War: From Homer to Oeming." In *Classics and Comics*, edited by George Kovacs and C. W. Marshall, 103–114. New York: Oxford University Press.

Slatkin, Laura. 1996. "Composition by Theme and the *Mêtis* of the Odyssey." In *Reading the Odyssey*, edited by S. L. Schein, 223–237. Princeton, NJ: Princeton University Press.

Sorum, Christina Elliott. 1993. "Myth, Choice, and Meaning in Euripides' *Iphigenia at Aulis*." *American Journal of Philology* 113, no. 4: 527–542.

Spanakos, Tony. 2009. "Super-Vigilantes and the Keene Act." In *Watchmen and Philosophy: A Rorschach Test*, edited by Mark D. White, 33–46. Hoboken, NJ: John Wiley.

Spencer, Diana. 2002. *The Roman Alexander: Reading a Cultural Myth*. Exeter, UK: University of Exeter Press.

Steel, James. 2005. "Let's Party! Astérix and the World Cup (France 1998)." In *The Francophone Bande Dessinée*, edited by C. Forsdick, L. Grove, and L. McQuillan, 210–218. New York: Rodopi.

Steinbeck, John. 1952. *East of Eden*. New York: Penguin.

Stevenson, Warren. 1968. "Shakespeare's Hand in *The Spanish Tragedy*." *Studies in English Literature, 1500–1900* 8: 307–321.

Stoll, André. 1974. *Asterix, das Trivialepos Frankreichs: Die Bild- und Sprachartistik eines Bestseller-Comics*. Cologne, Germany: M. DuMont Schauberg.

Stoll, André. 1978. *Astérix, l'épopée burlesque de la France*. Editions Complexe: Brussells.

Stoneman, Richard. 2008. *Alexander the Great: A Life in Legend*. New Haven, CT: Yale University Press.

Sullivan, J. P. 1965. "Introduction." In *Petronius*, The Satyricon, *and Seneca*, Apocolocyntosis, 11–32. Harmondsworth, UK: Penguin.

Sulprizio, Chiara. 2011. "*Eros* Conquers All: Sex and Love in Eric Shanower's *Age of Bronze*." In *Classics and Comics*, edited by George Kovacs and C. W. Marshall, 207–220. New York: Oxford University Press.

Svendsen, James T. 1990. "Euripides' Clytemnestra on the Page, on the Stage and on the Screen." In *Views of Clytemnestra Ancient and Modern*, edited by Sally MacEwen, 42–64. *Studies in Comparative Literature* 9.

Tabachnick, Steve. T. 2001. "The Gothic Modernism of T. S. Eliot's *Waste Land* and What Martin Rowson's Graphic Novel Tells Us about It and Other Matters." *Readerly/Writerly Texts* 8: 79–92.

Tarn, W. W. 1933. "Alexander the Great and the Unity of Mankind." *Proceedings of the British Academy* 19: 123–166.

Tarn, W. W. 1948. *Alexander the Great*. Cambridge: Cambridge University Press.

Teitler, Hans. 2002. "Raising on a Shield: Origin and Afterlife of a Coronation Ceremony." *International Journal of the Classical Tradition* 8: 501–521.

Tenniel, John. 1868. *Cartoons from Punch by John Tenniel*. London: Bradbury & Evans.

Tenniel, John. 1870. *Cartoons from Punch*. London: Bradbury & Evans.

Tenniel, John. 1895. *Cartoons from "Punch" by John Tenniel, 1871–1881*. London: Bradbury & Agnew.

Theisen, Nicholas. 2011. "Declassicizing the Classical in Japanese Comics." In *Classics and Comics*, edited by George Kovacs and C. W. Marshall, 59–72. New York: Oxford University Press.

Thomson, Iain. 2005. "Deconstructing the Hero." In *Comics as Philosophy*, edited by Jeff Mclaughlin, 100–129. Jackson: University Press of Mississippi.

Thompson, Jason. 2007. *Manga: The Complete Guide*. New York: Del Rey.

Thompson, Maley Hayes. 2011. "The Shakespearean Additions to *The Spanish Tragedy*." Master's thesis. University of Texas, Austin.

Tierney, J. J. 1960. "The Celtic Ethnography of Posidonius." *Proceedings of the Royal Irish Academy* 60: 251–270.

Tomasso, V. 2014. "Alexander in the '80s: Interpreting Micro-References to Classical Antiquity in Modern Popular Culture." Presidential Panel at the Classical Association of the Middle, West, and South. March. Waco, TX.

Umurhan, O. 2012. "Heavy Metal Music and the Appropriation of Greece and Rome." *Syllecta Classica* 23: 127–152.

Uncenta Gómez, L. 2007. "Mito clásico y cultura popular: Reminiscencias mitológicas en el cómic estadounidense." *Epos* 23: 333–344.

Uncenta Gómez, L. 2012. "*Greek Street*: El mito griego visita los bajos fondos." *Minerva* 25: 187–207.

Vals, Marie. 1966. "Astérix et sa vérité historix." *L'Echo de la Mode* (December 31): 6.

Van Ness, Sara J. 2010. Watchmen *as Literature: A Critical Study of the Graphic Novel*. Jefferson, NC: McFarland.

Van Royen, René, and Sunnyva van der Vegt. 1997. *Asterix en de waarheid*. Amsterdam: Bakker.

Venuti, Laurence. 1995 [2nd ed. 2008]. *The Translator's Invisibility: A History of Translation*. New York: Routledge.

Vernant, Jean-Pierre. 1996. "Death with two faces." Translated by Janet Lloyd. In *Reading* The Odyssey: *Selected Interpretive Essays*, edited by Seth L. Schein, 55–61. Princeton, NJ: Princeton University Press.

Versaci, Rocco. 2007. *This Book Contains Graphic Language: Comics as Literature*. New York and London: Continuum.

Vidal-Naquet, Pierre. 1996. "Land and Sacrifice in the *Odyssey*: A Study of Religious and Mythical Meanings." In *Reading the* Odyssey: *Selected Interpretive Readings*, edited by Seth L. Schein, 33–54. Princeton, NJ: Princeton University Press.

Vines, Lois Davis. 2010. "Recent *Astérix*: Franco-American Relations and Globalization." *Contemporary French Civilization* 34, no. 1: 203–224.

Wall, Melissa A. 2005. "'Asterix Repelling the Invaders': Globalization and Nationalism in News Coverage of Jose Bove and the McDonald's Incident." *Popular Communication* 3, no. 2: 97–116.

Waterfield, Robin. 2011. *Dividing the Spoils: The War for Alexander the Great's Empire*. Oxford: Oxford University Press.

West, Martin. 1981. "Tragica V." *Bulletin of the Institute of Classical studies* 28: 61–78.

White, Mark D. 2009. "The Virtues of Nite Owl's Potbelly." In *Watchmen and Philosophy: A Rorschach Test*, edited by Mark D. White, 79–90. Hoboken, NJ: John Wiley.

Wiater, Stan, and Stephen Bissette. 1993. *Comic Book Rebels: Conversations with the Creators of the New Comics*. New York: Donald I. Fine.

Wiedemann, T. 1986. "Between Men and Beasts: Barbarians in Ammianus Marcelinus." In *Past Perspectives. Studies in Greek and Roman Historical Writing*, edited by I. S. Moxon, J. D. Smart, and A. J. Woodman, 189–201. Cambridge: Cambridge University Press.

Wilkins, John. 1990. "The State and the Individual: Euripides' Plays of Voluntary Self-Sacrifice." In *Euripides, Women, and Sexuality*, edited by A. Powell, 177–194. London and New York: Routledge.

Williams, Raymond. 1989. *Politics of Modernism: Against the New Conformists*. London: Verso.

Winnington-Ingram, R. P. 1980. *Sophocles: An Interpretation*. Cambridge: Cambridge University Press.

Wittkower, D. E. 2010. "Human Alchemy and the Deadly Sins of Capitalism." In *Anime and Philosophy*, edited by J. Steiff and T. D. Tamplin, 205–217. Chicago: Open Court.

Wohl, V. 1998. *Intimate Commerce: Exchange, Gender, and Subjectivity in Greek Tragedy*. Austin: University of Texas Press.

Wolf-Meyer, Matthew. 2003. "The World Ozymandias Made: Utopias in the Superhero Comic, Subculture and the Conservation of Difference." *Journal of Popular Culture* 36, no. 3: 497–517.

Wong, Amos. 2006. "Equivalent Exchange." *Newtype USA* 5, no. 1 (January): 134-135.

Woolf, Greg. 2007. *Et Tu, Brute? A Short History of Political Murder*. Cambridge, MA: Harvard University Press.

Yalouris, N., et al. 1980. *The Search for Alexander: An Exhibition*. New York: Little, Brown.

Yurkovich, D. 2007. *Mantlo: A Life in Comics*. Los Angeles: Sleeping Giant.

Zanettin, Federico. 2008. "Comics in Translation: An Overview." In *Comics in Translation*, edited by Federico Zanettin, 1–32. Manchester, UK: St. Jerome.

Zanker, Paul. 1990. *The Power of Images in the Age of Augustus*. Ann Arbor: University of Michigan Press.

Zeitlin, Froma. 1980. "The Closet of Masks: Role Playing and Mythmaking in the *Orestes* of Euripides." *Ramus* 9: 51–77.

Zeitlin, Froma. 1996. "The Dynamics of Misogyny." In *Playing the Other: Gender and Society in Classical Greek Literature*, 87–119. Chicago: University of Chicago Press.

Zijderfeld, Anton. 1979. *On Clichés: The Supersedure of Meaning by Function in Modernity*. London: Routledge.

Ziolkowsi, Theodore. 1993. *Virgil and the Moderns*. Princeton, NJ: Princeton University Press.

Zitawi, Jehan. 2008. "Disney Comics in the Arab Culture(s): A Pragmatic Perspective." In *Comics in Translation*, edited by Federico Zanettin, 152–171. Manchester, UK: St. Jerome.

Zukofsky, Celia, and Lewis Zukofsky. 1969. *Catullus*. London: Cape Golard.

Index